MINORITY STATUS AN

REFERENCE BOOKS IN
INTERNATIONAL EDUCATION
(VOL. 7)

GARLAND REFERENCE LIBRARY
OF SOCIAL SCIENCE
(VOL. 618)

Reference Books in International Education

Edward R. Beauchamp
General Editor

MINORITY STATUS AND SCHOOLING
A Comparative Study of
Immigrant and Involuntary Minorities

Margaret A. Gibson
John U. Ogbu

GARLAND PUBLISHING, INC. • NEW YORK & LONDON
1991

Library of Congress Cataloging-in-Publication Data

Minority status and schooling : a comparative study of immigrant and
involuntary minorities / [edited by] Margaret A. Gibson, John U. Ogbu.
   p.   cm. — (Reference books in international education ; vol.
7) (Garland reference library of social science ; vol. 618)
   ISBN 0-8240-3534-8 (alk. paper); ISBN 0-8153-0464-1 (pbk. alk. paper)
   1. Children of immigrants—Education—Case studies.
2. Minorities—Education—Case studies. I. Gibson, Margaret A.
II. Ogbu, John U. III. Series. IV. Series: Garland reference
library of social science ; v. 618.
LC3745.M56   1991
371.97—dc20   90-25254
                                                    CIP

Printed on acid-free, 250-year-life paper
Manufactured in the United States of America

CONTENTS

SERIES EDITOR'S FOREWORD

This series of scholarly works in comparative and international education has grown well beyond the initial conception of a collection of reference books. Although retaining its original purpose of providing a resource to scholars, students, and a variety of other professionals who need to understand the role played by education in various societies or regions of the world, it also strives to provide up-to-date information on a wide variety of selected educational issues, problems, and experiments within an international context.

Contributors to this series are well-known scholars who have devoted their professional lives to the study of their specialization. Without exception these men and women possess an intimate understanding of the subject of their research and writing. Without exception they have not only studied their subject in dusty archives, but they have also lived and travelled widely in their quest for knowledge. In short, they are "experts" in the best sense of that often overused word.

In our increasingly interdependent world, it is now widely understood that it is a matter of survival that we not only understand better what makes other societies tick, but that we also make a serious effort to understand how others, be they Japanese, German, or Chilean, attempt to solve the same kinds of educational problems that we face in North America. As the late George Z.F. Bereday wrote: "[E]ducation is a mirror held against the face of a people. Nations may put on blustering shows of strength to conceal public weakness, erect grand façades to conceal shabby backyards, and profess peace while secretly arming for conquest, but how they take care of their children tells unerringly who they are" (*Comparative Methods in Education*, New York: Holt, Rinehart & Winston, 1964, page 5).

Perhaps equally important, however, is the valuable perspective that studying another education system (or its problems) provides us in understanding our own system (or its problems). To step outside of our own limited experience and our commonly held assumptions about schools and learning in order to look back at our system in contrast to another places it in a very different light. To learn, for example, how the Soviet Union or Belgium handles the education of a multilingual society; how the French provide for the funding of public education; or how the Japanese control admissions into their universities enables us to understand that there are alternatives to our own familiar way of doing things. Not that we can often "borrow" directly from other societies; indeed, educational arrangements are inevitably a reflection of deeply rooted political, economic, and cultural factors that are unique to a society. But a conscious recognition that there are other ways of doing things can serve to open our minds and provoke our imaginations in ways that can result in new approaches that we would not have otherwise considered.

Since this series is intended to be a useful research tool, the editor and contributors welcome suggestions for future volumes as well as ways in which this series can be improved.

Edward R. Beauchamp
University of Hawaii

PREFACE

This volume is the outgrowth of a symposium organized by the editors at the annual meeting of the American Anthropological Association held in Chicago in 1983. The purpose of the symposium was to present and discuss ethnographic findings on the school experiences of different minority groups in order to shed light on why some groups are more successful in school than others. Since findings from previous research pointed to differences between *immigrant* and *involuntary minorities*, we decided to focus our analysis on these two types of minorities. Papers were presented by established educational anthropologists as well as by doctoral students working on dissertation research. Some chapters in the present volume are revisions of the symposium papers; others were prepared specifically for the volume.

Following the Chicago symposium, this volume addresses the central question of why some minority groups do relatively well in school, in spite of facing substantial barriers related to such factors as their different cultures and languages, the prejudiced attitudes of the dominant group toward minorities and unequal access to jobs, while other minorities confronting similar barriers do far less well in school. We believe that this question can be answered to a large extent by examining and comparing the school-adaptation patterns of minorities who are relatively successful academically with the adaptation patterns of others who are less successful. Because the variability between immigrant and involuntary minorities appears to be an international phenomenon, we have included studies from Australia, New Zealand, Japan, Britain and the Caribbean as well as the United States.

The field of minority education has grown considerably since the 1960s but few works in this field are comparative. A major reason for preparing this book is to encourage further comparative research within the field of minority education. Another reason is to make available a body of research that looks beyond classroom experiences for insights into why some minority students have an easier time than others in transcending cultural, linguistic and social barriers in school. We hope, with the increasing availability of ethnographic research of the kind included herein, that scholars from various disciplines will begin to reexamine comparatively and systematically some long-held assumptions about the forces promoting and impeding success in school for minority children. We also hope that the case studies and comparative perspective in this volume will prove useful to educational policy makers, program planners and school practitioners. Finally, we hope that minority-group members will find this work useful in advancing their cause in education.

The book is organized into three sections. Section one consists of an introductory chapter which discusses the theoretical framework. Section two comprises ten case studies: the first three deal with immigrant minorities, the next three compare immigrant and involuntary minorities and the final four focus on involuntary minorities. Most but not all of the case studies are based on ethnographic data collected by the authors. The final section summarizes the book and discusses some implications for policy and practice.

The preparation of this book was carried out with support from the Anthropology Department and the Survey Research Center, University of California, Berkeley, and the Bilingual Research Group and Division of Social Sciences, University of California, Santa Cruz. The editors wish especially to acknowledge the assistance of Robert Breckenridge and Deanna Niebuhr, who typed the final version of the manuscript. We also extend our deepest gratitude to the authors of the case studies for their substantive contributions and for their patience in seeing their chapters into print.

Margaret A. Gibson
John U. Ogbu

Part I
Introduction

Chapter One
Immigrant and Involuntary Minorities in Comparative Perspective

John U. Ogbu
University of California, Berkeley

Anthropologists have been concerned with the problems encountered in school by non-mainstream children—lower class, minority and immigrant children—from the beginning of the twentieth century (see Hewitt, 1905). Although they did not conduct ethnographic studies in schools until recent decades, leading anthropologists of every generation since the turn of the century have written about the school experience of these children (e.g., Boas, 1928; Benedict, 1943; Mead, 1943; Powdermaker, 1943; Redfield, 1943). Ethnographic research on minority education began in the 1950s, expanded in the 1960s and 1970s and has grown substantially since then. Moreover, anthropologists have become actively involved in the application of their knowledge to the solution of various problems faced by minorities in school.

These developments have resulted in constructive and empirically based criticisms of the way in which schools educate minority children. Suggestions for and efforts to improve minority children's school experience are also now based on ethnographic evidence rather than on speculation. Yet, upon close inspection, there appears to be at least one important reason for caution: most anthropological research has focused on the school experience of minority groups who are not particularly successful in school—usually nonimmigrants. That is, we have been concerned primarily with the

3

school experience of those minority groups who did not choose to come voluntarily to the countries in which they now reside in order to improve their social, economic and political status or to achieve other desired ends. Ethnographers have generally found that among nonimmigrant minorities a disproportionate number of children experience social adjustment problems and are not academically successful compared with other children. They have also discovered that these minority children often differ in significant ways from dominant-group children in culture and communication and in terms of power relations. From these observations, ethnographers have concluded that the minority student's disproportionate school failure is caused by discontinuities in culture, communication and power relations. And sophisticated ethnographic techniques have been developed to study and demonstrate how these discontinuities cause school failure as well as how school failure can be prevented.

Recent ethnographic studies among immigrant minorities suggest, however, that our conclusions about the relationship between discontinuities in culture, language and power relations on the one hand, and on the other, minorities' disproportionate school failure or success may not be applicable to all minority groups. Some of these ethnographic studies indicate, specifically, that there may be different patterns of adaptation in school which lead to differential school success for immigrant and nonimmigrant minorities, partly because of different historical experiences which lead to different adaptive responses. The main task of this volume, then, is to make a comparative examination of the extent and nature of the differences and similarities in the general adaptive responses and their impact on the schooling of the two types of minorities. The major question is why immigrant minorities are relatively more successful in school than nonimmigrant minorities in spite of the apparent similarities in the cultural, linguistic and structural barriers facing both types of minorities.

A Comparative Framework

In order to achieve our comparative goal the authors of the chapters in this volume were asked, as far as possible, to address the same issues, to use the same framework and the same concepts in organizing their chapters and to provide the same kinds of quantitative data. More specifically, each case-study author was asked to consider the following: the history of the minority group, its contemporary status and its pattern of school performance. Other factors to be addressed were the barriers to school adjustment and school success the minority group faced, such as societal, within-school and community barriers, including cultural and language factors, the factors facilitating school adjustment and success and the minority group's folk theories of success. Not all the case studies addressed these issues to the same degree because the nature of the data available to each author differed. It needs to be pointed out, moreover, that the initial studies were not designed with the present comparative framework in mind.

Conventional Explanations of Variability in Minority School Performance

Several explanations have been proposed to account for the variability in the school performance of minority children. Jensen, for instance, has claimed that black Americans are less successful in school than white Americans because they are not endowed with the type of genes that enhance white "intelligence" and success in school (1969). However, a theory based on genetic differences, such as Jensen's, cannot explain why the Japanese Buraku outcastes do less well than the majority of Japanese when attending schools in Japan (Shimahara, in this volume) but are as successful as the majority of Japanese when both groups attend schools in the United States (Ito, 1967). Some scholars have argued that cultural and language differences create conflicts in teaching and learning situations and that these conflicts, in turn, adversely affect the school success of minority children (e.g., Erickson and Mohatt, 1982). The proponents of this view do not explain why and how other minorities in similar situations manage to cross cultural and language boundaries and do relatively well in school (see Gibson, in this volume; Suarez-Orozco, in this volume).

Some social scientists promote the view that the academic problems of minorities and lower-class children, the so-called "children at risk," are attributable to social class variables. It is said, for example, that black children do less well in school than white children because more blacks than whites come from lower-class or "underclass" backgrounds (Bond, 1981). Middle-class blacks are said to be as successful in school as their white middle-class counterparts (Van den Berghe, 1980; Wilson, 1980). Unfortunately, this argument is not supported by available data. Research generally shows that at any given class level black students, on the average, do less well than their white counterparts (Jensen, 1969; Slade, 1982; Wigdor and Garner, 1982). Furthermore, the academic achievement gap between the lower class and the middle class is smaller among blacks than among whites, and black students' school success is not strongly correlated with social class, i.e., with parents' education, income or socioeconomic status (Slade, 1982; Haycock and Navarro, 1988).

From a comparative perspective these and other explanations of variability in minority school performance are lacking in three ways. First, they ignore the historical and wider societal forces that can encourage or discourage the minorities from striving for school success. Second, they do not consider a group's collective orientation toward schooling and striving for school success as a factor in academic achievement. They assume that school success is a matter of family background and individual ability and effort. And third, the theories fail to consider the minorities' own notions of the meaning of and the "how-to" of schooling in the context of their own social reality.

Thus, conventional explanations have given insufficient attention to understanding why minorities behave the way they do from the point of view of the minorities themselves; instead, they have evaluated the behaviors of minorities from the perspective of the dominant group's perceptions of their own social reality or from the perceptions and interpretations that the dominant group members have of the social reality of minorities. Consequently, current explanations of the variability in the school performance of minority students have usually been constructed without the benefit of what the minorities themselves think, and, from my point of view, these theories cannot adequately account for the variability in the school performance of minorities who are members of the same social class as dominant group peers or who are from different social classes. Nor can they explain adequately the variability in the school performance of children from minority groups who experience cultural and language differences or conflicts in school, nor the performance variability among members of the same minority group either from the same social class or from different social classes. To construct a more adequate explanation of the variability in the school success of minority children, it is necessary to incorporate the perceptions and understanding that the minorities have of their social realities and of their schooling. Toward this end, I suggest the concept of "cultural model" as a useful tool.

Cultural Model

In plural societies such as the United States, Japan and New Zealand, different segments of the society, such as the dominant group and the ethnic/racial minorities, tend to have their own cultural models—their respective understandings of how their society or any particular domain or institution works and their respective understandings of their places in that working order. The cultural model of the dominant group, like the cultural model of a given minority group, is neither better nor worse than other models. As Bohannan (1957:5) put it in his study of the justice system among the Tiv of colonial Nigeria, "The folk systems [or cultural models] are *never* right nor wrong. They exist." Their purpose is to guide behaviors and interpretations.

In the domain of education or schooling the cultural model of the dominant group coexists with those of various minorities. The cultural model of each group—minority as well as majority—exists to provide group members with the framework for interpreting educational events, situations and experiences and to guide behavior in the schooling context and process. Since differing cultural models provoke different behaviors, the cultural model of a particular group is connected to some degree with the relative academic success or academic failure of its members. The theories reviewed earlier do not necessarily reflect the realities they attempt to explain because they do not include the cultural models of the minorities and their consequences for the academic behaviors of the minorities (Ogbu, 1974).

An Emerging Explanation from Comparative Research

Findings from comparative research indicate that what distinguishes minority groups who are doing relatively well in school from others who do less well is not that the former possess a particular type of genetic endowment, nor that they inhabit a cultural environment which enables them to develop the type of cognitive, linguistic, motivational and socio-emotional attributes characteristic of the middle-class members of the dominant group, nor that they attend schools that are without defects. Nor are the major distinguishing features the particular minority groups' experiences of economic, political or other discriminatory treatment at the hands of the members of the dominant group, nor the cultural and language barriers they encounter in school—although all these factors are important. Rather, the more academically successful minorities differ from the less academically successful minorities in the type of cultural model that guides them, that is, in the type of understanding they have of the workings of the larger society and of their place as minorities in that working order. In addition, the minorities differ in their cultural models of their social realities because of differences in their histories. Note, however, that within a given minority group, too, there are subgroup and individual differences in school success attributable in part to differences in the influence of the cultural model.

Minority Status and Cultural Models

There are two forms of historical forces which shape the different cultural models of minority groups who are relatively successful or unsuccessful in school. One is the initial terms of incorporation of these minorities into the society in which they now exist; the other is the pattern of adaptive responses that the minorities have made to subsequent discriminatory treatment by members of the dominant group.

Initial Terms of Incorporation

Minority groups have been incorporated into their various societies either voluntarily or involuntarily. Those who have been incorporated voluntarily are immigrants. *Immigrant minorities* have generally moved to their present societies because they believed that the move would lead to more economic well-being, better overall opportunities or greater political freedom. These expectations continue to influence the way they perceive and respond to treatment by members of the dominant group and by the institutions controlled by members of the dominant group. In the present volume the immigrants are represented by Hispanics from Central America in San Francisco (Suarez-Orozco), Mexicans in the Central Coast area of California (Matute-Bianchi), Koreans in the United States (Lee), Sikhs in Britain and in the United States (Gibson and Bhachu), Turks in Australia (Inglis and Manderson) and West Indians or "Down Islanders" in the U.S. Virgin Islands (Gibson).

In contrast, nonimmigrant minorities, whom I designate *involuntary minorities,* are people who were brought into their present society through slavery, conquest or colonization. They usually resent the loss of their former freedom, and they perceive the social, political and economic barriers against them as part of their undeserved oppression. Involuntary minorities in this volume include American Indians (the Ute) in Utah (Kramer), blacks in Stockton, California (Ogbu), Burakumin in Japan (Shimahara), Koreans in Japan (Lee), Maoris in New Zealand (Barrington), Crucians in St. Croix (Gibson), and "Chicanos" in California's Pajaro Valley (Matute-Bianchi).

Subsequent Discriminatory Treatment

Both immigrant and involuntary minorities experience prejudice and discrimination at the hands of members of the dominant group. Both may be relegated to menial jobs, for example. They may also be confronted with social and political barriers, given inferior education and derogated intellectually and culturally, and they may be excluded from true assimilation into the mainstream society.

Unfortunately, not all contributors to the volume have documented the discriminatory treatment of immigrant minorities in society at large and in the schools, although we know from other sources that this discrimination exists. Inglis and Manderson tell us, instead, that Turkish immigrants in Australia are employed mostly in unskilled and semiskilled jobs because of their low educational attainment and that the Australian government provides assistance to the immigrants. I suspect that research with an ethnographic base would reveal discriminatory treatment. "Down Islanders" in St. Croix, according to Gibson, hold jobs in tourism that the native Crucians regard as a new form of slavery. And Koreans in the United States are underemployed and underpaid for their educational qualifications. Although almost all the authors are silent about discriminatory treatment of immigrant minorities in school (Gibson and Bhachu provide the fullest discussion), it does not follow that the immigrants are not discriminated against (see Ogbu, 1983).

There is more documentation of the discriminatory treatment of involuntary minorities by the dominant group. The discriminatory treatment of black Americans is perhaps the best known and the most extensively documented (Frazier, 1957; Newman et al., 1976; Drake and Cayton, 1970). I will use the concept of a *job ceiling* to illustrate their treatment in the economic sector. A job ceiling includes both formal statutes and informal practices employed by members of the dominant group/whites to limit the access of blacks to desirable jobs, to truncate their opportunities and to narrowly channel the potential returns they can expect from their education and abilities (Mickelson, 1984; Ogbu, 1978). Using a job ceiling, whites have effectively denied generations of blacks equal opportunities to compete for desirable jobs, as well as equal wages and opportunities for promotion on the job based on education and ability. The case of AT&T settled by the Equal Employment Opportunities Commission in 1974 is a good illustration of the economic exploitation of minorities through a job ceiling. It was found that the giant company "saved" over $362,000,000 a year by not paying black, Hispanic and female workers what they would have earned if they had been white males (DeWare, 1978). The discriminatory treatment of blacks in Stockton, California that is described in this volume follows the national pattern: blacks in Stockton faced a job ceiling and residential segregation, as well as cultural and intellectual derogation. Other involuntary minorities described in this volume have also faced a job ceiling and derogatory treatment: Mexican Americans in the Central Coast area of California; the Burakumin and Koreans in Japan; Maoris in New Zealand; and Ute Indians in Utah. Many of these minorities have also faced inferior and segregated schools as well as discriminatory treatment within the schools, in the form of discipline, for example.

Minority Responses: Immigrants

When confronted with these collective problems, immigrant minorities and involuntary minorities tend to interpret them differently. These responses form part of the contents of the cultural models of the minorities. The immigrants appear to interpret the economic, political and social barriers against them as more or less temporary problems, as problems they will or can overcome with the passage of time, hard work, or more education. Furthermore, the immigrants have a positive dual frame of reference which allows them to develop or maintain an optimistic view of their future possibilities. This frame of reference entails comparing their present situation with their own former situation or with that of their peers "back home." When they make this comparison they find a great deal of evidence that enables them to believe that they have more and better opportunities in their host society for themselves or for their children. And because of this positive dual frame of reference with respect to status mobility, the immigrants think that even if they are allowed only marginal jobs they are better off in their host society than they would be in their homeland. This viewpoint is reported among Punjabi Sikhs in "Valleyside," California (Gibson and Bhachu, in this volume) and Central American Hispanics in San Francisco (Suarez-Orozco, in this volume). With regard to Central American Hispanic immigrants, Suarez-Orozco (in this volume) writes:

> Recent Central American immigrants developed a dual frame of reference with which they evaluated their current lot and anticipated the future. The overwhelming majority of my informants came to believe that they had more and better opportunities to get ahead in the United States than at home.

Another significant feature of the immigrants' response to barriers is that they tend to interpret their exclusion from better jobs and other positions as attributable to the fact that they are "foreigners," or that they do not speak the language of their host society well, or because they were educated elsewhere. From these perceptions and interpretations, there emerges among the immigrants a folk theory of getting ahead in the host society in which education plays a central role. Suarez-Orozco (in this volume) reports that among Central American Hispanics in San Francisco "education was the single most significant avenue to status mobility in the new land." The Sikhs also believe that their best weapon against job discrimination is good education. As Gibson states: ". . . most believed that employers generally hire those best qualified. They assumed that their children, armed with U.S. credentials, would be competitive in the American job market. They respect U.S. laws safeguarding individual rights. They believed, moreover, that employment opportunities in America are far better than in India, or in Britain" (Gibson and Bhachu, in this volume). It is important to note that the immigrants do not necessarily bring the folk theory stressing success through education from their homeland. Rather, they tend to develop this theory when they arrive in their host society. This theory contrasts with their experiences and perceptions of their homeland situation.

The immigrants also develop survival strategies to cope with some of their problems. With respect to barriers in the structure of opportunity that exist in the new country, their survival strategies include the option of returning to their homeland or emigrating to other societies. In addition, immigrants tend to explore economic resources and niches not wanted by members of the dominant group or other members of their host society. Thus, as indicated earlier, "Down Islanders" take jobs in the tourist industry which the native Crucians regard as "another slavery" (Gibson, in this volume).

The response of immigrant minorities to cultural and language differences is influenced by the fact that they arrive in their host societies with prior differences in culture and language as compared to the dominant group. I have designated the immigrants as characterized by *primary cultural/language differences* (Ogbu, 1982) because the differences between the cultural systems of the immigrants and the dominant group members of their host society existed *before* the immigrants emigrated. The Punjabi Indians in California, for example, speak the Punjabi language, practice the Sikh, Hindu, and Moslem religions, have arranged marriages and, in the case of male Sikhs, wear turbans. These practices all existed *before* the Punjabis emigrated from India. Once having arrived in the United States Punjabis continue these beliefs and practices to some extent. However, like other immigrant minorities, Punjabis interpret some of the cultural and language differences that they encounter in school and the workplace as barriers they have to overcome in order to achieve the goals of their emigration (Gibson and Bhachu, in this volume). They try to overcome them by selectively learning the English language and other cultural features of the American mainstream without interpreting such behaviors as giving up their own culture and language.

Another factor that aids the immigrants is the nature of their social identity. They bring with them a sense of who they are which they had before emigration, and they seem to retain this social identity at least during the first generation, even though they are learning the language and culture of the mainstream of their host society. Thus, the Sikhs of Valleyside (Gibson and Bhachu, in this volume) held on to their "positive sense of cultural identity, even superiority [which] protects them to some extent from the impact of majority-group pressures to assimilate." One informant told Gibson, "if we become like them, we shall fail," referring to the ways of the American majority. Gibson goes on to say that the Sikhs know very well what they like and dislike about American mainstream culture.

Similarly, West Indians/Afro-Caribbeans in the United States clearly recognize their different identity and want to retain it. Fordham (1984), Bryce-Laporte (1973), Raphael (1963) and others report that West Indians in the United States try to maintain their separate identity by disassociating themselves from native black Americans. Rather than seeking to become citizens, they prefer their "foreigner" status, since citizenship would result in their being treated like native black Americans. And they have a pragmatic reason for wanting to retain their separate identity as "Afro-Caribbeans"—it helps them improve their economic status. The point to stress is, however, that in all these cases—Sikh, West Indian, and others—the social identity existed *before* emigration and was not developed in opposition to the social identity of the dominant-group members of the host society.

One other thing that distinguishes immigrants and helps them to adjust and adapt is the degree of trust or acquiescence they have toward members of the dominant group and the institutions the latter control, such as the schools. The immigrants appear to rationalize and to acquiesce to the prejudice and discrimination against them by saying, for example, that they are strangers in a foreign land and have no choice but to tolerate prejudice and discrimination as a price worth paying in order to achieve the goals of their emigration (Gibson, in this volume; Suarez-Orozco, in this volume).

Minority Responses: Involuntary Minorities

Involuntary minorities differ from the immigrants in their perceptions, interpretations and responses to each of the sets of factors discussed above. To begin with, involuntary minorities interpret the economic, social and political barriers against them differently. Because they do not have a "homeland" with which to compare their present situation, involuntary minorities do not interpret their menial jobs and low wages as "better" than the situation of others like them in a foreign country. Instead, they compare their status with that of the members of the dominant group and usually conclude that they are worse off than they ought to be for no other reason than that they belong to a subordinate and disparaged minority group. Involuntary minorities thus have a negative dual frame of reference with respect to status mobility. Unlike immigrants, they do not see their situation as temporary; on the contrary, they tend to interpret the discrimination against them as permanent and institutionalized.

In discussing their folk theory of getting ahead, involuntary minorities often express the wish that they could get ahead through education and ability as members of the dominant group do, but they know that they cannot. They have, therefore, come to realize or believe that it requires more than education, individual effort and hard work to overcome the barriers against them in the society's opportunity structure. Consequently, they develop a folk theory of getting ahead which differs from that of the members of the dominant group in some important respects. For instance, their folk theory tends to stress collective effort as providing the best chances for overcoming the opportunity barriers. Blacks in Stockton, California (Ogbu, in this volume) and Burakumin in Japan (Shimahara, in this volume) illustrate this tendency.

Because involuntary minorities do not believe that the societal rules for self-advancement work for them, as they do for members of the dominant group, they usually try to change the rules. For example, they may try to change the criteria for school credentials and for employment in the mainstream techno-economic system. The "collective struggle" strategy is used effectively by involuntary minorities, such as blacks in the United States and Burakumin in Japan, to change those rules for advancement that these minorities believe work against them. Collective struggle is, however, one of several survival strategies that involuntary minorities develop to eliminate, lower, or circumvent the barriers they face in trying to get a good education, to obtain desirable jobs, and to advance in other ways. In the case of involuntary minorities in the United States, collective struggle includes what white Americans legitimate as "civil rights activities," but for the minorities it includes rioting and other forms of collective action that promise to increase opportunities or the pool of resources available to the minorities. Other survival strategies are found in patron-client relationships, sports, entertainment, hustling, drug dealing and the like.

As for cultural and language responses, involuntary minorities are characterized by secondary cultural difference systems. A *secondary cultural system* is one in which the cultural differences arose *after* the group has become an involuntary minority. In other words, involuntary minorities tend to develop certain beliefs and practices, including particular ways of communicating or speaking as coping mechanisms under subordination. These beliefs and practices may be new creations or reinterpretations of old ones. For example, Gibson (in this volume) reports that Crucians developed their oppositional culture ("reputation" as against "respectability") through a combination of their "African past" and a coping response to their subordination. The secondary cultural system, on the whole, constitutes a new cultural frame of reference or ideal way of believing and acting that affirms one as a bona fide member of the group. Involuntary minorities perceive their cultural frame of reference not merely as different from but as in opposition to the cultural frame of reference of their dominant-group "oppressors." The cultural and language differences emerging under this condition also serve as a boundary-maintaining mechanism. For this reason, involuntary minorities do not, unlike the immigrants, interpret the language and cultural differences they encounter in school and society as barriers they have to overcome. Rather, they interpret these differences *as symbols of identity to be maintained*. The cultural frame of reference gives the minorities both a sense of collective or social identity and a sense of self-worth.

With regard to identity, involuntary minorities develop a new sense of peoplehood, or social identity, *after* their involuntary incorporation into the society where they now live. This identity is based on their interpretations of subsequent discriminatory treatment, including denial of equal treatment and true admission into mainstream society. Koreans in Japan, for example, are permanently classified as "aliens" by the Alien Registration Act of 1947 (Lee, in this volume). In some cases, involuntary minorities may develop a new sense of peoplehood in the face of forced integration or forced assimilation into mainstream society. This oppositional identity seems to have been partly operative in the case of the Maoris of New Zealand (Barrington, in this volume) and Ute Indians in the United States (Kramer, in this volume; see also Castile and Kushner, 1981; De Vos, 1967, 1984; Spicer, 1966, 1971).

Involuntary minorities also develop an oppositional identity because they perceive and experience their treatment by members of the dominant group as collective and enduring. They believe that they cannot expect to be treated like members of the dominant group regardless of their individual differences in ability, training or education, regardless of differences in place of origin or residence, and regardless of differences in economic status or physical appearance (Green, 1981). Furthermore, involuntary minorities know that they cannot easily escape from their birth-ascribed membership in a subordinate and disparaged group by "passing" or by returning to a "homeland" (see De Vos, 1967; Ogbu, 1984). They do not see their social identity as merely different from the social identity of their "oppressors," but rather as oppositional to the social identity of the dominant group members. The oppositional identity combines with the oppositional cultural frame of reference to make crossing cultural boundaries and engaging in cross-cultural learning more problematic for involuntary minorities than for the immigrants, since utilizing the cultural frame of reference of the dominant group is threatening to their minority identity and security as well as to their solidarity. Therefore, individuals who try to behave as members of the dominant group do are discouraged by peer group pressures or by "affective dissonance" (De Vos, 1978:22, 1984).

Finally, involuntary minorities distrust members of the dominant group and the societal institutions controlled by the latter. In their history, involuntary minorities have experienced many situations that have left them with the feeling that they cannot trust members of the dominant group and their institutions. The schools are usually not trusted to provide minority children with a good education. Unlike the immigrants, involuntary minorities find no justification for the prejudice or discrimination that they experience against them in school and society other than the fact that they are disparaged groups. Furthermore, unlike the immigrants, they see the prejudice and discrimination against them as institutionalized and enduring. The discriminatory treatment and prejudice have, of course, usually been documented, as is the case for black Americans (Frazier, 1957; Drake and Cayton, 1970; Newman et al., 1978; Ogbu, in this volume).

In sum, the cultural models of immigrant minorities and those of involuntary minorities differ in these key elements: (1) a frame of reference for comparing present status and future possibilities, (2) a folk theory of getting ahead, especially through education, (3) a sense of collective identity, (4) a cultural frame of reference for judging appropriate behavior and affirming group membership and solidarity, and (5) an assessment of the extent to which one may trust members of the dominant group and the institutions they control, such as the schools. The different cultural models resulting from these differing theories and frameworks are learned by the children of the respective minority types, and these shape the attitudes, knowledge, and competencies the children bring to school.

Minority Status, Cultural Models and School Success

Immigrant Minorities

The cultural model of the immigrants enters into their schooling by influencing their educational attitudes and strategies. The nature of the contents of the cultural model—the frame of comparison with respect to status mobility, the folk theory of getting ahead in the host society, survival strategies, trusting/acquiescing relations, social identity and cultural frame of reference—affects the minorities' orientations toward schooling and their responses to schooling. The nature of the contents of their cultural model leads the immigrants to adopt pragmatic or instrumental attitudes and strategies that are quite conducive to school success.

The immigrants' dual status-mobility frame of reference, folk theory of success, and survival strategies lead them to emphasize education for their children. Among the Sikhs for instance, there is a belief that school success determines later success in the job market. Parents, therefore, strongly admonish their children to follow school rules of behavior for academic achievement even when such behaviors are contrary to parents' own cultural values. Parents advise their children: "Obey your teachers. Do your schoolwork. Stay out of trouble. You're there to learn and not to fight. Keep trying harder. Keep pushing yourself." According to Gibson and Bhachu (in this volume),

Sikhs counsel their young to place schoolwork first, ahead of housework, jobs and especially social activities, including those sponsored by the schools. They expect their children to do well academically. They urge them to do better by seeking help from their teachers.

Although they recognize language and cultural difficulties the children experience in school and discriminatory treatment by the school, parents place academic responsibility on the children themselves. As Gibson and Bhachu report with respect to Sikh parents in California:

> Sikh parents are not naive about the difficulties their children encounter in school. They simply brook no excuses for poor performance. Their children, as they see it, have far better schooling available to them in Valleyside than would have been the case in India. It is their responsibility to make the most of their opportunities.

Likewise, in Britain, Sikh parents believe responsibility for school performance rests with the child. Poor performance is strongly discouraged:

> Being a poor student is tantamount to being a failure as a social being. Children who bring home poor report cards are told they have not tried hard enough and are made to feel a failure. When word of their poor performance reaches relatives and family friends, Sikh young people may even be ignored socially. This sanction proves an excellent deterrent for bad behavior and helps instill a desire in the young to acquire educational qualifications. Such pressures fall most heavily on boys, for whom educational achievement is considered essential. (Gibson and Bhachu, in this volume)

It is of greater significance that parents do not stop at verbal admonition but carefully monitor the academic behavior of their children. Thus, Gibson and Bhachu write that:

> Parents monitor their children's out-of-school activities carefully, even during the late teenage years, in order for them to avoid "bad company" that might distract from the main goal of getting on in the educational system. Young people are taught that their teens are a time for diligence in school and that they will be able to enjoy themselves socially later on, once they are through with their studies. They are particularly discouraged

from wasting emotional energy at this point in their lives on cross-gender relationships.

The educational attitudes and strategies of other immigrant minorities are similar. Gibson (in this volume) reports that Down Islanders are influenced by their cultural model to pursue education. They emphasize education because they believe that good education will enable them to overcome the effects of job discrimination. For Koreans in the United States (Lee, in this volume) and Hispanics in San Francisco (Suarez-Orozco, in this volume), obtaining American education was a primary goal of emigration. As Suarez-Orozco reports for the Central American immigrants in San Francisco:

> Many Central American parents articulated the notion that a primary factor in the decision to emigrate was the future welfare of their children. As one mother from Nicaragua put it, "We came here for them," referring to her five children. She added, "So that they may become somebody tomorrow."

The nature of the immigrants' cultural and language differences as well as their collective/social identity also enables them to cross cultural/language boundaries and learn successfully in the schools of their host society. The primary cultural differences of the immigrants initially cause problems both in their relationships with their teachers and other students and in the actual process of learning. But the problems are attributable to differences in cultural assumptions, not to social opposition and, because they are not oppositional, they tend to diminish over time. For example, Central American Hispanic immigrant children enter San Francisco public schools from a cultural background that stresses getting ahead on the basis of who you know or "because of your name," rather than on the basis of educational credentials.

Punjabi Sikhs enter Valleyside public schools with the cultural assumption that children must defer to teachers and other adults, in contrast to the schools' expectation that children will defend their ideas even when such ideas conflict with those of the teacher. Sikh children also face problems of gender relations in school. They are brought up to avoid eye contact with members of the opposite sex, but in the classroom they are expected to look directly at teachers and classmates of the opposite sex when addressing them and when being addressed or be thought impolite. Still another problem is that immigrant minority children may bring to school a style of learning that is quite different from the style emphasized in school. In the case of Chinese immigrant children for example, their traditional style of learning emphasizes external forms and rote memorization rather than the observation, analysis and comprehension stressed in American schools (Ogbu, 1983). Then, too, immigrant minority children come to school lacking fluency in the language of instruction. In the case of the Chinese and some other minorities, the children's language differs from the English language structurally and in other important respects.

Immigrant minority children, therefore, initially have difficulties in school because of these cultural and language differences, but they eventually adjust and learn more or less successfully. Why? First, the immigrants succeed in overcoming cultural and language barriers because of the response of the schools to these problems. The extent to which the immigrants cross cultural/language boundaries and learn depends in part on what schools do to help them. But, second, it also depends on the minorities' own perceptions of and responses to the cultural and language differences facing them. In the latter case, the immigrants are aided by the non-oppositional nature of their cultural/language differences and identity as well as by the goals of their emigration.

As we have seen, the cultural and language differences faced by the immigrants existed before they emigrated; they did not arise as a part of the immigrants' coping mechanisms under subordination or to protect their identity. Consequently, the immigrants see the cultural/language differences as *barriers to be overcome* in order to achieve their long-range goals of employment, good wages and other benefits, rather than as *markers of social identity to be maintained*. For the immigrants, overcoming the cultural/language differences is not only essential for their social adjustment and academic success but is non-threatening to their own culture, language and identity. They generally adopt what Gibson (in this volume) calls the strategy of "accommodation without assimilation." That is, while they may not give up their cultural beliefs, cultural practices and language, they are willing and actually do strive to "play the classroom game by the rules" and try to overcome "all kinds of difficulties in school because they believe so strongly that there will be a payoff later."

Thus, in the Sikh community in Britain, it is strongly believed that one should understand the way the majority society operates and gain the social skills and personal networks that open doors. Gibson and Bhachu go on to say that a successful and respected Punjabi is one who demonstrates competence in the ways of the non-Punjabi world. Consequently, parents expect their young to become proficient in both the cultures of the Punjabi immigrants and Punjabi settlers, as well as that of the wider white community in which they find themselves.

Because the immigrants perceive the cultural and language differences as barriers they have to overcome, they do not go to school expecting to be taught in their own language and culture. Rather, they usually expect and are willing to learn the school culture and language, although they do not necessarily do so without difficulties. The immigrants are able to cross cultural boundaries because primary cultural differences and the problems they cause tend to be specific in nature so that they can be identified through careful ethnographic research. This identifiability and specificity make it possible to develop appropriate policies and programs to eliminate them or reduce their adverse effects.

Finally, the immigrants' trusting or acquiescing relationship with the schools and with members of the dominant group who control the schools also facilitates their school success. Although immigrant minorities may be attending segregated and/or inferior schools, their overall evaluation of their educational opportunity is not disillusioned for three reasons. One is that the immigrants, at least in the United States, tend to regard the public schools as offering an education far superior to what they knew of schools in their homeland. They may not recognize the segregated and inferior schools as inferior, since their frame of comparison is the education in their homeland, not the education of the dominant-group members of their host society. A second factor is that the immigrants believe that they are treated better in the public schools than they would be treated by the schools of their homeland. Immigrant minorities often say that they are both surprised and appreciative of the fact that they receive free textbooks and other supplies (Suarez-Orozco, in this volume). Third, even when the immigrants recognize, experience and resent prejudice and discrimination in school, as in the case of the Sikhs, they appear to respond in a manner that does not discourage them from doing well in school. They rationalize the prejudice and discrimination by saying that as "guests in a foreign land they have no choice but to tolerate prejudice and discrimination." Sikh parents impress this attitude on their children and place the responsibility for school success on their children themselves (Gibson and Bhachu, in this volume).

As a result of these perceptions, responses, or adaptations, the immigrant community, family, and children adopt schooling strategies that enhance academic success and promote social adjustment. At the community and family levels some of these categories include encouraging or guiding children to develop good academic work habits and perseverance through gossip and related techniques. Parents and other adult members of the community communicate to children clear instrumental messages about education: namely that education is a sine qua non of getting ahead in the host society and that it is also a means of overcoming or reducing discrimination in employment. Parents and community members tend to insist that children follow school rules of behavior that enhance academic success. For their part, immigrant minority children seem to respond positively to their parents' advice and training and to parental and community pressures. The children try to develop and maintain serious academic attitudes, value making good grades, respect school authority, follow school rules of behavior and standard practices, and invest a good deal of time and effort in their schoolwork. If language problems persist, older children tend to select courses requiring less use of language. They also avoid fields of study which prepare them for jobs where there is a job ceiling or discrimination against members of their group.

Involuntary Minorities

Like the immigrants, involuntary minorities encounter economic and social barriers in the society at large, and at school they encounter interpersonal and intergroup problems as well as academic learning problems because of cultural/language differences, but they are less able than the immigrants to overcome these problems. Therefore, they tend to experience more prolonged social adjustment problems and persistently higher rates of school failure. While they generally verbalize their desire to make good grades, there is less community and family pressure to achieve such a goal. As for peer groups, their collective orientation is actually the opposite of what it is among the immigrants: it is anti-academic success. Consequently, peer pressures among involuntary minority students are used to discourage utilization of those strategies that enhance school success. There are complex "community forces" which make it more difficult for involuntary minority students to overcome their initial school problems. I will now discuss some of the community forces that arise from the involuntary minorities' cultural models and show how such forces enter and affect their educational process.

Dual Status-Mobility Frame. As noted earlier, involuntary minorities, unlike immigrant minorities, did not choose to move to their present societies motivated by the hope of economic success or political freedom. Nor do they compare their situation to the conditions of their peers "back home," or to a less favorable former status. The only comparative frame of reference they have is to the members of the dominant group of their respective societies; and when they compare themselves with dominant-group members, involuntary minorities invariably conclude that they are worse off then they ought to be because of the way they are treated by the dominant group. They become resentful, especially because they attribute their poorer conditions to what they perceive as institutionalized discrimination perpetuated against them by dominant-group members and by dominant-group-controlled institutions such as schools. This assessment leads to disillusionment and lack of optimism about effort.

A comparison of two Hispanic groups studied by Suarez-Orozco (in this volume) illustrates the problem of involuntary minorities. Suarez-Orozco notes that Mexican American informants, members of an involuntary minority-group, "had no 'here' and 'there' reference matrix. Rather, while considering educational issues there was a perception of a basic continuity in the pattern of exploitation and crushed efforts; and they could produce countless vignettes of systematic exploitation, both expressive and instrumental." In contrast: "Central American immigrants endured hardships, racism, and marginality in reference to two issues: a perception that no matter how bad things seem to be [in the United States], they are not as bad as they would be at home [i.e., in Central America], *and* anticipation of a better tomorrow in which they came to view the United States as a land of opportunity." Among blacks in Stockton, an involuntary minority group, the perception of a job ceiling as relatively permanent produced disillusionment and low optimism about effort. A similar situation exists for the Koreans and Burakumin in Japan (Lee, in this volume; Shimahara, in this volume).

The Folk Theory of Success. Involuntary minorities emphasize the importance of education in expressing their folk theory of getting ahead but this verbal endorsement is not usually accompanied by the necessary effort. This discrepancy is attributable in part to the fact that historically involuntary minorities did not get the same opportunity to benefit from their education as members of the dominant group with respect to jobs, wages and other working conditions. Eventually the minorities came to believe that discrimination against them is institutionalized, and that it is not eliminated entirely by getting an education (Ogbu, 1982). Thus, during my fieldwork in Stockton, blacks complained that they had to work twice as hard as the whites or be twice as good as the whites if they competed for the same job or social position. One result is that the minorities did not develop "effort optimism" toward academic work (Shack, 1970). That is, they did not develop a strong tradition of cultural know-how, hard work and perseverance toward academic tasks. In Stockton, minority parents also appeared to be giving their children contradictory messages about getting ahead through education. While doing fieldwork there, I found that on the one hand parents were telling their children to get a good education in order to get a good job. On the other hand, the actual texture of the parents' lives with respect to low-level jobs, underemployment and unemployment, conveyed a contradictory message, which was powerful enough to undo their exhortation. Unavoidably, minority parents discuss their problems with "the system" as well as the problems of their relatives, friends and neighbors in the presence of their children. The result is that involuntary minority group children increasingly become disillusioned about their ability to succeed in adult life through the mainstream strategy of schooling (Hunter, 1980). This problem is not, of course, limited to black Americans, but can also be seen in the experiences of other involuntary minority groups such as the Burakumin (Shimahara, in this volume) and Koreans in Japan (Lee, in this volume).

Incongruent, Detracting, Competing Survival Strategies. The folk theory of getting ahead among involuntary minorities stresses other means of getting ahead than schooling, namely, survival strategies within and outside the mainstream techno-economic system, as discussed earlier. Most of the available data on survival strategies relate to black Americans, but there are indications that other involuntary minorities have them as well (see Ogbu and Matute-Bianchi, 1986).

These survival strategies affect minority youths' schooling in a number of ways. One is that they tend to generate attitudes and behaviors that are not necessarily conducive to good classroom teaching and learning. When survival strategies such as the collective struggle that the civil rights movement entailed succeed in increasing the pool of jobs and other resources available to minorities, they may encourage minority youths to work hard in school. However, such success can also lead the youths to slacken their efforts, blame "the system" and rationalize their lack of serious effort at schoolwork. Other survival strategies such as clientship or Uncle Toming among black Americans are not particularly conducive to academic success because they do not create good role models for school success through good study habits and hard work. Instead, clientship, for example, teaches minority children manipulative attitudes, knowledge and skills to deal with the members of the dominant group and their institutions. As the children become familiar with other survival strategies like hustling and pimping as well as drug dealing, their attitudes toward schooling are adversely affected. For example, in the norms that support some of these survival strategies, such as hustling, the work ethic is reversed by the insistence that one should make it without working, especially without "doing the white man's work." Furthermore, for students who are into hustling, social interactions in the classroom are seen as opportunities for exploitation, i.e., opportunities to gain prestige by putting the other person or persons down. This may lead to class disruption and suspensions (Ogbu, 1981, 1987; see also Matute-Bianchi's description of Chicano students, in this volume).

Another problem is that survival strategies may compete seriously with schooling as methods of getting ahead, leading young people to channel their time and efforts into non-academic activities. That is particularly true as involuntary minority children get older and become more aware of how some adults in their local communities "make it" without mainstream school credentials and employment (Bouie, 1981; Ogbu, 1974). Kramer, for example, reports (in this volume) that Ute Indians felt that education was not particularly important as indicated by their frequent reference to the fact that some of their Tribal Council leaders had only a few years of elementary school. Among black Americans there is some evidence that many young people view sports and entertainment, rather than education, as the way to get ahead, and their perceptions are reinforced by the media and by the realities they observe in the community and society at large. Blacks are over-represented in such lucrative sports as baseball, basketball and football as well as in boxing. The average annual salary in the NBA and in basketball is over $300,000 and in the NFL it is over $90,000. Many of the superstars who earn between $1 million and $2 million a year are black and these people may have had little education. While the number of such highly paid athletes are few, media exposure makes them and the entertainers more visible to black youngsters than black lawyers, doctors, engineers and scientists (Wong, 1987). There is some preliminary evidence, too, that black parents encourage their children's athletic activities in the belief that such activities should lead to a career in professional sports (Wong, 1987).

Under these circumstances, involuntary minority students, like their parents, may express high interest in doing well in school and in obtaining good school credentials for future employment in mainstream economy, but they do not back up their wishes and aspirations with effort, even though they know that it requires hard work and perseverance to succeed academically (Ogbu, 1977). The lack of serious academic attitudes and effort appears to increase as the students get older and become more aware of their own social reality or come to accept the prevailing beliefs about their social reality.

Oppositional Cultural Frame of Reference and Identity. Crossing cultural/language boundaries represents another barrier to social adjustment and high academic performance among involuntary minority group students because such minority groups form and maintain an oppositional cultural frame of reference and identity. Unlike the immigrants, involuntary minority students do not interpret the cultural and language differences they encounter in school as barriers they have to overcome and do not, apparently, make concerted efforts to overcome them. Rather, they interpret the cultural and language differences as markers of identity to be maintained. Moreover, they do not appear to make a clear distinction, as the immigrants do, between what they have to learn or do in order to succeed in school (such as learning the standard language and the standard behavior practices of the school) and the dominant-group's cultural frame of reference (which may be seen as the cultural frame of reference of their "oppressors"). As noted earlier, involuntary minority students appear to interpret learning certain aspects of the dominant group's cultural frame of reference as detrimental to their own culture, language and identity.

Therefore, when they *equate* the standard language and behavior practices required at school with the dominant group's language and culture, this results in conscious or unconscious opposition or in ambivalence toward school learning. I should add, however, that in Stockton, blacks express opposition to school learning because they interpret this learning as obeying white people's orders as blacks did in the days of slavery. Gibson (in this volume) also reports that among the Crucians there is some feeling that homework or other forms of schoolwork are slavery. It follows that involuntary minority students who adopt attitudes conducive to school success or who behave in a manner conducive to academic success are often accused by their peers of acting like their enemy, i.e., like their "oppressors." Among U.S. blacks, such students may be accused of acting white or acting like Uncle Toms (Fordham and Ogbu, 1986; Petroni, 1970). They are accused of being disloyal to the group and to the cause of the group, and they risk being isolated from their peers. But it is not only social pressures or peer pressures that keep involuntary minority students from striving to achieve academic success. There are also psychological pressures. For example, De Vos (1967) has noted that even in the absence of peer pressures, involuntary minority students may avoid adopting serious academic attitudes and avoid persevering in academic tasks partly because they have internalized their group's interpretations of such attitudes and behaviors and partly because they are uncertain that they would be accepted by members of the dominant group if they succeeded in learning to act like them. They fear that if they did act like the dominant group, they would lose the support of their own groups. This state of affairs results in "affective dissonance" for the individual (De Vos, 1978:22). Difficulties in the educational context arising from this oppositional process are explicitly reported in this volume for most of the involuntary minorities—the Crucians, black Americans, Maoris, Mexican Americans and the Utes.

Thus, as Petroni (1970) has pointed out, the dilemma of involuntary minority students is that they have to choose between academic success and maintaining their minority cultural frame of reference and identity—a choice that does not arise for the immigrants. Under this circumstance, involuntary minority students who want to achieve academic success are compelled to adopt strategies that promise to shield them from peer criticism and ostracism.

Distrusting the System. The deep distrust that involuntary minorities have for members of the dominant group and the schools they control adds to the minorities' difficulties in school. The minorities distrust the schools more than the immigrants do because the former lack the advantage of the dual frame of reference that allows the immigrants to compare the schools they now attend with the schools they knew "back home." Indeed, involuntary minorities compare their schools with those of the members of the dominant group and usually conclude that theirs are inferior for no other reason than that they are minorities. Having concluded that their schools and education are inferior, they divert their emotion and efforts in a continual quest for "better schools and better education." The message is also communicated to children quite early that the schools they attend and the education they are receiving are inferior, a message that contributes to the development of distrust for the system.

Since involuntary minorities do not trust the schools and those who control the schools, they are usually skeptical about the schools' ability to educate their children. This skepticism is communicated through family and community discussions and gossip, as well as through public debates over minority education. Even minority school employees participate in the transmission of skepticism to the children, as I found in my research in Stockton: black school employees were very skeptical about the efficacy of the educational programs they were implementing. Another factor discouraging academic effort is that involuntary minorities—parents and students alike—tend to question school rules of behavior and standard practices, rather than accept and follow them as the immigrants appear to do. Indeed, involuntary minorities sometimes interpret the school rules and standard practices as an imposition of the dominant group members' cultural frame of reference, which does not necessarily meet their real educational needs.

I have suggested elsewhere (Ogbu, 1988) that under these circumstances, it is probably difficult for children of involuntary minorities, especially the older ones, to accept and follow school rules of behavior and to persevere at their academic tasks.

Variability Within the Adaptation

In the preceding pages, I have argued that the cultural models of two types of minorities—immigrant and involuntary minorities—enter differentially into the process of schooling and affect their school adjustment and performance differently. However, I do not claim that all immigrant minority students are academically successful and all involuntary minorities are academically unsuccessful. What I have described is what appears to be the dominant pattern for each type. Within each type, as within each minority group, there are several culturally available strategies that enhance school success. But the two types of minorities differ in the degree of support, especially peer support, for individuals utilizing the strategies that enhance school success.

Among the immigrants, the collective orientation appears to be toward making good grades or doing well in school. There are pressures from the community (e.g., gossip), from the family (e.g., placing responsibility for success on the individual child) and from peer groups (e.g., ridicule and isolation) that support making good grades. Individuals who are subjected to criticism and possible peer isolation are youths who do not achieve academically (Yu, 1987). Partly because of the community, family and peer pressures, immigrant minority youths tend to utilize those strategies that enhance academic success (Ogbu, 1987).

Among involuntary minorities, on the other hand, the situation is different. While making good grades is generally verbalized as a goal, there is less community, family and peer pressure to achieve this goal. There is, for example, no stigma nor is there gossip against youths who do not make good grades. As for peer groups, the collective orientation is actually anti-academic success. Consequently, peer pressures are used to discourage strategies that enhance school success. And youths who are successful or who are behaving as if they wanted to succeed are the ones subjected to peer criticism and possible isolation. In this situation, youths who want to succeed academically are compelled to adopt a variety of secondary strategies that enable them to conceal their real attitudes and efforts from their peers and thus shield themselves from peer pressures and other detracting forces. The secondary strategies are utilized in addition to the conventional strategies adopted by immigrant minorities, which include serious academic attitudes, hard work and perseverance. The secondary strategies provide the context in which the minority youths can practice the conventional strategies without penalty.

A good example of secondary strategies is camouflage among black youths. One technique of camouflage is to become involved in athletic or other team-oriented activities approved by peers. Involvement in athletic activities reassures peer group members that one is not simply pursuing individual interests and success in order to get ahead of others. Another technique of camouflage is to become a jester or the class clown. By playing the role of the clown the jester satisfies the expectations of his or her peers by pretending not to be concerned with academic excellence which the peers do not endorse. However, the student is merely concealing his or her real academic interest, efforts and attitudes. Such an individual is careful not to brag about his academic success and the success can then be attributed to the fact that he or she is naturally smart since no one thinks that he or she studies or is serious about academic success.

References

Benedict, R. 1943. "Transmitting Our Democratic Heritage in the Schools." *The American Journal of Sociology* 48:722–27.

Boas, F. 1928. *Anthropology and Modern Life.* New York: Norton and Co.

Bohannan, P. 1957. *Justice and Judgment Among the Tiv.* London: Oxford University Press.

Bond, G.C. 1981. "Social Economic Status and Educational Achievement: A Review Article." *Anthropology and Education Quarterly* 12(4):227–57.

Bouie, A. 1981. "Student Perceptions of Behavior and Misbehavior in the Schools: An Exploratory Study and Discussion." San Francisco: Far West Laboratory for Educational Research and Development.

Bryce-Laporte, R.S. 1973. "Black Immigrants." In *Through Different Eyes*, ed. P.I. Rose, S. Rothman, and W.J. Wilson, pp. 44–61. New York: Oxford University Press.

Castile, G.P., and G. Kushner. 1981. *Persistent Peoples: Cultural Enclaves in Perspective.* Tucson: University of Arizona Press.

De Vos, G.A. 1967. "Minority Status and Attitude Toward Authority." In *Japan's Invisible Race*, ed. G.A. De Vos and H. Wagatsuma, pp. 258–72. Berkeley: University of California Press.

———. 1978. "Selective Permeability and Reference Group Sanctioning: Psychocultural Continuities in Role Degradation." In *Major Social Issues*, ed. J.M. Yinger and S.J. Cutler, pp. 7–24. New York: Free Press.

———. 1984. "Ethnic Persistence and Role Degradation: An Illustration from Japan." A paper presented at the American-Soviet Symposium on Contemporary Ethnic Processes in the USA and the USSR. New Orleans, LA, 14–16 April.

DeWare, H. 1978. "Affirmative Action Plan A.T. and T. is Permitted." *The Washington Post*, 4 July, pp. A1, A7.

Drake, St. Claire, and H.R. Cayton. 1970. *Black Metropolis: A Study of Negro Life in a Northern City*. New York: Harcourt.

Erickson, F., and J. Mohatt. 1982. "Cultural Organization of Participant Structure in Two Classrooms of Indian Students." In *Doing the Ethnography of Schooling: Educational Anthropology in Action*, ed. G. D. Spindler, pp. 132–75. New York: Holt, Rinehart and Winston.

Fordham, S. 1984. "Ethnography in a Black High School: Learning Not to be a Native." A paper presented at the 83rd Annual Meeting, American Anthropological Association, Denver, Colorado, 14–18 Nov.

Fordham, S., and Ogbu, J.U. 1986. "Black Students' School Success: Coping with the Burden of 'Acting White,'" *The Urban Review* 18(3):176–206.

Frazier, E.F. 1957. *The Negro in the United States*. New York: Macmillan.

Green, J., and C. Wallat. 1981. *Ethnography and Language in the Educational Setting*. Norwood, N.J.: ABLEX.

Haycock, K., and M.S. Navarro. 1988. "Unfinished Business." Report from The Achievement Council, Oakland, Calif.

Hewett, E. 1905. "Ethnic Factors in Education." *American Anthropologist* 7(1). Reprinted in *Educational Patterns and Cultural Configurations: The Anthropology of Education*, ed. J.I. Roberts and S.K. Akinsanya, pp. 27–36. New York: David McKay Co., 1976.

Hunter, D. 1980. "Ducks vs. Hard Rocks." *Newsweek*, 18 Aug.

Ito, H. 1967. "Japan's Outcastes in the United States." In *Japan's Invisible Race*, ed. G.A. De Vos and H. Wagatsuma. pp. 200–21. Berkeley: University of California Press.

Jensen, A.R. 1969. "How Much Can We Boost IQ and Scholastic Achievement?" *Harvard Educational Review* 39:1–123.

Mead, M. 1943. "Our Educational Emphases in Primitive Perspective." *The American Journal of Sociology* 8:633–39.

Mickelson, R.A. 1984. "Race, Class and Gender Differences in Adolescent Academic Achievement Attitudes and Behaviors." Ph.D. diss. Graduate School of Education, University of California, Los Angeles.

Newman, D.K., et al. 1978. *Protest, Politics and Prosperity: Black Americans and White Institutions*. New York: Pantheon.

Ogbu, J.U. 1974. *The Next Generation: An Ethnography of Education in an Urban Neighborhood*. New York: Academic Press.

—. 1977. "Racial Stratification and Education: The Case of Stockton, California." *ICRD Bulletin* 12(3):1–26.

—. 1978. *Minority Education and Caste: The American System in Cross-Cultural Perspective*. New York: Academic Press.

—. 1981. "Education, Clientage and Social Mobility: Caste and Social Change in the United States and Nigeria." In *Social Inequality: Comparative and Developmental Approaches*, ed. G.D. Berreman, pp. 277–306. New York: Academic Press.

—. 1982. "Socialization: A Cultural Ecological Approach." In *The Social Life of Children in a Changing Society*, ed. K.M. Borman, pp. 253–67. Hillsdale, N.J.: Lawrence Erlbaum Associates.

—. 1983. "Minority Status and Schooling in Plural Societies." *Comparative Education Review* 27(2):168–90.

—. 1984. "Understanding Community Forces Affecting Minority Students' Academic Effort." The Achievement Council, Oakland, Calif., Unpublished manuscript.

—. 1987. "Opportunity Structure, Cultural Boundaries and Literacy." In *Language, Literacy and Culture: Issues of Society and Schooling*, ed. J.A. Langer, pp. 149–77. Norwood, N.J.: ABLEX.

—. 1988. "Diversity and Equity in Public Education: Community Forces and Minority School Adjustment and Performance." In *Policies for America's Public Schools: Teachers, Equity and Indicators*, ed. R. Haskins and D. McRae, pp. 127–70. Norwood, N.J.: ABLEX Publishing Corp.

—. In Press. "Cultural Models, Identity and Literacy." In *Cultural Psychology: The Chicago Symposia*, ed. J. Stigler, G. Herdt, and R.A. Schweder. New York: Cambridge University Press.

Ogbu, J.U., and M.E. Matute-Bianchi. 1986. "Understanding Sociocultural Factors: Knowledge, Identity and School Adjustment." In *Beyond Language: Social and Cultural Factors in Schooling Language Minority Students*, pp. 73–142. Bilingual Education Office, California State Department of Education, Sacramento, California.

Petroni, F. A. 1970. "Uncle Toms: White Stereotypes in the Black Movement." *Human Organization* 29:260–66.

Powdermaker, H. 1943. "The Channeling of Negro Aggression by the Cultural Process." *The American Journal of Sociology* 48:750-58.

—. 1968. *After Freedom: A Cultural Study in the Deep South*. New York: Atheneum.

Raphael, L. 1963. "To Be or Not to Be an American Negro." *Negro Digest* 13(1):30–34.

Redfield, R. 1943. "Culture and Education in the Midwestern Highlands of Guatemala." *The American Journal of Sociology* 48:640–48.

Shack, W.A. 1970. "On Black American Values in White America: Some Perspectives on the Cultural Aspects of Learning Behavior and Compensatory Education." A paper prepared for the Social Science Research Council: Subcommittee on Values and Compensatory Education, 1970–71.

Slade, M. 1982. "Aptitude, Intelligence or What?" *New York Times*, 24 Oct.

Spicer, E.H. 1966. "The Process of Cultural Enclavement in Middle America." 36th Congress. *International de Maricanistas* (Seville) 3:267–79.

———. 1971. "Persistent Cultural Systems: A Comparative Study of Identity Systems That Can Adapt to Contrasting Environments." *Science* 174:795–800.

Van den Berghe, Pierre. 1980. "A Review of Minority Education and Caste: The American System in Cross-Cultural Perspective." *Comparative Education Review* 24(1):126–30.

Wigdor, A.K., and Garner, W.R. 1982. *Ability Testing: Uses, Consequences and Controversies*. Washington, D.C.: The National Academic Press, part 11: Documentation.

Wilson, W.J. 1980. "Race, Class and Public Policy in Education." Lecture presented at the National Institute of Education, Vera Brown Memorial Seminar Series, Washington, D.C.

Wong, M.L. 1987. "Education Versus Sports." Special Project, University of California, Berkeley. Unpublished manuscript.

Yu, E. 1987. Personal communication.

Part II
Case Studies

Chapter Two
Immigrant Adaptation to Schooling:
A Hispanic Case

Marcelo M. Suarez-Orozco
University of California, San Diego

Introduction

The educational functioning of Hispanic Americans has gained increasing attention in the past two decades (see, for example, Suarez-Orozco, 1989; Lefkowitz, 1985; Hispanic Policy Development Project [HPDP], 1984; Brown et al., 1980; Carter and Segura, 1979). Although much research has been done to further understanding of the issues facing Hispanic Americans in schools, many areas of the problem remain virtually unexplored. One such area which I have argued demands proper systematic treatment is related to the *differences* emerging from a consideration of the educational adaptation of the various Hispanic American groups (Suarez-Orozco, 1987c). Mexican Americans, Puerto Rican Americans, Americans of Cuban descent and Americans of South American origin, as well as the recent immigrants and refugees from troubled Central American nations, are distinct populations, face different issues and should be understood as such.

Although for political purposes Hispanic American leaders typically overlook the issue of diversity, more strict heuristic reasoning demands a consideration of differences, as well as similarities, in patterns of educational adaptation emerging among these distinct populations.

This chapter explores issues relating to the school functioning of Central American immigrants in the ethnographic tradition of anthropological research. For purposes of comparison, I shall also interject findings from earlier ethnographic work among Mexican Americans (Suarez-Orozco, 1987a and 1987b).

The 1980s witnessed an impressive and continuous flow of immigrants and refugees from Central America to the United States (Suarez-Orozco, 1989; Leslie and Leitch, 1989). The United Nations High Commissioner for Refugees reported that over 500,000 Salvadorans fled their country between 1979 and 1983 (Mohn, 1983:42), with an estimated 300,000 to 400,000 taking refuge in the United States (Mohn, 1983:43). A 1987 report on Central American refugees estimated that there are perhaps as many as 700,000 Salvadoran refugees in the United States (Universidad para la Paz, 1987:177). The United States is also home to increasing numbers of Guatemalans. Reports estimate that as many as one million Guatemalans have become refugees as a result of the warfare in that country (Mohn, 1983:42; Universidad para la Paz, 1987:49; Manz, 1988). Many, although not a majority, of these Guatemalans have settled in the United States. Turning to Nicaragua, it has been noted that during the bloody war to overthrow Somoza, an estimated 40,000 Nicaraguans were killed (see Buckley, 1984:332; LaFeber, 1984:226–42), and some 200,000 people left their country in search of refuge in Mexico, other Central American nations and the United States (Aguayo, 1986; Quezada, 1985:37). Since the *Sandinista* takeover in 1987, thousands more have died in the U.S.-backed Contra war (Dickey, 1987; Kempton, 1986:5–11). Recent estimates put the number of Nicaraguan refugees in Miami alone at over 30,000 (Universidad para la Paz, 1987:178).

This chapter considers certain key educational issues facing a cohort of these recent arrivals. I shall report on their perceptions of schools and on their responses to schooling. This will lead me to explore the emergence of an immigrant ethic in the context of social change. As immigrants move into a new socio-geographical landscape, they develop ideas on the nature of opportunity and the future. I will also explore the emergence of significant socio-familial motivational dynamics among the immigrants. Lastly, I will consider certain issues relating to school problems and non-learning.

Throughout the chapter, I shall explore the theoretical significance of these patterns juxtaposing two complementary approaches to the study of minority school functioning: a psychosocial model of ethnic adaptation and minority status in plural societies (De Vos, 1980, 1982 and 1983; De Vos and Suarez-Orozco, 1990) and a cultural ecological approach to the study of minority adaptation to schooling (Ogbu, 1978, 1981, this volume).

The Problem of Hispanic School Failure

The school functioning of Hispanic Americans, largely Mexican Americans and Puerto Rican Americans, has been amply documented in the scholarly literature (see Matute-Bianchi, this volume). For example, Brown et al. reported in 1980 that almost one-fourth of all Mexican Americans nationwide aged twenty-five years or older had less than five years of schooling (1980:25). In the Southwest of the United States only 60 percent of Mexican American youth graduate from high school compared to 86 percent of Anglo American youth (Knowlton, 1979). Mexican American children also have been found to perform poorly on a number of achievement scales ranging from measures of reading achievement to participation in extracurricular activities (Maestas, 1981).

The dropout rate for Mexican American students is much higher, moreover, than for "other Hispanics" including those of Central and South American origin (HPDP, 1984:57). Researchers have reported other differences between Mexican Americans and "other Hispanics." For example, only 6 percent of the "other Hispanic" category aged twenty-five or older has completed less than five years of school compared with 23 percent of the Mexican American population of that age group (Brown et al., 1980). These are significant differences, pointing to the fact that the Hispanic Americans are a heterogeneous group facing various problems.

In the first phase of my ethnographic research among working class Mexican American students in an industrial center of Northern California, I also encountered an alarming pattern of poor academic performance. Large numbers of Mexican American children were failing in school. The teachers, mostly Anglo, defensively blamed the parents for the problems. The parents, quite enraged at the teachers for not educating their children, pushed for greater ethnic control over the school (Suarez-Orozco, 1987b).

As my research progressed, I became increasingly aware that recent immigrants from Central America did not follow the same pattern of school performance as the Mexican American students. I also began to see that the issues facing more recent Central American immigrant students were quite different from those facing Mexican American students. In short, I realized that the two groups faced quite distinct interpersonal issues, vis-à-vis the schools and the larger encompassing social environment. This posed a number of important empirical and theoretical questions: are there indeed patterned differences in the interpersonal concerns of these groups as they relate to the schooling processes? Do their schooling strategies differ? Are there differences in the perceptions of schooling between the two groups? Are there differences in the motivational patterns found among students in these two groups? If such differences do exist, what can they reveal about minority schooling and the serious problem of minority non-learning in plural societies?

In order to explore these issues I conducted an ethnographic study of the adaptation patterns of recent immigrants from Central America. The research began with participant observation at two schools with high concentrations of Central American students. After six months of observation, excited by what the ethnographic record was suggesting, I began an in-depth study of the psycho-pedagogical adaptation of about 50 students. Brilliant students, average students and poor students were all represented in our sample. The second phase of the study lasted approximately six additional months.

A Psychosocial Framework

John Ogbu (1974, 1978, 1981, this volume) has demonstrated from a comparative perspective the cultural ecological basis of castelike or involuntary minority school failure. Ogbu identifies castelike or involuntary minorities as minorities who have been exploited and depreciated systematically over generations through slavery, e.g., blacks in the United States, and colonization, e.g., Mexicans in the Southwest after the Anglo colonization of the Mexican territories and

Koreans in Japan. For heuristic purposes, involuntary minorities are differentiated from immigrant minorities such as Salvadorans, Guatemalans and Nicaraguans in the United States, Sicilians in Brazil, and Japanese in Argentina.

Involuntary minorities, as contrasted with immigrant minorities, were incorporated into a host society not by their own choice, and they must operate in an encompassing social context in which there is a basic continuity in a long history of instrumental and expressive exploitation and depreciation by the dominant group. Employment opportunities have been limited historically to certain less desirable sectors, usually those requiring little formal schooling. Ogbu (1983, this volume) has cogently argued that this "job ceiling" has direct consequences on a group's perceptions of schooling. Such perceptions may be translated into behavioral strategies which in some cases serve to further remove minority youngsters from the schooling process.

Immigrant minorities, on the other hand, "choose" to leave their original environment to enter a new socioeconomic and cultural milieu. Immigrants are free from a history of depreciation over generations in the new social environment (De Vos and Suarez-Orozco, 1990). Furthermore, in the context of changes brought about by the migratory experience, immigrants develop what I have termed a *dual frame of reference* (Suarez-Orozco, 1989). That is to say, immigrants commonly interpret conditions and events in the new country in direct reference to prior experiences in their country of origin.

These facts have been shown to have an effect on the emergence of a folk epistemology regarding schooling and how to "make it" in the new land. This is the case among the Salvadorans, Nicaraguans and Guatemalans reported on in this chapter. Free from such experience of job ceiling exploitation and having a comparative perspective ("homeland" vs. "new land") on the nature of their current situation and future opportunities, working-class Central American informants have developed beliefs about schooling which are quite different from those reported among nonimmigrant working-class Hispanic informants (see Matute-Bianchi, this volume).

The work of George De Vos (1978, 1980, 1982, 1983 and 1984; De Vos and Suarez-Orozco, 1990) illuminates the complex psychosocial consequences of prolonged exploitation and disparagement. De Vos has argued that continuous depreciation has concrete psychosocial consequences in the classroom. According to De

Vos (1984), patterns of "expressive exploitation" lead to forms of "ego rigidification" and the emergence of non-learning strategies among minority students such as Mexican Americans. In the context of continued depreciation, certain minority students engage in what may be termed "defensive non-learning" in the classroom (Suarez-Orozco, 1987b; De Vos and Suarez-Orozco, 1990).

In an atmosphere of discrimination, intolerance and mutual distrust, involuntary minorities come to experience formal schooling not only as irrelevant, but worse. The traditional educational system, run by Anglos, becomes psychologically a threat to the students' sense of ethnic belonging. When schools become a stage enacting the inequality and depreciation in the encompassing social structure (Suarez-Orozco, 1987b), success in school may induce what De Vos (1978:22) has termed a state of "affective dissonance." In such a context, engaging in the behaviors required for success in school becomes dangerous; it may be read as indicating a wish to "pass," a wish "to do the white man's thing," an attempt to leave one's ethnic group (De Vos and Suarez-Orozco, 1990).

Fernandez and Marenco (1980) argue that rather than viewing schooling as a ladder for upward social mobility, certain disparaged minorities experience schooling as one further tool of the oppressor to maintain the inequality of the status quo (see also Ogbu, this volume; Ogbu and Matute-Bianchi, 1986). During the course of my research, Mexican American parents repeatedly told me that the schools were not teaching their children. For example, one informant noted that his children were given the same textbooks to use year after year. He pointed out this and other facts to show that the schools were interested in maintaining Mexican American children at lower levels.

Romo (1984) found a pattern of severe alienation from school among Chicano families in Texas. She reports that for Texan Chicano families "their own school experiences reinforced negative perceptions of school interactions and sensitized them to prejudices and discrimination. Of all families interviewed, Chicano parents expressed the most alienation from schools" (1984:646). The narratives of these informants relating to schooling stand in binary opposition to the schooling *para llegar a ser alguien* (to become somebody) motif I found among recent Central American immigrants.

The Immigrant Ethic and Its Impact on Schooling

Immigrants from troubled Central America have entered the United States to escape war and limited opportunities, searching for a better tomorrow. At two school sites, which at the time of my research served several hundred recent Central American arrivals, teachers reported that despite the many problems they face the new immigrants were "desirable students." Two experienced teachers confided that they could never go back to teaching "North American students" (read U.S. minority students) because the immigrant students (mostly Central American and Asian) were so eager to learn, so appreciative and polite that they could not face regular classes again in their rough inner-city high school. The student body in this high school was about 30 percent black, 30 percent Filipino, Vietnamese, Cambodian, and Chinese, and 30 percent Hispanic (Chicanos, Mexicans, South Americans and Central Americans). The remaining 10 percent were Samoan, Indian, Palestinian and Anglo students.

A number of teacher-informants reported early on that the Central American students were motivated to learn (particularly English). These teachers noted that immigrant students expended more effort, studied harder and often received better grades than other minority students. Teachers reported, too, that immigrant students were much more respectful and "nicer to have around" than either Anglo or other minority students. More objective measures seem to confirm these impressions. For example, at one school site, the Central American students were statistically under-represented in numbers of school suspensions.

As the research progressed and I became more intimate with the students, their backgrounds and their families, the specific problems facing these students at school became more understandable. As my knowledge of poor inner-city school dynamics increased, I became increasingly surprised that these students stayed in school and tried to learn at all.

Many Central American students were learning English at a fast pace. In fact, so rapid was their English acquisition that teachers at both school sites reported that school counselors systematically held students in English as a Second Language (ESL) classes and lower-level bilingual classes much longer than was necessary due to lack of space in the regular English classes. This was part of a systematic pattern of subtle discrimination that emerged in the course of fieldwork. The powerless immigrant children were not a priority; they were assigned to lower-level classes, even when they had successfully completed the same classes in their country of origin (Suarez-Orozco, 1989). Less subtle forms of racism also permeated the school atmosphere. For example, one rather insensitive staff member indicated that the school's basic priority was to "housebreak the little immigrants that come down from the Central American mountains."

Recent arrivals from Central America were routinely routed to overcrowded, understaffed classes in overcrowded, understaffed poor inner-city schools. Students found themselves trying to learn in a rather poisonous environment. Drugs and sex were on display for sale all around the schools. At both sites, violence was a common occurrence. Teachers were afraid of their students. Teachers complained that they had to operate with far more students than they had been trained to teach. For example, in one school there were 30 to 40 students in each of five ESL classes. Because the English department had no room for more students, even those who were ready and eager to enter the regular English program were held back at lower levels. This was a major complaint quietly reported to me by many students and parents. A number of informants repeatedly noted that they wanted to take harder, more advanced classes but that school officials would not let them. Some informants became hopelessly bored after months of repetitive, monotonous, often quite irrational but ostensibly pedagogical tasks (see Suarez-Orozco, 1989).

Despite a poisonous school atmosphere of drugs, violence, low expectations, calculated tracking of students to unacademic subjects (in already unacademic schools), bitter teachers and seductive offers by more acculturated peers to join the street culture, many immigrant students persevered. It was impressive to note the achievement motivation of many recent Central American students. Their wish to learn, especially to learn English, and to do well in school emerged over and over again in my conversations with them.

I thus decided to test the achievement motivation of Central American students by means of the Thematic Apperception Test (TAT). An analysis of test records indicates a high achievement motivation and the emergence of a specific motivational pattern in which the need to achieve is not patterned along an individualistic need for independence and self-advancement. Rather, it is rooted in a psychocultural matrix that orients the self to others in the family and the community. In the case of the Central American students, achievement is correlated with a wish to help others—typically less fortunate members of their families and community. In short, the association between the need to achieve and a need for independence found by McClelland (1961) and associates was not replicated in my study (see also Suarez-Orozco, 1985, 1987c, 1989).

My ethnographic research among recent arrivals from Central America indicates that their adaptive strategies to schooling are quite different from that of minorities with a long history of degradation by the Anglo world, such as American Indians, blacks and Mexican Americans. Whereas too many involuntary minorities eventually learn the lesson that schooling is not for them and give up, immigrant students "put all their chips" in the educational system, at times succeeding practically against all odds. Many Central American students did remarkably well considering that they carried with them a tragic legacy of war and misery from their native lands, in addition to facing serious ongoing hardships in the new land. Most informants had to deal with marginality (economic, linguistic, legal, political), violence in the schools (most of my informants had been mugged), burnt-out teachers and a patterned intolerance of cultural diversity.

Recent Central American immigrants developed a dual frame of reference in which they evaluated their current lot and anticipated the future (see Suarez-Orozco, 1989:87–101). The overwhelming majority of my informants believed that they had more and better opportunities to get ahead in the United States than at home.

Many Central American parents noted that the future welfare of their children was a primary factor in their decision to emigrate. As one mother from Nicaragua put it, "We came here for them," referring to her five children. She added, "so that they may become somebody tomorrow. . . . I am too old. At my age, it is too late for me. . . . If anything, it is harder for me here than there. . . ."

A dual frame of reference comparing present and past realities emerges to help the Central American immigrants face and interpret current conditions. Because they left their country in search of a better tomorrow and because their parents sacrificed a great deal for the journey, recent immigrant students thought the advantages in this country were self-evident and required little elaboration. For them it was very simple: despite current difficulties, there were more opportunities to study, more help to do so, better training facilities and more and better job opportunities in this country than at home. More than once informants seemed puzzled by my question: "Are there more opportunities for your future in your country or in this country?"

Many parents seemed to overlook difficulties and emphasized the positive. Parents generally perceived the Anglo American world as fairer than the Latin American. Many parents could point to at least one American teacher whom they thought was genuinely interested in their children. These factors added to the development of beliefs in a better tomorrow in the host land. For example, some informants had expected that they would have to pay to send their children to school since "we are foreigners." They were happy to find out that there were no additional school fees for foreign children. Others noted that their children were loaned textbooks for the entire semester without having to pay a cent. One father was overjoyed as we walked through the school's library telling me that his children could "use any book they wanted." Many noted that both in El Salvador and Nicaragua they had to pay for their children's books. One student pointed out that he was given a hot lunch every school day at no cost to his parents. This, he said, would be unbelievable in El Salvador.

Once this theme of a "better tomorrow" became apparent, I concentrated on identifying a specific folk theory of status mobility. Given that there was a collectively held perception among immigrants that more opportunities for advancement existed in the United States than in El Salvador, Nicaragua or Guatemala, the next issue was to document beliefs on the nature of how one "makes it" in this country. Universally, informants reported that *education* was the single most significant avenue to status mobility in the new land. It is important to note that the majority of my parent-informants had been pushed out of school in their native lands. Some had not been able to afford the luxury of schooling in remote rural areas. Others had faced hard physical labor at an early age to contribute to the family's income. The overwhelming majority had not finished elementary school. Most of the parents were unskilled or semiskilled laborers. Most were illiterate or semiliterate in their native Spanish. Their command of the English language was limited. Some parents attended night school to take language courses (see Leslie and Leitch, 1989).

It is important to emphasize that the belief in education as the key method of status mobility was often constructed in *opposition* to the conceived system of status mobility in the country of origin. As one Salvadoran informant succinctly put it: "Here [in the United States] it's *what* you know; there [in El Salvador], it's *who* you know." In the United States, the combination of schooling, knowledge and individual effort emerged as the primary avenue to status mobility. On the other hand, in the country of origin, one "made it" through networks and friends of friends, or through nepotism or *por appellido* (because of one's last name) and not because of effort or knowledge.

To summarize, I have isolated the emergence of an immigrant ethic. The self-evident fact that immigrants leave their land for a better tomorrow is of fundamental importance in understanding subsequent immigrant functioning. A dual frame of reference, comparing present and prior (often brutal) realities emerges as a matrix in which to evaluate and face experience. In thinking about the meaning of schooling and the future, the immigrants often paused and made comparative evaluations between the "here" and the "there." In sharp contrast, Mexican American informants had no "here" and "there" reference matrix. Rather, while considering educational issues there was a perception of a basic continuity in the pattern of exploitation and crushed efforts; and they could produce countless vignettes of systematic exploitation, both expressive and instrumental. Central American immigrants, on the other hand, endured hardships, racism and marginality with reference to two factors: first, a perception that no matter how bad things seem to be now, they are not as bad as they would be at home, and, second, anticipations of a better tomorrow in what they had come to view as a land of opportunity.

An immigrant world view has been identified in which entrance into the new socioeconomic order fuels the development of certain ideas and strategies for advancement. We shall now explore the motivational dynamics governing the achievement patterns of recent Hispanic immigrants.

Parental Sacrifice, Familial Duty and Achievement: The Psycho-Social Context of Motivation among Recent Central American Immigrants

Most of the older students were keenly aware of the degree of parental sacrifice involved in getting out of the country of origin. Many

parent-informants explicitly stated that they came to the United States
so their children could get an education and "become somebody" in this
country of peace and greater opportunity. Parents framed all sacrifices
in reference to the future of their children. The majority of informants
noted that they emigrated from Central America to avoid war, military
service (for the boys) and because, in some areas, their children could
no longer study in peace.

Although all informants were greatly appreciative of their new
lot in the United States, all continued to live through the hardships that
had to be endured in order to survive in a foreign land. Students saw
their parents take jobs, sometimes two jobs, as janitors, maids, and
busboys so that they could go to school. Being witness to continued
parental sacrifices led many students to develop an inner conviction that
their parents did it all for them.

Other student-informants were here without their entire nuclear
family. Female-centered households were in fact common. Students in
this situation often worked at least four hours or so a day to help their
mothers. Others, particularly young men, were living with distant
relatives. In some of these cases, parents had used their entire life
savings to send their children to the safety of the United States.

For example, a Salvadoran student was sent away by his parents
after drunk soldiers tortured him and his cousins. He was living in the
United States with an aunt, while his relatives remained in El Salvador.
He was intensely grateful for the self-evident advantages of living and
studying in this country, but he remained anxious about his cousins'
safety. His efforts went into studying hard so that he could get a good
job and bring his family to the United States (for other specific cases,
see Suarez-Orozco, 1989).

Such circumstances put a particular psychological burden on
these students. An intense sense of duty to less fortunate relatives
gained center stage in the psychological profile of many informants.
Psychological tests, interview records and participant observation
allowed a careful consideration of the psychosocial profiles of these
students. Many showed an intense sense of duty to their parents and
family members as evidenced, for example, by their efforts to get loved
ones out of their war-torn countries and by their remittances back home.
This fueled a need to do well in school, in order to repay parents and
relatives so that the sacrifices of the loved ones would be worthwhile.

A Nicaraguan student was sent to the United States to live with an uncle in order to avoid military service and the war. His less fortunate sister had been drafted to pick the coffee crop. His sense of guilt over his sister's suffering came up over and over again in discussions and psychological tests. He was particularly tortured by the fact that she had been a good student and had wanted to go to college to become an architect. With the situation in his country, that was out of the question. This young man worked at night to save money so that he could bribe his sister's way out of Nicaragua. Guided by a strong sense of duty, he had earned an A- record in school. All his teachers had warm feelings for this hard working and polite young man. He had applied to college to study computer science. That way, he said, he would get a good-paying job and would be able to help his family back home. He had no doubt about the fact that there were so many *oportunidades* in this country that he would get ahead.

Three Guatemalan children, Jose, Maria and Pedro, stayed home with their maternal grandmother when their entrepreneur mother left for the long, uncertain, and dangerous journey to the United States, escaping misery and a drunken, abusive husband. Some years later, after she found enough security, she was able to bring her children to the United States. Here the mother "cleaned the houses of other people" so that her children could go to school, become educated and one day "be somebody," as she said. Jose, the oldest, was able to earn an impressive A average (with an A+ in Algebra, U.S. History and Civics) in his first year of bilingual schooling in the United States. His sister Maria, seventeen years old, who was also a senior, earned a B-average (with an A+ in English) in her first year of American schooling. Pedro, the youngest, was sixteen years old. His grade point average (GPA) during his first year in the United States was a 3.60 out of a possible 4.00. Their mother had only finished elementary school before poverty had forced her to join the labor force.

From a psychodynamic perspective the unifying theme in the interpersonal lives of these students, evident in testing and other data, was an intense feeling of guilt and duty to the sacrificing mother. With tears in his eyes, Jose one day told me that it was just "not right" that his mother had to continue to sacrifice herself so much cleaning houses all day in order for them to go to school. Four months later, in order to help out, he and his younger brother found a job delivering newspapers. They worked from 5:00 A.M. until 7:30 A.M. each morning and gave their earnings to their mother. In their eyes and in the eyes of their mother, they could pay her back and make her suffering worthwhile by going to school and *llegando a ser alguien* (becoming somebody). In so many words, and independently of one another, all three explained that their dream was to become *universitarios* [professionals] to better themselves and, most importantly, to take care of their mother, who had worked so hard for so many years.

Let us consider another case. Angel was a seventeen-year-old young man from El Salvador who had come to the United States in 1981 with his mother and his older sister. None of them spoke any English. His father, a hard-drinking taxi driver, stayed behind in San Salvador. Angel's father had left school after sixth grade and his mother after seventh grade in order to work full time to help their respective families. In the United States, his mother, Rafaela, worked as a maid six days a week and his sister, who had graduated from high school in El Salvador, worked as a "salad girl" in a restaurant. Rafaela normally left home at about 6 A.M. and returned after sundown. The work schedule was particularly hard during the winter months. Because Rafaela did not have access to a car, she had to take public transportation to the different homes she cleaned. Moreover, because the homes were usually in upper-middle-class neighborhoods and she lived in the inner city, she often had to take two, at times even three, buses to get to work.

Angel completed ninth through twelfth grades in the United States. His senior year he earned a cumulative grade point average of 3.74 and was accepted in a prestigious American university. Rafaela did not allow Angel to work during the academic year. She noted that they had come to the United States "so that he can study in peace and make a better tomorrow," referring to the war and the very limited economic opportunities in their native land. War and a wrecked economy in El Salvador had pushed away any fantasies that her children could get ahead in their native country. As she concluded, "Angel now has to dedicate himself to school." Rafaela had hoped that Angel might attend a university, and she was full of pride when he was accepted. "He'll be the first *universitario* in the family," she observed with great joy. Like many other informants, Angel was fully aware of why his mother wanted him to study: "She does not want me to lead a life such as the one [my parents] had to live when they were young. They had to work hard, sacrifice themselves," he said.

Angel's dream was to become a professional: "I believe the most important thing I can do for my parents is to become a doctor; that would make them happy." Like many other informants, Angel said that he wanted to become a professional in order "to work with my community, to help the Latin community here as a doctor." In order to achieve this, Angel studied for four or five hours each day after school. In fact, his major responsibility was to study, and he took this responsibility very seriously, spending each one of his summers in the United States going to special summer programs at a local private university to learn more English and science. Yet he felt a sense of guilt because he did not have a job: "I feel bad about this, . . . my mother and sister working hard all the time. . . . But now I must study."

Angel's Thematic Apperception Test Results

Angel was given the TAT in late 1984. The test consists of a series of 20 vague drawings which are presented sequentially to the informant. The informant is simply asked to "make up a story" based on what he/she sees in the drawings. The narrative should have a past, a present and a future. The TAT rests on the logic that given vague stimuli, informants will talk about themselves. They will articulate their latent wishes, fears, dreams and worries. The TAT has been widely used as an anthropological tool complementing ethnographic participant observations to systematically capture patterned interpersonal concerns of informants (see De Vos, 1973; Suarez-Orozco, 1990a). Key parts of Angel's TAT:

Card 1 (boy contemplating a violin).

[Angel takes a long look, more than 30 seconds.] May I begin? This is about a family that lives in a small town outside San Francisco. The family is composed of two brothers, the father and the mother. The family has financial problems. Up to now the children do not know anything about this. But the father and the mother are worried about this and they cannot hide their worry. During one of the conversations between the mother and the father, one of the boys realizes the nature of the problem. At that point, the child that found out about the problem went to tell his brother. They begin to talk about the problem and about what they will do about it. That same evening one of the brothers is doing his school work. He cannot concentrate on his school work because he is thinking about the economic troubles facing his family. The two brothers then organize a campaign. They read the want ads in the paper, and they find that there is a job for two kids to deliver newspapers after school. They begin to work after school so that the mother and father do not realize it. That way they get together enough money between the two of them to pay their parents' debt.

Analysis. This story captures the interpersonal context of achievement motivation among many Central American informants. The motivation to achieve is often directly related to a wish to help relieve parental suffering. In this case, although the parents wanted to protect the children from their worries, the children are perceptive and the parents "cannot hide their worries" from them. There is no question that they should both intervene and do their lot to help out. Their solution to the problem is appropriate to the ethos of cooperation and mutual support; they get a job together and between the two of them save the money to pay for their parents' debt.

Psychologically it is significant that in Angel's story the children feel they must keep their work a secret; the parents must not know. Why should this be the case? Bear in mind that Angel's mother did not want him to work so he could devote all his energies to studying. Angel feels some uncomfortable guilt that he is the only one not working. His sister must work. His mother works hard six days a week and, indeed, has been working hard ever since she was a girl. His father also had to drop out of school during his elementary school years to go to work to help out his family. Young Angel is aware that he is living off his mother's labor so that he can go to college. This creates a fantasy—to work and materially help out behind her back. The fantasy helps ventilate some of the guilt associated with the fact that now he is the only one in the family not helping out economically.

Card 2 (a farm scene: a young woman is in the foreground with books. In the background a man is working the land. A woman leans on a tree).

This is about a girl named Maria. She was a country girl, a very beautiful farmer who lived with her mother and her brother. Maria's family was a hard-working farm family. They cultivated the land. Maria's brother was a hard-working man, he worked very hard next to his mother. They had a hard life.

Maria was a studious woman. She looked at her family's future and her own future. One day Maria went to the city. In the city she realized how different life there was from life on her farm. She said, "one day I shall have the conveniences city families have." Seeing the difference between the city and her farm, Maria began studying and studying. She studied more and harder than ever. She went to the most prestigious universities of her country, with scholarships and working part time. Finally Maria was able to move her family, her mother and brother, from the farm to the city. They lived a long time with Maria. But the family did not really like city life; they went back to the country. Maria was very sad, so she went back to her farm to help them there, to work with them there, to teach there.

Analysis. The hard-working family lived off their work on the land. Maria, a studious person, is concerned about "her family's future." One day she goes to the city and sees how life in the city can be different—significantly, not only for herself but for her sacrificing mother and brother. There she observes the convenience of city life. She sees a difference. As is the case with many informants, a comparative perception of opportunity leads the *dramatis persona* to study. Studying becomes the way out of a hard existence. The perception of opportunity juxtaposed with a realization of familial sacrifice is the framework in which motivation flourishes. Here is a chance to change the hard life of one's relatives. Studying hard prepares Maria to attend "the most prestigious universities," and with the help of available scholarships and part-time work she makes it. Finally she was able to move her family from the farm to the city. Clearly, the objective was not mere self-advancement and independence but releasing the family from hard farm work. This is the meaning of success.

Upon close scrutiny the structure of the motivational pattern in both Maria's and Angel's life is isomorphic. Both *dramatis personae* are witnesses to the hard work the family must endure to survive. Both are further motivated by perception of opportunity in a new land. In neither case is the achieving motive rooted in an individualistic wish for self-betterment, or in a wish for becoming independent. Rather, the aim is to end, through education, the family's hardships.

Card 8BM (a young man in the foreground, three men in the background).

Rafael was a cinema actor. He was very popular in his time. He was around beautiful women and beautiful things in life. Rafael was originally from a poor *barrio* [neighborhood] in the city. As a boy he had to work singing in bars at night. Sometimes he even sang in the bus. One day, while singing in a bus, a movie mogul saw him and invited him to his studio. Then Rafael's success began. Rafael, not forgetting his family, his friends and his *barrio*, took them all from their poverty and established them in a safe and comfortable place. One day Rafael had to go on tour in Europe. He went to many cities. On the trip between Spain and Russia his plane had an accident. A majority of the passengers in that plane died, but not Rafael, although he was seriously wounded. The Red Cross took him to the nearest hospital where doctors operated on him, but could not save him. . . . The doctors tried, . . . but could not do anything about the burns. Rafael left a son, a boy with his same name "Rafael." Little Rafael, following in his father's footsteps, became a good singer and an actor. He achieved this to honor his father.

Analysis. The little boy sings his way up to a grand tour of Europe via bars and buses. A benevolent figure identifies the potential of this young fellow and gives him the opportunity that would put him on the road to fame. Rather than forgetting his people, Rafael turns to his people, takes them out of their poverty and "established them in a safe and comfortable place" as soon as he could. Rafael does not forget; rather he shares at once the fruits of his achievements. Ultimately the hero must turn to his people to validate his success by sharing with them the fruits of his achievements.

Let us underline the emergence of a pattern in which achievements are neither individualistic nor for the sole purpose of independence or self-advancement. Rather, achievements are embedded in a pattern of cooperation and mutual nurturing. One "makes it" with the precious help of significant others, and must turn to them to complete the cycle.

Card 13B (A barefoot boy, sitting down in front of a door).

This is about a boy, Rodolfo. He lives in a hamlet outside the city. He is a poor boy from a very poor family. So he had to work from a young age. At five years of age he had to go to work and live a street life. His mother is sick. His father had left her when he was born. Rodolfo has to work shining shoes and selling candy in buses. Sometimes he even works at night to earn enough to have a tortilla to eat. One day Rodolfo began thinking about the future. Will he be a good man? Or will he be a bad man? He also thinks about school and the streets and the differences that exist between the two. After thinking about all this he discovered that there was a great difference between the street and school. That difference is knowledge. Knowing what is good and what is bad. After meditating about this Rodolfo told his mother that he was going to do his best to continue in school. He told her not to worry about anything because he would also work. . . . He would work . . . and study, no matter how hard it was to do both or how much he would suffer. This is what Rodolfo did. Years passed and he was a model student in his school. After finishing high school he went to the university to study law. He chose law because he thought that it would be the best way to help as many poor children (as he once was) as possible.

Analysis. Little Rodolfo had to work since the age of five to buy food. His poor mother was sick and his father left them. Rodolfo pondered about his future and concluded that the fundamental difference between the street and school is knowledge. Knowledge represents a capacity to tell good from bad. Rodolfo thus chooses school over street life. He tells his poor sick mother not to worry because he will be able both to study and to work. He becomes a model student and chooses a career which will help many poor children.

The pattern emerging is identical to the previous stories. The boy from a poor home has the insight that education is the route out of misery. Through hard work and study he becomes an attorney. Rather than turning away from his people, he both studies and works so his poor sick mother will not "worry." At the end his achievement is translated into helping "as many" poor children as possible. The culmination is not some sort of self-centered indulgence but rather the conversion of success into concrete help for his people.

The interpersonal concerns of Angel, as revealed by ethnographic observations, TAT responses, and other materials gathered in formal and informal interviews and informal chats confirm the presence of a strong motive to achieve. In reality, Angel's motivation has already been translated into concrete results as evidenced by the fact that he has been accepted by a leading U.S. university. The son of a maid and a taxi driver, Angel was taken out of his native El Salvador by his mother to avoid misery and the war and to continue his studies in peace. Angel was keenly aware of the sacrifices his family endured to establish him in a foreign land so that he could become the family's first *universitario*. His evaluations of the socioeconomic possibilities in the new land were no facile simplifications of reality. He was well aware of the hardships that must be endured. His own mother was a living example of the sacrifices that must be made to meet basic living needs in the new land. At the same time, he had become certain that hard, disciplined, studious behavior and initiative were amply rewarded in the new society, much more so, he had concluded, than in his native country. As evidence of greater opportunities, he pointed out the fact that he was able to earn scholarships to attend the university. The emergence of an immigrant world view of opportunity became intertwined with a severe sense of duty to his mother, his sister and his community. They were taking care of him now, but one day he would be able to take care of his family financially. He would also have made his mother's sacrifices worthwhile by becoming a *universitario*.

Further Themes in Immigrant School Adaptation and the Emergence of Problems

A majority of my Central American informants stated strongly that schooling was the key to a better future for themselves and their families. Encounters with discrimination, hostility, and other obstacles that would enrage more acculturated Hispanics were often dismissed as irrelevant or as minor evidence of U.S. ignorance or arrogance. A Salvadoran informant, commenting on the discriminatory reputation of a teacher, said with some sarcasm in his voice, "She thinks we are all Mexicans; she can't tell a Salvadoran from a Venezuelan from an Argentine."

Keenly aware of a rather miserable situation in their native lands, recent immigrants from Central America can often afford to take a more instrumental view of their present hardships and marginality (political, economic, legal and linguistic). This is in part because things here are much better than at home, as an informant put it.

Nonetheless, Central American students, particularly younger ones, are affected by teachers' hostilities, overcrowded schools, poor urban living conditions, lack of parental supervision (attributable mostly to work schedules), and peer group pressures. Often lacking the sense of responsibility their older siblings possess, other issues emerge as significant to these students. Students doing poorly in school reported a great deal of boredom. They noted that teachers did not really care about their welfare. Many became depressed; that is, they turned their anger inward when they were enrolled by hostile counselors in classes dealing with subjects they had already studied (and often passed) in their countries. Cutting classes became a strategy to cope with boredom.

All youngsters had been traumatized by the Central American wars (see Suarez-Orozco, 1990a, 1990b; Arroyo and Eth, 1985). Other problems that confronted recent immigrant students were related to the fact that in some cases war and poverty pushed them out of the classrooms for different periods of time. Many had worked full time and had the responsibilities associated with adult status. Once in the United States, they had to catch up academically after years of being away from school. This created unique psycho-pedagogical problems. They felt like adults, yet in the classroom they were essentially treated as children. Some teachers became impatient with these students' problems. Other students felt guilty not working full time to aid their families. Eventually some Central Americans dropped out of school to work full time. Not one of my informants reported receiving any sort of public assistance.

Many informants, as they neared graduation, became aware that without the necessary legal documentation they would not be able to enroll in a university, and they became depressed. In short, most informants were in the United States without the required documents. This "legal ceiling" created a sense of helplessness in students wishing to continue their education. This feeling was particularly acute in students with excellent grades and a sincere wish to attend universities. Some informants began "to give up" on school. As one junior put it a few weeks after she discovered she did not possess the required documentation to enter college, "Why should I study now? I can't get into college." Looking for a job became the major concern of many such youngsters. Other students found ways to maneuver around this "legal ceiling" (Suarez-Orozco, 1989).

Conclusion

If we are to formulate successful educational programs we must sensitize ourselves and our teachers to the different social histories, present realities and adaptive strategies of the various Hispanic American groups. A broad distinction, the one proposed herein as a first attempt, is to differentiate between those Hispanic Americans who have experienced a history of depreciation vis-à-vis the Anglo environment and the more recent immigrants.

This chapter has identified a number of fundamental differences in the issues facing these two populations. Ogbu (this volume) has argued that members of disparaged involuntary minorities respond to inequality by formulating conceptions regarding the educational system that further remove them from investing in schooling as the way to a better tomorrow. Thus, the alarmingly high rates of non-learning and school failure. On the other hand, the more recent immigrants from Central America have great expectations of the American educational system. This frame of reference helps many immigrants overcome cultural and social barriers. Other barriers, however, in some cases legal, may prevent large numbers of qualified and motivated immigrant students from pursuing higher education.

Analysis of immigrant groups and their strategies for coping contribute to the refinement of theories of ethnic adaptation and minority school failure. As this analysis indicates, the problems facing Mexican Americans in inner city schools are distinct from those facing recent immigrants from Central America. The Central American students have escaped a situation of war and scarcity. That reality overshadows many of the subsequent real hardships and marginality they encounter in the new land. For many informants the sacrifices of family members and the folks "back home" remain a significant point of reference against which to check more current developments. In their eyes, the relative advantages of life in the United States are self-evident. In this context they developed notions in which schooling emerges as the most important avenue to make it in this society and, in turn, to help less fortunate relatives.

References

Aguayo, Sergio. 1986. "Salvadorans in Mexico," *Refugees* (New York) 34(Oct.):30–31.

Arroyo, William. 1985. "Children Traumatized by Central American Warfare." In *Post-Traumatic Stress Disorder in Children*, ed. Spencer Eth and Robert S. Pynoos, pp. 103–20. Washington, D.C.: American Psychiatric Press.

Brown, George H., et al. 1980. *The Condition of Education for Hispanic Americans*. Washington, D.C.: United States Department of Education, National Center for Education Statistics.

Buckley, Tom. 1984. *Violent Neighbors: El Salvador, Central America and the United States*. New York: Times Books.

Carter, Thomas P., and Roberto D. Segura. 1979. *Mexican Americans in School: A Decade of Change*. New York: College Entrance Examination Board.

De Vos, George A. 1973. *Socialization for Achievement: Essays on the Cultural Psychology of the Japanese*. Berkeley: University of California Press.

———. 1978. "Selective Permeability and Reference Group Sanctioning: Psychocultural Continuities in Role Degradation." In *Major Social Issues*, ed. John Milton Yinger, pp. 7–24. New York: The Free Press.

———. 1980. "Ethnic Adaptation and Minority Status." *Journal of Cross-Cultural Psychology* 11:101–124.

———. 1982. "Adaptive Strategies in United States Minorities." In *Minority Mental Health*, ed. Enrico E. Jones and Sheldon J. Korchin, pp. 74–112. New York: Praeger.

———. 1983. "Ethnic Identity and Minority Status: Some Psycho-Cultural Considerations." In *Identity: Personal and Socio Cultural*, ed. Anita Jacobson-Widding, pp. 90–113. Upsala: Almqvist & Wiskell Tryckeri AB.

———. 1984. "Ethnic Persistence and Role Degradation: An Illustration from Japan." Paper read at the American-Soviet Symposium on Contemporary Ethnic Processes in the USA and the USSR. New Orleans, Louisiana, 14–16 April.

De Vos, G.A., and M. Suarez-Orozco. 1990. *Status Inequality: The Self in Culture*. Newbury Park, Calif.: Sage.

Dickey, Christopher. 1987. *With the Contras: A Reporter in the Wilds of Nicaragua*. New York: Simon and Schuster.

Fernandez, Celestino, and Eduardo Marenco. 1980. "Group Conflict, Education and Mexican Americans: A Discussion Paper." San Francisco: Mexican American Legal Defense and Educational Fund, Inc.

Goho, Tom, and David Smith. 1973. "A College Degree: Does it Substantially Enhance the Economic Achievement of Chicanos?" New Mexico State University, Las Cruces. Center for Business Services Occasional Paper No. 503.

Hispanic Policy Development Project. 1984. *Make Something Happen: Hispanics and Urban High School Reform.* 2 vols. New York: The Hispanic Policy Development Project, Inc.

Kempton, Murray. 1986. "Scenes from Nicaragua." *The New York Review of Books* 33(13):5–11.

Knowlton, Clark S. 1979. "Some Demographic, Economic, and Educational Considerations on Mexican American Youth." Paper read at the South-Western Sociological Association Meeting, Fort Worth, Tex.

LaFeber, Walter. 1984. *Inevitable Revolutions: The United States in Central America.* New York: W.W. Norton and Company.

Lefkowitz, Bernard. 1985. "Renegotiating Society's Contract with Public Schools: The National Commission on Secondary Education for Hispanics and the National Board of Inquiry into Schools." *Carnegie Quarterly* 29(4):2–11.

Leslie, L.A., and M. Laurie Leitch. 1989. "A Demographic Profile of Recent Central American Immigrants: Clinical Services and Implications." *Hispanic Journal of Behavioral Sciences* 11(4):315–329.

McClelland, David C. 1961. *The Achieving Society.* Princeton, N.J.: D. Van Nostrand Co.

Maestas, Leo C. 1981. "Ethnicity and High School Student Achievement Across Rural and Urban Districts." *Education Research Quarterly* 6:32–42.

Manz, Beatriz. 1988. *Refugees of a Hidden War: The Aftermath of Counterinsurgency in Guatemala.* Albany, N.Y.: State University of New York Press.

Mohn, Sid L. 1983. "Central American Refugees: The Search for Appropriate Responses." *World Refugee Survey*, 25th anniversary issue, pp. 42–47.

Ogbu, John U. 1974. *The Next Generation: An Ethnography of Education in an Urban Neighborhood.* New York: Academic Press.

————. 1978. *Minority Education and Caste: The American System in Cross Cultural Perspective.* New York: Academic Press.

————. 1981. "Origins of Human Competence: A Cultural-Ecological Perspective." *Child Development* 52:413–29.

————. 1983. "Indigenous and Immigrant Minority Education: A Comparative Perspective." Paper read at 82nd Annual Meeting of the American Anthropological Association, Chicago, Ill., 16–20 Nov.

Ogbu, John U. and Maria Matute-Bianchi. 1986. "Understanding Sociocultural Factors: Knowledge, Identity, and School Adjustment." In *Beyond Language: Social and Cultural Factors in Schooling Language Minority*

Students, pp.73–142. Sacramento, Calif. State Department of Education, Bilingual Education Office.

Quezada, Sergio A. 1985. "Exodo centroamericano." *NEXOS* 3:37–42.

Rodriguez, Richard. 1982. *Hunger of Memory: The Education of Richard Rodriguez, An Autobiography.* Boston: Godine.

Romo, Harriet. 1984. "The Mexican Origin Population's Differing Perceptions of Their Children's Schooling." *Social Science Quarterly*, 65(2):635–49.

Suarez-Orozco, Marcelo M. 1985. "Opportunity, Family Dynamics and School Achievement: The Socio-cultural Context of Motivation among Recent Immigrants from Central America." Paper read at the University of California Symposium on Linguistic Minorities and Education, Tahoe City, Calif., 30 May–1 June.

———. 1987a. "Transformations in Perception of Self and Social Environment in Mexican Immigrants." In *People In Upheaval*, ed. S. Morgan and E.F. Colson, pp. 129–143. Staten Island, N.Y.: Center for Migration Studies.

———. 1987b. "Towards a Psycho-social Understanding of Hispanic Adaptation to United States Schooling." In *Success or Failure? Learning and the Language Minority Student*, ed. Henry T. Trueba, pp. 156–68. Cambridge, Mass.: Newbury House.

———. 1987c. "Hispanic Americans: Comparative Considerations and the Educational Problems of Children." *International Migration* (Geneva) XXV(2):141–63.

———. 1989. *Central American Refugees and U.S. High Schools: A Psychosocial Study of Motivation and Achievement.* Stanford: Stanford University Press.

———. 1990a. "Speaking of the Unspeakable: Towards a Psychosocial Understanding of Responses to Terror." *Ethos* [forthcoming].

———. 1990b. "Some Psychocultural Strategies for Research with Children in War." Invited paper presented to the conference on "Children in War." Sigmund Freud Center, Hebrew University of Jerusalem, Israel, 27 June.

Universidad para la Paz. 1987. *Los Refugiados Centroamericanos.* San José, Costa Rica: Universidad Nacional.

Chapter Three
The Dynamics of Educational Decision Making: A Comparative Study of Sikhs in Britain and the United States

Margaret A. Gibson
University of California, Santa Cruz
and
Parminder K. Bhachu
University of California, Los Angeles

Research in Britain and in the United States indicates wide variations in the school-adaptation patterns of different minority groups. While the overall performance of some minorities surpasses national norms, other groups do far less well. To understand these disparities, we need to look not only at the local opportunity structure and the stratified nature of schools and society but also at the minority group's theories of success and the interplay between these theories, its educational strategies and the actual school-adaptation patterns of its young. This chapter focuses on these relationships for one group of South Asians—the Punjabi Sikhs.

Sikh youths raised in Britain and the United States are comparatively successful in school, more successful by a number of criteria than their majority-group agemates. Research on ethnicity and school performance in inner-London secondary schools reveals, for example, that Sikhs and other Indian students do better on examinations taken at age sixteen than students of English, Scottish, Welsh and Irish origin. Research on ethnicity and school performance in a California high school shows similar results. In the British case, not only do more Indians take their "O levels"—the exams that determine if secondary students are eligible for advanced academic course work—but they also sit for exams in more subjects and receive higher grades than white British agemates. The Indian students' achievement, furthermore, is significantly better than can be predicted on the basis of their "verbal reasoning ability" at the end of primary school, while the majority students' achievement is significantly worse than would be predicted using this same criterion (Inner London Education Authority [ILEA], 1987).

The academic achievements of Asian Indians settled in Britain have received considerable attention in recent years, in particular because Indian students have demonstrated a high degree of success in surmounting both the influence of prejudice and discrimination in British society and that of low socioeconomic status (Ballard and Vellins, 1985; Swann Report, 1985; Taylor and Hegarty, 1985). Although most of the British literature on minority school achievement fails to distinguish South Asian students by ethnic or religious background, our own research makes clear that the general pattern of academic achievement among British Indians pertains to Sikhs.[1]

Our research indicates, moreover, many similarities between the school performance patterns of Sikhs settled in metropolitan Britain and those settled in rural California. In both settings Sikh students perform better than can be predicted based on such factors as parents' education, income, occupation and English-language proficiency (Bhachu, 1985a; Gibson, 1987a, 1988a; Gibson and Bhachu, 1986).

Sikh theories of success and attitudes about the value of formal education have their roots in well-defined cultural processes predating migration. To a very great degree, although not entirely, they cut across deep caste and class lines. No matter where Sikhs have settled, they hold many views in common regarding the value of formal education, reflected in folk sayings that often lace their conversations. "The difference between an educated and an uneducated person," Sikhs say, "is the difference between the earth and the sky." They say, furthermore, with reference to education, that "If you are blind yourself, how can you lead others?" and that education "opens new worlds."

It must be noted that folk theories of success, although clearly influenced by cultural and religious traditions, including beliefs about the role of formal education in promoting socioeconomic mobility, are by no means static. This chapter calls attention to the dynamic nature of Sikh success theories and educational strategies. More specifically, it examines the interrelationship between the cultural background of the Sikhs and their experiences prior to migration, the structure of the host societies in which they have settled, including economic and social conditions, the Sikhs' current situations in these countries, and the reciprocal influence of these forces on educational strategies and performance.

Attention to gender differences in academic achievement and aspiration highlights the interaction between cultural and contextual variables. Very rapid and dramatic changes have occurred within one generation in attitudes about education and employment for women. Comparison of the American and British settings also points up differences in perspectives between recently arrived immigrants and those whose children are now largely second generation.

The California Case

The earliest Asian Indians to settle in California arrived around the turn of the century. Most, however, have come since the passage of the 1965 Immigration and Naturalization Act. Between 1965 and 1985 the number of Asian Indians residing in the United States grew from less than 20,000 to more than 500,000 (Gibson, 1988b). About two thirds of the recent arrivals were born in India, the remainder in other countries where Indians have established overseas settlements. They come, as they themselves say, because of economic opportunities. Many come also because they have relatives already settled in the United States.

Such is the case in "Valleyside," California, a small farming community located in the fertile Central Valley about two hours by road from San Francisco.[2] Between 1965 and 1980 the number of Asian Indians living in and around Valleyside increased tenfold, to more than 6,000 by local estimates. School district records show a growth in Asian student enrollment for grades kindergarten through twelve from only 2.4 percent in 1972 to nearly 13 percent by 1981. Most of the new students are of Indian descent.

Almost all Valleyside Indians are emigrants from the state of Punjab in northwest India and 85 to 90 percent are Sikhs. By tradition, most are farmers, members by birth of a landowning group in northern India known as Jats. Historically a group of tribes, Jats are commonly regarded as a caste within the Indian social system. A proud, independent and self-reliant people, Jats are dominant in number and power in most Punjabi villages. Although those who have emigrated to Valleyside had land holdings of only small to moderate size in Punjab, they considered themselves, and were considered by others, to be members of the highest ranking group within the social structure of their villages. They come to the United States not so much to flee either low status or poverty as to maintain or improve their family's economic condition.

They bring with them, however, few salable skills, apart from farming, and little or no cash. Many are in debt to relatives who have helped pay for their air fares. Upon their arrival in the United States they have little choice but to take backbreaking work in the fruit orchards surrounding Valleyside. Recent arrivals often work for less than minimum wage—$3.35 at the time of fieldwork—because peach farmers generally pay seasonal labor by the piece, a practice that favors the faster and more experienced workers. For the first year or two, most Sikh families have an extremely difficult time making ends meet. Even after five to ten years in Valleyside, most families earned no more than $15,000 a year, including unemployment compensation and the earnings of older children, as well as of both parents.

Findings reported here come largely from a core sample of 42 Punjabi families, all with children in their senior year at Valleyside High School, and from school records for 231 Punjabi high school students, grades nine through twelve. Some 10 to 15 percent of these students were Hindus and Muslims; the rest Sikhs. But irrespective of religious identity, all shared a common Punjabi heritage. About one-half of the students had been in the United States less than five years; only 12 percent were American born. Fieldwork was carried out during an 18-month period (1980-82) by a team of researchers, Punjabi and non-Punjabi, male and female, insiders and outsiders to the Valleyside setting.

A majority of the mothers in the core sample and quite a few of the fathers were illiterate or semiliterate. More than one-third of the mothers had no formal education and only one in ten had attended middle school or beyond. One fourth of the fathers had attended school for five years or less and fewer than half had completed secondary school, which in India means ten years.

The large majority of families had never lived outside of a Punjabi village prior to emigrating to America and few had had any substantial contact with Western ways. More urbanized and sophisticated North Indians, in India and abroad, view these "peasant" farm families as backwards, "all brawn and no brains" (Ramakrishna, 1979:27).

In spite of their rusticity, more than half and perhaps as many as three-quarters of the Jat Sikhs who had arrived in Valleyside during the 1960s or earlier were self-employed orchard farmers at the time of fieldwork. Between 1974 and 1980 Valleyside Sikhs more than doubled their landholdings, and by the early 1980s they owned approximately half the peach orchards in the area, plus additional acres of prunes, pears, almonds and walnuts. Even so, most have only small ranches, 40 acres or less, and few are secure financially due to the many economic difficulties facing small farmowners in America today.

More recent arrivals—and it is this group that forms the majority of Valleyside Sikhs—had been unable by 1980 to purchase even small farms. The rapid escalation in the cost of good orchard land during the latter half of the 1970s, coupled with the unprecedented rise in interest rates and major changes in the national and international markets for canned fruit, priced these newcomers out of the market. Most had no option but to remain agricultural laborers or, in the case of those with at least a high school education and some facility with English, to shift into factory work, when they could find it. Since Valleyside offers few unskilled or semiskilled employment opportunities, apart from agriculture, recent immigrants wishing nonagricultural employment find they must relocate to urban areas where the cost of living is far higher than in Valleyside (see Gibson, 1988b, for fuller discussion of these economic-adaptation patterns).

In spite of their high status within the social structure of a Punjabi village and the ability of the pre-1970 immigrants to purchase farm land in Valleyside, the parents in the sampled families share few of the background characteristics commonly associated in America with success in school. In addition to low incomes, limited formal education, and lack of familiarity with Western culture, most Sikh adults were also handicapped by a limited knowledge of English. Few spoke English with ease, even those who had lived in the United States for many years. Punjabi was the language of the home, and most of the Sikh students attending Valleyside High had entered American schools with little or no facility in English. Those who had entered Valleyside schools during their elementary years, furthermore, had received no instruction in their mother tongue and little or no specialized assistance in learning English as a second language. (The school district has subsequently instituted English as a Second Language [ESL] and bilingual instruction in the elementary grades.)

The Valleyside study has revealed, nevertheless, that the Sikh students who had received *all* their schooling in the United States did relatively well academically by the time they reached high school. These American-educated Sikh children were nearly as likely on entering ninth grade to be placed in college preparatory classes as white Valleysiders. For example, analysis of school records revealed that while somewhat more Sikhs than majority-group students were placed into remedial or ESL English classes, more majority students were placed into remedial math. During high school, Sikh students' grades equaled or, in the case of boys, surpassed those of majority peers.

The Sikh boys, furthermore, as a group, took significantly more advanced academic courses than their white Valleysider classmates, male or female. Thirty-seven percent of those sampled took four years each of science and math compared to less than 15 percent of their majority-group classmates (Gibson, 1988a). Sikh girls, on the other hand, took fewer science and math classes than their white peers. Most of the girls pursued vocational rather than college-preparatory courses during the final two years of high school.[3] The gender differences relate to Sikh parents' assumptions about the necessity and desirability of postsecondary education for their daughters (see below).

In most other respects, the school-adaptation patterns of the Sikh boys and girls are similar. Sikh students, on average, newcomers and second generation, male and female, spend more time on homework than majority-group peers and have far better attendance records. While one-fifth of the Sikh students in the class of 1981 never missed a day of school during their senior year, not one majority-group student in a random sample of 44 seniors had a perfect attendance record. The median number of days absent for the majority students was 14; for Sikhs, only three. Moreover, an estimated 85 to 90 percent of all Sikh students, including the freshest arrivals from village India, graduate from high school, compared to 70 to 75 percent of the majority students.

The overall academic performance and persistence of these students, girls in particular, is impressive given their family backgrounds. In school, furthermore, Sikh children have to cope not only with mastering a new language, but must contend as well with sometimes severe racial prejudice and conflicts between the values of their parents and those of their teachers and majority peers.

A climate of prejudice permeates the school experience of all Sikh students. In school, Sikh children are told directly by white classmates and indirectly by their teachers that they stink. They are verbally and physically abused by majority students, who refuse to sit by them in class or on buses, crowd in front of them in lines, spit at them, stick them with pins, throw food at them, and worse. Only a handful of white youths participate actively in the harassment, but the majority either condones their classmates' behavior or feels powerless to alter the status quo. Teachers and administrators, although disturbed by the situation, seem almost equally powerless to turn things around. They deal with the most blatant hostilities, but otherwise encourage Sikh students to be understanding of their majority peers' "ignorance." Sikh students who seek to defend themselves fear that they will be labeled troublemakers.

In addition, Sikh children must contend with being told in one way or another that India and Indian culture are inferior to Western and American ways. They are criticized for their values, their diet, and their dress. They are faulted because they defer to the authority of elders, accept arranged marriages, engage in group decision making, and place family ahead of individual interests. They are condemned most especially for not joining in majority-dominated extracurricular activities and for withstanding as best they can the pressures to conform to the dominant culture.

Although Sikh children who receive all their schooling in Valleyside manage, in spite of the barriers, to persevere and even do reasonably well academically, later arrivals often find the barriers insurmountable. Many of those transferring from Indian to American schools after fourth grade, for example, never break out of a remedial or ESL instructional track during high school. These students manage, by and large, to complete requirements for a high school diploma, but they graduate without the academic, vocational, or English language skills needed to be competitive in the job market. These later arrivals, moreover, are generally those subjected to the worst hostilities by ignorant and racist classmates.

The difficulties faced by Sikh students, both newcomers and second generation, are discussed in detail elsewhere (Gibson, 1987a, 1988a). Our chief purpose here is not to analyze the barriers to school success encountered by Sikh young people but to offer some explanation for the relative success in school of those Sikhs who have received all their education in Valleyside. How is it that these students, even in the face of major obstacles related to the structure of school programs, racism, home-school cultural differences and low socioeconomic status, perform on a par with their majority counterparts?

Punjabi Perspectives on Life in America

Punjabi Sikhs say of themselves, "Wherever we go we are successful." Only a small minority of Valleyside Sikhs have become economically successful in American terms, but they generally judge their success using their own criteria. Their reference group is other Sikhs, those settled abroad and those left behind in India. Earning only a minimum hourly wage, Valleyside Sikhs are able quite rapidly to accumulate some savings and improve their economic condition. Within five years of reaching the United States, for example, almost every Sikh family has become a homeowner. From their perspective, furthermore, farm labor is but a stepping stone to a better life, for their children if not themselves. Cases of Sikhs who have prospered in America bolster these beliefs.

Valleyside Sikhs welcome what they perceive to be the opportunity to compete for jobs on the basis of objective criteria. While a few of those interviewed thought that Sikhs suffer job discrimination, most believed that employers generally hire those best qualified regardless of race. They assume that their children, armed with U.S. credentials, will be competitive in the American job market. They respect U.S. laws safeguarding individual rights. Employment opportunities in America, as they see it, are far better than in India or in Britain.

This is not to say that Valleyside Sikhs have no first-hand experience of racial prejudice and discrimination. Almost every Sikh interviewed spoke of hostile actions directed toward them or members of their families in Valleyside, but Sikh accounts of harassment are almost always balanced with examples of majority-group friendliness. "Not all whites are alike," Sikhs are quick to report. "Some are good, some bad, just like Punjabis."

The following remarks by a Sikh farmer are indicative of the older generation's response to prejudice:

> If some white children pass by in a car and shout, "Hey, Hindu" and give us the finger, it would make things worse if we go after them in our car. If they abuse us and we abuse them, then we will have bad feelings amongst us. If I start swearing at them, do you think they will treat me well? If we don't allow anyone to cough, no one else is going to let us cough either.[4]

The Sikh response to prejudice is both calculated and deliberate. Some of those interviewed stated explicitly that to fight back, individually or collectively, would only exacerbate the situation and quite possibly interfere with educational and economic opportunities.

Sikhs do not shy away from confrontation when they feel their identity or interests threatened. In Valleyside, however, most Sikhs believe that, in spite of widespread prejudice and almost constant pressure to conform to the dominant culture, they have the ability to maintain essential aspects of a Punjabi Sikh way of life and to improve their lot economically. Sikhs pursue a strategy of *accommodation and acculturation without assimilation*. "Being in America means you have to compromise a little," they say. "Learn from the Americans, but don't become like them." "Dress to please the people, but eat to please yourself." Interviews with Sikh parents and students were filled with such comments and sayings.

Sikh Ideology

In discussing their views, Sikhs point frequently to the teachings of their gurus and their scripture. They are guided in their daily lives by an ideology of egalitarianism, service to others, and making the most of one's circumstances. A commonly cited phrase which epitomizes Sikh ideals is "Work hard for your living, share your earnings and worldly possessions with fellow community members, and also worship God." Sikhs are expected to be actively involved in the secular world of whatever community or country they find themselves and not to withdraw into a life of prayer, celibacy or seclusion. This ethos contributes to the Sikhs' ability to adapt to life in overseas settings.

So, too, do the Sikhs' experiences in pluralistic India, a country where 17 major languages are spoken and where all students, beginning in their middle-school years, routinely study Hindi and English in addition to their provincial language. Sikhs have well-developed strategies for maintaining their ethnic and religious identities within a heterogeneous, competitive, and highly stratified society. They have a long and self-conscious history of perseverance in the face of adversity and effective institutions for preserving, honoring, and teaching this history. In India, furthermore, Sikhs comprise only two percent of the population and the management of their minority status is by no means a new challenge for them when they settle abroad. Whether in India, Britain, the United States, or elsewhere within the Sikh diaspora, Sikhs expect to have to fight for their rights. Similarly, they expect to have to work hard to maintain their separate identity and to get ahead economically.

Sikhs settled in Valleyside, like those in Britain, welcome the opportunities available to those willing to work hard, take risks, and sacrifice material comforts for the sake of future reward. Their folk beliefs reflect this ethos: "Work hard and eat sweet buttered *chappattis* [bread]." Sikhs say, similarly, that "hardship breeds success" and that a person "can only become successful when he has known hardship."

Folk Beliefs, Gender and Educational Performance

Almost all Valleyside Sikh parents believe that their own employment opportunities in America have been severely restricted by their limited schooling. Although British-style Western schooling has existed in Punjab since the mid-19th century (Metha, 1926:9), only recently has even a primary education become universally available throughout rural Punjab. While Jat Sikhs espouse great respect for schooling—"education is the third eye," they say, and "with only a simple education, one can expect only a simple job"—book learning has not been considered a necessity for those who farm. Indeed, many Valleyside Sikhs stated strongly their belief that farming is the province of the least educated. Although the views of rural Punjabis have shifted somewhat in recent years, partly as a consequence of the green revolution in Indian Punjab, village schools remain poorly attended (Gibson, 1988a).

In Valleyside, too, as recently as 10 or 20 years ago, it was not uncommon for sons of Sikh farmers to leave high school before receiving their diplomas. These young men expected to farm for a living and for that no credentials were necessary. Today the situation has changed. Few Valleyside Sikhs, even those with large landholdings, expect their sons to farm. Young people themselves want a more secure and remunerative livelihood than farming can offer. They perceive, moreover, a strong, positive correlation between the amount of education one has and the type of employment one can expect to obtain. Parents and children alike view formal education as an investment in the future.

Most of the Sikhs in Gibson's senior sample, male and female, aspired to a college education. There was no four-year college in Valleyside, however, and few of the girls actually expected that their parents would allow them to go away to college. Many were even uncertain if their parents would permit them to attend the local community college. This reluctance on their parents' part stemmed from the traditional Punjabi view that "too much" education will make a girl too independent in her views and behavior, thus tarnishing her reputation and quite possibly jeopardizing arrangements for her marriage. Sikh parents take very seriously their responsibility to arrange their children's marriages.

Not only were Valleyside Sikhs concerned that if their daughters went away to college they might fall in love and wish to arrange their own marriages, but also that they might become so Americanized that they would no longer fit into the Punjabi community. In addition, a highly educated woman could find it difficult to take up her proper role within her future husband's family. She might say, for example, as one parent explained, "I've just finished college. How can I make the *roti* [bread]?" It is customary for a woman in village Punjab when first married to carry a heavy share of the cooking and other daily chores in her in-laws' house, including cooking for the male members of the household and their friends. In this context to "make the *roti*" takes on a very broad cultural meaning.

The belief that too much education may make a woman "snobbish" and "spoiled" is characteristic of Punjabi Indians of rural background. A less educated woman, Valleyside parents asserted, would be less likely to question her role and more comfortable with the joint decision-making processes that are the norm within Punjabi households. Accordingly, many Valleyside Sikhs said that if their daughters wished to pursue higher education, beyond the community college level, they should do so after they were married. The decision could then be made jointly by the girl, her husband, and her in-laws. This is the traditional village pattern, but young women raised and educated in Valleyside were helping to reshape parents' traditional attitudes. So, too, were the employment opportunities available to older, uneducated women.

In Punjab, as recently as the early 1970s, less than two percent of the women were "in the labor force," compared with 13.2 percent for India as a whole, and most Jat landowners continue to "consider it below their dignity to allow their women to work outside the home," even if their farms are small (Singh, 1979:3).[5] Until recently Valleyside Jats have shared this attitude about their wives and daughters working outside the home, and the first Valleyside Sikh women to break with village tradition became the object of much teasing. Attitudes shifted rapidly, however, as families learned that a woman's earnings could contribute substantially to a family's income. At the time of fieldwork the overwhelming majority of Sikh women, whether the wives of farm owners or farm laborers, were engaged in some sort of agricultural work during the summer months, helping on their own farms, working for others, or employed seasonally by a local cannery. One old-timer commented about this change: "Now that they [the women] see others working, they say, 'Why shouldn't I earn money too?' But it took us [the men] time to adjust to this."

Valleyside Sikh parents recognize that educated women have far better employment opportunities than uneducated women. Almost all those interviewed wanted their daughters to finish high school—this itself represents a dramatic shift in attitudes—and the majority either favored some postsecondary education for their daughters or acquiesced to their daughters' wishes to attend community college before they married. Fully 80 percent of the girls sampled actually attended college the year following their high school graduation, as did 74 percent of the boys. All of these girls and all but three of the boys attended the local community college.

A sharp gender difference existed, nonetheless, in the courses taken by Sikh students during high school. Boys elected a combination of college-preparatory courses and shop classes, the latter providing practical skills in such fields as welding, small engine repair and auto mechanics. Most Sikh girls, on the other hand, even the most academically gifted, including those who aspired to postgraduate degrees, selected secretarial classes. Few actually espoused interest in secretarial work, but these courses seemed a practical choice for young women who were unsure even at the time of their high school graduation whether or not they would be permitted by their parents to enroll at Valleyside Community College the following fall. "Why take college-preparatory math and science," these girls explained, "if our parents aren't going to let us go to college?" The ultimate decision depended in part at least on the girls' "good" behavior during high school. Sensing this, the girls were careful not to deviate too far from accepted community standards for adolescent female behavior, but at the same time they were reluctant to take the more advanced academic courses that were prerequisite to their career aspirations.

Many of the girls who had been reared from childhood in America felt pulled between two worlds, Punjabi and American. At school and through the media they received one set of messages: be independent; make your own decisions; go as far as you can with your education; postpone marriage and children until your career is begun. Their parents told them something else: don't get involved in social activities; avoid all contact with the opposite sex; come home directly from school; expect to marry soon after high school; defer to adult authority. Preoccupied by how best to cope with these conflicting sets of expectations, many of the American-reared girls found it difficult to apply themselves to their studies. As a group, these girls had poorer attendance, poorer grades, and a lower satisfaction level with their high school experience than American-reared boys or girls who had migrated from India at an older age.

Boys had far more freedom than girls to make decisions for themselves regarding their social life, course selection, career choice, and the age at which they wished to marry. Most believed that their parents would back them if they wished to pursue four years of college, or more, and demonstrated both ability and diligence. Most also felt a strong pressure to become successful financially.

In spite of these differences, boys and girls received much the same advice from their elders with respect to proper school behavior: "Obey your teachers." "Do your school work." "Stay out of trouble."

"You're there to learn and not to fight." "Keep trying harder." "Keep pushing yourself." All Sikh students agreed that these were the sorts of things their parents repeatedly told them. Most adhered to parental advice.

Sikhs urge their young to place school work first, ahead of housework, jobs, and most especially social activities, including those sponsored by the schools. They expect their children to do well academically. They admonish them to do better by trying harder and by seeking help from their teachers. Most Valleyside Sikh parents, because of their own limited education and limited English, cannot help their children with their studies. "We send the children to school and leave the rest to God," one farmer reported. When a child does poorly, parents generally blame the child: "If the child does not wish to study, then what can the teacher do?" "Those who wish to learn, will learn," parents explain.

The importance of upholding family respect serves as a strong incentive to diligence in school. Sikh children are instructed repeatedly that their good deeds will bring honor to their family, and, conversely, that poor behavior will bring a bad name to their parents, their household, and their community. Girls, especially, feel the pressure to adhere to community standards for proper behavior. "All our honor is in their hands," parents observe, with reference to their daughters. Sikh young people, boys as well as girls, also learn from an early age that if word of misbehavior reaches home, no matter the explanation, they can expect to be punished.

Although Sikh parents were deeply concerned about the problems their children encountered in school, racial hostilities in particular, they viewed the problems as no excuse for poor academic performance. In spite of all difficulties, their children, as they saw it, had far greater opportunities for a good education and, following that, good employment in America than in India. Schoolwork was to be treated as a job and hard work was expected. "God is not going to make you a man [or woman] a second time," parents reminded their young. They reminded them, too, that if they were "only interested in play and clothes" they could not "become successful."

Valleyside Sikhs were deeply troubled by pressures placed on their children to adopt majority-group cultural standards. "Take up their good values," they urge their children, but "leave the rest," the assumption being that "If we just follow the whites and do as they do, then we are going to be lost." Parents noted as well that "When our children get together with the white children, they start doing things that affect our family honor." Accordingly, parents urge their adolescent children to mix with white peers while in school, but outside of school they were expected to socialize with other Sikhs. In Valleyside's tight-knit Sikh community, gossip spreads rapidly and works as a powerful force to maintain community standards for appropriate behavior. All Sikh adolescents can cite examples of culturally-deviant students who have been withdrawn from school. Sikh youngsters realize that if they get out of line their parents may arrange an early marriage or put them to work in the fruit orchards. "The fields are waiting," parents warn.

The British Case

Sikhs resident in Britain are a more heterogeneous group than those settled in Valleyside. A significant minority migrated to Britain from East Africa (Bhachu, 1985b). Others came from urban India. Those who came direct from Punjab villages settled in Britain some 20 years ago. Thus, even those of rural origin are now quite urbanized and the younger generation—those currently in school—are almost entirely United-Kingdom born. The British Sikh population is also diversified along caste and class lines.

Findings reported here come from a sample of 35 Sikh families based in London and the West Midlands. The sample included factory workers, white-collar workers, professionals and businessmen. The research involved two years of anthropological fieldwork (1982–84), during which time Bhachu regularly attended community functions and conducted informal interviews with parents, their children, and key members of the Sikh community. The interviews focused on parents' aspirations and expectations for their children. All 35 families had children who were attending or had previously attended British schools. Unlike Gibson's study in Valleyside, which was larger in scope, Bhachu's study included no school component. The British and American studies were similar, however, in their focus on the role of parents and community in shaping school performance patterns.

Bhachu's sample of families included Khatris (merchants) and Ramgarhias (artisans), as well as Jats (agriculturalists). Unlike Jats, the

Khatris and Ramgarhias were urban-based in India, and formal education has long been an avenue to their occupational mobility. Educated members of these groups, in India and in East Africa, have occupied business and professional niches, as well as public-sector employment. These employment patterns have been reproduced in Britain.[6] Jats, on the other hand, who constitute the largest group of Sikhs in Britain, were predominantly rural based in India and had far less access to secondary and higher education. In Britain, they have tended to seek employment as skilled and unskilled workers in factories and heavy industry.[7]

In spite of these differences in background and current socioeconomic situation, British Sikh parents, as a group, share high educational expectations for their children. They encourage their children, daughters as well as sons, to acquire university credentials that can lead to well-paid employment. Even if they themselves have little formal education, the parents nearly always have access to highly educated individuals through their extended kin group or through the local *gurdwara* (Sikh temple). Such individuals are held up as role models for their children.

Children are constantly told stories of those who have overcome adversity—perhaps the death of one's father at an early age or being born of parents in very humble circumstances—to become highly respected doctors and lawyers. Likewise, children are told of young people who, in spite of their privileged backgrounds, have amounted to little. What matters, their parents remind them, is what one does for oneself. Every Sikh thinks himself or herself to be as good as anyone else. It is achieved, not inherited, status that is important, they instruct their children.

The egalitarian principles of the Sikh religion, projected especially strongly in their religious institutions, act as an equalizing influence on the Sikh community and weaken the potential development of restricted educational categories and socioeconomic groupings. The Sikh religion encourages the intermixing of individuals of different caste and class backgrounds. Almost all children have direct contact, through the *gurdwara*, if not their own kin network, with adults who have overcome substantial obstacles. There is a strong sense within the British Sikh community that to be successful, one has not only to understand the way the majority society operates but, in addition, to gain the social skills and personal networks that open doors. Education is viewed as instrumental to these goals.

In the Sikh view, a successful and respected individual is one who demonstrates command over the non-Punjabi world of the British mainstream while maintaining strong roots within the Punjabi community. Such a perspective is strongly reflected in the teachings and writings of Sikh leaders settled overseas as the following comments on the educational needs of Sikhs in Britain clearly indicate:

> Education is meant to widen his [a Sikh's] outlook and make him a philanthropist. He has to remain always in high spirits and work for the welfare of humanity as a whole. He has to raise his voice against any discrimination of caste and color. The schools, colleges and Universities in Britain should look towards him and his children as part and parcel of the British society and prepare him as an equal partner in the destiny of this country. Whereas he has carved his place in the world as a sturdy and hard working Punjabi, he can also rise and become a great British workman engineer, doctor, lawyer, educationist and scientist. (Kohli, 1985/86:23)

Parents today in Britain expect their young to become proficient in both the cultures of Punjabi migrants and settlers, and those of the wider community in which they find themselves. A decade or two ago, when the Sikh community in Britain was less well established, there was much discussion about the potential negative impact of British and Western culture on the younger generation. Today, these fears have subsided and few parents worry about losing their children from the Sikh community. It is now accepted as fact that Sikhs born and raised in the United Kingdom can be Punjabi *and* British.

British Sikhs also see education as bringing credit to the whole family. One man explained the relationship as follows:

> If one *rhistedhar* [relative] . . . gets educated, a whole *kul* [sub-caste] raises its status. We can get better matches for our daughters and sons. We will get more respect as well. We can also get help from the educated person and give his or her example to the younger generation to create an even more educated set of people.

The same might well have been said by a Valleyside Sikh, so similar are their perspectives on the value of education.

British Sikhs, however, place more pressure on their young to excel academically than is the case in Valleyside. They note that an uneducated person, even one with many talents, has no value. A child who brings home a poor report card is told he or she has not tried hard enough and is made to feel a failure. When word of poor performance reaches relatives and family friends, Sikh young people may even be ignored socially. This sanction generally serves as a deterrent to mediocre academic performance and helps instill a desire to acquire top marks.

Parents monitor their children's out-of-school activities carefully, even during the late teenage years, in order for them to avoid "bad company" that might distract from the main goal of getting on in the educational system. Young people are taught that their teens are a time for diligence in school and that they will be able to enjoy themselves socially later on, once they are through with their studies. Although Sikh youths participate quite freely in extracurricular activities during the school year—a distinction between them and the Valleyside group—they withdraw from these activities as exam time nears in order to devote themselves singlemindedly to their studies.

Like the Valleyside group, British Sikh young people are particularly discouraged from wasting emotional energy at this point in their lives on cross-gender relationships. They are discouraged, too, from emulating the negative educational values of working-class white British peers. Take "what is good from *chitas* [white people] and leave the bad," parents say. As in Valleyside, Sikh young people interact with white classmates at school, but outside of school they remain largely within their own kinship networks. Although the popular peer group culture of non-Sikhs is not without its impact, its influence is mitigated by the strong orientation of the Sikh community toward academic diligence and the acquisition of educational credentials.

Intragroup Variation

It should be stressed that not all Sikhs are interested in education, despite the intense collective pressure placed on them by their families and the Sikh community at large to do well in school. There are some young Sikhs, moreover, who simply are unable to manage the educational system successfully, and these young people are the most receptive to the influence of peer subcultures beyond the parameters of the Sikh community. For example, during the course of fieldwork Bhachu came to know several young men who had been made to feel outcast because of poor marks on their "O level" and "A level" examinations—those that determine if a student is eligible for advanced academic course work at age sixteen and, following that, university admission. These young men, after failing their exams, drifted farther and farther from the symbols of the Sikh faith and the norms that govern Sikh behavior.

The case of Jagjit Singh is illustrative here. A year after he failed his "A levels," Jagjit cut his hair (he had previously worn his hair long in concert with orthodox Sikh principles), began smoking (which is forbidden by the Sikh religion), had his left ear pierced, and turned his attention increasingly to the Reggae music popular among Afro-Caribbean youths. His aunt described him as "turning black." Jagjit himself said that he is ignored at religious and family functions because "he is not bright" (his words) and because he has not become a professional like Gurcharan, his "cousin brother" who is a dentist. Dubbed "the Reggae Singh" by relatives, Jagjit is characterized as "bad company" and a poor influence on younger cousins with whom he often socializes.

Not all young Sikh men who do poorly academically are made to feel outcast or socially invisible. And even those who receive failing marks in school can redeem themselves in adult life by becoming successful in some trade or business. Sikhs greatly admire those who demonstrate money-making abilities, leadership skills, and service to others. One with such attributes can become a respected and powerful figure within the Sikh community regardless of educational achievements.

Alternative Mobility Strategies

Not all Sikh parents stress education as the channel to upward mobility. There are big building contractors and industrialists such as the Thekedhars (a business category that cuts across caste lines) who do not and have not in the past emphasized to their young the importance of schooling. Such an attitude applies regardless of caste background, urban experience or familiarity with Western education. Because of their expectation that they will join the family business, most Thekedhar males find little incentive to pursue postsecondary education. Even those with professional training tend to be absorbed into the family business rather than pursue a career in line with their degrees. This alternative of entering the family business does not exist for other Sikhs in Britain, and for them, upward mobility, at least until recently, has been primarily through educational channels.

The situation of the Thekedhars has some parallel to that of Jat Sikhs males in India who know that they can take up farming even if they fail to do well in school, an option that exists to a certain extent for California Jats as well, although not at all for British Jats. This is a major point of difference between urban British Sikhs and rural California ones.

Bhattra Sikhs are another group at variance with the mainstream of the Sikh community in their lack of interest in using education as a means to economic and social mobility. A low-caste and very orthodox group, Bhattras have maintained their distinctive identity by restricting their social arena to other Bhattras and by adhering rigidly to their religious and social ways. They pride themselves in being custodians of orthodox Sikh traditions and in so doing help to compensate for their low-caste status (Ghuman, 1980). In Britain they tend to be self-employed, running small businesses that require little or no formal education, such as a market stall or clothing outlet.

In sharp contrast with other Sikh youths, Bhattras have a high rate of truancy and generally drop out of school in their teens although a few British-born Bhattra males have gone on to attend university. Rather than encouraging their children to become proficient in both British and Punjabi worlds, Bhattra parents see British schools as a threat to their way of life and their tightly knit community and, thus, seek to minimize their children's exposure to this force for anglicization (Ghuman, 1980).

Thus, even though there is a pervasive Sikh pattern of valuing formal education, which applies almost regardless of class and caste status, there are also differences that follow individual clusters of families and caste groupings. There are differences, too, in strategies used to foster academic achievement.

Parental Involvement Strategies

Many of the more urbanized British Sikhs, in an effort to improve their children's opportunities for scholastic success, have adopted what may be characterized as an *interventionist approach to schooling*, similar to that of the English middle class (Bhachu, 1985a). These parents regularly attend school meetings, assist their children with homework, and join in peripheral school activities. A significant percentage has also placed their children in private, fee-paying schools, which they consider more credentials-oriented and less racist than state-run institutions.

Prejudice and discrimination against South Asians in Britain and British schools are well documented in the literature on race relations and there are some indications that South Asians settled in Britain may experience even more frequent acts of unprovoked racial hostility than West Indians in Britain (Brake, 1980:76–79; Brown, 1984:247–58; Pearson, 1976; Rampton Report, 1981; Swann Report, 1985; Willis 1977:49) or Punjabis in Valleyside (Gibson, 1988a). Understandably, British Sikh parents, like their Valleyside counterparts, are extremely concerned about the impact of racial hostilities on their children's emotional, social and educational development. In Valleyside, however, Sikh parents really had no alternative to the public (state-run) schools due to their own limited resources and the limited availability of private schools in Valleyside. In Britain, too, tuition payments create a financial hardship for families of modest means, but Sikh parents assume that there will be ample return in the future in terms of an easier, happier life for their children.

Not all British Sikh parents become directly involved in their children's schooling. Those of rural background, with little formal education and prior exposure to urban and Western lifestyles, rarely visit their children's schools. This was particularly true in the early days of settlement in the United Kingdom when their understanding of the British educational system was minimal. Like their Valleyside counterparts, these parents adopted a *noninterventionist approach* to schooling.

This characterization of rural Sikhs as "less educated" does not apply to their command over religious and scriptural knowledge, agricultural skills and traditional cultural values. The latter are crucial in fashioning their children's educational attitudes and success strategies. The noninterventionist approach of the rural migrants has proved just as effective within the British context in motivating children to do well in school and to pursue higher education as the more middle-class, urban interventionist approach (Bhachu, 1985a).

Changing Educational Strategies

Although the dominant Sikh pattern of enormous respect for educational qualifications and a strong interest in "getting children through studies successfully" persists in Britain, there are an increasing number of Sikh youngsters who have opted not to go into tertiary educational institutions. These young people have chosen to take up employment either at age sixteen, after completing their CSE (Certificate for Secondary Education) or "O (Ordinary) level" examinations (the CSE is a somewhat lower-level, more vocationally oriented examination than the "O level"), or after taking their "A levels" at age eighteen. Their justification for bypassing higher education and heading directly into the job market stems from a number of factors. One is that young Sikhs now emerging from the British educational system feel knowledgeable about the skills required to operate in the labor market successfully. They are astute not only about the qualifications needed to get financially rewarding employment but also about the disadvantages of pursuing an educational program that may lead to no clear-cut job.

It has become increasingly difficult in Britain in recent years for university-degree holders to find jobs which match their qualifications and this has deterred some young Sikhs from going to university. At the same time, their diminishing respect for advanced education reflects an attitude prevalent among white, working-class peers. Some working-class Sikh youths choose not to pursue their studies for precisely the same reasons as white youths within their class group. Class position and peer subcultures are having increasing impact on Sikh youths' educational aspirations and strategies. The point to be emphasized is that the educational and career strategies of Sikh young people are influenced not only by their cultural backgrounds but by their position within the British class hierarchy, the values of their peers, both in and out of school, and popular culture beyond their own ethnic group.

Parents' perspectives on the value of higher education, furthermore, no longer are determined by the experience of India and East Africa, where educated Indians had prestigious jobs and were among the most high status employees in the British colonial bureaucracies. Life in the United Kingdom has taught them that doors do not necessarily open up for educated individuals, particularly those of Asian or minority background. Racial discrimination in Britain operates as powerfully on the highly-educated as on the least educated. The force of this factor has led to changes in the Punjabi educational belief system and to a diversification in career choices. Young Sikhs today, irrespective of class or caste status, are turning increasingly to commercial enterprise, a strategy that takes them away from white-controlled employment sectors. Not only is this a response to racism in employment and the ceiling on job promotion which Sikhs experience, but it also reflects the general lack of employment opportunities in Britain and the Thatcher government's encouragement of the enterprise culture. In addition, it indicates a Sikh desire to be "one's own boss in one's own business . . . away from *gora* [white] bosses."

Increasing numbers of young Sikhs, including college graduates who are unable to find work in the fields for which they have trained, are opening up small businesses, mostly retail outlets such as a corner grocery store, a tire shop or a neighborhood post office. These enterprises are generally set up with financial backing from the extended family and often in partnership with one's brothers. This overall pattern has led to a shift in the Sikhs' educational strategies and in some cases is accompanied by the loss of respect for higher education and in others a reorientation toward courses of study that more closely fulfill market demand.

Women and Education

Another development in the United Kingdom that has led to a change in educational values and strategies is the dramatic entry over the past decade of Sikh women into the labor market as wage earners. Sixty-two percent of the Asian women of Indian origin and 67 percent of those of East African origin, ages twenty-five to forty-four years, are now economically active (Labour Force Survey, cited in Barber, 1985).[8] As in Valleyside, the large majority of these women had not worked outside their homes prior to migration (Bhachu, 1986, 1988). Without formal education and job skills, most of the older women have found their opportunities restricted to unskilled factory work, a fact that has had major impact on mothers' aspirations for their daughters. There now is great interest in higher education for women, at least to the B.A. level and in a number of cases the postgraduate level as well, so that they can get reasonable jobs away from the unskilled factory work that most of the older women are involved in.

So strong is this orientation that Sikh parents in Britain, in sharp contrast to those in Valleyside, are quick to point out that "if one girl gets educated in one family, it influences seven generations of people to come." In Britain today, a young woman's educational credentials have become an important criterion in the arrangement of her marriage. Far from saying that an educated woman may have difficulty fitting into her husband's household, as in Valleyside, British Sikhs feel that education enhances their daughter's attractiveness in the marriage market. In the past, when men were the sole wage earners, it was common for highly educated men to marry women with little or no schooling. Today in Britain, however, two incomes are essential to the maintenance of the household and education for girls has become an imperative. These changes have led, moreover, to decreasing emphasis on family and kinship group status as a criterion of spouse selection and increasing attention to the individual achievements of the young people concerned (Bhachu, 1985b).

Also, whereas in the Indian subcontinent and in East Africa education had to be paid for, in Britain this is not the case. Girls in particular are benefiting from state grants for higher education which permit them to pursue their studies independent of parental financial support. In the past, few Sikh families considered investing in the education of their daughters, even when they were brighter than the sons. In both India and Africa, it was customary for men of the household to be encouraged to enter tertiary institutions and, family resources permitting, to be sent abroad to British universities. This is not to suggest that women were never educated beyond the secondary level, but that such cases were rare, whereas today this has become a common pattern. Recent studies show not only that Indian females in Britain are taking their "A levels" in considerable numbers but that they are outperforming their male counterparts (ILEA, 1987).

The next decade will see the production of a highly educated and high-earning population of British Sikh women partly because of the Indian interest in education and partly because of their freedom from romantic love. The fact that Indian girls lose no vital time during their school years in the pursuit of "Prince Charming," as is the case for the majority of white adolescent girls, is a factor that clearly enhances their educational success. As British educator Hazel Taylor (1983:8) observes, South Asian girls "achieve better in school, and are far more likely to take up science subjects and do well in Math, than white girls. . . . Freedom from the myth of Mr. Right and romantic love allows energy to be directed to other more positive occupations."

This type of attitude toward education is further buttressed in the case of Sikhs by religious tenets which accord women equal status to that of men. Sikh women in Britain are active both in public institutions, for example, as key officeholders and committee members in *gurdwaras*, and in the labor market.

A final point that needs to be made is that the educational and career choices of Sikh women are influenced not only by the factors discussed here, but also by structural forces operative in British mainstream society. As noted above in the discussion of changing educational strategies, the younger generation of Sikhs are the products of British society and they, like their white agemates, are affected by peer group subcultures that discourage educational diligence. Thus, when a Sikh girl fails to pursue higher education, this is not necessarily because of parental restrictions or the older cultural pattern that discouraged female education. Working-class Sikh girls may choose to leave school at age sixteen, whereas middle-class girls may not consider arresting their education before the tertiary stage.

It should be stressed, however, that in spite of the increasing influence of class position on Sikhs' educational aspirations and strategies, the majority of Sikhs maintain their ferocious interest in education. On the whole there is strong congruence between parents' views and those of their children, most of whom have been successfully socialized to view education as the primary avenue to upward social mobility. It is precisely this belief that has produced the high level of academic achievement among British Sikh students.

Discussion

The Sikh case study demonstrates a close relationship between a minority group's theories of success, its strategies for getting ahead in society, and the school-adaptation patterns of its young. In the present case, the dominant perspective in the British and American settings is one that encourages academic persistence even in the face of majority-group prejudice and discrimination. Sikh parents in both settings assume that formal education is the primary avenue to upward mobility. They also assume that success in school stems from the individual student's hard work and perseverance, and that schooling is one arena where children have the opportunity to compete on an equal footing regardless of family background.

Not all subgroups of Sikhs share this dominant view. While most overseas Sikhs, and indeed most immigrant minorities, focus on the instrumental value of schooling and its role in promoting socioeconomic mobility for their young, the Bhattra Sikhs have regarded Western schooling as a threat to the maintenance of their separate cultural and religious identities. In equating school learning with acculturation and this, in turn, with assimilation, the Bhattra response appears to be similar to that of many involuntary minorities whose school performance continues from generation to generation to lag behind national norms (see Ogbu in this volume). Why some minority groups see the acquisition of academic learning and skills in the majority culture in a linear fashion leading ultimately to assimilation, while others see school learning and acculturation in a multidimensional fashion whereby new skills and values are incorporated into the old culture is an issue of pressing concern. Those minorities that view schooling in a *subtractive* rather than *additive* fashion also tend to be those who persistently underperform in school (Gibson, 1987b:273–74, 1988a, 1989:130–31). Although immigrant minorities tend generally to distinguish school learning from assimilation, the Bhattra example suggests that this is not necessarily the case.

We have also noted variation in the instrumental value attached to schooling by other subgroups of Sikhs. The Thekedhars, a group known for its entrepreneurial success, have generally encouraged their young to enter family business at the end of their secondary schooling rather than pursue a tertiary level of education. In a somewhat similar vein, Jat Sikhs have assumed that those of their offspring who will take up their traditional vocation as farmers have little need for formal education. Although Jat parents in India may have great respect for formal education and may believe, as their counterparts in England and America, that schooling is an arena where children can compete on an equal footing irrespective of family status, they have not provided equal encouragement to all their children to excel academically.

As the Sikh case makes clear, however, a group's theories of success, including its educational beliefs, are not rigidly defined, but are in a constant process of negotiation. Mobility strategies change as the societal context changes and as the group's situation within a particular society itself changes. In turn, folk theories of success themselves are modified. We can see this clearly with respect to the education of Sikh women. In rural India, where women have few opportunities to work outside the home, schooling has been viewed not only as having little practical value but as potentially disruptive to traditional age and sex roles. In spite of Sikh religious beliefs regarding the equality of the sexes, Sikh girls in India, particularly in the rural areas where the large majority of the population continues to live, have not received the same encouragement and support as their brothers to pursue an education. Although this gender difference persists in overseas settings, the entry of Sikh women into the labor market in Britain and in the United States has led to a dramatic shift in attitudes about the necessity of educational qualifications. Valleyside Sikh parents, even recent migrants from rural Punjab, expect their daughters to become wage earners. The same is true in Britain. In both settings the parents recognize that a wide variety of employment opportunities are available, to women as well as men. They recognize, in addition, based in large measure on their own employment experiences, that their children must be well educated if they are to compete successfully for desirable jobs. Although Valleyside Sikhs may still say that too much education can make a girl snobbish and outspoken, few today stand in the way of their daughters attending community college and, once married, pursuing more advanced degrees.

In Britain, moreover, where Sikhs have a longer experience of urbanization, parents actively encourage higher education for women before marriage, noting not only that educational credentials enhance marriage opportunities, but that an educated woman can provide a positive influence on her family for generations to come. Another facet of change that has encouraged education for women is the shift to residence in nuclear households immediately or soon after marriage and the increasing "couple orientation" of young Sikhs raised in Western societies. A focus on the individual achievements of spouses at marriage, women as well as men, is replacing the earlier Punjabi focus on the status of the extended family.

Gender differences persist in terms of occupational goals. These in turn have direct bearing on students' course selection and decisions regarding university attendance. Moreover, a higher proportion of Sikh males than females continue to pursue professional degrees. By most other measures, however, the educational performance of Sikh girls now matches and, in some instances, surpasses, that of their brothers. In metropolitan London, for example, where the majority of Indian youths, including Sikhs, are now British-born (unlike in Valleyside where most Sikh adolescents continue to be rather freshly arrived from rural Punjab and thus strongly influenced by rural Punjabi values), girls not only persist to the fifth year of secondary school in numbers equal to Indian boys, but their average performance on fifth year examinations surpasses that of the boys (1985 mean scores of 26.3 and 22.5, respectively). In addition, both perform significantly better on their examinations than majority-group girls and boys, whose respective mean scores in 1985 were 16.9 and 13.6 (ILEA, 1987:11, 19).

Our analysis demonstrates a strong relationship between the Sikhs' perseverance in school and their perceptions of the instrumental value of educational credentials or of a particular course of study in obtaining employment. The Sikhs whom we studied, moreover, saw the acquisition of skills in the majority-group language and culture as essential to their children's successful participation in the larger society. At the same time, they counseled the maintenance of strong roots within the Sikh community and severely sanctioned those who deviated too far from community norms.

Although the general trend in Valleyside, and even more so in Britain, has been toward more and more years of schooling, Sikhs have demonstrated a readiness to shift their strategies in response to changing market conditions. They are increasingly aware, moreover, that educational credentials are no insurance against job discrimination. The direct experience of a ceiling on job promotions for Asians, including those with professional qualifications, has led some young Sikhs, males in particular, to lose respect for higher education and to opt for jobs that are outside the areas of white control.

This pattern of diminishing respect for education is a product of current economic conditions in Britain and of the realization that, even with degrees, minorities are denied equal opportunities for advancement within British society. It reflects as well an internalization of some facets of the prevalent white British youth culture, especially that of the working classes.

Structural position within the British class hierarchy is an increasingly important determinant of educational and career choices for young British Sikhs, most of whom are now second generation. Raised in Britain, their reference group no longer is those left behind in India, as is the case with their parents. Although the egalitarian ideology of the Sikh religion and Sikh social institutions mitigate against the development of clear class structures and restricted educational categories, Sikh youths in Britain today are increasingly influenced by the class cultures of the white majority.

In the California setting the influence of class-related belief systems is far less strong. At the same time, however, the impact of dominant American values is readily apparent. For example, those raised in the United States feel strongly the pressures to place individual interests ahead of those of the group and to get out on their own, versus taking their places within the extended family grouping. Young American-born Sikhs, when questioned about their hopes and plans for the future, often sounded more like majority-group peers than their recently arrived cousins from Punjab (Gibson, 1988a).

This chapter has focused on how the educational strategies and school adaptation patterns of the student generation are directly and strongly influenced by cultural models of their families and ethnic community, but we have noted also the impact of peer values, the popular culture beyond one's own ethnic group, and socioeconomic conditions in the society at large. We have suggested, too, that research on community forces and school performance must consider the interplay of gender, class and ethnicity. The point we wish to emphasize in closing is that efforts to reform educational practice and to meet the needs of underachieving students must take into account the sociocultural and economic structures that cause students to embrace or reject schooling.

Notes

Acknowledgments: Although written expressly for the present volume, a version of this chapter appeared in *Ethnic and Racial Studies* 11(3): 239–62, 1988, under the title "Ethnicity and School Performance: A Comparative Study of South Asian Pupils in Britain and America." Permission to reprint was granted by the publisher of *Ethnic and Racial Studies*. The authors are indebted to the National Institute of Education (grant G80-0123) for support of research on educational equity for Punjabi youth in "Valleyside," California, and to the Economic and Social Research Council (grant C00222005) for support of research on parental perspectives on schooling, Thomas Coram Research Unit, Institute of Education, University of London.

1. As of 1984, there were an estimated 1,271,000 South Asians living in Britain, including 169,600 Sikhs (Knott, 1987).

2. Valleyside is a pseudonym.

3. No similar gender disparity was found to exist among the white Valleysiders.

4. Many white Valleysiders use the term "Hindu" in a derogatory fashion when referring to Valleyside Indians, be they Sikh, Hindu or Muslim.

5. Most rural Punjabi women in fact do work, most of them for very long hours, but not for wages. Jat women's labor in managing the household is essential to the successful operation of a Punjabi farm.

6. Jat Sikhs, who are and have been predominantly rural-based, constitute the majority Sikh community both in India and overseas. The Khatris, a mercantile group, and the Ramgarhias, who represent a consolidation of three artisan groups—blacksmiths, carpenters, and bricklayers—are today largely urban-based. The Jats and Khatris rank above the Ramgarhias and above the Ravi Dasis (scheduled or lower castes) in the traditional Indian caste hierarchy, although the latter groups have benefited from migration to East Africa and the United Kingdom. Ramgharias, in particular, while in East Africa became familiar with bureaucratic processes and acquired educational skills and were able to transfer the knowledge and the skills with them when they migrated to the United Kingdom.

7. This is not to suggest that there is an absence of educated individuals within the Jat Sikh group but rather that the large majority of those who have settled in Britain were, like those in Valleyside, direct migrants from the rural areas. The minority of urban migrant Jats in the United Kingdom and in the

United States have a much longer tradition of using formal education as an avenue to professional positions. 8. The percentage of Muslim women in the labor market is far smaller: only 17 percent of women aged twenty-five to forty-four of Pakistani and Bangladeshi origin are economically active (Bhachu, 1988).

References

Ballard, Roger, and Selma Vellins. 1985. "South Asian Entrants to British Universities: A Comparative Note." *New Community* 12(2):260–65.

Barber, Ann. 1985. "Ethnic Origin and Economic Status." *Employment Gazette*, December, pp. 467–77.

Bhachu, Parminder. 1985a. "Parental Educational Strategies: The Case of Punjabi Sikhs in Britain." Research Paper 3, Centre for Research in Ethnic Relations, University of Warwick.

————. 1985b. *Twice Migrants: East African Sikh Settlers in Britain.* London: Tavistock Press.

————. 1986. "Work, Dowry and Marriage among East African Sikh Women in the United Kingdom." In *International Migration: The Female Experience*, ed. R.J. Simon and C.B. Brettell, pp. 22–40. Totowa, N.J.: Rowman and Allanheld.

————. 1988. "Apni Marzi Kardhi. Home and Work: Sikh Women in Britain." In *Enterprising Women: Ethnicity, Economy and Gender Relations*, ed. S. Westwood and P. Bhachu, pp. 76–102. London and New York: Routledge.

Brake, Mike. 1980. *The Sociology of Youth Culture and Youth Subcultures.* London: Routledge and Kegan Paul.

Brown, Colin. 1984. *Black and White Britain: The Third PSI Survey.* London: Heinemann.

Ghuman, Paul A.S. 1980. "Bhattra Sikhs in Cardiff: Family and Kinship Organization." *New Community* 8(2):308–16.

Gibson, Margaret A. 1987a. "Punjabi Immigrants in an American High School." In *Interpretive Ethnography of Education: At Home and Abroad*, ed. George Spindler and Louise Spindler, pp. 281–310. Hillsdale, N.J.: Lawrence Erlbaum.

————. 1987b. "The School Performance of Immigrant Minorities: A Comparative View." *Anthropology and Education Quarterly* 18(4):262–75.

———. 1988a. *Accommodation without Assimilation: Sikh Immigrants in an American High School.* Ithaca: Cornell University Press.

———. 1988b. "Punjabi Orchard Farmers: An Immigrant Enclave in Rural California." *International Migration Review* 22(1):28–50.

———. 1989. "School Persistence versus Dropping Out: A Comparative Perspective." In *What Do Anthropologists Have to Say about Dropouts?*, ed. Henry T. Trueba, George and Louise Spindler, pp. 126–34. New York: Falmer Press.

Gibson, Margaret A., and Parminder K. Bhachu. 1986. "Community Forces and School Performance: Punjabi Sikhs in Rural California and Urban Britain." *New Community* 13(1):27–39.

Inner London Education Authority. 1987. "Ethnic Background and Examination Results: 1985 and 1986." Report P-7078, prepared by ILEA Research and Statistics, 1 July. London.

Knott, Kim. 1987. "Calculating Sikh Population Statistics." *Sikh Bulletin* 4:13–22, W.O. Cole and E. Nesbitt, eds.

Kohli, Surindar Singh. 1985/86. "Religious, Cultural and Educational Needs of the Sikhs in Great Britain." *Sikh Messenger*, Winter/Spring, pp. 20–24.

Metha, H. 1926. "A History of the Growth and Development of Western Education in the Punjab, 1846–1884." Punjab Government Record Office, Monograph no. 5. Languages Department, Punjab.

Pearson, G. 1976. "'Paki-Bashing' in a North East Lancashire Cotton Town." In *Working Class Youth Culture*, ed. G. Mungham and G. Pearson. London: Routledge and Kegan Paul.

Ramakrishna, Jayashree. 1979. "Health Behavior and Practices of the Sikh Community of the Yuba City Area of California." Ph.D. diss. University of California, Berkeley.

Rampton Report. 1981. *West Indian Children in Our Schools. Interim Report of the Committee of Inquiry into Education of Children from Ethnic Minority Groups.* Cmnd. 8273. London: Her Majesty's Stationery Office.

Singh, K.P. 1979. "Economic Development and Female Labour Force Participation in Punjab." Paper presented at seminar, Regional Development: Socio-Economic Aspects, 4–6 March. Chandigarh, Punjab: Indian Council of Social Science Research—North Western Regional Center, Punjab University.

Swann Committee Report. 1985. *Education for All. Report of the Committee of Inquiry into the Education of Children from Ethnic Minority Groups.* Cmnd. 9453. London: Her Majesty's Stationery Office.

Taylor, Hazel. 1983. "Sexism and Racism: Partners of Oppression." *Cassoe Newsletter*, May–June, pp. 5–8.

Taylor, Monica, and Seamus Hegarty. 1985. *The Best of Both Worlds . . .? A Review of Research into the Education of Pupils of South Asian Origin.* Windsor: NFER-Nelson.

Willis, Paul E. 1977. *Learning to Labour: How Working Class Kids Get Working Class Jobs.* Westmead: Saxon House.

Chapter Four
Turkish Immigrants in Australia

Christine Inglis
University of Sydney
and
Lenore Manderson
University of Queensland

Turkish immigration to Australia is a result of the extensive immigration program which Australia embarked upon after World War II. The program played a major part in the growth of Australia's population from 7.5 million in 1947 to 15.7 million in 1985. The initial intention in the formulation of immigration policy was to preserve the predominantly Anglo-Celtic character of Australian society but, in seeking to meet population targets, it became necessary for the government to seek and accept increasing numbers of migrants from continental Europe. A feature of this immigration became the ever changing origins of the waves of migrants as the government extended the search from Britain to northwest and eastern Europe, then to southern Europe, and more recently, to the Middle East and Asia. By 1981, 2.4 percent of Australia's population had been born in Asia and the Middle East.

Extensive Turkish immigration to Australia began after the signing of a bilateral agreement between Australia and Turkey in 1967. Whereas the Turkish-born population was 2,475 in 1966, by the time of the 1981 census, it had grown to 24,313. While official statistics do not provide information on the numbers of Turks from Cyprus nor on the children born in Australia to parents of Turkish origin, the figure of

50,000 is often cited by the Turkish community as indicating the total population of Turkish origin (Young, 1983:33; Australia Department of Education and Youth Affairs, 1983:16).

The Turkish immigrants, like many earlier immigrants to Australia, predominantly found employment in unskilled and semiskilled occupations. Although many Turks received Australian government assistance with fares, accommodation and settlement services, there was a tendency to perceive them as a group experiencing considerable difficulties in adjustment.

Explanations for their disadvantage emphasized their rural background, their limited Turkish education and their lack of English. The difficulties of these people were compounded by the lack of longer-resident or professional members in the Australian community and the lack of established Islamic religious organizations to assist in the settlement of the new arrivals, who were seen as being culturally alien to the majority of the population. A further difficultly facing the Turks was that their arrival commenced toward the end of the period of postwar economic growth and prosperity, which meant that opportunities for economic and social mobility were restricted. The disadvantaged label which Turks rapidly acquired also was extended to their children, who were seen to face particular problems in education and employment.

This chapter is concerned with the educational experience of these Turkish children and, in particular, it focuses on the nature of the family cultural background as an important component in the children's educational experiences and levels of attainment. As one of many immigrant groups in Australia, the experiences of the Turks need to be placed in relation to the experiences of other immigrant groups; these experiences also need to be seen in the context of the changing responses of the Australian schools to immigrant children.

Australian Education and Children from Migrant Backgrounds

The response of Australian schools to the influx of large numbers of children from migrant families has passed through a number of stages which moved from no accommodation to them to the present situation where special programs have been instituted to overcome identified areas of difficulty. The initial lack of response to the needs of migrant children was linked to the then-dominant ideological and policy position that migrants should assimilate into the Anglo-Australian culture. As the policy corollary of this, there was a denial that existing institutions should make any special provisions for the migrant (Martin, 1978). By the late 1960s, however, when the majority of Turkish immigrants began to arrive, the situation was changing, partly as a result of increasing public and educational awareness of the difficulties faced by migrant children and their teachers (Martin, 1978). The first major step toward assisting the migrant children was the funding of English as a Second Language (ESL) programs by the federal government through its Child Migrant Education Program in 1970. These programs have continued and have been expanded to cater also to Australian-born children from non-English speaking backgrounds.

By the mid-1970s, the educational system had begun to respond in more varied ways to the presence of children from diverse ethnic backgrounds, and policies of multicultural education began to be adopted. The programs sponsored under these policies extended the provisions beyond the teaching of remedial English to curriculum changes with two main aims. The first was to make all Australian children aware of, and receptive to, the cultural diversity which existed in Australia. The second aim was to provide opportunities for children from specific migrant backgrounds to study the language, history and culture of their own heritage. The extent to which these policy changes have been effective in realizing the not-necessarily interrelated objectives of (1) improving educational attainment, while (2) raising the personal and social esteem of children from migrant backgrounds and (3) promoting intercultural understanding is an issue currently debated in Australian education. Certainly, it is clear that the extent to which children are exposed to the various programs, especially those other than the ESL programs, depends on the school they attend and the composition of its student population. As the Turkish migrants often live in relatively concentrated areas of Turkish residential settlement, many children have attended the few schools which by the early 1980s either were providing Turkish language programs or had Turkish ethnic aides available to assist the teachers.

Australian studies of migrant children's educational experiences, which have played a part in the analysis of and impetus for educational change, have examined two aspects of these experiences in schools where English is used almost exclusively for instruction and communication and where, despite recent changes, Anglo-Celtic values and content still dominate the curriculum. The material emphasizes the personal and social traumas experienced by children, especially those from non-English speaking backgrounds where home and school are viewed as especially likely to be in conflict (Brotherhood of St. Laurence, 1971). The second area of study has been the children's level of educational attainment and how this varies between ethnic groups (including the Australian born of Anglo-Celtic origin). While differences were not perceived initially, more recently the very low levels of educational attainment in terms of both schooling levels and qualifications, particularly among those of Southern European background, have begun to receive attention. The absence of a national data base makes it difficult to come to definitive conclusions about the extent of inequalities in educational outcomes and scholastic attainment (Jakubowicz, 1985). The varying methodologies, measures of attainment/disadvantage, and focus on different ethnic groups make comparison extremely difficult. However, a number of studies have highlighted the extent to which there is diversity in educational attainment and disadvantage among ethnic groups (Taft, 1975a and 1975b; Martin and Meade, 1979; Taft and Cahill, 1978; Turney et al., 1978; Majoribanks, 1980; Meade, 1981, 1982, 1983). In contrast, there is a growing perception among educators and the general public that students of certain ethnic groups, including Greeks and Asians, especially Chinese, achieve even better than Australian-born children of Anglo-Celtic origins. Further, two recent surveys of the literature on ethnic education and disadvantage argue that there is little evidence of a clear-cut link between ethnic origin and educational disadvantage (Poole, 1981; Sturman, 1985). The importance of cultural background and the differences between and within ethnic groups, even those whose members share similar economic circumstances in Australia, illustrate the need to determine the complex interplay of class, ethnicity and gender in understanding educational outcomes. As Sturman (1985:37) notes, the critical educational issue in both theory and policy is whether the existing disadvantage of many overseas-born lower-class migrants will be transmitted to their children's educational and vocational attainments.

An important feature of the studies of educational disadvantage has been a concern with the cultural attributes of migrant parents. This has involved an examination of the nature of parental attitudes with respect to specific aspects of education, including their aspirations for their children. In certain cases, studies also concern the broader cultural background of the family, particularly as it relates to the social aspects of schooling for both parents and their children. This focus provides a link with the more general studies of educational achievement which have displayed an increasing interest in the cultural background of the family when considering the role of education in cultural and structural reproduction. The interest in family cultural attributes is evident in recent Australian studies which ignore ethnicity (Connell et al., 1982). Such studies are pursuing trends similar to those found elsewhere, where concern has moved from the use of demographic and large-scale survey date (e.g., Coleman, 1966; Bowles and Gintis, 1976) to more detailed studies of the sociocultural environment of specific groups, which often employ ethnographic models in schools (Willis, 1977; Corrigan, 1979). A major concern in these studies is to examine the cultural framework or ideologies of the group members especially as they relate to education and the work environment. Complementing this approach is the consideration of "cultural capital" which the family passes on to the children (Bourdieu and Passeron, 1977). The value of the cultural capital which the child acquires from the family depends on whether it coincides with the cultural attributes which are valued by the schools and form the basis for the schools' selection, evaluation and rewarding of students. These methodological and conceptual concerns provide a useful basis for examining the potential effect on educational experiences of not only class but also ethnicity among an immigrant minority group such as the Turks.

Turkish Educational Attainment in Australia

The 1986 Census contains an enormous wealth of data relating to ethnicity in Australia but only a small amount of this information has as yet been released and is available for this paper. The existing data providing information on educational attainment are only available for those born in Turkey, and these data do not distinguish those individuals whose education was obtained in whole or in part overseas from those educated in Australia. The data also exclude the Australian-born children of Turkish parents. Nevertheless, they provide an indication of the general educational levels within the Turkish community, showing that educational attainment has risen considerably in recent years in certain respects. Indeed, among fifteen- to nineteen-year-olds born in Turkey, a slightly higher proportion of boys and girls, compared with the Australian-born population as a whole, has obtained educational qualifications, although these credentials are typically trade or other certificates. However, among the twenty- to twenty-four-year-old age group of both men and women who have had the opportunity to complete the longer tertiary diploma and degree courses, the level of qualifications reported is only two-thirds that of their Australian-born peers and the absence of tertiary qualifications for the Turkish born is evident. Progressively older groups of Turkish born show a steadily declining level of educational qualification attainment in comparison with the Australian-born population.

Paralleling this decline in educational qualifications with age, there is a decrease in the age of leaving school. However, among the fifteen- to nineteen-year-old age group the percentage of young men and women leaving school after seventeen is virtually comparable for the Turkish and Australian born, which again indicates an increasing convergence between the two birthplace groups. The most noticeable deviation in this age group is among the Turkish-born girls, some 6 percent of whom had left school before the age of thirteen, although even this figure was markedly lower than for the two older age groups, where 14 percent and 22 percent respectively (of the twenty to twenty-four and twenty-five- to twenty-nine-year-old age groups) had left school before the age of thirteen. Information on ways in which the level of qualifications is affected by period of residence in Australia among the fifteen- to twenty-nine-year-old age group is equivocal for, while nearly one-quarter of the men resident five years or less have qualifications, the figure is lower for those resident in Australia for longer periods. This may suggest that the newer residents completed their education prior to migrating to Australia and so avoided the consequences of educational disruption. However, among the women, the picture is reversed since those resident longer in Australia are 50 percent more likely to have obtained postsecondary educational qualifications than the more recent arrivals. Their general level of attainment is only slightly below the men which may suggest that the women's educational opportunities are greater in Australia than Turkey, although trade and other certificates are still their most common type of qualifications.

Statistics on those who are still studying in Australia provide the best indicator of how the Turkish born are faring within Australian educational institutions. What these data show is that for the fifteen- to twenty-four-year-old age group, the percentage of Turkish men who are still students (38 percent) is slightly higher than for the Australian born or total population (37 percent). For the Turkish-born women, only 30 percent are still students compared with 35 percent for the Australian born and total population; based on these figures, educational equality is still eluding the Turkish-born women. A more detailed examination of the location of the students shows that the Turkish-born men and women are under-represented in the university and college of advanced education (CAE) sectors of education, in contrast with the technical and further education (TAFE) sectors, although it is not clear whether this is a result of choice or, as seems more likely in the context of the high aspirations to be discussed below, it is a result of their lower levels of secondary attainment. Figures on assessment of ability to speak English well or very well suggest that for those who have spent less than six years in Australia in particular, limitation in English may be a critical handicap, since only one third of those aged fifteen to nineteen and one quarter of those twenty to twenty-four feel they speak English to these standards.

For a more detailed consideration of the factors which are associated with and underline these census figures, it is necessary to turn to specific research concerning Turkish education in Australia. Material on the educational experiences of Turkish children in Australia is limited because they are recently arrived and are fewer in number than other groups such as Greeks or Italians. Apart from the paucity of data, an added problem is that studies tend not to make clear whether they are referring to the educational experiences of Australian-born children of Turkish origin or, as is more common among a recently arrived group, Turkish-born children who have spent varying amounts of time in Australian schools.

One of the first studies that examined issues relating to Turkish educational attainment was undertaken in 1974–1975 in Melbourne. It had as its starting point the high level of school absences and early leaving reported for Turkish girls, especially at secondary level. In one area, for example, only 12 of the 62 students in six secondary schools were girls (Wolf, n.d.:1). A survey five years later of the employment and education of Turkish youth aged fifteen to twenty in Melbourne reported similarly low levels of educational attainment among Turkish-born youth, particularly girls (Young, 1983). Interviews with 100 Turkish boys revealed that some had come to Australia when they were too old to continue their schooling, while others had migrated at a relatively late age and had stayed in school for a short time only (Young, 1983:53). The probability of leaving school early was inversely proportional to the number of years of schooling in Australia.

Associated with this limited education, it was found that few of the youths were in the jobs to which they had aspired. The same situation was also found among the small number of girls included in the initial study (Young, Petty, and Faulkner, 1980:182, 235; Young, 1985). In general, the young men aspired to white-collar, lower-professional jobs and skilled trades, rather than to high-level professional jobs such as doctors and lawyers. Among the girls, a similar emphasis on white-collar, clerical jobs was found. The study concluded that longer residence was associated with improved education and jobs. Since it excluded those who were continuing with their studies, it inevitably underestimated the level of educational and, possibly, occupational attainment.

A slightly more encouraging picture emerges from a 1981 survey of Turkish families in Melbourne, although the numbers are very small. In this study only six of the 50 families included had children old enough to complete post-secondary education. Of those, two had actually done so; one had completed university while the other had done a secretarial training course (Mackie, 1983:50). Both were boys; the number of girls, if any, is unknown. Two other studies provide information on teachers' estimates of the educational performance of Turkish primary students (Wolf, n.d.) and secondary students (Browning, 1979). These studies, which suggest that Turkish students perform at relatively low levels, had only small numbers of students in their sample (fourteen and twenty-one, respectively) and this makes it difficult to assess the influence on the results of other factors such as teacher or school characteristics.

Despite the limited levels of Turkish scholastic achievement suggested in these studies, there is considerable evidence that Turkish parents have high aspirations for their children (Browning, 1979; Cox,

1975; Ethnic Affairs Commission of New South Wales, 1985; Mackie, 1983; M.S.J. Keys Young Planners, 1980; Wolf, n.d.). In one study, these were equal to those of Greek parents, renowned in Australian research for high aspirations (Browning, 1979:208). However, there is some indication that lower aspirations may be held for girls (Babacan, 1983:4; Young et al., 1980:235).

The continuing disjuncture in the aspirations and experiences of Turkish parents and their children in Australia directs attention to the factors which inhibit the realization of these aspirations and to those factors which allow the aspirations to be sustained in the face of numerous examples of their non-realization. An understanding of the processes involved is important in considering whether the patterns reported in these studies are likely to continue or will alter with time as the Census suggests may be occurring. The role of the family as a source of cultural capital for Turkish boys and girls is clearly a critical issue in the educational process. This issue will now be explored further, using material collected by the authors as part of a study of Turkish women in Sydney.

Characteristics of the Turkish Families in Sydney

In 1981, the Sydney Turkish community numbered 9,455, which constituted the second largest concentration after Melbourne's Turkish population (11,449). Our research in Sydney commenced in 1980. The information on the cultural background and educational experience of a group of Turkish families presented below draws particularly on data collected in 1981 from extensive interviews with 40 women. These interviews were conducted with the assistance of bilingual interviewers, using a structured schedule designed to elicit detailed information on the involvement of the women in the workforce and the ways in which this involvement was linked to the rearing and education of their children. In particular, we wanted to determine how the women's experiences were related to their own ideas about child-rearing and education in a situation where many of these activities were, of necessity, undertaken by other people, who were often from very different cultural backgrounds.

The women included in this survey were selected on a quota basis through contacts with schools and Turkish welfare agencies. All were born overseas, three quarters in Turkey and the rest in Cyprus. All were married with at least two children, one of preschool age and one of school age. Usually the older child was at primary school, although a number of women also had older children, and one family had a child who had already left school. Since all women had at least one child of school age, this meant that they all had, through their children, some contact with the Australian education system. A further requirement of the quota sampling procedure was that approximately half the women were currently employed and half were unemployed. The women in the sample and their families were found to have had fairly homogeneous work experiences which were typical of those of Turkish migrants in general (Manderson and Inglis, 1984).

All the women and their husbands had some education, which they had completed prior to immigration to Australia. A large proportion of men (36 percent) and the majority of women (60 percent) had no more than primary schooling, although both the men and the women were better educated than the Turkish averages.[1] In addition to basic schooling, 40 percent of the women had received some vocational training. This mostly involved trade skills such as sewing or dressmaking, but 12 percent had completed university or had received similar extensive training. The comparable figure for men was somewhat lower, with one third having vocational qualifications of some type and 8 percent having tertiary level education. Typically, though, spouses had comparable levels of education.

The majority of spouses (88 percent) spoke Turkish to each other. In half the families, conversations with children by parents were likely also to be solely in Turkish, while in the rest either English and Turkish or English only were used. Children were more likely to be bilingual but to use English to speak to each other and, according to one respondent, to their parents "especially when they are angry." Most parents used some English outside the home, but only 40 percent of the women and 55 percent of the men claimed to be able to read simple English, with a slightly lower proportion feeling that they were capable of writing a simple letter. The children, then, came from homes where exposure to English, especially in its written form, was limited (see also Ethnic Affairs Commission, 1985:32–44).

While the Turkish families studied have many similarities once they have settled in Australia, their backgrounds prior to migration do differ. The differences are not only in terms of their education and occupation but also in their birthplace, for in addition to some being born in Cyprus and others in Turkey, a number had been born and were brought up in rural areas (40 percent of the women and 27 percent of the men). However, many of these people had spent some time in major urban centers such as Istanbul and Ankara prior to their emigration. Despite variations in background, a striking feature in the interviews with the women was the homogeneity of their views concerning the important role of women in childcare and rearing and their common extensive involvement in domestic work (Manderson and Inglis, 1985). Their views on motherhood and women's role in reproduction coexist with their participation in the production process, highlighting the lack of integration between the domestic and productive spheres of the women's lives (Manderson and Inglis, 1985). Such lack of integration renders problematic the way they may view the education of their daughters. Taken in conjunction with the evidence of differences in the educational experiences of Turkish boys and girls, the issue of gender requires attention when considering the cultural capital of Turkish families. Two major areas of educational concern relevant to examining the women's role in their children's education are their aspirations for their children and their perceptions of the schools and educational processes.

Educational and Occupational Aspirations

The most striking features of the women's views about education were the consistently high levels of educational and occupational aspirations that they held for their children—both sons and daughters (cf. Brookes, 1985; Hartley, 1987). When asked about appropriate educational levels for boys, just over half the respondents said that they should obtain university or other qualifications, while two-fifths said that it was up to the boy or that "he should go as far as possible." Specific high educational qualifications were typically linked by the women to their preferred career paths for their sons, because a higher education would allow them "to secure their well-being" financially, "to manage life without difficulty," or "because a high education is necessary in today's society." When queried about appropriate educational levels for girls, the women's responses were comparable although a marginally lower proportion mentioned tertiary-level education. Three-quarters of the women thought that the same educational levels were appropriate for boys and girls; one respondent, who stressed that "I don't differentiate between boys and girls," had in fact remigrated to Australia to ensure that her daughter would have an opportunity for a university education that was equal to her son's.

Women frequently related education to employment prospects, stressing higher education so that their daughters "don't have to work in a factory doing dirty jobs." Some stressed the greater importance of education for their daughters: "Girls need a higher education than boys because they don't have such a large choice in work." For other women, the reasoning related to personal experience. One respondent, with a primary education only, had come from a poor family and had married a wealthy man some 20 years her senior, as his third wife, and had migrated to Australia with him while her parents took up residence rent free in his house in Turkey. She stressed the importance of education for her daughters because "a girl [should] get as much education as she can, because if she marries and if her husband deserts her, then she can look after herself." In a similar vein, another respondent suggested that "a girl should be well-educated so she will not have any need of others." But other women tended to view less education as being necessary for girls, as indicated by the one-fifth of the women who thought that secondary-level experiences was sufficient for girls while only 2 percent thought that this was so for boys. Women who placed less importance on their daughters' education typically invoked reasons that related to their expectations of their daughters' future: "They'll end up being married anyway"; "If a girl doesn't continue, it is not so important, she can be a sewing teacher or a craft teacher whereas a boy can't."

The limited proportion of women seeing different levels of education as appropriate for boys and girls is interesting given that the women were frequently from rural and working-class backgrounds in Turkey, where more traditional views might be assumed to be more common. It has been asserted that education is not considered critical for girls, at least in a traditional setting, and Turkish educators in the past have complained of the refusal of parents to send their daughters to school (Magnarella, 1974:158). Babacan (1983) maintains that this attitude continues in Australia. However, other more recent evidence from Turkey[2] illustrates the high educational aspirations of parents for their children and the limited distinction made between boys and girls, as articulated by the women in this study.

Women we interviewed shared high aspirations for their children despite their varied educational and occupational background. The only indication of some difference was that women who had been born in rural areas and had then moved to the cities were somewhat more likely to specify a particular level of education for boys, with other women leaving it "up to the child."

The women's high educational aspirations in general were matched by comparable occupational aspirations for their children. This inevitably involved a preference for social mobility into white-collar and high status occupations. Underlying this mobility was a preference for what was widely described by the women as "clean work," since white-collar occupations have a clear status connotation independent of a perception of them as also being financially more rewarding. In contrast to the educational aspirations, there were differences in women's preferred occupational aspirations for their children on the basis of sex. Of the women who had sons, over half hoped their sons would be professionals, such as doctors or lawyers; a further one-fifth said that it was "up to him." The remainder were virtually evenly divided between those who nominated managerial or white-collar jobs and those who nominated trades.

In contrast, only one-fifth of the women who had daughters mentioned professional occupations. Two-fifths nominated semi-professional jobs. Teaching was considered an especially suitable vocation for a woman, as the following comments indicate: it is "a respectable job for a woman"; as a teacher, a woman would be "useful to herself and to others also, and would have long holidays and money"; and again "she can have long holidays to spend with [her] children." The next most common response, as with sons, was the nonspecific "it's up to her"; the remaining women were more or less evenly divided between white-collar and skilled jobs.[3] None referred to marriage as the desired vocation for their daughters, although marriage featured prominently in their general aspirations for their children.

Just over half the women with both sons and daughters distinguished between them in their indicated job preferences. Women's aspirations for boys were not related to their own level of education, prior residence, or occupation but were related to their occupational history following migration. Thus, among women with semiskilled occupational backgrounds in Australia, two-thirds indicated specific preferences for professional jobs and only one-ninth recommended "leaving it up to him." In contrast, the small number of women in white-collar and professional jobs in Australia were more evenly divided between specifying professional employment for their sons and leaving the decision with the child, suggesting a "freer" approach which may reflect their own sense of security in Australian society. Women's expectations for their daughters were not related to their occupations in Australia, although there was a similar trend for women in white-collar jobs to feel that career choice was up to their daughters themselves. The women's educational level, however, was related to their job aspirations for their daughters. Women with tertiary education were especially likely to nominate a specific professional or semiprofessional job. Similarly, women with secondary-level education nominated semiprofessional jobs for their daughters although their second preference was for the freer "it's up to her" approach, followed then by white-collar occupations. As with the boys, there is tentative evidence that women of higher class or status may be less prescriptive with regard to their daughters' future occupation.

A comparison of the more general hopes which women held for their children showed that the most common desire for both sons and daughters was to be established in a career and to be in a position of high social status. After that, however, the importance of particular aims varied. For daughters, having a good husband and a happy family life was considered the most important, followed by being a good wife and also being liked and well respected (cf. Kagitcibasi, 1981–82:266). Community respect was the second most commonly mentioned aspiration for sons but it was considerably less important. Instead, for sons, being wealthy, having a good education and being a good parent all ranked ahead of concern with their marital situation. This order of preference highlights the importance which is implicitly attached to women's marital status and their dependence on a husband for personal happiness. This was captured by one respondent whose aspiration for her daughters was "to be a bride in a good way," and by the number of women who placed high value on their daughters being "good wives, good mothers and good housewives." In this context, it is perhaps not surprising that having a good education or being wealthy are seen by the women as less important hopes for their daughters, even despite the initial emphasis on job success for their daughters.

The concern of women for their daughters' education and future employment needs to be considered against their concern with the daughters' future marriages. One factor in the women's somewhat paradoxical emphasis on the importance of marriage and career may lie in the way that a better-educated daughter is seen as well placed to make a good marriage because of the value attached to her education by potential spouses and their families. As one respondent put it, a daughter with a good education could "pick and choose" among men. Having a good job, however, can also be seen as important for a woman should her marriage not be a success. This point was made explicit by two informants whose own marriages were on the verge of collapse and who were faced with the prospect of being the sole supporters of themselves and their children. However, a factor stressed by other women was the independence that education and a successful career gave women. These women may have been mindful that within the Turkish community in Australia, the incidence of marital breakdown is considered to be increasing, with women typically being the ones left with children. The emphasis on semiprofessional employment such as teaching and nursing can be seen not merely as following the usual patterns of female employment but also as reflecting the way these jobs fit well with women's roles as mother and nurturer. In this context, it is pertinent that the majority of the women interviewed had themselves experienced real problems in combining workforce participation and childrearing, when no such "fit" operated (Inglis and Manderson, 1984).

While aspirations may indicate a certain ideal situation, it is also important to know how attainable this situation seems to be. Women, when asked whether they expected their children to achieve their educational and occupational aspirations, gave little indication that they saw specific barriers or impediments. One mother felt that it was unlikely that her daughter would proceed as desired to a university, because "girls usually don't go to school that far." Five percent of women with sons felt that they would not reach their aspirations. In the case of educational aspirations, significant proportions of women (nearly half with sons and one third with daughters) indicated that it was "too soon" to tell. This was a reasonable response, given the generally young age of their children, but it is significant, too, that no women, including those employed at the time of the study in a semiprofessional capacity, perceived cultural or structural impediments to their children's scholastic progress.

When asked about the occupational aspirations, one-third of the mothers of sons and somewhat less than half of those with daughters considered that they would meet these expectations; the remainder emphasized that it was "too soon" or else that they "hoped so." Only one mother felt that her expectations of her daughter with respect to occupation were unrealistic, but was unable to articulate the basis of this feeling.

Perceptions of Schools and Education

Because of the potential importance of schooling as constituting a barrier to educational and occupational success, it is relevant here to consider the women's views on the schools their children attend. As a general indicator of satisfaction, only some 15 percent of mothers indicated that they had considered changing their child's school. However, this figure needs to be treated cautiously since all the children were attending government schools where change to another government school serving a different geographical area can often be difficult. The alternative of attending a fee-paying private school would also involve considerable financial strains for the majority of these Turkish families.

Women's more specific attitudes to the schools were obtained by asking them what they liked and disliked about their children's schools. Most frequently (29 percent) women noted "proximity" as a reason for liking the school. Its importance is perhaps understandable, given the proportion of working women often involved in complex child-care arrangements. The teacher and school administrators were the next most frequently given reason (22 percent) for liking the school. While 10 percent of the women said that they liked everything about the school, 16 percent said that they did not know and one woman said that there was "nothing" that she liked.

A somewhat more positive picture of the schools emerged when the women were asked what they did not like about the schools. Nearly half were unable to pinpoint any cause of dissatisfaction. Among the remainder, the only item mentioned with any frequency was "discipline," referred to by nearly one in five of the women. Other studies (e.g., Brookes, 1985:30ff; Hartley, 1987; M.S.J. Keys Young Planners, 1980:71; Tsolidis, 1986:68; Turney et al., 1978) have highlighted the way parents frequently focus on discipline, or more specifically the lack of it, as a cause of dissatisfaction with the school. Partly this is explained by the fact that "discipline" is a more easily accessible and visible part of the school to parents than are other areas such as curriculum or teaching methods. For the Turkish women its significance is more complex.

Apart from the language of instruction, discipline and the use of corporal punishment are by far the most obvious distinguishing features between Turkish and Australian schools, followed by the emphasis on rote learning in the schools that the women had attended in Turkey. Half the women mentioned discipline as a major difference between the two educational systems, compared with one-fifth who referred to curriculum differences and one-eighth who mentioned the language of instruction. By comparison with the Turkish schools, Australian schools are far milder in the forms of punishment used and are also less rigid in their requirements. The Turkish women's concern with the Australian schools' approach to discipline cannot be seen as mere conservatism. The significance of discipline became apparent when we asked the women what they thought it was important for a child to learn at school. Apart from "school subjects" which one third mentioned, "etiquette" and "respect" were the next most important responses and these were mentioned by one-quarter of the women; a few also referred explicitly to "discipline." Etiquette and respect are not the same as "discipline," but these concepts were very closely linked for the women. Women pointed to children's misbehavior in the home, including lack of respect for their parents (as evidenced by swearing in English) and for other adults, as indicators of the lack of discipline within the school system. This they contrasted with their own upbringing, where respectful behavior was emphasized within the home and reinforced within the school (Eminov, 1983:137, 141). The women also considered that "discipline" was a prerequisite to learning and, thus, that scholastic difficulty was associated with lack of institutional discipline.

Additional information on the women's views of education was obtained by asking them what activities were considered appropriate for children of different ages. Among children of preschool age, "play" was typically considered the most appropriate activity. This tended to continue to be so for children of primary-school age when they were not at school or doing homework. Other major activities seen as appropriate for this older age group were helping with the housework (particularly for daughters) and learning specific skills such as ballet, cooking, sports, and "about their own culture." Among the younger children few of the mothers felt that differences were appropriate between the activities of boys and girls. More distinguished between older sons and daughters, and referred both to girls doing housework and to undertaking different activities, such as ballet, while their brothers played soccer.

We have argued elsewhere (Inglis and Manderson, 1984) that the Turkish mothers' emphasis on "play" for younger children generally does not focus on the educative possibilities of play. The exception is among those Turkish families where the parents are more educated. The views of these parents are closer to those of educators and also to many Anglo-Australian mothers, particularly those from middle-class backgrounds.

Among the families in our sample, education was not regarded as being confined only to formal schooling. Just over half the families had children attending extra classes; for the majority these were Turkish language classes. Three families also sent the children to Islamic religious classes. Children from eight families attended classes in activities such as soccer (for boys) and dancing (for girls). The enrollment of children in extra-curricular activities such as religious and Turkish language classes and the women's comments on the importance of respect and concomitant concern with "discipline" do not necessarily represent departures from what their concerns might have been in Turkey. Magnarella (1974:159), for example, notes that while parents desired for their children maximum access to a "modern" education as an avenue to social mobility, they also stressed the continued importance of Turkish (and Islamic) traditions, values, customs and practices.[4] Apart from the indication that better-educated parents were more likely to see play as educative, the women generally agreed in their views on schooling and education. Occupations, educational level, and prior rural or urban residence in Turkey were not a basis for distinguishing among them.

The Influence of Class, Ethnicity and Gender on Turkish Women's Beliefs about Education

In seeking to understand the processes which have led to the development of the Turkish women's beliefs about their children's schooling, this paper has presented in some detail the individual aspects of the larger pattern of beliefs. As already indicated, neither class situation nor premigration background alone determines the women's beliefs. The interaction of various areas including class, ethnicity and gender is critical and, as we shall see, the mode of interaction varies between one area of belief and another.

The most obvious starting point for seeking to determine the origins of the women's educational views is the apparent incongruity, evident in other studies as well as here, between their aspirations for their children and the likelihood of realization. The women's generally high expectations for sons and daughters and the lack of any perceived major barriers to success are interesting, given the apparent "unreality" of such experiences in the Australian situation where the majority of Turks are employed in unskilled laboring jobs and few have progressed through to tertiary study. The origins of the aspirations and their resistance to modification are linked to the women's class and Turkish ethnic background. The importance of their ethnic background lies in the way the women base their frame of reference for their children's future on Turkish experience and the possibility of return to Turkey. This was not always expressed consciously since many of the families were envisaging relatively long-term settlement in Australia. But, at a more general level, their Turkish experience sustained their beliefs about their children's schooling since there are generally very high expectations for education in Turkey as this is virtually the only way to social mobility (Australia Department of Education and Youth Affairs, 1983:16; Cosar, 1978; Gencer, 1980:4; Yaka, 1977:25).

The importance of the women's class background in contributing to their aspirations highlights the complexities involved in determining the cultural effects of class position. Among educators and researchers, high educational aspirations are usually associated with middle-class families and culture, yet the Turks in Australia are predominantly working class. Such a position has not, however, always characterized the families in the Sydney study. Many of the women are married to men who had been self-employed in Turkey and thus may be considered more appropriately as members of the *petite bourgeoisie* rather than working class. It should additionally be noted that improved social and economic life chances have generally played an important part in the women's decision to come to Australia. The importance of seeking better educational opportunities for their children was for many of the women an explicit reason for coming to Australia and highlights the importance they attach to education.

The families' class membership in Turkey and their hopes for social mobility which underlay their migration to Australia further reinforce their aspirations for their children. Both those from self-employed and from peasant or working-class backgrounds expressed their desire to become independent entrepreneurs in Turkey if not in Australia. For their children, they desire a move into middle-class white-collar positions. In Turkey, this is possible only through education. Australian conditions reinforce and confirm their understanding of the importance of education, since schooling provides access to English, which parents recognize is an important prerequisite to mobility in a country where English is the official and dominant language.

The complexity of the women's educational views is further highlighted by the significance of gender in women's aspirations for their daughters. The women had initially high educational aspirations for their daughters. While fears of divorce were related to these aspirations, women did not in equal fashion stress high occupational and lifetime aspirations. The reason lies in the continuity of their attitudes about women's domestic and reproductive roles which they saw as being major areas of women's responsibility—even while they themselves continued to be employed either from choice or, as in most cases, from financial necessity (see also Engelbrektsson, 1982:212, 238). The importance of gender and the ethnic determinants of these views is clear regardless of the class of women in either Australia or Turkey (Manderson and Inglis, 1985:205).

Women's general perceptions of the role of schools and education are also characterized by extensive homogeneity. This homogeneity reflects the influence of Turkish cultural patterns relating to both general and gender-specific areas of social life rather than to class-based determinants of culture. Only in the cases of attitudes to "play" is there an indication of the significance of cultural differences related to educational status and indirectly to class in Turkey and

Cyprus. The homogeneity in both educational aspirations and in beliefs about schooling related to the women's common Turkish heritage. These views persist in Australia, in part because the women operate within a community of ideas and interests which only at certain points intersect with that of the larger Australian group (Elley, 1984:53). Given the close-knit networks with minimal social choice in which many Turkish migrants live, it may be that there is even greater consensus in ideology within the Australian Turkish community than in Turkey. Certainly, the congruence between the views of the women we studied and those reported in studies of the Melbourne community points to considerable consensus (e.g., Brookes, 1985; Elley, 1985; Hartley, 1987). The continuity of ideas from Turkey to Australia, despite a change in the class situation of the families as they migrate, highlights the complexity which exists in determining class and the cultural background associated with it. This is particularly salient in considering educational ideologies since migration may involve only a temporary alteration in class position.

The relevance of class designation is critical to a discussion of the extent and operation of cultural and structural reproduction as it applies to Australia. Such a discussion implies an element of stability or immobility in class position over generations both in Australia and overseas which may not apply to the situation of a recently arrived immigrant group such as the Turks. Many Turks in Australia may regain their premigration occupational status after occupying a working-class position in society. Others, despite their continued membership in the Australian working class, may retain their ambitions for social mobility by operating an independent business either in Australia or upon their eventual return to Turkey.

Premigration class position can also influence educational beliefs and ideology. In Australia, discussions of the cultural and social reproduction of immigrants have tended to focus only on the Australian class situation of groups. Current research on cultural transmission highlights the idea that cultural attributes of class emerge as a result of the ongoing processes involved in social relations. As this examination of the cultural beliefs of Turkish women indicates, these insights need to be applied also to immigrant groups.

An important complicating factor in the case of immigrant groups arises from the different historical situation in which their class position in their homeland was articulated and the way that constitutes a very distinctive set of cultural patterns in the Australian context. These patterns are further reinforced through the tight-knit nature of the local community networks and require a separate description which acknowledges that their cultural origins are embedded within patterns of ethnically based social relations. Just as with the cultural construction of class beliefs, so the construction of ethnic beliefs is a process which may vary over time. While such beliefs may ultimately be subordinated to class-based cultural beliefs, this is clearly not yet the case for Turkish groups in Australia.

Cultural Capital and the Potential for Turkish Educational Attainment

In Australia, the starting point of the discussion of the role of education in the social reproduction of migrants is the assumed lack of mobility of working-class migrant children. This assumption is derived from the observation that large numbers of children from specific ethnic backgrounds have not been achieving educationally and that this lack of success has long-term implications for occupational and social positions. As a result the children are seen as locked into their parents' working-class situation. There is, however, increasing evidence that among Australian-born children of even "disadvantaged" migrant groups, the relative disadvantage in terms of postsecondary qualifications is not evident (Kocbek, 1981). In the context of the above discussion of the overly simple attribution of a class culture to migrants based on their Australian situation this lack of disadvantage may not be surprising since the children's parents may transmit a cultural background which, whether through its class or ethnic components, provides the children with considerable cultural capital. This, in turn, allows them to achieve educationally and so move out of the working-class position which their family occupies in Australia.

The recency of Turkish migration precludes amassing detailed information on the class mobility of children of Turkish parents who have had most of their schooling in Australia, in contrast with those who arrived at a later stage in their schooling. Most of the families of the women included in our survey had children not yet old enough to attend secondary school and hence it is not possible to determine conclusively how the women's educational beliefs affect the educational attainment of their children. Only four of the families included in this study had children who were fifteen or older and thus legally able to leave school. In three of the cases, the children, all boys, had experienced virtually all their schooling in Australia—a fifteen- and a sixteen-year-old had both arrived when they were eight while the other fifteen-year-old had been in Australia since he was three. All were still attending school, where they were doing well, and their mothers expected them to continue their education to a higher level.

In the other family, a Turkish Cypriot family which had been in Australia for 12 years, there were two adult daughters and one son in addition to a primary- and a preschool-aged child. The eldest daughter was married; the second was still studying and was encouraged by her mother to go "as far as she can." At the time of the study, the son was working with his father as a mechanic; he had left school because he was "not interested" in it. Clearly little can be generalized about the effects of family cultural backgrounds from the experiences of this small number of children. However, it is possible to examine the extent to which the beliefs may constitute cultural capital for the children and so assist them to achieve their parents' high educational aspirations. Furthermore, given the homogeneity evident in the Turkish migrants' educational ideology, they can be applied more generally to Turkish youth in Australia.

An important prior issue is the similarity of the women's and men's backgrounds and relevant attitudes. Husbands and wives typically were matched in their educational and occupational qualifications and status. However, men may well have rather different attitudes than the women, especially as they relate to their children. In particular, fathers may have different views about the appropriate levels and types of jobs desirable for their daughters and, indeed, how much education is appropriate for girls. While we did not interview the husbands nor ask the women whether their spouses shared their ideas, evidence collected by Mackie (1983:62) indicated that men did have somewhat different aspirations for their daughters. But, contrary to expectations, her data indicate that men were less likely than women to countenance different and lower expectations for girls compared with boys. On the basis of these findings, the women's educational aspirations for their daughters represent a minimum rather than a maximum level of family aspirations. However, other researchers report instances where fathers discourage or prevent their daughters from continuing with their education (Brookes, 1985:76).

The high educational aspirations of the Turkish families and their associated encouragement to continue with schooling are obvious examples of cultural capital available to the children. However, in the light of reports from school officials that Turkish girls may be withdrawn from school on reaching puberty it seems that, for daughters at least, the educational aspirations may be modified in practice as a result of other considerations relating to their gender (see also Babacan, 1983). In our study, while there was an indication that educational aspirations were high for girls, this was not universally so. Furthermore, the mothers' occupational and life aspirations for their daughters differed from those they held for their sons.

One explanation for these different aspirations and the earlier school-leaving age for Turkish girls relates to the mothers' beliefs about domestic roles. Girls may be kept from school in cases of illness or other crises when the mother's job or her own illness prevents her from fulfilling her domestic duties. Abadan-Unat (1977:42–43) has documented the extent to which older daughters among Turks in Europe are penalized educationally as a consequence of their mother's workforce participation; examples of such absences were also reported to us, although not by members of our sample. Where such absences do occur, the consequent gaps in the daughters' schooling potentially compound other difficulties they may experience educationally and lead to their opting out of the school system. The importance of this disadvantage for Turkish girls should not be overstated in the future, however, since, of the women whom we interviewed, an increasing number had moved out of the labor force to remain at home fulltime; moreover, none indicated that they had ever kept their daughters away from school for domestic duties (see also Wolf, n.d.:111). The departure of women from the labor force was for some a result of work-related illness, but in many cases it reflected the opportunity to cease work which was provided by the family's increasingly established financial security in Australia. This appears to be the general trend among Turks as their period of residence in Australia increases. With the withdrawal of women from the workforce, the pressure on daughters to assist at home is likely to be reduced.

While pressure for the Turkish girls to assist with domestic duties might decline, another factor may continue to interfere with the realization of the aspirations which the women hold for their daughters. This factor is parental concern about the behavior of daughters as they get older and reach puberty. Although coeducational schools are a basic principle of Turkish education, some segregation does exist (Australia Department of Education and Youth Affairs, 1983:15). Many Turkish parents in Australia are concerned by the extent to which secondary-school children may be required to attend coeducational high schools, since their perceptions about looser discipline and the more lax moral standards of Australian children cause them grave concern about their daughters mixing with boys once puberty is reached (Wolf, n.d.:7). The effects on the family honor of a girl's potential misbehavior with boys are sufficiently serious for male kin to pressure families to remove their girls from school. In doing so, families are willing to forego the honor which could be derived from the educational successes of their daughters to ensure that the more important family honor is not impaired (Brookes, 1985).

The beliefs underlying this practice show considerable resistance to change in Australia. Again, the importance of the tight-knit Turkish community for the individual family facilitates the reassertion of such values, and gossip is widely reported as an important factor in this process (Brookes, 1985; Hartley, 1987). Even so, the census figures cited earlier for the Turkish-born women indicated a marked decline in their tendency to very early school-leaving; studies in Melbourne, as well as our own, concluded that the practice was no longer widespread. Nevertheless, fear of possible gossip was an important consideration for the Turkish girls and their families.

A potential area in which the family's cultural background can assist the children, apart from encouraging them to continue with their schooling, is in providing them with cultural resources valued by the school. In this area of cultural capital, the Turkish families are less well placed to assist their children since the families often lack familiarity and fluency in English, the language of instruction in schools. In addition, the mothers' perception about the appropriate activities of preschool children do not equip the children with information that prepares them for the tasks which they face when they first enter school. These tasks, including counting, categorizing and recognizing shapes, may also be taught at organized preschool programs but, since few Turkish families have access to such programs (Inglis and

Manderson, 1984), this alternative source of preparation is closed to these children.[5]

The significance of this preparation for later schooling, as compared with the impact of limited English, has not been studied, but it is evident that the parents' ideas about what is educationally appropriate for preschool children and their ideas on play and patterns of language usage do not provide any extensive capital for their children within the Australian school system. Where the schools, in the absence of this capital, classify children as lacking sufficient ability to be encouraged beyond certain relatively low levels of scholastic achievement, the children and the parents may receive more or less overt messages which encourage the children to conclude their schooling before reaching the levels of educational attainment which their families hope they will achieve (Ethnic Affairs Commission, 1985:157).

Teachers, of course, frequently operate with stereotypes of children's abilities and of the "problems" characterizing children of specific ethnic or social backgrounds; thus, the classification of Turkish schoolchildren as lacking in academic potential is not unique. However, one aspect of this classification is the failure of teachers to perceive the high educational aspirations of children and their parents and so they categorize them as lacking in motivation (Tsolidis, 1986:80; Turney et al., 1978:66; Factor, pers. comm.).

The effectiveness of this "cooling out" process in which children are discouraged from continuing school, however, depends on whether the parents and children receive the message in the first place and then whether they accept and act on it. A considerable amount of evidence suggests that parents and children of migrant background may not actually receive the message, if only because of the problems of communication. Misunderstandings which arise out of the school's communications being transmitted in English (even if an interpreter, who is often the child involved in the communication, is used) may be further compounded by the parents' lack of understanding of the Australian school system. Thus, where parents are used to a system such as Turkey's in which promotion from one class to another is dependent on achieving a certain level in schooling, they may misunderstand the Australian system, where promotion is automatic except in extreme cases of underattainment. In such circumstances, the parents perceive the child's promotion as indicating that he or she is coping satisfactorily with his or her schooling.

Even if the school's message is accurately received, the parents may be unwilling to accept such a message since this may conflict with their ambitions for their children and themselves. The lack of success of other Turkish children may not be sufficient to dampen their hopes since, to the extent that other children are viewed as individuals, their experiences may not be seen as similar or likely for one's own child. In these circumstances, attributes which at first glance do not appear to constitute "cultural capital" can become capital by operating in reverse, enabling parents to ignore or withstand attempts by the school to discourage their child from continuing with academic education.

Martin and Meade (1979:5) have referred to this phenomenon as involving a rejection of the "institutional ideology." In the case of migrant groups such as the Turks, the rejection contrasts with that reported in much of the writing on the resistance of working-class groups to the school which has emphasized the way such resistance detracts from the educational achievement of the children (Giroux, 1983). A further difference is that the migrant "rejection" of the institutional ideology occurs more through ignorance of the school and its culture than through direct and conscious resistance and confrontation. Certainly, while parents may not understand, or even accept, the methods which Australian schools use to discipline or instruct, they do accept the instrumental outcome which they see the school providing for their children if only the children can progress through the school system successfully.

The above review indicates the complex cultural background which Australian Turkish families transmit to their children. The extent of cultural capital is not clear since the weighting of parental expectations, especially where unaligned with detailed knowledge of the educational system, is problematic. The study of Turkish youth by Young (Young et al., 1980; Young, 1980, 1983) is of interest for its suggestion that the young Turkish people may have a lower set of aspirations than their parents. Such lower aspirations indicate their closer contacts with non-Turkish networks and institutions such as schools and may reflect, too, a more realistic appraisal of their employment opportunities and prospects. Indeed, Brookes (1985:43) and Hartley (1987) report that students' aspirations decline and become more disparate from those of their parents as they progress through secondary school and presumably become more aware of their abilities and the levels of attainment required for particular jobs.

Ultimately, however, the working out of the various dimensions of cultural background is affected by the children's experiences in school and the effects of larger socioeconomic and labor market pressures. The complexity and importance of the school's role are increasingly being realized as a result of detailed ethnographic studies of students and teachers within the school setting (e.g., Walker, 1987). In the absence of a detailed Australian study of a school that includes a focus on Turkish students, the more detailed analysis of processes which may affect the educational attainment of Turkish students is problematic. We have already noted that teachers' stereotypes may affect their treatment of specific groups of students. To the extent that Turkish students are perceived as members of a particularly disadvantaged migrant group, the teacher may well put them into a category typified by disadvantaged characteristics (Hartley, 1987). Whereas teachers once held undifferentiated views about children from various ethnic backgrounds, it is now common to find that certain groups are positively differentiated. Thus, Chinese students are perceived as good at mathematics, while Greek students and their parents are categorized as ambitious and having high aspirations, but these more positive connotations are unlikely to develop for Turkish students and enter the realm of public knowledge until those with more extensive Australian schooling realize their families' higher educational aspirations. Where longer exposure to Australian schooling gives students a better chance to acquire the culture of educational success, then it is likely that the possibility of success for Turkish children will expand even if the improvement is more marked for boys than girls.

By comparison with the school experience of the earlier arrivals, recent changes in the organization and curriculum of schools potentially provide more support for Turkish students, especially for those who attend schools with a sizeable Turkish student population. Such schools are more likely to have Turkish-speaking aides who can inform parents about the operation of the school and so reduce potential conflict between parents and the school. These schools are also more likely to have bilingual Turkish language programs. These programs are designed to be transitional in English, but they nevertheless ease parents' concerns about their child's loss of the mother tongue. At the same time, they facilitate the child's acquisition of English without hindering his or her cognitive development, as can occur with a totally monolingual approach to English language teaching.

Larger social trends may also be significant in determining the Turkish children's educational attainment. The economic recession which Australia is currently facing has been characterized by an extremely high level of youth unemployment. A response common to the government and many parents has been to encourage students to stay longer at school to become better qualified and more competitive in the labor market. Those Turkish families who have become more securely established economically are less likely to exert pressure on children to take a job to help the family survive. But where the family has become a casualty of the economic recession, the pressures for children to seek jobs are heavy. If there is an extension of years of education in the Turkish community as a consequence of the recession and earlier educational developments (Young, 1983), this longer period of schooling need not necessarily indicate that the Turks are overcoming the extensive disadvantages faced by their older siblings. To overcome such disadvantages, Turkish children will need to attain higher levels of education as compared with both older Turkish children and with the children from other ethnic backgrounds.

This chapter has argued that the cultural background of Turkish families that is relevant to their children's education involves a highly complex set of processes which have their origins in both class and ethnic patterns of social relations occurring in Australia and Turkey. These cultural beliefs and attitudes have the potential to sustain and, to a more limited extent, to assist Turkish children in their endeavor to attain educationally. Paradoxically, even though this is not an immediate prospect, the assimilation of the parents into Australian society would limit the general efficacy of these beliefs. The effects of such assimilation would be less on girls than boys, because of Turkish families' beliefs and practices related to gender and the impact of such beliefs on education and schooling.

Some indication of whether a process of change is occurring within the Turkish community should be evident from additional 1986 census material, which should include data on how the Australian-born Turkish children are achieving educationally. A longitudinal study of a group of children from primary through to the postsecondary level would also be valuable. Another possibility would be to follow up the women and families involved in earlier studies to determine what the subsequent experiences of their children, now teenagers, have been.

Notes

Acknowledgment: An earlier version of this chapter was published under the title "Turkish Families, their Children and Education in Australia" in *Turkish Community in Australia*, conference papers, ed. Rahmi Akcelik and Joy Elley, Australian-Turkish Friendship Society Publications No. 3, Melbourne, Australia, 1988.

1. According to the 1970 census, nearly 64 percent of women and 29 percent of men were illiterate and by 1975, 46 percent of women and 13 percent of men still had no formal education (Kagitcibasi, 1981–1982:62).
2. Magnarella (1974:156) reports that in the small town he studied, some 93 percent of townsmen desired a university education for their sons, and a smaller proportion, but still the majority (56 percent) wanted the same for their daughters. Cosar (1978:126) suggests that in the village education for girls is not taken as seriously as that for boys but in towns and cities, and especially among immigrants, female education is highly valued. A related lack of preference for sons is also reported by Kagitcibasi (1986:491) as being more common among urbanized women working in the formal labor force.
3. Again, these types of parental job aspirations closely follow those reported from Turkey. Magnarella (1974:65) reports that over 76 percent of townsmen nominated a professional occupation for their sons, and nearly 47 percent specified the occupations of doctor, lawyer and pharmacist for their daughters, the most popular choice after that of housewife. Kandiyoti (1977:65) notes that teaching, employment in the civil service and secretarial work have high prestige for women, and these were all areas of employment mentioned frequently by the women in this study.
4. Eminov also notes the importance that Turkish parents place on language maintenance for their children in Bulgaria, where other Turkish and Islamic traditions have eroded and where language is "one of the most important remaining sources of their identity" (1983:45).
5. In Melbourne, the wider availability of Turkish child care centers than in Sydney means that more Turkish children do have access to this form of cultural capital.

References

Abadan-Unat, N. 1977. "Implications of Migration on Emancipation and Pseudo-Emancipation of Turkish Women." *Migration Review* 11(1):31–57.

Australia Department of Education and Youth Affairs. 1983. *Cultural Background Papers: Turkey.* Canberra: Australian Government Publishing Service.

Babacan, H. 1983. "Turkish Families." *Ms. Muffet* 18 March, p. 4.

Bourdieu, P., and J.C. Passeron. 1977. *Reproduction in Education, Society and Culture.* London: Sage.

Bowles, S., and H. Gintis. 1976. *Schooling in Capitalist America.* London: Routledge and Kegan Paul.

Brookes, A. 1985. *Educational Disadvantages of Turkish Girls in Melbourne's Northwestern Suburbs.* Melbourne: Department of Community Services.

Brotherhood of St. Laurence. 1971. *Two Worlds: School and the Migrant Family.* Melbourne: Stockland Press.

Browning, K. 1979. "Parental Attitudes to and Aspirations for their Children's Education." In *Mosaic or Melting Pot: Cultural Evolution in Australia,* ed. P.R. de Lacey and M. Poole. Sydney: Harcourt Brace Jovanovich.

Coleman, J.S. 1966. *Report on Equality of Educational Opportunity.* Washington, D.C.: Government Printing Office.

Connell, R.W., et al. 1982. *Making the Difference: Schools, Families and Social Division.* Sydney: Allen and Unwin.

Corrigan, P. 1979. *Schooling the Smash Street Kids.* London: Macmillan.

Cosar, F.M. 1978. "Women in Turkish Society." In *Women in the Muslim World,* ed. L. Beck and N. Keddie, pp. 124–40. Cambridge, Mass.: Harvard University Press.

Cox, D. 1975. "Turks in Australia." In *Welfare of Immigrants. Commission of Inquiry. Vol. 1. The Role of Ethnic Groups in Migrant Welfare,* ed. D. Cox, pp. 70–77. Canberra: Australian Government Publishing Service.

Elley, J. 1984. "The Maintenance of Turkish Identity in the Migration Situation." In *Change and Persistence of Turkish Culture,* Seminar papers, ed. R. Akpcelik. Melbourne: Australia-Turkish Friendship Society Publications, No. 1.

Eminov, A. 1983. "The Education of Turkish Speakers in Bulgaria." *Ethnic Groups* 53:129–50.

Engelbrektsson, U.B. 1982. *The Force of Tradition: Turkish Migrants at Home and Abroad.* Goteborg: Acta Universitatis Gothoburgensis.

Ethnic Affairs Commission of New South Wales. 1985. *Onsekiz Yil Sonra . . . Eighteen Years After. The Turkish Settlement Experience in New South*

Wales. Interim Report. Sydney: Ethnic Affairs Commission of New South Wales.

Gencer, G. 1980. "Turkish Background Paper." In *Communication and Cultural Diversity*, pp. 37–41. Sydney: Sydney Teachers' College.

Giroux, A. 1983. "Theories of Reproduction and Resistance in the New Sociology of Education: A Critical Analysis." *Harvard Educational Review* 53(3):257–93.

Hartley, R. 1987. *"They Could Go a Lot Further . . .": Factors Influencing Decisions Which Ethnic Families Make About Children's Schooling and Post-School Futures.* Report for Ministerial Advisory Committee on Multicultural and Minority Education, Ministry of Education, Victoria.

Inglis, C., and L. Manderson. 1984. "Patterns of Child Care Amongst Women in the Sydney Turkish Community." *Australian Journal of Social Issues* 19(2):113–24.

Jakubowicz, A. 1985. "Education and Ethnic Minorities—Issues of Participation and Equity." Discussion paper No. 1. Canberra: National Advisory and Coordinating Committee on Multicultural Education.

Kagitcibasi, C. 1981–82. "Women and Development in Turkey." *International Journal of Turkish Studies* 2(2):59–70.

———. 1986. "Status of Women in Turkey: Cross-Cultural Perspectives." *International Journal of Middle East Studies* 18:485–99.

Kandiyoti, D. 1977. "Sex Roles and Social Change: A Comparative Appraisal of Turkey's Women." *Signs: Journal of Women in Culture and Society* 3(1):57–73.

Kocbek, I. 1981. "Class, Status and Ethnicity: An Exploratory Study of University Students." B.A. honors thesis. Sydney: University of Sydney.

Mackie, F. 1983. *Structure, Culture and Religion in the Welfare of Muslim Families.* Canberra: Department of Immigration and Ethnic Affairs.

Magnarella, P. 1974. *Tradition and Change in a Turkish Town.* New York: John Wiley and Sons.

Majoribanks, K. 1980. *Ethnic Families and Children's Achievement.* Sydney: Allen and Unwin.

Manderson, L., and C. Inglis. 1984. "Turkish Migration and Workforce Participation in Sydney." *International Migration Review* 18(2):258–75.

———. 1985. "Workforce Participation and Child-Rearing amongst Turkish Women in Sydney, Australia." *Ethnic and Racial Studies* 8(2):194–204.

Martin, J. 1978. *The Migrant Presence.* Sydney: Allen and Unwin.

Martin, J., and P. Meade. 1979. *The Educational Experience of Sydney High School Students: Report No. 1.* Canberra: Australian Government Publishing Service.

Meade, P. 1981. *The Educational Experience of Sydney High School Students: Report No. 2.* Canberra: Commonwealth Department of Education and Academy of Social Sciences in Australia.

————. 1982. "Comparative Education Experiences of Students of Non-English-Speaking Migrant Origin and Students with Australian-Born Parents." Paper prepared for the Alf Sampson Leadership Institute on Multicultural and Intercultural Education, 9–12 May, Ballarat, Victoria.

————. 1983. *The Educational Experience of Sydney High School Students: Report No. 3.* Canberra: Commonwealth Department of Education and Academy of Social Sciences in Australia.

M.S.J. Keys Young Planners. 1980. *The Settlement Process of the Turkish in the Outer Suburbs of Melbourne.* Report prepared for the Department of Immigration and Ethnic Affairs, Surrey Hills, New South Wales.

Poole, M.E. 1981. "Educational Opportunity for Minority Groups: Australian Research Reviewed." In *Education of Minorities*, ed. Jacquetta Megarry. *World Yearbook of Education.* London: Kogan Page.

Sturman, A. 1985. "Immigrant Australians, Education and the Transition to Work." Discussion paper 3. Canberra: National Advisory and Coordinating Committee on Multicultural Education.

Taft, R. 1975a. "The Career Aspirations of Immigrant School Children in Victoria." La Trobe Sociology Papers No. 12. Bundoora, Victoria: La Trobe University.

————. 1975b. "Aspirations of Secondary School Children of Immigrant Families." *Education News* 15(1):38–41.

Taft, R., and D. Cahill. 1978. *Initial Adjustment to Schooling of Immigrant Families.* Canberra: Department of Education and Academy of the Social Sciences in Australia.

Tsolidis, S. 1986. *Educating Voula: A Report on Non-English-Speaking Background Girls and Education.* Ministerial Advisory Committee on Multicultural and Minority Education, Ministry of Education, Victoria.

Turney, C., C. Inglis, K. Sinclair, and R. Straton. 1978. *Inner-City Schools: Children, Teachers and Parents.* Sydney: University Press.

Walker, J.C. 1987. *Louts and Legends: Male Youth Culture in an Inner City School.* Sydney: Allen and Unwin.

Willis, P. 1977. *Learning to Labour.* Westmead: Saxon House.

Wolf, S. n.d. "Study of a Turkish Girl 1974–75." Unpublished paper. Melbourne: Counseling, Guidance and Clinical Services, Migrant Resources Section.

Yaka, R. 1977. "Turkish People in Australia." In *Australia 2000: The Ethnic Impact*, Proceedings of the First National Conference on Cultural Pluralism and Ethnic Groups in Australia, ed. Margarita Bowen, Armidale, N.S.W.: University of New England Press.

Young, C. 1980. "School to Work Transition Among Migrant Youth in Australia, with Special Reference to the Turks and Lebanese." In *Australian Association for Research in Education*, ed. I.D. Smith. Papers presented to the 1980 annual conference in Sydney, 6–9 Nov.

———. 1983. "Education, Employment and the Turkish Community in Australia." *International Journal of Turkish Studies* 2(2):33–57.

———. 1985. "Turkish Teenage Girls in Australia: Experience, Attitudes and Expectations." In *Australia in Transition: Culture and Life Possibilities*, ed. M.E. Poole, P.R. de Lacey, and B.S. Randhawa. Sydney: Harcourt Brace Jovanovich.

Young, C., M. Petty, and A. Faulkner. 1980. *Education and Employment of Turkish and Lebanese Youth*. Canberra: Australian Government Publishing Service.

Chapter Five
Koreans in Japan and the United States

Yongsook Lee
Korean Educational Development Institute

Introduction

In the United States, Asian Americans (Koreans, Japanese and Chinese in particular) are the only minority group whose academic achievement surpasses that of the majority whites. They not only have higher college attendance rates but also higher achievement test scores than the majority. In California, for example, Korean, Chinese and Japanese students who speak fluent English were ranked on average in the 90th percentile in reading, written language and math test scores in 1979–80 (California Assessment Program, 1980a).

Interestingly, Koreans, who achieve as well academically as Japanese in the United States, are reported to have considerably lower achievement rates than Japanese in Japan (Rohlen, 1981). For example, the college attendance rate of Korean high school graduates was less than 60 percent of that of Japanese high school graduates in Hyogo Prefecture in 1976 (Rohlen, 1981). This chapter attempts to explain the different academic achievement of Korean students in these two countries.

In light of the significance of the issue, it is unfortunate that literature on the academic performance of Koreans in either the United States or Japan is scarce. Because available data are limited, I have based some of my analysis on logical argument rather than specific data. It is hoped that this initial work will stimulate more comparative research on Korean academic achievement.

In order to analyze Korean academic achievement patterns I draw upon a model which I developed to help explain Asian Americans' academic achievement patterns (Lee, 1984). This model traces and links the reasons behind a minority group's academic achievement based on three interrelated factors: the structure of the society; the culture of the people; and interactions among individuals, namely children, parents, teachers and children's peer groups.

An understanding of the Korean case can provide insight into the educational achievements of minority students because it goes beyond simplistic heredity and cultural deprivation explanations of minority educational failure.

Theoretical Background

Four major sets of theories have been used to explain the high educational achievement levels of Asian Americans and the low achievement levels of blacks and other minorities in the United States. The first, heredity theory (Jensen, 1969; Jensen and Inouye, 1979), suggests that racial variations in intelligence are mainly caused by hereditary differences in conceptual and problem-solving skills, grasping relations and symbolic thinking. It has been claimed that blacks have lower abilities in these areas than Chinese Americans, Japanese Americans and whites (Jensen, 1969; Jensen and Inouye, 1979).

Unlike hereditary theory, cultural deprivation theory (Coleman et al., 1966; Deutsch, 1969; Glazer and Moynihan, 1963; Moynihan, 1965; Lewis, 1966; Reissman, 1962) attributes the low achievement of black, Hispanic and American Indian children to "deficient" home or cultural backgrounds. These children are said to lack the cognitive, linguistic and other skills necessary for school success because their parents do not possess these skills to a sufficient degree to teach them to their children. On the other hand, cultural advantage theory, which is a corollary of cultural deprivation theory (Schwartz, 1971; Vernon, 1982), attributes the high academic achievement of Asian Americans to their unique culture. Most commonly cited are a traditional family system oriented toward collectivity, an acceptance of authority structure, firm parental control, a motivation for educational achievement and the need for hard work to gain success and to honor the family.

Criticizing cultural deprivation explanations, cultural conflict theorists (Valentine, 1968) have argued that minority children fail to do well in school because their culture is different from the mainstream culture and the attitudes, values and learning styles which they acquire at home are in conflict with those required for success in the public schools and in the wider society. The cultural conflict theory has been reversed by those who use the idea of cultural compatibility or similarity to explain the high socioeconomic and educational achievements of Japanese Americans. Cultural compatibility theories propose that Japanese American academic success can be explained by cultural similarity through assimilation (Kitano, 1969) or by original compatibility between Japanese and American middle-class culture (De Vos and Caudill, 1973).

The fourth set of theories includes two separate trends, both of which draw upon structural explanations to explain minority educational achievement. One trend (Bowles and Gintis, 1976; Lindblom, 1977) attributes achievement levels of blacks and other minorities to the organization of school and society, which perpetuates racial and class inequalities through educational discrimination. The other trend (Ogbu, 1978; Ryan, 1976) emphasizes minority perceptions of the opportunities available to them within this stratified society. Ogbu (1978) argues that blacks, Hispanics and American Indians, whom he calls "castelike" or "involuntary" minorities, are not allowed to compete for the most desirable roles in society on the basis of their individual training and abilities.

A major problem with these different theories is their tendency to draw upon only one dominant factor to explain the situation. The genetic difference theory is inadequate in large part because it is not possible to include sufficient controls to distinguish biological differences from environmental differences. There appears to be considerable merit in the structural explanation, although it tends to ignore the unique cultural characteristics of each minority group. The cultural explanation also seems to be valuable, although it does not provide enough explanation by itself. Rather than maximizing one explanation and minimizing the other, both cultural and structural explanations need to be viewed in concert to provide a powerful theory. Ignoring one or the other results in incomplete explanations.

Explanation of the educational achievement of a minority group must include attention to three interrelated factors. On the macrolevel, one should understand the structure of the host society and the cultural background of the minority group. Both structure and culture can be understood only in the context of history, however. This macrolevel understanding of minority education must also be supplemented by an understanding of the process of interaction among children, parents, teachers and children's peer groups. Since this process is continuously created and influenced by the structure and culture of the society, and since this process forms the structure and culture, these three aspects cannot be separated.

Figure 1 presents a model which integrates these three factors. The model is based on a review of present theories and on ethnographic fieldwork in public schools (Lee, 1984). Slaughter and Schneider's "Model of the Private Schooling Process" also provided an important insight (1982).

Numeric notations in Figure 1 refer to processes which integrate the background variables of each minority group with their academic achievement. Thirteen processes are identified in this model as follows:

(1)   A minority group's educational values affect parents' educational expectations for their children.

(2)   The educational expectations of minority group parents are affected by income distribution (i.e., their ability to pay for children's education) and their perception of economic return from education for their group.

(3)   Teachers' educational expectations for children of certain minority groups are affected by their perception of economic return from education for the minority group (i.e., expected job opportunities) and individual children's ability to pay for their education (i.e., parents' socioeconomic status).

(4)   Teachers' and parents' educational expectations of students are interrelated.

(5)   Children's perceptions of parents' educational expectations affect their self-expectations.

FIGURE 1

Sociocultural Interactive Model for a Minority Group's Academic Achievement Process

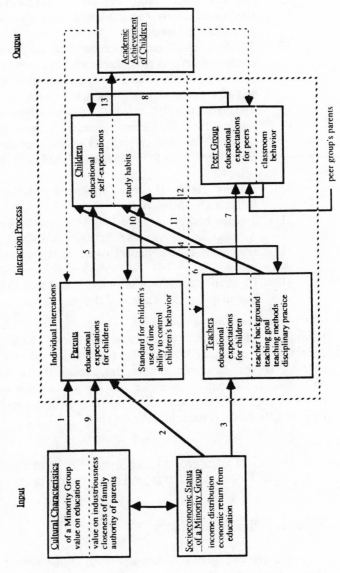

(6)   Children's perceptions of teachers' expectations of their educational achievement affect their self-expectations of educational achievement.

(7)   Teachers' educational expectations of certain groups of children affect peer group expectations for those children.

(8)   Peer groups' educational expectations affect children's self-expectations of educational achievement.

(9)   The value placed on industriousness affects parents' standard for their children's use of time. The closeness of the family and the authority of minority group parents affect the ability of the parents to control their children's behavior.

(10) Parents' ability to control children's behavior affects children's study habits.

(11) Teacher backgrounds, teaching goals, teaching methods and disciplinary practices affect children's study habits.

(12) Peer group's classroom behavior affects children's study habits.

(13) Children's educational self-expectations and study habits lead to their actual academic achievement.

The interaction process works on two levels: one level is the transmission of educational expectations which form children's self-expectations; the other level is the actualization of educational expectations into academic achievement through the formation of children's study habits. Because the input variables—cultural characteristics and socioeconomic status of a minority group—vary over time, the model is fundamentally dynamic.

Historical Background and Socioeconomic Status of Koreans in Japan and the United States

Koreans in the United States

The first immigration of Koreans to the United States began in 1882 with a handful of students and political refugees. The first large-scale immigration to the United States and its territories began in 1903. Between 1903 and 1905, 7,226 immigrants (6,048 male adults, 637 female adults and 541 children) arrived in Hawaii as sugar plantation contract laborers. They were mostly common laborers and displaced peasants from Korean port cities and towns. Less then 14 percent were farmers; 65 percent were illiterate; more than half were Christians. Less than 60 percent of these immigrants remained in Hawaii. Approximately 1,000 returned to Korea, while 2,000 moved to the mainland United States (Houchins and Houchins, 1976; Kim, 1981).

Between 1910 and 1924, more than 1,000 women came to Hawaii as brides, somewhat ameliorating the massive gender imbalance. They were from impoverished southern Korean provinces. This period was also marked by rapid urbanization of Korean immigrants, who escaped miserable working conditions and the low wages of sugar plantations. In the cities, Koreans found work as canning factory workers, stevedores, cooks, waiters, janitors and domestic servants. Those who accumulated sufficient capital started small-scale business operations such as laundries, rooming houses, barber shops, restaurants and retail grocery stores. Second- and third-generation Koreans later held more diverse occupations, including professional ones (Houchins and Houchins, 1976; Kang, 1978).

Despite the influx of about 2,000 Koreans to the mainland before 1907, the Korean population in the continental United States was only 1,806 in 1930, including 1,097 in California. During the 1930s, Korean college graduates could only find jobs in Hawaii if they wanted to be employed in the professions for which they had been trained. In the continental United States, Koreans had to accept manual and service jobs or start their own small-scale businesses, such as fruit and vegetable stands, grocery stores, laundries and restaurants. Nonetheless, and in spite of their lack of financial resources, one in ten of the Koreans residing in the continental United States in the late 1930s attended an institution of higher learning. The average college attendance rate for all Americans was then only one in 100 (Givens, 1939).

Between 1924 and 1952, there was practically no Korean immigration to the United States or its territories because of the Exclusion Act of 1924. This act prohibited further entry of Koreans and other Asians, with the exception of Filipinos. Up to the Korean War in 1950–53, Koreans were an invisible minority group in the mainland United States because of their small number. Moreover, Koreans were hardly recognized as Koreans by the American public since Korea regained its independence only in 1945. Koreans were often mistaken for Chinese or Japanese because of their physical similarities. After the American participation in the Korean War, however, Korea became better known to the American public, mainly as a poor country in need of help. This negative image lasted even after the Korean War was over, because of its legacy in the movies and in TV series based on the Korean War, such as *M*A*S*H*, and because Americans who had participated in the Korean War had a vivid memory of poverty and destruction.

The Korean community in the United States started to grow after the McCarran Act of 1952, which allocated a quota of 105 immigrants per year from Korea and allowed naturalization of Koreans (Daniels, 1976; Kim, 1981). In addition, nonquota immigrants such as war brides and relatives of citizens were able to come to the United States in relatively large numbers. Moreover, considerable numbers of students, tourists, retired government officials and businessmen obtained permanent residency after they came to the United States. As a result, between 1950 and 1965, 18,797 Koreans were admitted to the United States as permanent residents (Kim, 1981).

Full-scale Korean immigration started only after the passage of the Immigration Act in 1965, which took effect in 1968. By 1980 the Korean community in the United States had grown to more than 350,000 people (United States Bureau of Census, 1984). Because the Immigration Act allows immigration of only two major categories—people who have advanced education, skills or money to benefit American society and family members of American citizens or permanent residents—the majority of Korean immigrants have been from the well-educated and skilled urban middle class. Doctors have been especially welcome. In addition, nurses, pharmacists, engineers, mechanics and businessmen have chosen to settle in the United States. While parents, children and siblings of these groups may have more diverse occupations, they are generally from a similar socioeconomic class (Kim, 1980; Kim, 1981; Reimers, 1981). For this reason, Korean Americans do not have major subgroups based on socioeconomic status.

There are several reasons for the large-scale emigration of Koreans, among which are overpopulation, political instability and, in particular, the constant threat of war caused by the division of South and North Korea. North Koreans who fled to South Korea are particularly afraid of another Korean War because they would be the first victims in the event of North Korean victory. This may be the reason why a large proportion of North Korean refugees and their descendants are to be found among Korean immigrants to the United States. In addition, North Korean refugees have neither relatives nor a solid economic foundation to forfeit if they leave South Korea. Most are Protestants, who were previously exposed to American culture through the influence of American missionaries (Kim, 1981).

Korean Protestant churches in the United States have become a primary center for Korean immigrants' social life, whereas only a small portion of Chinese Americans and Japanese Americans are members of Christian churches. Even non-Christian Korean immigrants tend to go to Korean church every Sunday because it provides a unique opportunity for social interaction among Korean immigrants (Kim, 1980; Kim, 1981).

The image of Koreans held by the American population has become increasingly positive due, most probably, to two factors: Korea has emerged as a rapidly developing country since the late 1960s, with economic and strategic importance for the United States, and most Koreans in the United States are educated people with middle-class backgrounds. Even with their middle-class and educated backgrounds, most Korean immigrants, except for doctors, have found it difficult to enter the mainstream of the American middle class. The language barrier, an inability to transfer skills acquired in their country of origin and discrimination against them in large business firms are the major obstacles that they have encountered (Kim, 1981).

Despite the myth of Asian-American economic success (Lindsey, 1982; *Newsweek*, 1982; Petersen, 1966), Asian Americans, including Koreans, have not enjoyed the same occupational or financial success as whites. For example, in the Los Angeles area, which has the largest Korean population in the United States, the 1970 median annual income of Korean males was only $6,512 compared to $7,890 of the majority males (Moulton, 1978). Considering the higher educational levels of Koreans (median 12.9 years in 1970) than whites (median 12.1 years in 1970), Koreans were underpaid. The 1980 census figures also reveal that new Korean immigrants (post-1970 arrivals) have lower income and occupational levels than new European immigrants in spite of the Koreans' higher educational levels. When we compare median incomes of males fifteen years old and over who were year-round fulltime workers in 1979, Korean immigrants earned $1,467 less than European immigrants. Moreover, a lower percentage of Korean immigrants than European immigrants had either administrative or craft occupations, whereas a higher percentage of Korean immigrants had sales and service occupations. Unlike Korean immigrants, European immigrants enjoyed comparable income and occupational levels with the U.S. population as a whole.

Koreans in Japan

Korea and Japan share not only a long history of interaction but also, according to the archeological and linguistic evidence, common origins. Japanese culture was influenced by Korean residents in Japan as early as the sixth century. Between 1592 and 1598, during the Japanese invasion of Korea, groups of Korean potters, scholars and others were forcibly sent to Japan. However, at the time of Japan's annexation of Korea in 1910, there were only 790 Korean residents in Japan. Most of them were students and political refugees (De Vos and Lee, 1981a, 1981b).

Large-scale Korean immigration to Japan started in 1911 when Japanese industrialists, in the midst of a rapid industrial expansion, began to recruit Korean laborers who had become impoverished by Japanese colonial policies. An increasingly large segment of Korean farmers were reduced to the status of debt-ridden tenants. Most Koreans in Japan came from three southern provinces—Cholla-Namdo, Kyongsang-Namdo and Kyongsang-Bukdo—where Japanese administrators had consolidated practically the entire countryside under their supervision. These provinces, which had the best agricultural land in Korea, are located nearest to Japan (De Vos and Lee, 1981b; K. Lee, 1983).

The Korean population in Japan increased rapidly from 30,175 in 1920 to 298,091 in 1930 and 799,865 in 1938 (De Vos and Lee, 1981b). Most Koreans in Japan worked as unskilled laborers, especially as coal miners, stevedores and manual laborers. Korean laborers received considerably smaller wages than Japanese holding similar jobs, sometimes only a little more than half of the average wage. Moreover, the Koreans in Japan were continually exploited by labor brokers who exacted a percentage of the Koreans' pitiful daily income (De Vos and Lee, 1981b; K. Lee, 1983).

A high illiteracy rate continued because of ineffective Japanese governmental policies in raising the educational levels of Koreans either in Korea or Japan. By 1936, only 60 percent of Korean children in Japan were attending elementary schools and only a handful of them were attending secondary or higher-level institutions. Koreans were not encouraged to send their children to school and sometimes were even prevented from doing so. The extreme poverty of most Koreans, the overt disparagement and contempt of Japanese schoolmates and Korean parents' reluctance to indoctrinate their children with a chauvinistic Japanese education were also major factors lowering educational levels of Koreans (De Vos and Lee, 1981b).

Koreans comported themselves in a rougher and more overtly aggressive manner than was customary for the more obsequious and diffident lower-class Japanese. Because they were aware of the subjugation of their country and the ruthless practices of oppression from 1910 on, Koreans could only feel helpless rage at their condition (De Vos and Lee, 1981b).

In the eyes of Japanese laborers, the existence of Koreans in Japan threatened their job security by either taking their jobs away or lowering wages. Such factors as extreme poverty, abnormal living conditions caused by the imbalance in the gender ratio (only 11 percent of Koreans in Japan were females in 1920) and the different customs of Korean migrants induced the Japanese population's hatred and contempt of Korean migrants. One extreme expression of Japanese hatred toward Koreans was the 1923 massacre of 4,500 to 20,000 Koreans (there are several different statistical estimates) after the Kanto earthquakes (De Vos and Lee, 1981b; K. Lee, 1983).

With the beginning of World War II, involuntary migration of Koreans to Japan started. Between 1939 and 1945, approximately 822,000 Koreans were brought to Japan as labor and military conscripts (De Vos and Lee, 1981b). As a result, more than 2,000,000 Koreans were in Japan by the end of World War II (Lee, 1981a; K. Lee, 1983).

The end of World War II meant the liberation of Korea from Japanese colonialism. Immediately, Koreans started to return to Korea. According to the Korean government's report, 1,414,258 Koreans returned from Japan by the end of 1946 (K. Lee, 1983). Among these were most of the Koreans who had been brought to Japan as labor and military conscripts. There were factors, however, that discouraged some Koreans from returning home. First, the Supreme Command for the

Allied Powers in Japan forbade any repatriates from taking with them more than 1,000 yen or objects of equivalent value. With that amount, one could scarcely buy more than a few cartons of cigarettes in Korea. Second, the incoming Japanese repatriates from Korea reported disheartening news about the situation in Korea—riots, strikes, epidemic diseases, floods and famine—which made Koreans in Japan anticipate conditions worse than those they had experienced in Japan (Lee, 1981a; K. Lee, 1983). As a result, 611,758 Koreans remained in Japan after the end of the repatriation program in 1946, according to the report of the Japanese Attorney General's Office (Goldstein, 1972).

Although almost 100,000 Koreans were repatriated to North Korea between 1959 and 1967 (Lee, 1981b), 670,890 Koreans still remained in Japan in 1981 (K. Lee, 1983). Over three quarters of them were born in Japan (Lee, 1981a; K. Lee, 1983). In addition, by 1980, there were 102,544 naturalized Koreans in Japan (K. Lee, 1983).

In modern times, Koreans in Japan still remain a segregated, poor and persecuted minority in the midst of an increasingly affluent Japan (Goldstein, 1972). The split of Koreans into two organizations— "Mindan," which is attached to South Korea (the Republic of Korea), and "Ch'ongnyon," which is attached to North Korea, is one obstacle to the development of the Korean community, but ongoing legal and social discrimination against Koreans by the Japanese is a much more significant obstacle. During the colonial period, Koreans were considered Japanese nationals. However, nationals of colonial origin were differentiated from Japanese citizens through a rigid family registry system (Lee, 1981c). Since the enactment of the Alien Registration Law in 1947, Koreans have been legally classified as aliens. Koreans who went to Japan before 1945, and their children born before 1952, were permitted to reside in Japan by a supplementary law in 1952. Children born after 1952 had to renew their registration every three years, subject to approval by the Ministry of Justice. After the Republic of Korea-Japan Normalization Treaty in 1965, Koreans who had been resident in Japan continuously since 1945 and their children (but not future generations) could apply for permanent residence. Up to the deadline for application in 1971, there were 351,262 Koreans who filed applications and 342,366 among them were granted permanent residence. About 250,000 Koreans did not apply because of ineligibility, allegiance to North Korea or other reasons (Lee, 1981c; K. Lee, 1983).

Two major obstacles prevent naturalization for Koreans. First, the National Law enacted in 1950 includes a clause of "good behavior" without a clear definition of what constitutes "good behavior." Therefore, anyone with a simple police record is unlikely to pass the rigorous scrutiny of the Ministry of Justice. A violation of a traffic law often causes a problem. Moreover, under the Immigration Control Law of 1952, even an alien who fails to carry a registration card is subject to arrest. Second, even when a person qualifies under the provisions of the law, the application for naturalization is subject to approval by the Ministry of Justice (K. Lee, 1983).

There are additional factors that make Koreans reluctant to apply for naturalization. To become naturalized is to give up one's Korean citizenship and to identify with the Japanese, who despise Koreans. One's sense of self-worth is threatened by the knowledge of how much Koreans are despised. In addition, naturalization means only legal acceptance as a Japanese citizen, not social acceptance. In Japan, a copy of one's "Koseki" (family registration) is required when applying for a job, for school admission or for membership in any group. One's country of origin is thereby revealed. Moreover, naturalized Koreans are held in contempt by Koreans who are not naturalized. Therefore, socially, they belong neither to the Japanese community nor to the Korean community.

Between 1952 and 1980, about 100,000 Koreans were naturalized. The number of naturalized Koreans is increasing gradually each year, especially among the second and third generations (K. Lee, 1983). Over 670,000 Koreans who remain unnaturalized in Japan suffer extreme legal and social discrimination. Koreans are not eligible for most of the social welfare benefits, including pensions, insurance and public housing, although they are subject to taxation. However, the biggest problem for them is discrimination in employment. As non-Japanese citizens, Koreans are prohibited from being hired by national and local governments, including public corporations, public schools and national and public universities (K. Lee, 1983; Rohlen, 1981).

Korean graduates face serious employment barriers at almost every level of society and in almost every form possible (Rohlen, 1981:199). Private Japanese companies tend to hire Koreans with low levels of education only when there are shortages of laborers. Koreans with higher education have even less chance to be employed unless they pursue skills that can be used in individual private practice such as medicine, architecture and engineering. Moreover, employed Koreans often experience discrimination in promotion. As a result, the jobs Koreans hold are characterized by low social status, low pay and little security of employment. Compared to the Japanese population as a whole, Koreans experience more poverty, more broken homes and a higher crime rate (Rohlen, 1981).

Koreans have also experienced discrimination in the area of education. Between 1948 and 1955, Korean schools either were not accredited or were forced to close down unless they complied with all pertinent Japanese directives. From 1952 to 1965, Korean students were admitted to the public schools only if space and facilities were available. In addition, parents and students had to pledge not to disturb the public order, and they could not demand Korean ethnic studies (Lee, 1981d).

Since the Republic of Korea-Japan Normalization Treaty in 1965, Koreans have been legally entitled to public school education. As a result, by 1981 about 80 percent of Korean students were attending Japanese schools and the others attended Korean schools (K. Lee, 1983). Because Japanese schooling is considered by Koreans to contribute to their integration and upward mobility in Japanese society (Rohlen, 1981), their enrollment in Japanese schools had increased from 75 percent in 1974. Another reason for the increase may be that Korean schools do not have the status of regular schools and many universities disqualify graduates of Korean schools. Graduates of Korean schools are even disqualified from the qualifying examinations for nurses, beauticians, barbers, chefs and masseurs (K. Lee, 1983).

Koreans who want to attend Japanese schools experience a great deal of overt and covert discrimination, starting with gaining admission to these schools. There are some private primary and junior high schools which openly refuse admission to Koreans. Other schools, including public schools, admit Korean students only when they pledge not to disturb school order or when they pay higher tuition than Japanese students. The strongest discrimination occurs at the beginning of the senior high level, because education is compulsory only through junior high school. In one prefecture, 14 out of 35 senior high schools were reported to openly refuse admission to Korean students in 1978. In addition, some other schools required Korean students to have better grades than Japanese students, to conduct themselves well or to pledge not to make demands that the school be concerned about their employment after graduation (K. Lee, 1983). In 1974–75, only 69 percent of Korean senior high school students were in Japanese schools, compared to 76 percent of elementary and junior high school students. Academically less able Korean graduates transfer to Korean high schools because they cannot gain acceptance to public high schools (Rohlen, 1981). Pronounced discrimination in high school admission seems also to be a factor.

Korean students attending Japanese schools experience continuous overt and covert contempt by Japanese students and sometimes even by teachers. Japanese textbooks present Korean history in a negative light. They sometimes even change the facts to make it appear that Korea has always been a poor and miserable country, inferior to Japan (K. Lee, 1983). The effect of this has been the development of a negative self-image among Korean students in Japanese schools.

Discussion

The social position of Koreans in Japan is markedly different from that of Koreans in the United States. The timing of immigration, the class origin of the majority of the migrants and the relationship between Korea and the host countries are a few of the factors which have contributed to the different social positions. However, the most important factor is the level of discrimination against Koreans by the host society.

Ogbu's concepts of "immigrant" and "involuntary" minorities can be applied to some extent to a comparison of Koreans in the United States and Japan (Ogbu, 1978, and in this volume). Koreans in the United States can be categorized as an immigrant minority. They tend to consider discrimination and prejudice to be obstacles to overcome and a price that they may need to pay to achieve their ultimate objective of a better life for themselves and their children. Koreans in Japan can be categorized as an "involuntary" minority because they are not allowed to compete for desirable jobs on the basis of their individual training and abilities. Moreover, their seemingly voluntary immigration to Japan was brought about by Japanese colonial policies which impoverished Koreans.

Several factors have made the condition of Koreans in Japan less favorable than that of Koreans in the United States. First, the fact that

Koreans constitute 85 percent of foreign nationals and naturalized citizens in Japan (K. Lee, 1983) makes them a very visible target of resentment. The majority group's resentment against a minority group tends to be strongest toward the largest minority group that competes economically with the majority, thus lowering the majority's employment or wage levels (Hendrick, 1977). Since Koreans in the United States have never constituted more than 0.2 percent of the whole population, they are likely to attract either relatively favorable attention or no attention at all from the majority.

Second, unlike the United States, Japan is not an ethnically diverse society, and Japan has shown much less tolerance for ethnic minorities than the United States. This is the case even though Koreans are of the same race and similar culture to the majority of Japanese.

Third, even before large-scale Korean immigration to the United States began in the late 1960s, East-Asian Americans had gained the reputation of a successful minority group—industrious, quiet and education-oriented (Petersen, 1966; United States Commission on Civil Rights, 1980). Thus, from the beginning, most Korean immigrants could enjoy relatively favorable treatment from the majority. On the other hand, Koreans in Japan were that country's first colonial subjects. There were no immigrants before them, and from the beginning, the Japanese had contempt for Korean immigrants.

Fourth, Korea and the United States have always had a friendly relationship and Koreans have favorable attitudes about the United States. Therefore, Korean immigration to the United States has been voluntary. In sharp contrast, Koreans developed a feeling of hatred toward Japan when it exploited Korea as her colony. Korean immigration to Japan was enforced either by an exploitative colonial policy or by wartime conscription (K. Lee, 1983).

Fifth, most Korean immigrants to the United States came from the middle class or upper-middle class. By the late 1960s, when large-scale Korean immigration started, a solid educational system had been established in Korea. Therefore, most Korean immigrants to the United States brought with them at least minimal funds for a new life and good education. Most Korean immigrants to Japan went during the colonial period (1910–45) and were from the poorest class. They had neither funds nor education.

Sixth, the United States has provided the two-parent family an opportunity to earn enough money to start a small-scale business and/or to invest in their children's education, if both parents are willing to work long hours. Even the early Korean immigrants, who came with neither money nor education, were able in time to start small-scale businesses and to educate their children. Until recently, Japan's economy was not as strong as that of the United States. In Japan, Koreans were the first to be laid off whenever there were recessions and they got much lower wages than Japanese laborers, who in turn got lower wages than American laborers. Even those who have managed to start small-scale businesses in Japan have tended to have very low incomes (Rohlen, 1981). As a result, Koreans in Japan have had fewer opportunities to save money or to educate their children properly compared with Koreans in the United States.

Seventh, since 1952, Korean immigrants have been able to get American citizenship relatively easily after five years' residence (United States Commission on Civil Rights, 1980). Any child who is born in the United States automatically becomes an American citizen. Naturalization in Japan involves a selective process. A child born in Japan does not get Japanese citizenship unless one of his/her parents is Japanese. Moreover, permanent residents in the United States do not experience as many legal barriers as those in Japan.

Cultural Backgrounds

For more than 15 centuries, the Chinese written language, sociopolitical institutions and belief systems have provided the main framework with which Koreans and Japanese organize their world. The Chinese culture is reflected in every aspect of the lives of East Asians (Kang, 1978). This does not mean that Korea and Japan have identical cultures. Each has its own language, food, housing and clothing. Within a similar framework of a patrilineal descent system, the detail varies in each country. For example, in traditional Japan, only one son, son-in-law or adopted son chosen by the father (usually the eldest son) inherits all property. The other sons must either subordinate themselves to the chosen son or leave the village. In Korea, the eldest son inherits more property than other sons, but usually younger sons also are entitled to some property.

There is also a similar emphasis on vertical dyadic relationships which vary in detail. In feudalistic Japan, vertical systems of loyalty and personal commitment to one's lord or master were strongly developed at both the Samurai and merchant levels (De Vos and Lee, 1981c). In centralized Korea, loyalty and personal commitment were oriented more toward family and the king.

On the whole, however, Korea and Japan have more commonalities than differences in their Confucian-influenced cultures (De Vos and Lee, 1981a; Kang, 1978; Kim, 1977; Nandi, 1980). This is especially true in areas related to children's education such as intrafamily relationships, child rearing practices, the valuation of education and the status of teachers. In these, Koreans and Japanese have very similar attitudes and practices.

Interpersonal harmony is the greatest social virtue in the Confucian ideology (De Vos and Lee, 1981c). Interpersonal harmony and the closeness of family have been achieved by the sacrifice of the individual for the good of the family. The emphasis on filial piety, respect for the elderly, subordination to the father and parental care for children even after they are grown have been strongly emphasized both in Korea and Japan (Chun, 1980; Dore, 1965; Nandi, 1980).

In both Japan and Korea the early years of childhood have been characterized by permissiveness of parents toward their children. The child is seldom left alone or left to cry. It is almost always being fed, carried or soothed. Discipline does not become strong until the age of six or seven, after which absolute obedience to parents is expected. Close body contacts through long breast feeding, sleeping in the same bed with parents during infancy and allowing children to participate in much of adult life have been common practices. Most parents are ready to sacrifice economic or recreational comfort for the success of their children. These practices result in the establishment of an unconditional basic trust and a strong bond between parents (especially mothers) and children (Koh, 1979; Y. Lee, 1983; Nandi, 1980).

Strong emphasis on education has a long history in Korea and Japan. For more than 1,000 years, national examinations have been almost the only way to become a middle- or high-level bureaucrat in Korea. Although the examinations were not open to lower-class people before this century, well educated people have been greatly respected in Korea. In Japan, being a Samurai required not only military but also academic skills. Japan's literacy rate was higher than that of most European countries in 1870. Formal education developed as the principal mechanism of social mobility (Dore, 1965).

These traditions continue in modern Korea and Japan. In both countries, entrance examinations are required by schools, the government and large companies. A good education is the most important means to gain economic success and social respect (McGinn et al., 1980). Moreover, academic achievement is not a personal matter for children but is related to the honor of the family, especially that of the parents (Nandi, 1980). "The need for accomplishment in both Korean and Japanese people is expressed in the context of a strong sense of responsibility and obligation to one's family" (De Vos, 1983:68). Therefore, there is tremendous pressure on children to achieve well in school (Totman, 1978; Koh, 1979). At the same time, support for attempts at success are provided by parents, who have close ties with their children (McGinn et al., 1980).

Confucianism perceives the teacher-child relationship as the extension of the parent-child relationship. Thus, Japanese and Korean students are socialized to show extreme obedience and respect toward their teachers. Teachers have privileged social positions in both countries, although in Korea their status has been lower in recent years because of low salaries (McGinn et al., 1980; *Newsweek*, 1983; Singleton and Ebuchi, 1970). The close family relationships typical of Korea and Japan are often contrasted with those of the American/Western culture which are more individualistic and independence-oriented (De Vos, 1983; Hsu, 1970; Kang, 1978).

Although education is an important factor of success in the United States, it has never been emphasized to such a degree as it has in Japan or Korea. American teachers do not appear to enjoy a great deal of respect from either parents and children (*Newsweek*, 1981, 1983). Therefore, in the area of education, the differences between Korean and American culture are much wider than those between Korean and Japanese cultures. These cultural differences seem to work favorably for both Korean Americans and Japanese Americans in terms of educational achievement (Lee, 1984).

Academic Achievement of Koreans
in Japan and the United States

In this section, the process of Korean academic achievement in Japan and in the United States will be contrasted and discussed with regard to the socioeconomic and cultural backgrounds of the students.

Academic Achievement Patterns

There are no data available that compare the test scores or grades of Korean students in Japan to those of Japanese students. However, we can speculate about the lower academic achievement of Koreans by looking at their high school and college attendance rates. Competitive entrance examinations are required in Japan at two points of school transfer: from junior to senior high school and from senior high school to the university.

A school hierarchy exists in Japan. Night schools are generally at the bottom; public high schools are more desirable than private high schools (with the exception of a few elite institutions) and academic high schools are more desirable than vocational high schools (Rohlen, 1981). Similarly, the university is more desirable than junior college. Therefore, the percentage of Korean students going on to the higher-level schools and those enrolled in different kinds of schools are indicative of the academic achievement patterns of Korean students, as well as the socioeconomic status of their parents.

In 1976, 88 percent of the Koreans graduating from junior high schools in Hyogo Prefecture went on to high school, compared to 94 percent of the prefecture's total population. As shown in Table 1, twice as many Korean high school entrants as compared to the total population enrolled in public night schools. In addition, more Korean high school entrants enrolled in less desirable private schools and vocational schools. The Korean entrance rates in the public high schools were lower even than those of the Burakumin, historically the lowest-status group within Japanese social structure (see Shimahara, in this volume).

Table 1. Total High School Entrants, Burakumin Entrants, and Korean Entrants in Different Types of High Schools in Hyogo Prefecture, 1976

	Public Schools %	Private Schools %	Academic Schools %	Vocational Schools %	Night Schools %
Total	71.7	28.9	74.8	25.2	4.0
Burakumin	69.6	30.0	56.6	43.0	4.7
Korean	62.2	36.0	68.0	31.4	8.2

Source: Rohlen, 1981.

The disparity between the Koreans and the total population is even greater at the point of university entrance. The Korean entrance rate for university is less than half that of the total population (see Table 2). Again, the Korean rate is less favorable than that of the Burakumin students (Rohlen, 1981). These attendance data show clearly that Korean students have lower academic achievement levels than Japanese students.

Table 2. Total High School Graduates, Burakumin Graduates and Korean Graduates in Hyogo Prefecture, 1976

Graduates	University %	Junior College %	Total %
Total	29.4	16.4	45.8
Burakumin	18.7	13.4	32.1
Korean	12.7	13.6	26.3

Source: Rohlen, 1981:197.

In the United States, the picture is reversed. In California, for example, Korean-speaking elementary students who were fluent in English ranked in the 82nd to 96th percentiles in reading, written language and mathematics in 1980 (see Table 3). Similarly, in the two Chicago-area public schools where I carried out research (Lee, 1984, 1987), Korean students had considerably higher test scores and report card grades than "Anglo" (majority-group) students. This was the case even though the Anglo students came from higher socioeconomic backgrounds (see Table 4).

Table 3. California Survey of Basic Skills: State Percentile Scores for Reading, Writing and Mathematics, by Language and Grade Level, 1979–80

English Language Fluency And Other Language Spoken	Average Test Scores by State Percentile Rank		Written Language 3rd* Grade	Mathematics	
	Reading				
	3rd Grade	6th Grade		3rd Grade	6th Grade
State Total	44	39	45	46	48
English only	56	53	57	55	57
Fluent English, Total	28	17	27	33	28
Chinese	94	86	92	98	96
Japanese	93	89	92	96	94
Korean	90	82	88	96	92
Filipine Dialects	81	45	83	83	66
Vietnamese	71	49	63	82	85
Spanish	21	10	20	24	14
Others	63	35	66	71	60

Sources: Student Achievement in California Schools: 1979–1980; Survey of Basic Skills, Grade 3:1980; Interpretive Supplement to the Report on the Survey of Basic Skills, Grade 6:1980.

*No equivalent test score is provided at 6th grade.

These markedly different academic achievement patterns of Koreans in Japan and in the United States can be explained by two levels of interaction processes: formation of educational self-expectations and actualization of educational expectations.

Table 4. Mean Comparison of Korean and Anglo-American Students' Achievement Test Scores and Grade Point Averages

School	Grade	Ethnic Group	N[3]	Achievement Test Scores[1]				Grade Point Average[2]			
				Language/Reading		Math		Reading	Lang./[4] writing	Math	Conduct
				Grade Equiv.	Nat'l %tile	Grade equiv.	Nat'l %tile				
Sub- urban	6	Korean	5	9.9	86	9.3	93	2.6	2.4	3.1	--
	6	Anglo	14	8.1	74	7.4	75	2.4	2.5	2.5	--
	7	Korean	6	11.8	87	11.8	94	--	2.5	3.0	--
	7	Anglo	18	8.0	63	8.0	68	--	1.8	2.0	--
City	6	Korean	4	8.7	84	8.7	90	4.0	4.0	3.8	3.8
	6	Anglo	3	8.0	72	8.6	88	3.7	3.8	3.5	3.3
	7	Korean	10	8.5	62	10.2	94	3.6	3.4	3.8	3.3
	7	Anglo	14	9.2	74	9.5	85	2.8	2.9	3.1	2.9

1. Suburban students took the "Stanford (Language and Math) Test" in April 1983. City students took the "Iowa (Reading and Math) Test" in January 1983.
2. Suburban school: A=4.0, B=3.0, C=2.0, D=1.0, F=0.0
   City school: E=4.0, G=3.0, S=2.0, U=1.0
3. Data were not available for students who transferred to other schools by the end of the 1982–83 academic year.
4. "Language arts" for the suburban school and "written expression" for the city school.

Formation of Educational Self-Expectations

Minority parents' educational expectations for their children are influenced by the cultural and the socioeconomic characteristics of the minority group. In terms of cultural characteristics, Koreans in Japan do not have the advantages which their counterparts in the United States enjoy. This is because of the similarities between Korean and Japanese cultures in relation to childhood education. They, thus, enjoy no "cultural advantage." In terms of socioeconomic characteristics, both absolute and relative economic returns of education are much lower for Koreans in Japan than for Koreans in the United States. In addition, Koreans in Japan have lower average family incomes than Japanese, while Koreans in the United States enjoy a higher average family income than the majority.

Korean parents in the United States tend to have higher educational expectations for their children than Anglo parents. Unlike many Anglo parents, Korean parents are not satisfied with average grades (Lee, 1984). These high educational expectations of Korean parents can be attributed in part to their high valuation of education for self-improvement, self-esteem and family honor. The Koreans' high college attendance rate during the 1930s is indication of this high value placed on higher education despite the virtual impossibility for Korean college graduates at that time to find professional jobs in the mainland United States (Givens, 1939).

Since World War II more employment opportunities have been available to Koreans in the United States. Asian Americans, including Koreans, continue to be discriminated against in managerial, administrative and high-paying blue-collar jobs such as construction, wholesale trades and manufacturing industries (United States Commission on Civil Rights, 1980). Therefore, to avoid employment in low-paying jobs as laborers, unskilled and semiskilled factory workers and service workers, Koreans have chosen between self-employment in their own business and employment in professional and technical positions such as doctors, pharmacists, nurses, engineers and scientists (Miller, Vowell and Crist, 1976). Korean parents demand good grades from their children as a strategy for combatting occupational discrimination and so that they will be competitive in the fields of medicine and engineering, which require good grades (Lee, 1984, 1987).

Although Koreans in Japan are reported to have high educational expectations for their children, the expectations of Korean parents do not appear to surpass those of Japanese parents (K. Lee, 1983). If Korean parents value education highly for self-improvement, self-esteem and the honor of the family, so do Japanese parents. Because Korean families have lower incomes than Japanese families, they have fewer resources to pay tuition or to support their children's study financially. Moreover, they do not have an incentive for higher education because "the higher the educational achievement of the Korean student, the less likely will he be to gain a job" (Rohlen, 1981:199). It is estimated that less than 10 percent of Korean college graduates find employment in Japanese companies (K. Lee, 1983). About 50 percent are employed in companies owned by Koreans (K. Lee, 1983), which are characterized as undercapitalized, dependent on very low labor costs and relying on insecure sources of income (Rohlen, 1981). The remaining 40 percent either inherit their parents' business, are employed as laborers, are self-employed or are unemployed (K. Lee, 1983). Under these circumstances, it is difficult for Korean parents to have as high educational expectations for their children as Japanese parents.

In the American setting, most teachers and administrators perceive students of East-Asian descent, including Korean students, to be high academic achievers. They attribute this to the high value that parents place on education and strict discipline, both of which are considered to be East Asian cultural characteristics. American educators tend to welcome Korean parents and children because they perceive that Koreans respect teachers. Teachers praise Korean students for their industrious, quiet, respectful behavior. Most American teachers perceive that Korean Americans will have equal economic opportunity once they become proficient in English and, therefore, they have no reason to lower their educational expectations because of a perceived lack of future occupational opportunities (Y. Lee, 1983, 1984, 1987).

In the Japanese setting, the Japanese are brought up to despise Korean culture. Only the Korean cultural characteristics that are different from Japanese culture are emphasized and these are perceived in a negative light (K. Lee, 1983; Rohlen, 1981; Wagatsuma, 1981). Therefore, Japanese teachers are not likely to have positive attitudes toward Korean culture or to have high expectations for Korean children. In fact, Korean children can, on occasion, experience overt contempt (K. Lee, 1983). The fact that some Japanese schools demand that Korean parents or students pledge not to disturb the school order (K. Lee, 1983) is evidence that Japanese administrators and teachers do not welcome Korean students. Japanese teachers are well aware of discriminatory hiring practices against Koreans. Teachers themselves, moreover, play a critical role in the hiring process. In 1975, for example, 85 percent of Korean graduates from Japanese high schools in Hyogo Prefecture who took jobs were introduced to their employers by their schools. In such a fashion, many Japanese teachers help Korean graduates to obtain employment. On the other hand, teachers' perceptions of the movement of children in the society are reported to influence their educational expectations of the children and their teaching behavior (Eddy, 1967; Lightfoot, 1978; Rist, 1978; Roberts, 1970; Ryan, 1976). It is possible that Japanese teachers lower their educational expectations for Korean children because they see dim prospects for Korean children's employment in Japanese society.

In the United States, a very different situation prevails. Anglo parents welcome Korean students as friends of their children because they perceive Korean children to be high achievers and a good influence on their children. To a large extent, Korean children are integrated with Anglo children. Anglo children perceive Korean children to have behavior similar to their own and also perceive them as being high achievers (Y. Lee, 1983, 1984, 1987).

In Japan, more than half of all Korean children use Japanese names at school. Many hide their ethnicity as long as possible, because Japanese students despise Korean students and laugh at them harshly. Hiding their Korean identity means that they have to make fun of other Korean children, together with Japanese peers. There are many records of friendships being broken between Japanese and Korean students when a Korean student's identity is revealed. In an extreme case, two junior high school students killed themselves after a series of incidents in which they were mistreated by Japanese peers (K. Lee, 1983; Rohlen, 1981; Wagatsuma, 1981).

In the United States, Koreans tend to live in middle-class neighborhoods within the metropolitan area, and they are rapidly moving toward better suburban neighborhoods, which tend to be populated by a considerable number of Asian Americans (*Chicago Tribune*, 1983; Maruyama, 1979). School peer groups for Korean students thus tend to be comprised of Asian American and other middle-class students, who generally have high educational standards. In Japan, since about half of the Koreans live in poorer sections of Japanese cities (Rohlen, 1983), the Korean students' peer groups tend to be lower-class Japanese and other Korean students. These peer groups are likely to have lower academic standards than those of middle-class Japanese. Thus, Korean students in Japan are at a disadvantage compared to Korean students in the United States in terms of the formation of educational self-expectations. Korean students in the United States, influenced by the high educational expectations of parents, teachers and their peer groups, tend to develop high expectations for themselves (Lee, 1984, 1987). On the other hand, Korean students in Japan are likely to develop low educational expectations for themselves, following the low expectations of their parents, teachers and peer groups.

Actualization of Educational Expectations

High or low educational self-expectations are actualized through the study habits of students. The development of study habits is affected by parents, teachers and the peer group.

In the United States, Korean parents tend to control their children's time more strictly than Anglo parents. Korean children, on the whole, spend more time on lessons in music, computers, martial arts and (Korean) language instruction than Anglo children. Moreover, many more Korean parents than Anglo parents teach their children reading, writing and simple arithmetic skills before they enter school at age five (Y. Lee, 1983, 1984). From an early age Korean students become accustomed to using their time diligently. This strict control of children's behavior is possible partly because Korean culture emphasizes the authority of parents, filial piety and obedience to parents. An even more important factor may be the closeness of the Korean family. Because of this closeness between parents and children, and the self-sacrifice of parents for their children, Korean children tend to respond positively to their parents' high educational expectations. The low divorce rate among Korean parents provides evidence of their close family ties. In the two Chicago area schools mentioned previously, 92 percent of Korean parents, compared to only 25 percent of Anglo parents, indicated that they would sell their only house for the college education of their children if necessary (Y. Lee, 1983, 1984, 1987). This is another example of Korean parents' self-sacrifice.

In Japan, no data are available about the Korean parents' control of their children's use of time compared to that of Japanese parents. However, Korean parents do not appear to have any advantage because of the similarity of parent-child relationships in Korean and Japanese cultures. Moreover, it is likely that Korean parents in Japan do not have enough leisure time or energy to carefully control their children's use of time because they are too busy struggling for survival. The higher divorce rate among Koreans in Japan (K. Lee, 1983; Rohlen, 1981) may be evidence of the stressfulness of their lives.

Korean students in the United States tend to be grouped in top classes or instructional groups from an early age in part because they tend to spend more time on learning at home before school age and in the early stages of formal education (Y. Lee, 1983). Children placed initially in the top class tend to remain in the top class in the upper grades. Teachers generally use more challenging and problem-solving methods in the top class, while spending more time on custodial care in the lower classes. More experienced and prepared teachers are also often assigned to the top classes (Bowles and Gintis, 1976; Eddy, 1967; Roberts, 1970). Therefore, Korean American students, who, for the most part, attend top classes in middle-class neighborhood schools, have a better than average chance of developing creative and problem solving skills and of having higher motivation and interest in education. Thus, they may be willing to spend more time on active learning both in and outside the classroom. Moreover, Korean students have less chance to be distracted by other students in the classroom because the students in top classes and better neighborhood schools tend to be distracted less often than students in the low classes and ghetto schools (Y. Lee, 1983, 1984, 1987).

Korean students in Japan generally attend lower-class schools with high delinquency rates and discipline problems. Since teachers in those schools may need to use more time for custodial care, Korean students are likely to have lower motivation and interest in education. Thus, they may be less willing to spend time on learning. Another disadvantage for Korean students in Japan is that they are likely to have a higher chance of being distracted, because more students in their schools are likely to be inattentive.

Influenced by these contrasting family and school factors, Korean students in the United States and Japan are likely to develop different study habits to actualize their educational self-expectations into academic achievement. In the United States, Korean students make more and better use of their time for study, both in and outside of school, and actualize their high educational self-expectations into high academic achievement (Lee, 1984, 1987). Korean students in Japan are likely to make less and worse use of their time for study both in and outside schools, thus actualizing their low educational self-expectations into low academic achievement. This analysis, which is somewhat speculative due to the current lack of data on the school-adaptation patterns of Koreans in Japan, needs to be extended through further comparative research.

Conclusion and Implications

This study highlights two levels of interaction processes—the formation of educational self-expectations and the actualization of educational expectations—which lead to the high academic achievement of Koreans in the United States and the low academic achievement of Koreans in Japan.

Korean parents in the United States have higher educational expectations and standards for their children than majority parents for two reasons. One is their traditionally high valuation of education for self-improvement and family honor. The other is their realization that Koreans have occupational opportunities only in limited fields, such as medicine and engineering, which require high grades.

American teachers also have high educational expectations for Korean students because they have positive attitudes toward Asian cultural characteristics. The limited occupational opportunities for Korean students do not hold back their teacher's educational expectations for them, because teachers do not realize that there is discrimination against Koreans in many occupational fields. Teachers seem to believe in the popular image of Asian Americans as a successful minority (*Newsweek*, 1982; *Time*, 1983). Korean students' Korean peers also have high educational expectations which, coupled with the high educational expectations of their parents and teachers, leads Korean American students to develop high educational expectations for themselves.

Korean parents tend to be more successful than Anglo parents in controlling their children's use of time because of the close family ties and the strong authority of parents emphasized by Korean culture. The quiet, industrious, disciplined and orderly behavior emphasized by Korean culture is also rewarded at school, because American teachers tend to interpret these behaviors as traits of a good student. In addition, Korean students' teachers and peer groups appear to provide a favorable environment for learning. One reason is that Korean American students generally attend better schools. New arrivals from Korea tend to settle in middle-class neighborhoods immediately, or within a few years after their immigration. The other reason is that Korean students tend to be grouped into top classes from the early grades on because they usually spend more time on learning at home before the school age and in the early stages of formal education.

Thus, family, teacher and peer group factors interact together to motivate Korean American students to make effective use of their time for study both in and out of the classroom. Through disciplined study, Korean American students actualize their high self-expectations into high academic achievement.

On the other hand, Koreans in Japan tend to have lower educational expectations for their children than Japanese parents because of their extreme poverty and their realization that there is a highly restricted job ceiling for them. As mentioned before, less than 10 percent of Korean college graduates are hired by Japanese enterprises (K. Lee, 1983). In addition, Koreans who are permanent residents in Japan are not legally eligible for government jobs, including public school teaching. Korean cultural characteristics offer no advantage, because the Japanese have a similar culture.

Japanese teachers also have low educational expectations for Korean students because they tend to have negative attitudes toward Korean culture and recognize that a job ceiling exists for Korean students. The Japanese peers of Korean students also have low educational expectations for Korean students because they observe their parents' and teachers' negative attitude toward Korean students. Influenced by these low expectations of parents, teachers and peer groups, Korean students in Japan develop low educational expectations for themselves.

In Japan, Korean parents might be less successful than Japanese parents in controlling their children's use of time because their living conditions do not allow them to have enough leisure time and energy. Again, Korean students do not have the competitive edge they have in the United States because Japanese culture, like Korean culture, influences Japanese parents to control their children's time closely. Moreover, Korean students in Japan have unfavorable teacher and peer group environments because Korean students on average attend lower-class area schools with high delinquency rates. The reason for this attendance is that they are forced to live in urban ghettos by their parents' low incomes and by discrimination against Koreans in housing (K. Lee, 1983). Therefore, compared to Japanese students, Korean students are less motivated by parent, teacher and peer group factors to use their time for study. Thus, Korean students actualize their low self-expectations into low academic achievement.

Koreans in the United States appear to be more successful than Koreans in Japan not only in academic achievement but also in economic achievement. However, Koreans in the United States are not without problems. Korean students tend to concentrate disproportionately on mathematical or technical subjects. Korean parents' and students' realization of their limited occupational opportunities and educators' reinforcement of the "quiet model minority" (Y. Lee, 1983, 1984, 1987) appear to perpetuate this process. This results in a lack of opportunity to enter more language-oriented professions such as law and politics, or to obtain executive and managerial positions. Without gaining power through influential positions such as these, Koreans are unable to affect policy decisions, even when the policies are directly related to themselves.

If Koreans continue to fill mainly technical professions along with small-scale family businesses, they will form a "middleman minority" group, which acts as a buffer between a dominant group and minority groups at the bottom. Kitano (1976) suggests that this has happened to Japanese Americans. The disadvantage of being a middleman minority is that while such a group rises above the status of other minorities because of a competitive advantage, or because of a high adaptive capacity, it soon reaches a ceiling imposed, usually, by a combination of dominant group discrimination and the ethnic group culture (Kitano, 1976). If Koreans are not satisfied with the middleman minority position, they need to actively pursue language-oriented subjects instead of avoiding them simply because they do not see rewards in them in the near future.

Koreans in Japan are in a much worse position than Koreans in the United States. Economic and social rewards for education are necessary before Koreans in Japan can fully maximize their opportunities. The responsibility lies both within the Korean community and in Japanese society. The Japanese, in general, need to provide Korean minorities with more consistent economic rewards for educational achievement. The severe legal barrier to the employment of Koreans needs especially to be eliminated. Koreans themselves, however, need to maximize their opportunity by increased investment in higher education, even when the economic opportunity does not seem substantial.

The experience of East Asians in the United States provides evidence of the beneficial effects of extensive investment in education. Because of East Asian cultural characteristics, Koreans, Chinese and Japanese in the United States invested heavily in higher education before World War II. This was the case even though college graduates had to work at fruit stands (Miller, Vowell, and Crist, 1976). When labor shortages in technical areas arose during World War II, East Asians were able to take advantage of the new opportunities.

There are more benefits of strong investment in education. When Koreans in Japan begin to achieve more highly than the Japanese, the Japanese will lose the evidence which supports their prejudice, which is based on a stereotypic negative image of Koreans as low achievers. Also, the existence of a larger number of Korean graduates from top universities can become a significant pressure on the Japanese government and corporations to eliminate discriminatory practices.

The experiences of Koreans in Japan and in the United States have an important implication for low-status minority groups such as American blacks, because they show that a minority group can have very different achievement patterns in different host societies. The educational and economic achievement levels of Koreans in Japan are surprisingly similar to those of blacks in the United States. On the other hand, Koreans in the United States have much higher achievement levels than those of blacks. The colonial experiences of Koreans and the experiences of blacks in slavery, together with continued discrimination against both by the host society, seem to continuously acculturate them into an impoverished outcaste subculture of the dominant group (Van den Berghe, 1973). Therefore, as in the case of Koreans in Japan, blacks need to increase their investment in education even though the economic opportunity does not seem substantial, in addition to working for equal opportunity.

A culture is continuously changing, either by adopting some aspects of other cultures, or by losing some aspects of itself. Culture change is also affected by new technology, social organization and ideology. Therefore, in order to vitalize one's culture, it is important to make an effort to strengthen positive aspects of one's own culture and to adopt positive aspects of other cultures. In that sense, East Asian cultural characteristics which seem to increase academic achievement—high valuation of education, strict control of children's use of time and strong family ties—need to be carefully identified, emphasized and applied by both Koreans in Japan and other underachieving minorities such as blacks in the United States.

These suggestions are not intended to undermine blacks and Koreans' efforts in past decades, which have helped them to improve their socioeconomic status to some degree. The point is that the low-status minority groups have to use all available means to have higher educational achievement than that of the majority, in order to improve their socioeconomic status as much as possible.

References

Bowles, Samuel, and Herbert Gintis. 1976. *Schooling in Capitalist America.* New York: Basic Books.

California Assessment Program. 1980a. "Student Achievement in California Schools: 1979–1980." Annual Report. Sacramento, Calif.: State Department of Education.

———. 1980b. "Survey of Basic Skills, Grade 3: 1980." Sacramento, Calif.: State Department of Education.

———. 1980c. "Interpretive Supplement to the Report on the Survey of Basic Skills, Grade 6: 1980." Sacramento, Calif.: State Department of Education.

Chicago Tribune. 1983. "Skokie Becomes Asian Village," 27 Sept.

Chun, Shin-Ae. 1980. *A Passage Through the Hermit Kingdom.* Deerfield: Asian Press.

Coleman, James S., et al. 1966. *Equality of Educational Opportunity.* Washington, D.C.: United States Government Printing Office.

Daniels, Roger. 1976. "American Historians and East Asian Immigrants." In *The Asian American: The Historical Experience*, ed. Norris Hundley, Jr., pp. 1–25. Santa Barbara: Clio Books.

Deutsch, Martin. 1969. "Minority and Class Status as Related to Factors in Achievement." In *Achievement in American Society*, ed. B.C. Rosen, H.J. Crocket and C.L. Nunn, pp. 174–80. Cambridge, Mass.: Schenkman Publishing Company.

De Vos, George A. 1983. "Achievement Motivation and Intra-Family Attitudes in Immigrant Koreans." *The Journal of Psychoanalytic Anthropology* 6(1):25–71.

De Vos, George A., and William Caudill. 1973. "Achievement, Culture and Personality: The Case of the Japanese-Americans." In *Socialization for Achievement*, ed. G. De Vos, pp. 220–50. Berkeley: University of California Press.

De Vos, George A., and Changsoo Lee. 1981a. "Koreans and Japanese: The Formation of Ethnic Consciousness," In *Koreans in Japan*, ed. C. Lee and G. De Vos, pp. 3–30. Berkeley: University of California Press.

———. 1981b. "The Colonial Experiences: 1910–1945." In *Koreans in Japan*, ed. C. Lee and G. De Vos, pp. 31–57. Berkeley: University of California Press.

———. 1981c. "Conclusions: The Maintenance of a Korean Ethnic Identity in Japan." In *Koreans in Japan*, ed. C. Lee and G. De Vos, pp. 354–84. Berkeley: University of California Press.

Dore, R. 1965. *Education in Tokugawa Japan.* London: Routledge and Kegan Paul.

Eddy, Elizabeth M. 1967. *Walk the White Line: A Profile of Urban Education.* Garden City, N.Y.: Doubleday.

Givens, H.L. 1939. "The Korean Community in Los Angeles County." M.A. thesis, University of Southern California.

Glazer, Nathan, and Daniel P. Moynihan. 1963. *Beyond the Melting Pot: The Negroes, Puerto Ricans, Jews, Italians and Irish of New York City.* Cambridge: MIT Press and Harvard University Press.

Goldstein, Michael. 1972. *Minority Status and Radicalism in Japan.* Denver: University of Denver Press.

Hendrick, Irving. 1977. *The Education of Non-Whites in California, 1849–1970.* San Francisco: R & E Research Associates.

Houchins, Lee, and Changu-Su Houchins. 1976. "The Korean American in America, 1903–1924." In *The Asian Americans: The Historical Experience*, ed. N. Hundley, Jr., pp. 129–56. Santa Barbara: Clio Books.

Hsu, Francis L.K. 1970. *Americans and Chinese: Purpose and Fulfillment in Great Civilizations.* Garden City: The Natural History Press.

Jensen, Arthur R. 1969. "How Much Can We Boost IQ and Scholastic Achievement?" *Harvard Educational Review* 39(1):1–123.

Jensen, Arthur R., and Arlene R. Inouye. 1979. "Level I and Level II Abilities in Asian, White, and Black Children." ERIC Document ED 175948.

Kang, Shin Pyo. 1978. *The East Asian Culture and Its Transformation in the West: A Cognitive Approach to Changing World View Among East Asian Americans in Hawaii.* Seoul: American Studies Institute, Seoul National University.

Kim, Bok-Lim C. 1980. "The Korean American Child at School and at Home: An Analysis of Interaction and Intervention through Groups." A project report to Administration for Children, Youth and Families. United States Department of Health, Education and Welfare, Grant No. 90-C-1335(01).

Kim, Illsoo. 1981. *New Urban Immigrants: The Korean Community in New York.* Princeton: Princeton University Press.

Kitano, Harry H.L. 1969. *Japanese-Americans: The Evolution of a Subculture.* Englewood Cliffs: Prentice-Hall, Inc.

———. 1976. "Japanese Americans: The Development of a Middleman Minority." In *The Asian American: The Historical Experience,* ed. Norris Hundley, Jr., pp. 81–100. Santa Barbara: Clio Books.

Koh, Tong-He. 1979. "Child-Rearing Practices and Cognitive Psychological Development in Asian Children: Implications for Counseling." Paper presented at the National Rehabilitation Association, Pre-Conference Training Session, Chicago, 16 Sept.

Lee, Changsoo. 1981a. "The Period of Repatriation, 1945–1949." In *Koreans in Japan,* ed. C. Lee and G. De Vos, pp. 58–72. Berkeley: University of California Press.

———. 1981b. "The Politics of Repatriation." In *Koreans in Japan,* ed. C. Lee and G. De Vos, pp. 91–109. Berkeley: University of California Press.

———. 1981c. "The Legal Status of Koreans in Japan." In *Koreans in Japan,* ed. C. Lee and G. De Vos, pp. 133–58. Berkeley: University of California Press.

———. 1981d. "Ethnic Education and National Politics." In *Koreans in Japan,* ed. C. Lee and G. De Vos, pp. 159–81. Berkeley: University of California Press.

Lee, Kwang-Kyu. 1983. *Jaeil Hanguk'in* (Koreans in Japan). Seoul: Il Jo Gak.

Lee, Yongsook. 1982. "Academic Success of Asian-Americans: Structural, Historical and Cultural Explanations." Second-year qualifying paper submitted to Department of Anthropology, Northwestern University.

———. 1983. "Academic Success of Asian Americans: Cultural Transmission and Occupational Opportunities," Paper presented at the Annual Meeting of the American Anthropological Association, Chicago.

———. 1984. "A Comparative Study of East Asian American and Anglo American Academic Achievement: An Ethnographic Study." Ph.D. diss. Evanston, Ill.: Northwestern University.

———. 1987. *Academic Success of East Asian Americans.* American Studies Monograph Series No. 12. Seoul: American Studies Institute, Seoul National University.

Lewis, Oscar. 1966. *La Vida: A Puerto Rican Family in the Culture of Poverty.* San Juan: Random House.

Lightfoot, S. 1978. *Worlds Apart: Relationships between Families and Schools.* New York: Basic Books.

Lindblom, Charles E. 1977. *Politics and Markets.* New York: Basic Books, Inc.

Lindsey, Robert. 1982. "The New Asian Immigrants." *New York Times Magazine,* 9 May.

McGinn, Noel F., et al. 1980. *Education and Development in Korea.* Cambridge: Harvard University Press.

Maruyama, Koichi. 1979. "Domicilation Process of Japanese and Korean Americans in the Chicago Area." In *Ethnicity and Its Identity in the U.S.A.: A Report of the Field Research in the U.S.A.,* ed. Tsuneo Ayabe, pp. 145–73. Ibaraki, Japan: Institute of History and Anthropology, University of Tsukuba.

Miller, Wayne C., Faye N. Vowell, and Gary K. Crist. 1976. *A Comparative Bibliography for the Study of American Minorities.* New York: University Press.

Moulton, David M. 1978. "The Socioeconomic Status of Asian-American Families in Five Major SMSAS: With Regard to the Relevance of Commonly Used Indicators of Economic Welfare." ERIC Document ED 190 670.

Moynihan, Daniel P. 1965. *The Negro Family: The Case for National Action.* Washington, D.C.: Department of Labor.

Nandi, Proshanta K. 1980. *The Quality of Life of Asian Americans: An Exploratory Study in a Middle-Size Community.* Chicago: Pacific/Asian American Mental Health Research Center.

Newsweek. 1981. "The Problems and Education of Teachers," 27 April.

———. 1982. "Asian Americans: A Model Minority," 6 Dec.

———. 1983. "Can the Schools Be Saved?" 9 May.

Newsweek: On Campus. 1984. "Asian Americans: The Drive to Excel," April.

Ogbu, John U. 1978. *Minority Education and Caste.* New York: Academic Press.

Petersen, William. 1966. "Success Story, Japanese American Style." *New York Times Magazine,* 9 Jan.

Reimers, David M. 1981. "Post World War II Immigration to the United States: America's Latest Newcomers." *The Annals of the American Academy of Political and Social Science* 454(March):1–12.

Reissman, Frank. 1962. *The Culturally Deprived Child*. New York: Harper.

Rist, R. 1978. *The Invisible Children: School Integration in American Society* Cambridge: Harvard University Press.

Roberts, Joan I. 1970. *The Scene of the Battle: Group Behavior in Urban Classrooms*. Garden City: Doubleday.

Rohlen, Thomas. 1981. "Education: Policies and Prospects." In *Koreans in Japan*, ed. C. Lee and G. De Vos, pp. 182–222. Berkeley: University of California Press.

———. 1983. *Japan's High Schools*. Berkeley: University of California Press.

Ryan, William. 1976. *Blaming the Victim*. New York: Vintage Books.

Schwartz, Audrey J. 1971. "The Culturally Advantaged: A Study of Japanese-American Pupils." *Sociology and Social Research* 55(3):341–51.

Singleton, John, and Kasukimi Ebuchi. 1970. "The Study of Japanese Education." *Rice University Studies* 56(4):231–41.

Slaughter, Diana, and Barbara L. Schneider. 1982. "Newcomers: Blacks in Private Schools." Proposal to the National Institute of Education, Washington, D.C.

Time. 1983. "Confucian Work Ethic: Asian-born Students Head for the Head of the Class," 28 March.

Totman, Michiko. 1978. "Japanese Culture." In *The Second Annual Forum on Transcultural Adaptation: Asian Students in American Classrooms*, 23–24 May.

United States Bureau of Census. 1984. *1980 Census of Population*. Vol.1: *Characteristics of the Population, Detailed Population Characteristics: United States Summary*. Washington, D.C.

United States Commission on Civil Rights. 1980. *Success of Asian Americans: Fact and Fiction*. Washington, D.C.: Government Printing Office.

Valentine, Charles A. 1968. *Culture and Poverty: Critique and Counter-Proposals*. Chicago: University Press.

Van den Berghe, Pierre L. 1973. "Pluralism." In *Handbook of Social and Cultural Anthropology*, ed. J. Honigman, pp. 959–78. Chicago: Rand McNally.

Vernon, Philip E. 1982. *The Abilities and Achievements of Orientals in North America*. New York: Academic Press.

Wagatsuma, H. 1981. "Problems of Self-Identity Among Korean Youth in Japan." In *Koreans in Japan*, ed. C. Lee and G. De Vos, pp. 304–33. Berkeley: University of California Press.

Chapter Six
Ethnicity, Gender and Social Class: The School Adaptation Patterns of West Indian Youths

Margaret A. Gibson
University of California, Santa Cruz

> The aliens have ruined our schools. So many of
> them are overage, and they can't even do second-
> grade work.
>
> Crucian teacher

> Just because they were born here, the Crucians
> think they've got it made. Someone will look
> after them, get them a job, so they have this
> "don't care" attitude in school.
>
> Immigrant West Indian parent

Popular beliefs, such as these, were easy to come by in St. Croix during the mid-1970s, when I carried out fieldwork there on the relationship between ethnic identity, immigrant status and school performance.[1] The caricatures, however, obscured the facts. As a group, the immigrant West Indians, or "aliens" as they were locally called, did better academically and persisted in school longer than the native Crucian population. Within both groups, moreover, girls were meeting with greater success in school than boys. Gender proved more significant for native-born youths than for immigrants. This chapter explores these relationships, focusing on the central questions of why, in the St. Croix public school setting, black females are more academically successful than black males and immigrants are more successful than natives even though all subgroups are similar in class status, color and cultural background.

Full analysis of the St. Croix case and the interrelation of race, class, ethnicity and gender would require equal attention to the school-adaptation patterns of Puerto Rican students, who comprised close to 30 percent of the St. Croix public school population at the time of fieldwork, and to students within the private schools. Nearly every student who might be termed middle class attended a private school including almost all white students.[2] Almost all those who attended the public schools were black and from the lower classes and it is on this group that this analysis focuses.

Of major interest to the following discussion is the variation in performance that existed among black, lower-class students. As I learned soon after my arrival in St. Croix, it was not possible in analyzing school performance patterns to conceptualize race, class, gender or ethnicity as separate issues. By lumping all Crucians, all females, all blacks or all lower-class students together significant distinctions were obscured. Each of these statuses influenced students' responses to schooling, but no one of them was determinant. Nor was the impact of class status, for example, or race or gender the same for each ethnic group.

The Community Setting

Like other Afro-Caribbean societies, St. Croix is characterized by its relatively small size, its colonial and slave experience, a population predominantly African in descent and continued dependence on a colonial power. From roughly 1733, when the island was purchased from France by Denmark, until the abolition of slavery in 1848, St. Croix was a plantation society with sugar as its principal crop. Economic decline followed emancipation. The sale of St. Croix, along with St. Thomas and St. John, to the United States in 1917 did little for the abysmal economic situation. Efforts to Americanize the U.S. Virgin Islands and to bring them economic relief proceeded slowly prior to the 1960s (for a more detailed discussion of the history and development of St. Croix see Dookhan, 1974; Lewis, 1972; and Lewisohn, 1970).

Until a rise in tourism in the 1950s, the economy of St. Croix rested primarily on agriculture. In 1963 the last commercial crop of sugar was harvested and the old, agriculturally based economy was replaced forever by one based on industry, tourists, tourist-related services and local government. Tourism and industry together brought full employment but at a cost to the native population, which rapidly became a minority in its own homeland.

By 1975, the island's total population had surpassed 50,000, for a growth of more than 300 percent in the preceding fifteen years (U.S. Bureau of the Census, 1973; U.S. Department of the Interior, 1976). Much of the increase resulted from immigration to St. Croix by workers from neighboring, non-U.S. islands of the Caribbean. They came both as permanent residents and as "temporary" or "bonded" workers, whose stay was dependent upon the existence of jobs that no U.S. citizen or permanent U.S. resident was available to fill.

To the native Crucian population these immigrant workers and their families were "aliens." Regardless of their place of birth, Antigua or Trinidad, St. Lucia or Nevis, for example, all were lumped together by their Crucian hosts into one common alien group, a process that served to bind them together, Antiguan and Nevisian alike, and to set them apart from the native population. Even children born in St. Croix, and thus themselves American citizens, had the "alien" identity ascribed to them. By the mid-1970s, the alien label had gained such wide currency that some immigrant West Indians even used it to refer to themselves. Because of the term's negative connotations, I prefer instead to refer to this group collectively as "Down Islanders," a more neutral phrase which, although not widely used, was commonly understood. The phrase reflects the immigrants' ancestry and origins in the islands located south of or "down from" St. Croix.

At the time of fieldwork, Down Islanders (temporary workers and permanent residents together) comprised approximately 44 percent of the population; Crucians, 27 percent; Puerto Ricans, 22 percent; and continentals, 7 percent (Gibson, 1976). The Puerto Rican group included all persons of Puerto Rican ancestry living in St. Croix, whether recent arrivals or second generation. "Continental" was the local term for persons from the mainland or continental United States who had made St. Croix their primary place of residence.

Employment Niches

The population growth and expansion in the private economic sector had been accompanied by an equally sharp rise in the size of local government. Within the native group there existed a small professional and business elite, but for the most part, Crucians were employed in civil service jobs. From a scant 3 percent of the workforce in the 1940s, the local Virgin Islands government had grown to 25 percent of the total workforce in 1975 and an estimated 60 percent of the native-born workforce (Senior, 1947; U.S. Department of the Interior, 1976; U.S. Bureau of the Census, 1985). Continentals controlled industry, tourist-related businesses, and many of the island's other commercial enterprises. Many local businesses, both small and large, were owned and operated by Puerto Ricans. Down Islanders held most of the service jobs connected with tourism, such as waiters, maids and clerks in the island's duty free shops, as well as skilled and unskilled industrial jobs. Temporary residents also worked in construction or as gardeners and maids for resident continentals.

Crucians felt threatened by the unprecedented and largely uncontrolled expansion in the population, the rise in tourism and the encroachment of outsiders into nearly every segment of the local economy. Over 1,000,000 tourists visited the island in 1969, a sevenfold increase from 1959 (Dookhan, 1974:286). The tourist bonanza had caused property values to rocket from $25 an acre in 1940 to $20,000 an acre in 1970 (Hill, 1971:114). Crucians, few of whom could afford to buy land at these prices, resented the passing of their island's real estate into the hands of outsiders. From the perspective of many native Virgin Islanders, tourism was a "new form of slavery." White continental businessmen had simply replaced the European planters.

During the late 1960s Crucians were able to reap at least some benefits from a booming economy. By the early 1970s, however, a combination of factors sent the local economy into a tailspin. A series of well-publicized murders of resident white continentals by local black youths caused tourism to plummet and an economic recession in the United States, coupled with increased oil tariffs, forced new construction in general and expansion of the locally based Hess oil refinery in particular to grind to a virtual halt. By the mid-1970s unemployment was on the rise, especially among temporary workers, whose jobs were dependent on construction and tourism, and among young workers who were just entering the labor force. From 1972 to 1974 building permits decreased by 44 percent, and hotel occupancy fell below 40 percent. The depressed economy forced a halt in the expansion of local government. Even permanent government employees began to worry about the security of their jobs.

Ethnic Markers

By local estimates probably 70 percent of those who considered themselves Crucians had ancestors who had emigrated to St. Croix from other Caribbean islands. Cultural and family ties between the United States Virgin Islands and the Commonwealth West Indies reach back over 200 years, and prior to the 1960s immigrant British West Indians were readily absorbed into the local social structure. Few alien West Indians settled in St. Croix during the 1940s and 1950s, however, due to restrictive U.S. immigration laws.

With the rapid influx of alien West Indians during the 1960s, family ties and place of birth became increasingly significant symbols of belonging. During the 1970s, one frequently heard the expression "mi bo'n hea" [me born here], indicating identity as a Crucian. The "real Crucians" were identified by Crucians themselves as those whose parents and grandparents had been born in St. Croix. Crucians evoked birthplace and family connections as a strategy for maintaining both their separate identity and the employment niches which they continued to control, most notably local government.

Next to birthplace, dialect was the most important marker distinguishing Down Islanders from Crucians, although language differences were not pronounced. Most Down Islanders, like their Crucian hosts, spoke an English-based Creole. Down Islander children, moreover, quickly adopted a Crucian accent. "The older kids all sound alike now," teachers frequently commented. They looked alike as well. It was impossible to distinguish Crucian and Down Islander students by physical appearance.

Ethnic Relations

Had there not been prevailing economic and political reasons to impose the "alien" identity, the newcomers would likely have been

absorbed into the Crucian fold. As it was, less than half of the Down
Islander population enjoyed the security of permanent residence visas.
The remainder could be ordered off the island at any time, their legal
status contingent upon their continued employment. With the recession,
temporary workers became expendable. Those who were laid off had
60 days to find new positions. After that they were forced to leave the
island or to remain without proper documentation. In 1974, more than
2,000 illegal aliens were apprehended by the United States Department
of Immigration and Naturalization and deported from St. Croix (*Daily
News*, 3 Feb. 1975). Some of those whose jobs were terminated had
lived in St. Croix for as long as ten years. Many had children who were
American citizens.

Given their precarious status, temporary workers and even many
Down Islanders who held permanent residence status had little
incentive to invest locally. Savings were sent off-island, a fact that
caused much resentment among the native population. Such comments
as "aliens work like slaves," "all they care about is making money," and
"they send it home and it doubles" were indicative of Crucian hostility
toward Down Islanders. During the late 1960s, alien West Indians
exported an estimated $3,000,000 annually back to their islands of
birth, a sum equivalent to the total amount of direct subsidies received
by the Virgin Islands in Fiscal Year 1967 from the United States
(Social, Educational Research and Development, 1969:5; U.S.
Department of the Interior, 1976:76).

Many Crucians viewed the Down Islander newcomers as
"invaders" and "exploiters." They treated them rudely, referred to them
as *garots* and accused them of stealing the island's resources. Whether
or not the term "garot" was derived from a bird of prey by that same
name, there is no doubt that Crucians, like other Virgin Islanders,
considered Down Islanders to be predators (see Dirks, 1975:105).

Relations between the two groups were strained. One elderly
Crucian expressed her bitterness as follows:

> When I was young, I knew them all. If they did anything wrong,
> they were sent home. Now it's "F--- this" and "Mother that" in
> loud voices for all to hear, even with children around. They pee
> in your bushes and wear their hair all funny. They show no
> respect.

A younger Crucian noted similar resentment, saying: "Aliens don't
have any manners. Look at the way they walk in a room, or drive a

car!" By the mid-1970s, Crucians found Down Islanders to be a convenient target for their frustrations. That Crucian teachers described alien students as overage and underprepared was only symptomatic of their general dismay with the changing social conditions.

Down Islanders, for their part, had little good to say about Crucians. Many described the natives as surly and rude, occasionally venting even stronger sentiments:

> Crab has no head and so no brain. Crucian has a head and still no brain. [Man from Dominica, whose visa had lapsed. He supported himself and his family by doing yard work for white continentals]

> I can get along with white people better than Crucians. They're crazy, evil people, messing themselves up. [Maid from Antigua]

Feelings of mistrust and hostility ran in both directions. Each group's frustration with the other was caused in large part by economic competition and, in the Crucian case, by their ongoing dependency on the United States.

The Public School Setting

In 1969, fully 86 percent of the students attending public schools in St. Croix were either Crucians of Afro-Caribbean ancestry (49 percent), or Puerto Ricans, both first- and second-generation migrants from the neighboring islands of Puerto Rico (37 percent).[3] Only 12 percent were Down Islanders and a scant 2 percent continentals. Almost all continentals preferred to send their children to one of the island's private schools and had the means to do so. Older continental children were often sent off-island to attend schools in the mainland United States.

Unlike the continentals, many Down Islander families sent their children to private schools not out of preference but out of necessity. Until the fall of 1970, the public schools were open only to U.S. citizens and permanent residents. Temporary workers had to turn elsewhere for their children's education. This was the case even though they paid the same taxes as citizens and resided legally in St. Croix. Those who were unable to pay for private schooling (and even modest tuitions were difficult for most of these families) had no choice but to keep their children out of school or have them live with relatives back home in their island of origin and attend school there.

This situation changed in 1970 when, by court order, the public school system was required to admit all school-age children residing lawfully in St. Croix. Between 1969 and 1975, public school enrollment more than doubled. Fully two-thirds of the new students were noncitizens.

By the mid-1970s noncitizens formed the largest group within the public schools, a factor that contributed to Crucian resentment of Down Islanders. In just six years Crucians had dropped from 49 percent to 33 percent of the student body, grades kindergarten through twelve (see Table 1). Down Islanders had grown from 12 percent to approximately 40 percent of the total student enrollment (Gibson, 1976). No more than 10 percent of Down Islander students continued to attend private school, down from 60 percent. During this same period the proportion of Crucian and Puerto Rican families sending their children to private schools remained constant at about 20 percent (see Bramson, 1969; Olney, 1974).

Table 1. St. Croix Public School Enrollment: Percentage of Students Enrolled in 1969 and 1975

	1969 (n=5,203)	1975* (n=12,043)
Crucian	49	33
Puerto Rican	37	27
Down Islander	12	40
Continental	2	--

Sources: Bramson, 1969; Gibson, 1976.

*1975 percentages are approximations.

Most public school students were poor and many came from households whose annual income placed them below the official poverty line.[4] Crucian families, on the whole, were somewhat better off financially than the Down Islanders and Puerto Ricans, and somewhat better educated, but still, few of the Crucian parents had more than eight years of formal education (U.S. Bureau of the Census, 1973).[5] The more affluent and better educated parents, including most teachers and school administrators, sent their children to one of the island's private schools.

The rapid growth in student enrollment placed serious strains on the entire system of public education. Overcrowded, many of the schools were forced to use metal trailers as temporary classrooms. Several schools were operating on double shifts, one even serving as an elementary school in the morning and a junior high in the afternoon. Curriculum materials were sparse. To keep pace with rising enrollments, the school district was forced to import large numbers of teachers. By the mid-1970s only one in three teachers was a native Virgin Islander. Just over half (55 percent) were continentals, mostly white, some black. Only 7 percent were from Puerto Rico and only 2 percent from other islands of the Caribbean (Virgin Islands Department of Education, n.d.).

Most continentals came on short-term contracts and, while residing in St. Croix, remained socially separated from the Crucian population. During the mid-1970s the annual turnover rate for continental teachers ran close to 40 percent (Gibson, 1976:99).

The staffing of the schools by non-West Indians and their constant turnover meant that many teachers had little understanding of the students' cultural backgrounds, but, from the Crucian perspective, the hiring of continentals was preferable to the recruitment of Puerto Ricans and Down Islanders. These latter were more likely to settle permanently in St. Croix and thus posed a greater threat to local control over education. Many Crucians, moreover, felt closer ties to the English-speaking mainland than to Spanish-speaking Puerto Rico.

School Performance Patterns

Girls were doing notably better in school than boys and Down Islanders better than Crucians (Gibson, 1982, 1983). The differences, although small during the early primary years, became readily apparent by junior high. Track placement, annual promotion, and school persistence provide examples of these disparities.

In the fall of 1973, 70 percent of Down Islander and Crucian girls and 60 percent of Down Islander boys were placed into the top half of seventh grade at West End Junior High, one of the island's two junior high schools. Less than 30 percent of the Crucian boys were similarly placed.[6] By the following fall, 84 percent of the Down Islander girls, 82 percent of the Crucian girls, and 73 percent of the Down Islander boys had been promoted to and were attending eighth grade. In sharp contrast, only 34 percent of the Crucian boys could be found in grade eight (Gibson, 1982:7). Among the Crucian boys who were retained in seventh grade, one in three dropped out of school immediately. Most of the others, while officially listed on the school roll for 1974–75, failed to attend school with any regularity or, when there, to do the assigned work. The situation was no different at the other junior high.

The ethnic and gender differences in school performance continued through high school. About 80 percent of the Down Islander and Crucian girls persisted in school until at least tenth grade and an estimated 70 to 75 percent graduated from high school. Among Down Islander boys the figures were lower, but close to 60 percent reached tenth grade and an estimated 40 to 50 percent finished twelfth grade. Only some 20 percent of the Crucian boys reached tenth grade and possibly no more than 10 percent stayed on to complete requirements for a high school credential.

These findings come from a longitudinal study of 45 Crucian students and 22 Down Islander students, all of whom were enrolled in fourth grade in April 1969 (Gibson, 1976). The students were selected by stratified random sample from a 1969 ethnic census of St. Croix schools (Bramson, 1969). I carried out my study six years later.

By December, 1975, the students should have been in eleventh grade, if promoted each year, but, as shown in Table 2, only five of the 24 Crucian boys were still in school and only three were expected to graduate.[7] Among the Crucian girls a very different picture emerged. Eleven were attending eleventh grade; six, tenth grade and only four had dropped out of school. An even higher percentage of the Down Islander girls were in school, attending eleventh grade and expected to graduate. The Down Islander boys were less likely to remain in school than the Down Islander girls, but more likely than the Crucian boys.

Table 2. School Persistence by Ethnic Identity and Gender*

	Enrolled in school 12/74 %	Enrolled in school 12/75 %	Attending 11th grade 12/75 %
DI girls (n=10)	90	90	80
CR girls (n=21)	86	81	52
DI boys (n=12)	75	58	50
CR boys (n=24)	46	21	13

Source: Compiled from school records.

*All students were enrolled in fourth grade in April 1969.
DI = Down Islander; CR = Crucian

    Census data for 1980 provide some further indication of a gender difference in school persistence: 54 percent of all black females in the Virgin Islands, ages 18 to 24, were reported to be high school graduates, compared with 36 percent of black males of that same age group (U.S. Bureau of the Census, 1984, Table 33). Unfortunately, the published census data do not control for ethnic identity, place of birth or public versus private school attendance, and they thus obscure both the intragroup and intergroup disparities that emerged from my research. For example, I found girls of Puerto Rican ancestry nearly twice as likely to drop out of school as Crucian and Down Islander girls (Gibson, 1976, 1982; see also U.S. Bureau of the Census, 1984, Table 33). Since the black female census category includes not only Crucian and Down Islander students but many Puerto Ricans as well, it obscures the actual school completion rate for the non-Hispanic black girls. By lumping public and private school students together, the census tables also obscure the relationship between social-class background and school completion as well the interplay between class status, gender and ethnicity. The Crucian boys who attended private school—and approximately one in five did—were much more likely to finish high school than those who attended public school.[8]

    Although my samples of junior and senior high students were relatively small, the patterns that emerged were clear. Among public school students, Crucian boys were running into far more trouble than any other student subgroup. Interviews with students and former students, together with participant observation at the junior high and elementary levels, help to shed light on subgroup variations in school performance.

Dominant versus Subordinate Cultural Systems

Like other West Indian societies, St. Croix has been characterized by two separate but interrelated cultural systems, each with its own criteria for judging a person's worth (Gibson, 1976, 1982). The first, the culture of the dominant group, is a creolized version of European and, more recently in the St. Croix example, American values and behaviors. This system, termed *respectability* by Peter Wilson (1973), was historically that of the white European plantation owners and is today the culture of the native elite, most of whom share a mixed European and African ancestry. It is from their ranks that native teachers come.

The class stratification system in St. Croix continues to place the lower classes in a bind. To improve their status, members of the lower-class majority are required to adopt the values and behaviors of the dominant minority. At the same time, they have little hope of gaining positions of power and privilege. Wilson describes respectability as the summation of colonial dependence.

Unable to advance and uncomfortable with the values of their colonizers, the majority group evolved its own creolized Afro-West Indian cultural system, forged in part from their African past and in part as an expression of opposition to the superordinate group (Patterson, 1975). This system, which Wilson terms *reputation*, is a creative response to the elusiveness of high-class status. Although both males and females find themselves pulled between the opposing sets of values, the reputation system is largely male dominated. It is, moreover, younger, lower-class males who feel most strongly the pressure to reject or defy the values and behaviors required within the respectability system.

"You earn a reputation," one Crucian man commented, "by how well you talk, by how tough you are, by your willingness to fight, even if you lose, by how successful you are with women, by the dollars in your pocket and your willingness to spend them, and by your ability to lead others, no matter the direction." A man's worth, thus, is measured by his peers for the things he can do well. To be good in business and politics a man must have the status and authority that can only be earned within the reputation system. A woman's behavior, on the other hand, regardless of her age or social class, is judged largely by the canons of respectability. Women are expected to behave respectably, by other women and by men.

Schools as Agents for Cultural Assimilation

The schools in St. Croix, from the beginning of free and compulsory education in 1839 until the present day, have served as a strong acculturative force, leading students to understand, accept, and uphold the values of the dominant group. Formal education in the nineteenth century existed clearly for the purposes of Christian instruction and colonization. During the Danish period teachers were recruited first from Europe and later from Antigua, where there was a renowned teachers' college, or from the ranks of the native West Indian elite. Whether European or West Indian, teachers pressed their charges to adhere to the values of respectability.

Following its purchase of the Virgin Islands in 1917, the United States moved quickly to staff the schools with American teachers in a deliberate effort to Americanize the students. The first American director of education stated this goal quite explicitly in his annual report to the Governor:

> The value of the American teacher cannot be overstated. They possess a command of the English language and American ideals and standards that are very useful in the classroom. One of the objects of the public school is to make the pupils good prospective Americans. No one can do this better than the American teacher. (cited in Varlack, 1974:74)

As under Danish rule, the purpose of the schools remained one of acculturation to the standards of the ruling power. Within the lower classes, however, few children remained in school beyond the primary years.

The School-Adaptation Patterns of Crucian Students

Elsewhere I have discussed the influence of reputation and respectability on the school performance of Crucian students, showing how the two cultural systems were pitted against one another (Gibson, 1982). For Crucian adolescent males of lower-class background, the impact was severe. To gain respect and status within the reputation system, boys were obliged to reject or defy the values and behaviors required within the respectability system. Girls felt no similar pressure. Acceptable girl behavior coincided to a very great degree with acceptable school behavior.

Girls

Whether at home or at school, parents, boys and girls all expected girls to be "good," and girls earned respect by catering to these expectations. Not all girls conformed with school rules and regulations, but those who defied teacher authority usually did so discreetly. At the junior high I observed girls mimicking their teachers, but they were careful to do so when the teachers were not looking. Similarly, they ate in class—an infraction of school rules—but usually made sure the teacher did not care or would not see them. Even deliberate demonstrations of disrespect, such as putting on fingernail polish during class, tended not to be disruptive of the lesson.

Most girls enjoyed school. It provided an opportunity to socialize with friends. Most also saw schooling as instrumental to their goal of self-reliance. "The ideal woman," according to one junior high girl, was one "who is dependent on herself and does not depend on her man to support her always." A high school diploma, the girls believed, would help them get a job, preferably a government job, and thus the economic security they desired.

Pregnancy was the major reason Crucian and Down Islander girls dropped out of school, but, after the birth of her baby, a girl might reenroll or attend night school in order to complete requirements for a high school diploma. Even girls who were doing poorly academically persisted in school beyond the mandatory school attendance age of sixteen. In view of the Crucian boys, girls received their diplomas "for never being absent."

Junior high teachers readily admitted that students who attended regularly and were well-behaved were "never flunked." On the other hand, students who were truant or unruly were first assigned to the "slower" sections, as was the case with the large majority of the Crucian boys, and, if the unacceptable behavior persisted, retained in the same grade for another year. Few Crucian boys ever progressed through the system without repeating one or, as was often the case, more grades. Most boys left school or were "kicked out" when they turned sixteen.[9]

Boys

Just as girls were expected to be "good," boys were expected to be "bad," which meant challenging the standards of respectability. One young man explained:

Boys earn status by doing the silliest things. [They say] "He bad, mon. He goin' on bad" [which is to say good], because he broke the rules, or beat up a bigger boy, or played his radio, broke a window or lit a brush fire.

Other boys made similar statements.

No parents wanted their sons to get in trouble, or to drop out of school, but at the same time most Crucians with sons in public school appeared resigned to this eventuality. "Boys all come to ruination," one Crucian man explained. His son, like many Crucian teenage males in the mid-1970s, had been expelled from school. "A man earns a reputation," another explained, "by his ability to lead others, no matter the direction." Crucian boys, as they reached adolescence, felt pressure to prove their manliness.

Until their upper elementary years, most boys were willing to go along with the standards set forth by the public schools, but, from about fifth grade on, they began openly to challenge the system. By junior high their defiance of school rules became increasingly blatant. During any class period, on any school day, one could see boys who were supposed to be in class sitting outside reading comics, chatting with friends or playing ball. Less apparent were those behind the gym or on the roof gambling, drinking, smoking and, when occasion arose, teasing girls. Boys also wandered through the campus with radios blaring, threw rocks at the metal walls of the temporary classrooms and shouted obscenities at those who sought to discipline them. "You can't tell me what to do," they would assert. All these actions, although decried by school authorities, earned a boy status with other boys and also with girls.

Boys, especially those who had been assigned to the slowest sections, created disturbances inside class as well. These boys lacked discipline, their teachers explained:

> They can't sit still; they come and go during class as they please. They put their feet on the desks and refuse to remove them when asked. When questioned about an assignment they say, "I lose my book, I lose my pencil, or I finish," when in fact they haven't begun.

Classroom observation supported the teachers' descriptions.

Teachers at all levels, not only at the junior high, commented specifically on how difficult it was to motivate the boys. Some teachers, both Crucian and continental, especially the younger and less experienced ones, noted, too, that the boys deliberately harassed them. One high school teacher, a white continental, reported that if he inquired about homework, boys would reply: "That slavery, Mr. B," or "Slavery done, mon." If he asked them to help with some task, like moving the desks or chairs, the boys would say, "No suh, me'n carry dem chair. Me stay here. Me wanta learn." According to my teacher-informants, students also said directly that teachers were not their parents and, therefore, could not tell them what to do. To avoid hassles with their students and, quite likely with their parents as well, many teachers, particularly the continentals, shied away from disciplining unruly students.

"Playing White"

Within Crucian society those who make demands or criticize another's behavior are viewed as "playing white" and assuming a position of dominance (see Green, 1972:185). One woman, herself a member of the Crucian elite, explained: "You simply don't criticize. You don't tell someone what to do. You mustn't be direct or it might appear you are giving orders." Although this woman was referring to work situations and relationships between adults, the same rule applied to classroom situations. Since students might interpret any direct request as a demand or criticism, prompting some boy to remind the teacher that "slavery's done," many teachers, Crucian as well as continental, men as well as women, found it extremely difficult to cope. Some teachers, especially the Crucians, in an effort to bring unruly students into line, would resort to sarcasm and ridicule. In return, the boys became more disruptive or withdrawn, some simply refusing to attend the classes of those teachers who had embarrassed them in front of their peers.

Crucian boys appeared to equate acquiescence to school authority with the persistence of slavery and the domination of poor blacks by the ruling elite, be they white or black. They saw those who gave instructions as assuming an unwarranted and unacceptable position of power. Teachers who tried to assert their authority in a direct fashion, particularly if they were outsiders and thus had no status within the community, frequently had a great deal of trouble with classroom discipline.

By way of contrast, some of the most effective teachers were those who made requests indirectly and who avoided all comments that might be viewed as criticism of a students' behavior, dress or academic shortcomings. I observed in one English classroom where boys in the "worst" section of seventh grade attended class regularly and competed for a chance to read aloud, however haltingly. Most of these boys were seriously handicapped in basic academic skills and many went only infrequently to their other classes. The teacher, a young white continental woman with graduate training in linguistics, had gained the boys' respect by her nonjudgmental approach and her readiness to provide the boys with the help they knew they needed.

Crucian parents were quick to admit that their sons had "bad tempers" and that they hung around with a "bad crowd." In their view, however, the basic cause of their sons' educational difficulties lay not with the boys' behavior, but with the schools' response to them. "I know my son's not perfect," one Crucian woman explained, "but it doesn't matter what he does, they say he's wrong." This woman, whom I shall call Mrs. Brown, believed both race and social class played a hand in her son's troubles. "We're just poor black people [who live in the] ghetto," she said. Mrs. Brown accused Crucian school officials of deliberately discriminating against her boys because of "who they were" and because she herself had dared to stand up to school administrators. Mrs. Brown had four sons, all of whom had run afoul of school authorities (see Gibson, 1982:17–18). In sharp contrast, her daughters were all proceeding through the system with little apparent difficulty.

Boys in the Top Sections

The peer pressure to misbehave was strongest in the slower sections of the junior high. In top sections students did what was necessary to meet academic requirements. Teachers described students in the top sections as working "on grade level" and "ready for high school math and English." Classroom observation revealed a positive learning environment, good rapport between teachers and students and a fast pace of instruction. Boys would come late to class but not too late. They would crack jokes but without disrupting the lesson. Like their peers in the slower sections, these boys felt the pressure to challenge their teachers and the values of respectability.

Boys who conformed to school demands did so at the risk of being ridiculed by friends or even cut off entirely from their peer group. Those who were always neat and well-mannered, who did their homework and who never challenged their teachers were viewed with suspicion. Top students had either to disguise their academic effort or to find other means to gain and maintain peer respect. One Crucian teacher explained:

> Boys in the top sections will answer me back in front of their peers from lower sections, out in the hallway, to show they're not goody-goodies. Or they'll say to others, "I didn't do my homework," when in fact they have. Or they'll curse in front of teachers who get upset by it. They'll curse in front of the door to the classroom.

Cursing was a sure way to get a rise out of certain teachers. I also observed Crucian boys in the top sections pulling out their shirttails and donning hats as they entered the classes of teachers who were most disturbed by such infractions of the school dress code.

Not all Crucian boys openly resisted school authority or confronted the system. A few managed to earn a reputation and maintain their place within their peer group by being quick with words, a good athlete or a talented musician. The large majority found it necessary, however, both in a school setting and outside, to demonstrate their opposition to the dominant group and its institutions.

As they entered their teens, most boys also found more to interest them outside of school than in. Going fishing, playing ball or just hanging around with one's friends, what the boys called "liming," seemed far preferable to regular school attendance. Those who persisted in school worried that they were missing out on the action.

A Sense of Oppression

The Crucian boys saw less connection than the Crucian girls or the Down Islanders between schooling and work. Some assumed that they would be able to obtain government employment with no more than eight or nine years of formal education, like their fathers and older brothers had, based on family connections and their own reputations. During the decade prior to fieldwork, a time of economic expansion, almost all Crucian men had jobs and their average rate of pay exceeded that of most other population subgroups. Public school teachers and principals recalled boys in the 1960s asserting, "I don't need an education 'cause I can get a government job with a big title and earn more money than you do as a college graduate." Students of all ethnic groups concurred, moreover, that the best jobs went to Crucians because "people look out more for they own" and because "they are from here and have the preference."

Crucian girls, nonetheless, persisted with their education because they believed a high school diploma would help them secure office positions, preferably with the local government. Most boys of lower-class background, on the other hand, if they followed in the footsteps of their fathers and older brothers, expected to find blue-collar positions, preferably with the government, in which they could acquire skills and training on the job and for which there was no educational prerequisite.

At the time of fieldwork, however, unemployment was on the rise, anti-American and anti-white attitudes were becoming more prevalent and many Crucian boys felt uncertain about their future.[10] During the 1940s and 1950s, when there had been a shortage of jobs locally, many Crucians had migrated to the U.S. mainland and the number of Crucians in New York, I was told, equaled the number in St. Croix. By the mid-1970s, few Crucian boys saw migration as a desirable option. They wanted to stay at home, and they resented the fact that their island's economy was increasingly controlled by outsiders. Government jobs, moreover, were growing scarce and most

Crucian boys were unwilling to take low-level, nongovernment jobs where continentals or Down Islanders would boss them around. In addition, many if not most of these boys were antagonistic toward white Americans. Some (how many was unclear) consciously thought of themselves as oppressed.

The growing appeal of the Rastafarian movement in St. Croix in the mid-1970s seemed related to the boys' sense that they had little chance within the system to control their own futures.[11] To my inquiry about the Rastas, one Crucian junior high student responded, "They say a man should have the right to guide his own life and not have to do what the government or some white man tells you." When I asked why the boys dropped out of school, students responded: "They're Rastas and aren't supposed to go to school." Rastas, I was told, viewed the educational system as an instrument of their oppression. I am unclear to what degree the boys who were still attending school were being guided by Rastafarian principles and beliefs.

One Crucian, a woman who assisted with the student interviews and who characterized the American presence in St. Croix as having caused "a lot of trouble," described the Crucian boys as "hopelessly lost." They were, she explained, unable to see a place for themselves within the system. Another noted that the boys felt like they were in a police state: "They can't walk down the street without their shirts or the police harass them. If they wear their hair like Rastamen, police hassle them."

Other Crucian adults noted that the boys refused to accept work they viewed as demeaning. Yet most available jobs fell into this category. Some boys said quite openly that they would rather steal than take jobs requiring physical labor, "slave work," as they called it. Whites, they pointed out, had gotten rich off the labor of their ancestors and, in stealing, they were only taking back what was rightfully theirs.

Most white residents of the Virgin Islands were, in comparative terms, economically well off. The median income for resident white families in 1979 was double that of black families ($21,066 versus $10,824), and many far-wealthier white continentals had vacation homes in the Virgin Islands, visited the islands as tourists or owned local businesses.

A rising crime rate was symptomatic of the larger problems. By the mid-1970s most families, black and white alike, kept a watch dog. Bars on doors and windows were increasingly common while only a few years earlier, I was told, people had never even locked their doors. Many of the crimes were committed by young unemployed Crucian men and teenage boys.

The School-Adaptation Patterns of Down Islander Students

Crucian students readily admitted that noncitizens were more successful in school than natives. Their explanations: Down Islanders "come here to make the best of it" and "grab all that comes to them." Crucians noted, too, that Down Islander parents were "stricter" and that Down Islander youngsters studied more and were better behaved. Their good behavior, students observed, influenced their relationship with their teachers.

Although Crucian adults, including at least some teachers, stated straight out that they disliked "aliens" and resented their growing presence, these attitudes seem not to have been a predominant force in shaping teacher-student relationships. Some students, both Down Islander and Crucian, commented that teachers in fact appeared to prefer noncitizens to Crucians and Puerto Ricans.[12] As one Crucian male explained it, this was because teachers could get "aliens" to do whatever they said—"kiss their asses." Teachers, my young informant noted, tried to do the same with Crucians but could not "get away with it." Crucians, he observed, stood up for "their rights."

Classroom observation suggested that teachers did in fact prefer students who were willing to do what was requested of them, but this is hardly surprising. What is more interesting is that Down Islander boys were more likely than Crucian boys to be placed in the top sections and less likely than Crucian boys to come into open conflict with Crucian teachers. This was the case even though some native teachers expressed quite openly their belief that "aliens" were overage, underprepared and ruining the schools.

Although Down Islanders did comparatively well in school, they were by no means immune to the impact of Crucian hostility. Many Down Islander youths reported that native students had picked on them when they first arrived in St. Croix, called them names and told them to "go back" to their own islands. One young man described his reception at school as follows:

They teased me, destroyed my belongings. Students never liked
me. Crucians tease and fight new students. Crucians don't like
aliens. If we know more than them, they try to beat us up.

Another Down Islander described how Crucian boys had told
immigration officials he was an illegal, just to see him run. His papers
in fact were in order, but he was frightened by the situation. Many
Down Islander youths noted that they felt "unwelcome." Most tried to
steer clear of those who hassled them.

Immigrant Status, Gender and School Performance

In class status, color and cultural background Down Islanders
differed little from the mass of the Crucian population. All were black.
All were poor. Like their Crucian hosts, moreover, Down Islanders
shared a history of slavery and colonization. Back in their homelands
they, too, had been exposed to the opposing values of respectability and
reputation. The social networks and lifestyles of Down Islander men
closely resembled those of the native-born Crucians (see Green, 1972).

The major factor that distinguished Down Islanders from
Crucians was their status as voluntary immigrants. Unlike the Crucians,
who had been forced to accept American domination over their island
homeland, the Down Islanders had sought out residence in the United
States Virgin Islands as a strategy for improving their economic
situation. Most had migrated to St. Croix because they could not find
work in their countries of origin. In Antigua, for example, the
unemployment rate for 1973 was 40 percent; in St. Croix it was less
than 6 percent (Neumann, 1970:148; *Daily News*, 8 June, 1974). Hotel
maids in Antigua were then earning only $11 a week but likely
considered themselves fortunate to have any income at all. By way of
contrast, an unskilled construction worker in St. Croix during the early
to mid-1970s earned as much as $4.50 an hour plus overtime. These
same jobs the Crucian boys described as "slave work." It mattered little
to Down Islanders that they were required to work long hours under the
hot sun or that their continental employers overlooked traditional
Virgin Islands holidays. They saw in St. Croix a chance to get ahead
economically.

Down Islanders found employment opportunities readily
available in St. Croix during the 1960s and early 1970s because

Crucians, for the most part, had jobs. Those Crucians who were not part of the waged work force either were not looking for employment as was the case with quite a few of the women or refused low-status and frequently temporary positions connected with tourism and heavy industry. Crucians preferred government positions, which they viewed as high status even though such positions frequently paid less well than those connected with heavy industry. Most Crucians also resented the idea of working for white employers, especially in jobs requiring physical labor or service to tourists.[13]

Table 3. Parents' Place of Employment by Ethnic Identity, 1974–75

| | Crucian | | Down Islander | |
	Men (n=42) %	Women* (n=53) %	Men (n=19) %	Women* (n=22) %
Local Government	79	70	--	36
Business and Industry	12	28	89	59
Self Employed	9	2	11	5

Source: Compiled from interviews with Crucian and Down Islander students and former students, St. Croix, U.S. Virgin Islands.

*Omits mothers not in labor force.

Government service, according to some local informants, had become a new form of welfare for native Virgin Islanders. More than half of all wage earners born in the Virgin Islands were employed by the territorial government (U.S. Bureau of the Census, 1985), and among those in the thirty-five to fifty-five age bracket the percentage was substantially higher. Nearly 80 percent of the Crucian young people whom I interviewed reported that their fathers had government jobs of one sort or another (see Table 3). Close to 70 percent reported that their mothers worked outside the home and, of these, nearly 70 percent had government jobs. In sharp contrast, almost none of the Down Islander fathers were employed by the Virgin Islands government. Among those mothers who were—approximately one in three—most held unskilled positions.[14] Substantially more Crucians than Down Islanders, moreover, had jobs that may be classified as "white collar" (see Table 4). The 1980 census reports similar disparities between the employment levels of natives and immigrants (U.S. Bureau of the Census, 1985).

Table 4. Parents' Type of Employment by Ethnic Identity, 1974–75

| | Crucian | | Down Islander | |
	Men (n=44) %	Women* (n=52) %	Men (n=26) %	Women* (n=26) %
White Collar	39	31	23	8
Blue Collar	61	69	77	92

Source: Compiled from interviews with Crucian and Down Islander students and former students, St. Croix, U.S. Virgin Islands.

*Omits mothers not in labor force.

Like many other immigrant groups (see Ogbu, 1983; Gibson, 1988), the Down Islanders viewed social and economic hardships encountered in the new country from a distinctly different perspective than the native-born population. They were more willing than the Crucians to work hard in low-status and oftentimes low-paying jobs and to shrug off prejudice and discrimination so long as they were not barred entirely from moving ahead economically. As newcomers, they were able more readily than native-born Crucians to operate outside the host country's stratification system. They compared their status not to whites and native elites but to those left behind in their countries of origin. They knew, moreover, that they could always return home or, if lucky enough to have permanent U.S. residence papers, move to the American mainland. They were far less likely than Crucians to view white Americans as their exploiters.

Many of the same factors that contributed to the Down Islanders' economic industriousness and their sense of relative satisfaction with life in St. Croix seem also to have contributed to their children's academic diligence and persistence. In school Down Islanders worked hard, abided by the rules and were guided by a belief that they were getting ahead. They appeared to view schooling as instrumental to their future success, rather than, as in the case of native-born males, an instrument of their oppression and a threat to their identity. Down Islander young people assumed that natives would receive preference in the job market, but this only confirmed their belief in the importance of educational credentials. As aliens they had to be better prepared in order to compete successfully with natives. Moreover, if they, along with their parents, were forced to leave the Virgin Islands, they wished to do so with high school diplomas in hand.

Although raised in societies in many respects similar to St. Croix, where lower-class blacks were subordinated by native elites and white Europeans, the Down Islanders had experienced no direct history of exploitation at the hands of white Americans. Unlike the Crucians, they were not caught up in a struggle to protect their homeland from ongoing American colonization. By moving from one West Indian society to another, the Down Islanders also appeared to have freed themselves, to some degree at least, from their oppositional relationship with the ruling classes.

In school Down Islander boys were far more willing than Crucian boys to accept the authority of their teachers, be they Crucians or continentals. They did not feel that they had to defy school rules or resist formal instruction as a symbol of standing up for their rights. Nor did they appear to be as drawn to the Rastafarian movement and its messages of resistance.

Down Islander youths were also more comfortable with white teachers than were the Crucian students. One indication of this came from students' responses to a forced choice question on teacher preferences. Crucian young people, girls as well as boys, were quite clear in their preference for black teachers. Had they been in charge of hiring, they would have recruited white continentals last, after Crucians, Puerto Ricans, black continentals and West Indians from other islands, in that order. Down Islanders, on the other hand, would have hired black continentals and teachers from Down Island first, then white continentals, followed by Crucians and Puerto Ricans (Gibson, 1976). It was Crucian boys, moreover, not Down Islander boys, who depicted manual labor as slave work and who refused to follow teachers' instructions or requests because "slavery was done."

Conclusion

In their review of research on race, class and gender in education Carl Grant and Christine Sleeter note that the literature "tells us little about how and when the integration of these status groups is important. Race, social class, and gender tend to be examined separately" (1986). This leads, Grant and Sleeter suggest, to an oversimplification of the analysis of student performance and, in the end, may weaken efforts to improve educational opportunities. I agree.

The St. Croix case provides an unusual opportunity to analyze the influence on school performance of immigrant status and gender in a public school setting in which all students are black and from lower socioeconomic class backgrounds. What we have found is that the immigrant group, taken as a whole, performs better than the native group and that girls, on the whole, perform better than boys. Differences between the two sets of girls were minimal, while differences between the immigrant and nonimmigrant boys were substantial.

The study helps to illustrate how an oppositional identity and culture can serve as a major barrier to success in school for minority youths.[15] It has shown, too, that black males experience more difficulties in accommodating themselves to school rules for success than black females. Likewise, indigenous minorities and other minority groups that have been incorporated into a society involuntarily appear to experience more difficulties in school than immigrant minorities.[16]

Social-class background also has bearing in the present case although its impact varied among the student subgroups. Native males of lower-class background were more constrained in school by a culture of resistance and opposition than their middle-class counterparts. In the private schools, I was told, Crucian boys performed no less well than other student subgroups. As members of the Crucian elite, these boys quite likely did not feel the same pressures to challenge the values of respectability. Many lower-class Crucian males, on the other hand, beginning in their late elementary school years, felt compelled to resist school authority. Their resistance symbolized their opposition to the continued exploitation of poor blacks by native elites and white continentals. These differing school-adaptation patterns of elite and lower-class Crucian males merit further examination.

Immigrant lower-class males, although equally exploited both in St. Croix and back in their homelands, exhibited a distinctly different response to school authority than their Crucian male counterparts. Likewise, the Crucian and Down Islander females, although discriminated against in the job market for their gender as well as their color and class background, persisted in school because they saw formal education as instrumental to their goal of economic self-sufficiency.

Research in Other Settings

Research in the mainland United States suggests that the St. Croix findings may have applicability among American blacks, where females are more likely to persist in school than males and where middle-class blacks meet with more success in school than lower-class blacks. There is also some evidence to suggest that West Indian immigrants to the continental United States are more successful in school than native blacks (Fordham, 1984). It appears, moreover, that West Indians settled in America are more successful in school than the West Indians who have settled in Britain (Foner, 1983; Swann, 1985). In general, however, the school-adaptation patterns of West Indian Americans have received little attention in the social science literature, and there is a clear need for further comparative research in this area.

In Great Britain, considerably more attention has been given to the school performance of West Indian youths (Rampton, 1981; Swann, 1985; Taylor, 1983; Tomlinson, 1983a). As a group, West Indian students in Britain, most of whom are now second generation, do less well in school than either white, majority-group peers or students of South Asian origin. Although West Indians migrated to England from their homelands in the Caribbean in much the same way that they migrated to the American Virgin Islands and to the continental United States, their geographic relocation, in the British case, did not free them from their historical relationship with their white British colonizers. They went expecting a new beginning, but they found themselves instead placed in a subordinate position by the same dominant group that had once enslaved their ancestors. The situation of West Indians in Britain appears thus to be more similar to that of an involuntary minority group, such as blacks in the United States or Crucians in St. Croix, than to other voluntary immigrant groups (Gibson, 1988).

Many West Indian adolescents in Britain today, much like the Crucian males discussed here, feel that in order to survive they must resist white authority both within the schools and in the larger society (Mullard, 1982:131; see also Brake, 1980; Troyna, 1978). In his research on secondary school students Barry Troyna found that not all black youths became absorbed into a peer subculture of resistance, but he suggests that those who did well academically felt that they had to disassociate themselves from their black identity and from peers in the lower academic tracks. Those in the lower tracks, like Crucian males, were alienated from the larger society and were drawn to the teachings of the Rastas.

British research on West Indians indicates, in addition, clear differences in the academic performance, school persistence, and overall in-school behavior of males and females. In general, the West Indian females are more successful in school than West Indian males (Driver, 1977, 1980; Fuller, 1980; ILEA, 1987; Little, Mabey and Whitaker, 1968; Tomlinson, 1983b; see also Taylor, 1983:220–21; Tomlinson, 1983a:41). The girls see schooling as the way to obtain better jobs than their mothers have. Although frequently critical of the schools, they nonetheless do what they must to get ahead academically (Fuller, 1980). As Mary Fuller's work makes clear, however, for these girls school success is not viewed as acting white. Nor does it imply deemphasizing of their black identity.

Research in Jamaica also points to gender differences in school performance. Describing education during the 1940s, Eric Williams (1973) observes that "from every point of view, whether it be that of literacy, attendance, or the duration of study, the figures for females are higher than those for males." Christopher Bagley (1979) notes, moreover, that, as in the St. Croix case, Jamaican public school teachers appear to give preference to girls and that males of lower-class background are assigned in disproportionate numbers to the lower sections. Nancy Foner's work (1973) points, in addition, to different school-response patterns for Jamaican males and females: girls persist in school to obtain the credentials that boys find irrelevant to their own employment expectations.

Research in the Bahamas indicates a similar lack of congruence between educational achievement and economic opportunity for males. During the 1960s and early 1970s males with little formal education held high paying jobs in both the government and service sectors.

Females, on the other hand, as in St. Croix, found it necessary to stay on in school in order to obtain low-level white-collar jobs (Brown, 1978:47–48).

Immigrant vs. Nonimmigrant Minorities

There is increasing evidence in the United States and abroad that immigrant minorities persist in school longer and, once initial language handicaps are overcome, meet with a greater degree of academic success than nonimmigrant or involuntary minorities (see Ogbu, 1978, 1983; Gibson, 1987a, 1987b).[17] As explanation for these differences recent ethnographic research in the United States points to distinctly different perceptions of status and patterns of adaptation among immigrant and nonimmigrant minorities (Gibson, 1988; Matute-Bianchi, 1986; Ogbu and Matute-Bianchi, 1986; Suarez-Orozco, 1989; see also other case studies in this volume). The different perceptions and adaptations appear to be related less to the cultural attributes of the individual minority groups or the current structure of American society than to the particular historical context of contact between minority and majority, the minority's ongoing experience of subordination, and its perceptions of the opportunities available.

This West Indian case provides further evidence of the importance of the historical context of contact between the dominant and subordinate groups and its impact on group perceptions of opportunity. More importantly, it points to a complex and dynamic interaction among the students' multiple statuses, including gender and class as well as race and ethnicity. We have a great deal more to learn about how these several statuses interact to promote and impede educational achievement.

Notes

1. This chapter is based on a reanalysis of data gathered in 1974–75 (Gibson, 1976, 1982, 1983).
2. On the whole, Puerto Ricans attending the public schools did poorly academically. Puerto Rican females, while more successful in school than

Puerto Rican and Crucian males, were less successful than immigrant West Indian students, male or female, and less successful than Crucian females (Gibson, 1976, 1982). Fieldwork in the private schools was beyond the scope of my study.

3. The migration of Puerto Ricans to St. Croix began in the late 1920s after U.S. immigration laws restricted the flow of seasonal workers from the British West Indians. No longer able to import cheap alien labor, estate owners turned to Puerto Rico, which, like St. Croix, was an American dependency. The small Puerto Rican island of Vieques, having an even more depressed economy than St. Croix, provided a ready answer to St. Croix's need for cane cutters. Following the decline of agriculture, many Puerto Ricans took up jobs in food merchandising and, by the mid-1940s, Puerto Ricans had gained control over this important sector of St. Croix's economy (Senior, 1947).

4. One-third of all black families residing in St. Croix in 1979 had incomes below the poverty line and, in the west end of the island—the area where I carried out school and community observation—the percentage rose to 45 percent (U.S. Bureau of the Census, 1984).

5. The 1980 Census of Population in the Virgin Islands shows that of all black persons with income those born in the Virgin Islands had a median income of $7,458, compared to $6,351 for those born in Puerto Rico and $6,533 for those born in the West Indies. In all three groups males earned more than females (U.S. Bureau of the Census, 1985, Table 90).

6. These findings are drawn from analysis of school records for all 273 students who were enrolled in seventh grade at West End Junior High School (a pseudonym) during the 1973–74 school year. I also followed the students' progress in school during the following year.

7. I left St. Croix at the end of the 1974–75 school year but, with the assistance of a high school guidance counselor, was able to learn which students had returned to school the following fall. Several missing cases were omitted from the present analysis but were included in an earlier analysis that tracked students through April 1975 (Gibson, 1982).

8. Both the parents and teachers of private school students reported that discipline in the private schools was strict, attendance good and dropout rates low.

9. Only 12 percent of the Crucian boys in the longitudinal study, compared with 65 percent of the Crucian girls, reached tenth grade without ever being retained. These findings, drawn from school records and student interviews, include retentions from grade one onwards. No comparable data for Down Islanders were available because most had not begun their schooling in St. Croix.

10. In the U.S. Virgin Islands in 1970, more than 80 percent of black males ages twenty to twenty-four were employed. By 1980, this rate had fallen to 60 percent even though few young men of this age group were still attending

school. Employment rates for black women were lower than for black men—only 47 percent of those ages twenty to twenty-four were employed in 1980, but this was consistent with the 1970 employment rate for women of this age group (U.S. Bureau of the Census, 1973, 1984).

11. The Rastafarian movement was just surfacing in St. Croix in the mid-1970s and, to my knowledge, had not been studied. For accounts of the Rastafarian movement in Jamaica at about the same time, see Barrett (1977) and Nettleford (1970). See also Ernest Cashmore's discussion of the Rastas in England and their views of the English educational system (1979:75ff).

12. I am unclear if students were referring to the attitudes of Crucian teachers as much as continental, because their reference was to "teachers" in general.

13. 1970 census data for St. Croix indicate that more than 90 percent of all males and more than 50 percent of all females between the ages of twenty-two and forty-four were in the labor force (U.S. Bureau of the Census, 1973). These data are misleading in the case of women because very different patterns of employment existed between the Puerto Ricans, on the one hand, and the Crucians and Down Islanders on the other. I found, for example, that among mothers of public school students and former students only 35 percent of the Puerto Rican women were employed, compared with 71 percent of the Crucian women and 72 percent of the Down Islander women.

14. Information on parents' place and type of employment comes from interviews with students and former students.

15. See Ogbu (1987a, 1987b and this volume) for a discussion of collective oppositional identity and the school performance of nonimmigrant minorities in the United States.

16. Following Ogbu, I use the term *involuntary minority* to refer to those groups that have been incorporated into a society by colonization, conquest, annexation or slavery (Ogbu, 1987b). An *immigrant minority*, according to my usage, refers not only to the first generation—those who are actual immigrants—but also to a group whose ancestors settled by choice in a new country and which continues to maintain a separate minority-group identity.

17. *Nonimmigrant minority* in my usage refers not simply to those who are native-born but to those groups that have been incorporated into the host society involuntarily.

References

Bagley, C. 1979. "A Comparative Perspective on the Education of Black Children in Britain." *Comparative Education* 15(1):63–81.

Barrett, L.E. 1977. *The Rastafarians: The Dreadlocks of Jamaica.* London: Heinemann.

Brake, M. 1980. *The Sociology of Youth Culture and Youth Subcultures.* London: Routledge and Kegan Paul.

Bramson, L. 1969. "An Ethnic Census of St. Croix Schools." Appendix to "A Plan for Higher Education on St. Croix," R.O. Cornett. Unpublished manuscript. College of the Virgin Islands, St. Croix, U.S. Virgin Islands.

Brown, R. 1978. "Problems in Educational Development in the Bahamas." In *Perspectives in West Indian Education*, ed. Norma A. Niles and Trevor Gardner. East Lansing, Mich.: West Indian Association, Michigan State University.

Cashmore, E. 1979. *Rastaman: The Rastafarian Movement in England.* London: Unwin Paperbacks.

Daily News, 8 June 1974, 3 Feb. 1975.

Dirks, R. 1975. "Ethnicity and Ethnic Group Relations in the British Virgin Islands." In *The New Ethnicity*, ed. J.W. Bennett, pp. 95–109. St. Paul: West Publishing Co.

Dookhan, I. 1974. *A History of the Virgin Islands of the United States.* Epping, Essex, England: Caribbean Universities Press for the College of the Virgin Islands.

Driver, G. 1977. "Cultural Competence, Social Power and School Achievement: West Indian Secondary School Pupils in the Midlands." *New Community* 5(4):353–59.

————. 1980. *Beyond Underachievement: Case Studies of English, West Indian and Asian School-leavers at Sixteen Plus.* London: Commission for Racial Equality.

Foner, N. 1973. *Status and Power in Rural Jamaica: A Study of Educational and Political Change.* New York: Teachers College Press.

————. 1983. "Jamaican Migrants: A Comparative Analysis of the New York and London Experience." Occasional Paper no. 36. New York University, Center for Latin American and Caribbean Studies.

Fordham, S. 1984. "Afro-Caribbean and Native Black American School Performance in Washington, D.C.: Learning to Be or Not to Be a Native." Unpublished manuscript. Department of Anthropology, American University, Washington, D.C.

Fuller, M. 1980. "Black Girls in a London Comprehensive School." In *Schooling for Women's Work*, ed. R. Deem, pp. 52–65. London: Routledge and Kegan Paul.

Gibson, M.A. 1976. "Ethnicity and Schooling: A Caribbean Case Study." Ph.D. diss. University of Pittsburgh.

———. 1982. "Reputation and Respectability: How Competing Cultural Systems Affect Students' Performance in School." *Anthropology and Education Quarterly* 13(1):3–27.

———. 1983. "Ethnicity and Schooling: West Indian Immigrants in the United States Virgin Islands." *Ethnic Groups* 5(3):173–98.

———. 1987a. "Playing by the Rules." In *Education and Cultural Process* (Second Edition), ed. G.D. Spindler, pp. 274–81. Prospect Heights, Ill.: Waveland Press.

———. 1987b. "The School Performance of Immigrant Minorities: A Comparative View." In *Explaining the School Performance of Minority Students*, ed. E. Jacob and C. Jordan. Special Issue, *Anthropology and Education Quarterly* 18(4):262–75.

———. 1988. *Accommodation without Assimilation: Sikh Immigrants in an American High School*. Ithaca, N.Y.: Cornell University Press.

Grant, C.A., and C.E. Sleeter. 1986. "Race, Class, and Gender in Education Research: An Argument for Integrative Analysis." *Review of Educational Research* 56(2):195–211.

Green, J.W. 1972. "Social Networks in St. Croix, United States Virgin Islands." Ph.D. diss. University of Washington.

Hill, V.A., Sr. 1971. *Rise to Recognition: An Account of Virgin Islanders from Slavery to Self-Government*. St. Thomas, V.I. (n.p.)

Inner London Education Authority. 1987. "Ethnic Background and Examination Results: 1985 and 1986." Report P 7078, prepared by ILEA Research and Statistics, 1 July, London.

Lewis, G.K. 1972. *The Virgin Islands*. Evanston: Northwestern University Press.

Lewisohn, F. 1970. *St. Croix Under Seven Flags*. Hollywood, Fla.: Dukane Press.

Little, A., C. Mabey and G. Whitaker. 1968. "The Education of Immigrant Pupils in Inner London Primary Schools." *Race* 9(4):439–52.

Matute-Bianchi, M.E. 1986. "Ethnic Identities and Patterns of School Success and Failure among Mexican-Descent and Japanese American Students in a California High School." *American Journal of Education* 95(1):233–55.

Mullard, C. 1982. "Multiracial Education in Britain: From Assimilation to Cultural Pluralism." In *Race, Migration and Schooling*, ed. J. Tierney, pp. 120–33. London: Holt, Rinehart and Winston.

Nettleford, R. 1970. *Mirror, Mirror: Identity, Race and Protest in Jamaica.* Kingston: Sangster and Collins.

Neumann, B. 1970. "The Economy of the U. S. Virgin Islands: Some Basic Aspects." In *Virgin Islands: America's Caribbean Outpost,* ed. J.A. Bough and R.C. Macridis. Wakefield, Mass.: Walter F. Williams Publishing Co.

Ogbu, J.U. 1978. *Minority Education and Caste.* New York: Academic Press.

————. 1983. "Minority Status and Schooling in Plural Societies." *Comparative Education Review* 27(2):168–90.

————. 1987a. "Variability in Minority Responses to Schooling: Nonimmigrants Vs. Immigrants." In *Interpretive Ethnography of Education: At Home and Abroad,* ed. G. and L. Spindler, pp. 255–78. Hillsdale, N.J.: Lawrence Erlbaum.

————. 1987b. "Variability in Minority School Performance: A Problem in Search of an Explanation." *Anthropology and Education Quarterly* 18(4):312–34.

Ogbu, J.U., and M.E. Matute-Bianchi. 1986. "Understanding Sociocultural Factors: Knowledge, Identity, and School Adjustment." In *Beyond Language: Social and Cultural Factors in Schooling Language Minority Students,* pp. 73–142. Sacramento, Calif.: California State Department of Education, Bilingual Education Office.

Olney, J.L. 1974. "Interpersonal Relationships within Peer Groups in a Virgin Islands School." Unpublished manuscript. College of the Virgin Islands, St. Croix.

Patterson, O. 1975. "Context and Choice in Ethnic Allegiance: A Theoretical Framework and Caribbean Case Study." In *Ethnicity: Theory and Experience,* ed. N. Glazer and D. Moynihan, pp. 305–49. Cambridge, Mass.: Harvard University Press.

Rampton Report. 1981. *West Indian Children in Our Schools.* Interim Report of the Committee of Inquiry into the Education of Children from Ethnic Minority Groups. Cmnd. 8273. London: Her Majesty's Stationery Office.

Senior, C. 1947. "The Puerto Rican Migrant in St. Croix." Unpublished manuscript. Social Science Research Center, University of Puerto Rico.

Social, Educational Research and Development, Inc. 1969. "A Profile and Plans for the Temporary Alien Worker Problem in the U.S. Virgin Islands." Report to the Office of Economic Opportunity, Washington, D.C.

Suarez-Orozco, M.M. 1989. *Central American Refugees and U.S. High Schools.* Stanford: Stanford University Press.

Swann Report. 1985. *Education for All.* Report of the Committee of Inquiry into the Education of Children from Ethnic Minority Groups. Cmnd. 9453. London: Her Majesty's Stationery Office.

Taylor, M. 1983. *Caught Between: A Review of Research into the Education of Pupils of West Indian Origin.* Windsor: NFER-Nelson (first published 1981).

Tomlinson, S. 1983a. *Ethnic Minorities in British Schools.* London: Heinemann.

———. 1983b. "Black Women in Higher Education: Case Studies of University Women in Britain." In *Race, Class, and Education,* ed. S. Walker and L. Barton, pp. 66–80. London: Croom Helm.

Troyna, B. 1978. "Differential Commitment to Ethnic Identity by Black Youths in Britain." *New Community* 7(3):406–14.

U.S. Bureau of the Census. 1973. *1970 Census of Population.* Vol. 1: *Characteristics of the Population,* pt. 55, Outlying Areas, Virgin Islands. Washington, D.C.

———. 1984. *1980 Census of Population.* Vol. 1: *Characteristics of the Population,* chap. C: General Social and Economic Characteristics, pt. 55, Virgin Islands of the United States. Washington, D.C.

———. 1985. *1980 Census of Population.* Vol. 1: *Characteristics of the Population,* chap. D: Detailed Population Characteristics, pt. 55, Virgin Islands of the United States. Washington, D.C.

U.S. Department of the Interior. 1976. "Annual Report of the U.S. Government Comptroller for the Virgin Islands on the Government of the Virgin Islands," Fiscal Year Ended June 30, 1975. St. Thomas.

Varlack, P.I. 1974. "Teacher Education in the Virgin Islands: A Strategy for Curriculum Design." Ph.D. diss. University of Pittsburgh.

Virgin Islands Department of Education. n.d. "Public School Professional Personnel Report, 1973–74." St. Thomas.

Williams, E. 1973. "Education in the British West Indies." In *Consequences of Class and Color,* ed. D. Lowenthal and L. Comitas. Garden City, N.Y.: Anchor Books, 1973.

Wilson, P.J. 1973. *Crab Antics: The Social Anthropology of English-Speaking Negro Societies of the Caribbean.* New Haven: Yale University Press.

Chapter Seven
Situational Ethnicity and Patterns of School Performance among Immigrant and Nonimmigrant Mexican-Descent Students

Maria Eugenia Matute-Bianchi
University of California, Santa Cruz

Introduction

Persistent school failure among large numbers of Mexican-descent students and other Hispanic groups in the United States is a pervasive, well-documented and enduring problem (The Achievement Council, 1984; Arias, 1986; Brown et al., 1980; California Postsecondary Education Commission [CPEC], 1982; Carter, 1970; Carter and Segura, 1979; Coleman, 1966; Ogbu, 1974, 1978; Ogbu and Matute-Bianchi, 1986; U.S. Commission on Civil Rights, 1971). The majority of Hispanic students have suffered and continue to suffer the negative consequences of unsuccessful schooling experiences. As a group, these children participate less and do less well academically than any other group in the Southwest except for Native Americans, with indications of a widening achievement gap between these students and other groups in school (The Achievement Council, 1984).

The history of Mexican-descent students in California schools has been one of segregation and inequality, thus frustrating the achievement of economic and social advancement (Cameron, 1976;

Wollenberg, 1976). Many Mexican-descent children continue to attend segregated schools throughout the state, indicating that little progress has been made in integrating these students with more advantaged Anglo students in the public schools (Orfield, 1986). The descriptions of their schooling experiences, both from historical and contemporary perspectives, show clearly that many Mexican-descent students continue to perform less well in school than majority group students despite various intervention efforts to improve their academic achievement. Hence, the cycle of unsuccessful schooling continues for this group—a group which is now the fastest-growing school-age population in California and which is projected to become the state's largest ethnic group, representing almost 30 percent of the population by the year 2000 (Assembly Office of Research, 1986).

Despite the enduring cycle of disproportionate school failure among the Mexican-descent population, there is now evidence to suggest that not all of these students are unsuccessful in school (Matute-Bianchi, 1986; Ogbu, 1974; Romo, 1984; Valverde, 1987). My fieldwork in a California community, which has focused on variations in school performance patterns among Mexican-descent high school students, points to a relationship between academic performance and students' perceptions of ethnic identities (Matute-Bianchi, 1986). I found that more recent Mexican immigrants, as well as the descendants of Mexican immigrants who maintain a separate identity as *Mexicanos* within the context of their experiences in the United States, tend to perform relatively well in school and in many cases outperform nonimmigrant *Chicano* students. The emerging documentation of intragroup variability in patterns of school performance among Mexican-descent students requires that we define the group more precisely, describe more accurately the range of cultural orientations and intragroup variations and examine critically the traditional single-cause explanations of the underachievement of Mexican-descent students in U.S. schools. The analysis I present here is an attempt to contribute to these efforts.

As researchers have begun to examine the large Mexican-descent population in the United States, taking into account the context of historical and economic developments in both Mexico and the United States, the context of continuing immigration and the impact of subordination, discrimination and limited opportunity structures in the evolution of adaptive strategies that different groups of Mexican-descent persons have made to life in the United States, they have found and have begun to describe differences in a very heterogeneous population (Baca and Bryan, 1980; Bowman, 1981; Browning and de la Garza, 1986; Dinerman, 1982; Keefe and Padilla, 1987; Mines, 1981; Portes and Bach, 1985; Rios-Bustamante, 1981). The function of ethnic identity, for example, among different groups of Mexican-descent people in the United States suggests that there are different meanings for ethnic categories in different social settings for different individuals. As a result, we can observe variations in forms of ethnic identification and consciousness among various groups of Mexican-descent people in the United States: *Mexicanos, Mexican Americans, Pochos, Chicanos, Cholos, Low Riders, Homeboys,* etc. The emphasis on one ethnic category versus another, therefore, is best understood as an adaptive strategy; the specific ethnic label serves as a cognitive resource developed in an interactive response that is strategically exploited and manipulated within specific contexts as the various groups compete for scarce resources (material and/or social) within a system of structured inequality. These ethnic categories, which may change over time and be used for different purposes, are emblematic and have meaning both for members of the group and for analysts of situational contexts in which ethnicity emerges as a salient category. My particular interest in the study presented here is the different forms and functions of ethnic labels and identificational consciousness between immigrant Mexicanos and nonimmigrant Mexican-descent student groups in the United States and their relationship to variations in observed patterns of school performance.

The distinctions between immigrant and nonimmigrant Mexican people in the United States are complex and multifaceted. Yet it has only been relatively recently that researchers have begun to recognize these two groups as distinct communities in the United States or to describe the continuum of adaptive strategies and accommodations various subgroups within these communities have developed in response to the situations they find themselves in here. The earlier literature on Mexican-descent people, whether from assimilationist or ethnic-resistance perspectives, assumed an intragroup homogeneity and a cultural continuum of social, religious, linguistic and political values. Nonimmigrant Chicanos and other Mexican Americans were viewed as heirs or somewhat distant relatives of a Mexican heritage; immigrant Mexicanos were seen as bearers of the Mexican culture, a source of cultural replenishment for the Mexican-descent population in the United States (Bowman, 1981; Browning and de la Garza, 1986; Rodriguez and Nunez, 1986). The continuum was described in cultural terms with Mexican and American end-points. Distinctions within the group were described broadly in terms of relative placement along a linear acculturation/nonacculturation dimension, frequently obscuring more important historical and structural antecedents that shaped attitudinal and behavioral distinctions between the two groups, as well as leaving unexamined the different social, economic and cultural conditions of their experiences in the United States and differences in the manipulation of various ethnic labels as adaptive strategies of accommodations.

John Ogbu and I have proposed a theoretical framework for understanding the differences between immigrant Mexicanos and nonimmigrant Mexican Americans and Chicanos in terms of: (1) differences in minority status, (2) differences in the process of incorporation into the United States, and (3) differences in perceptions of and responses to the experiences of discrimination, limited opportunities and subordination in a system of structured inequality (Ogbu, 1978; Ogbu and Matute-Bianchi, 1986).

While more conventional theories of school performance explain differences between immigrant and nonimmigrant Mexican-descent students in terms of levels of acculturation and assimilation of American culture versus retention of Mexican cultural content, we have proposed an alternative interpretation (Ogbu, 1978, 1982, 1983; Ogbu and Matute-Bianchi, 1986). In our view, what distinguishes the two groups, in general, is their perception of their economic position in the United States as a subordinate, stigmatized minority and their responses to the legitimating, racist ideologies directed against them. Both immigrant Mexicanos and nonimmigrant persons of Mexican descent (Mexican Americans and Chicanos) are victims of instrumental and expressive exploitation, but they manifest different perceptions, interpretations and responses to such exploitation. The immigrant and nonimmigrant groups also utilize different strategies to respond to the barriers to assimilation and mobility. With respect to education, the response of many nonimmigrants has been to deemphasize striving for academic achievement as an essential component of their efforts to succeed. Many immigrant Mexicanos, on the other hand, see academic success and school credentials as very important elements in their strategies to improve their employment status and access to material benefits (see Ogbu and Matute-Bianchi, 1986:79–98).

Many earlier studies of Mexican-descent students in U.S. schools noted the persistence of "traditional" Mexican cultural traits and identified such traits as impeding the educational progress of these students. Intervention strategies designed to improve the educational performance of Mexican American children (e.g., Americanization and English-language training) assumed that greater knowledge of English and American cultural values would lead to more positive experiences in school. In fact, even the more recent federal Bilingual Education Act in 1968 was premised on the single-cause explanation of limited proficiency in speaking English as the primary cause of school failure among Mexican-descent students, thus obscuring the reality that many of these children are U.S.-born English speakers. These studies and the educational policies they generated assumed that virtually all persons of Mexican descent in the United States were relatively recent immigrants who lacked sufficient knowledge of the English language and the American culture. The academic progress of Mexican-descent students was perceived to be linked to higher levels of acculturation to the American mainstream and to fluency in English. The reality, of course, is that many people of Mexican descent have been in the United States for several generations, are fluent English speakers and are thoroughly familiar with the values and lifestyle of the American mainstream, yet continue to experience disproportionate school failure. The earlier literature also emphasized the school failure of Mexican-descent students and did not address the fact that some, albeit proportionately fewer, Mexican-descent students have succeeded in school.

The Mexican-descent population is, indeed, a heterogeneous one, and there are distinct subgroups within the population, manifesting different experiences and different adaptations and strategies to life in the United States. For example, Chicanos have developed a distinct ethnic consciousness which is neither Mexican nor American. It is an identity system in opposition to the American mainstream and has served as a strategic tool of resistance to the systemic exploitation, both instrumental and expressive, that people of Mexican descent have experienced in the United States. Others, as Browning and de la Garza (1986) note, have had different experiences during different periods in U.S. history, with some members achieving greater success and mobility than others, and with some becoming more integrated into

U.S. society than others. As a result, there are class differences, differences in cultural orientation and differences in ethnic identification and consciousness, as well as differences between immigrants and nonimmigrants in this large and growing population.

Variability in Patterns of School Achievement among Mexican-Descent Students: A Community Study

The analysis which follows draws upon my fieldwork in a largely agricultural community in the California central coast area, carried out between 1983 and 1985. It focuses on the differences between successful immigrant Mexicano students and unsuccessful nonimmigrant Chicano students at a high school that will be referred to here as Field High School. The study describes very diverse, distinctive social groups of Mexican-descent students within a single school, and it indicates differences in these students' expectations regarding the value of formal education in their adult lives, their self-definitions, and their perceptions of success and failure, as well as differences in the way the students are perceived by the school community. I interviewed a sub-sample of 35 Mexican-descent students over a two-year period to assess their aspirations for the future, their perceptions of their adult future, their knowledge of adult occupations, their understanding of strategies to achieve adult success, their definitions of adult success and failure and their perceptions of the value of schooling in achieving their expressed goals. I identified a range of ethnic identities and behaviors associated with several patterns of school performance among Mexican-descent students and found five major categories within which most of these students could be placed: (1) recent Mexican immigrants, (2) Mexican-oriented, (3) Mexican American, (4) Chicano and (5) Cholo.

In the analysis here, I highlight the pattern of school success I observed among immigrant Mexican-oriented students and the pattern of school failure among nonimmigrant Chicanos. I discuss these patterns within the context of differences in students' perceptions of their adult futures and differences in staff perceptions of these two groups of Mexican-descent students in the school. My analysis also indicates that the students in the Mexican American category do not fit neatly into either the immigrant or nonimmigrant ethnic identificational system. What this finding suggests raises important new research questions and policy considerations.

The Community's Historical and Structural Legacy

The historical and structural forces contextualizing this study have left the community with a legacy of paternalistic patterns of interaction between an Anglo majority and the Mexican minority, dating back to the 1848 annexation of California by the United States. Between 1848 and 1955 the region was transformed from a pastoral *Californio/Mexicano* cattle-raising economy to a predominantly Anglo-American farming community specializing in the production of apples, strawberries, berries and lettuce. The development of large-scale agriculture in the area has always depended on cheap immigrant labor, beginning with Chinese laborers in the 1860s, followed by Japanese workers at the turn of the century and later by Filipino workers in the 1920s. Although Mexicans have always been used as a source of exploitable agricultural labor in the area, they did not begin to settle permanently in the area until after World War II and the development of the Bracero Program. In this postwar period, technological changes in agricultural production created a demand for more Mexican labor to satisfy the region's expansion into one of the richest agricultural regions in California.

Although they made up a relatively small, ignored minority in the region prior to 1946, Mexican people have always been a presence in the community, albeit as a stigmatized subordinate group. With the transformation from the pastoral *Californio/Mexicano* society to a predominantly Anglo-American agricultural economy dependent on a racial division of labor, the social hierarchy was transformed into one in which Mexicans and subsequent nonwhite immigrant laborers were relegated to subordinate positions within all the major institutions in the community. The transformation provided a paternalistic context of interethnic social relations, with Anglo Americans dominating successive influxes of nonwhite immigrant labor.

During this early period there were few significant differences between Mexican-origin residents and the occasional migrant Mexican in search of seasonal work. In 1900, the Mexican-descent population comprised only 118 persons, or 3.3 percent of a total community population of 3,528; by 1940, the Mexican-descent population had increased to 757 persons or 8.4 percent out of a total community of 8,937 (Donato, 1987:40). A review of city directories from this period indicates very few businesses owned by Mexican-descent people, a lack that can be viewed as a result of both their sparse numbers and a discriminatory opportunity structure. In 1930, there were no Spanish-surnamed graduates of the community's one high school, Field High School; by 1940, out of a total of 202 graduates, only three were Spanish-surname (Donato, 1987:54). By all indications, the Mexican-origin population in this region between 1900 and World War II was an invisible minority, excluded from virtually all aspects of the Anglo American society.

It was not until well after World War II and the beginning of the Bracero Program that the Mexican-descent population began to grow rapidly in the area. By the 1960s the increasing population of Mexican-descent people began to develop some internal differentiation among those who were long-term residents and those who were relative newcomers (Takash, 1988). By the late 1960s, there was a phenomenal increase in the Mexican-descent population, and the community's stable pattern of paternalistic interethnic relations began to change. Not only was the Mexican presence greater, but the community found it was not immune to the larger social and political influences of the Civil Rights Movement, with its mobilization of ethnic consciousness and the ensuing controversies over desegregation, bilingual education, equal educational opportunity and affirmative action. This once quiet, conservative Anglo American farming community entered the decade of the seventies as a community of turmoil and interethnic tension.

The schools, in particular, have been a focus of continuing conflict for the past two decades, serving as a focal point of heated school/community controversies, as well as reflecting an emerging agenda for change among an increasingly more vocal Mexican American leadership. During this period, the conflicts have been heightened by periodic labor unrest in the agricultural fields, a bitter, protracted cannery strike and litigation against the city aimed at political enfranchisement of the Mexican-descent population in the community. The intensity of the conflicts has, of course, been stimulated by the dramatic increase in the Mexican-descent population in the schools as well as in the community as a whole. By 1980, the Mexican-descent student population represented the majority in 13 of the district's 24 schools and composed 51 percent of the community's population of 30,000. As the school district's proportion of Spanish-surnamed grew, their social and academic adjustment and development became a focus of great tension and debate. Issues of concern centered primarily on efforts to desegregate racially impacted schools and the development of bilingual education. The politics of this highly charged arena tended to obscure the differences between the immigrant and nonimmigrant Mexican-descent people in the community. The leadership which emerged on behalf of this population came from English-speaking Mexican-American and Chicano professionals, business people and activists (Donato, 1987).

The turmoil of the last 20 years of ethnic conflict in this community has been accompanied by a tremendous increase in the number of immigrant Mexicanos, both of legal and illegal status, seeking work in the fields or canneries. The Mexicanos tend to function in separate occupational contexts from nonimmigrant Chicanos and Mexican Americans who, if employed, are more likely to be found in blue-collar or semiskilled occupations. There is some indication that Mexicanos participate in separate social and organizational contexts, e.g., attending different masses at the same church and different dances in the community and congregating in different parks and plazas. Additionally, there is now a small but very visible Mexican-descent middle class in the community, represented by a few merchants, professionals, salaried white-collar workers and school district employees (administrators and teachers). Such internal differentiation within the community's Mexican-descent population reflects differences between immigrants and nonimmigrants in terms of both social and structural contexts in which they operate, as well as social class differences within the nonimmigrant group. Although there is now a small business and professional class within this population, the overwhelming majority are employed in low status, marginal jobs in agriculture and are stratified at the bottom of the employment structure, as indicated by the community's publicly employed labor force (see Table 1).

Table 1. Field Community Workforce Composition and Distribution, Full-time Employees, 1984

Job Category	Total Employees (n=232)	White %	Hispanic %	Asian American %	American Indian %
Officials and Administrators	11	100	0	0	0
Professionals	29	100	0	0	0
Technicians	21	76	10	14	0
Protective Services	41	73	17	10	0
Para-Professionals	9	77	11	11	0
Office and Clerical	41	78	15	7	0
Skilled Craft	43	65	28	5	2
Service/ Maintenance	37	43	49	8	0

Source: Equal Employment Opportunity Commission, State and Local Government Information (EEO-4), Community of Field.

These differences represent a complexity in the social context which defies easy description. On the one hand, there are observable differences between the various groups in terms of behavior (dress, language, self-presentation, etc.) and attitudes; on the other hand, there is a sense of collective peoplehood as members of a generic Mexican "family." This presumed bond of kinship is often invoked during times of intense controversy over such issues as local elections, immigration, bilingual education and litigation strategies against the city or school district. Hence, my impression is that the bonding agent in this community among the Mexican-descent people is their sense of sharing a common stigma as a low-status subordinate minority group. There are times when the bonding is more palpable and other times, more diffuse.

Categories of Mexican-Descent Students

There is a generic category of "Mexican" within Field High School and it is this category which is accorded lower status than Filipino Americans and Japanese Americans, the other obvious minority student groups in the school. Mexican-descent students are particularly sensitive to the negative perceptions of and stereotypes attributed to people of Mexican descent. While students recognize that not everyone holds pejorative views of Mexican people and culture, it is generally accepted that people of Mexican descent face discrimination, prejudice and other difficulties in much greater proportion than other groups in the school and community.

Despite membership in the low-status "Mexican" ranking in the school, not all students of Mexican descent are perceived to be the same. The ethnographic data indicate that many persons within the school community differentiate among the Mexican-descent clientele in the school and in the community, reflecting the great variability and cultural heterogeneity within the group. The five-category typology which I use below to describe the modal characteristics within the heterogenous "Mexican" student enrollment at Field High emerged from interviews with teachers, counselors, administrators, teacher aides and Mexican-descent students, as well as observations of classes and school functions.

Recent Mexican Immigrant

"Recent" immigrant, according to my usage, means one who has arrived within the last three to five years. Students in this category are also identified as "*recien llegados,*" "Mexican nationals," "citizens of Mexico," "Mexicanos" and "*mojados.*" These students identify themselves as Mexicanos and refer to Mexico as home. They are Spanish-speaking, Mexican-born and are frequently identified as L.E.P. (Limited English Proficient) by the school, according to diagnostic English placement tests. These students are identified by other Mexican-descent students and by some teachers and school staff as dressing differently from the rest of the student body and their clothing style is considered unstylish by other students. Recent immigrants frequently cite economic opportunity as the reason for their having come to the United States. Some have come here legally, others illegally. Some have established a relatively permanent base in the community and do not migrate seasonally back to Mexico.

Students within this group make distinctions among themselves, using the class-based reference framework of Mexico (e.g., rural versus urban, upper class versus working class, *mestizo* versus *indio*). Students in this immigrant Mexican category vary in their level of proficiency in Spanish. Some are functioning below grade level in Spanish, perhaps at the fourth- or fifth-grade level. These students are usually placed in a special curriculum which includes beginning E.S.L. (English as a Second Language). Students functioning approximately at grade level in Spanish are typically enrolled in one or two E.S.L. classes, bilingual math, bilingual science, and in beginning English reading. Among these recent immigrants, those who are relatively proficient in Spanish (both oral and written) tend to be more academically successful than those who are functioning well below grade level in Spanish. Hence, proficiency in their primary language appears to be related to their subsequent academic experience in the school. Many of these more proficient students have successfully completed *primaria* (grammar school) and in some cases, have entered the precollegiate curriculum of the *secundaria* or the *preparatoria* in Mexico.

Mexican-Oriented

Students in the second category are also self-identified as "Mexicanos," but they are distinct from the first group in several obvious ways. Most of the students in this group, which I have labeled "Mexican-oriented," tend to be bilingual. Because they have received most of their schooling in the United States, they are more likely than recent immigrants to be adept in carrying on academic work in English-only classes. They use English and Spanish interchangeably with their peers but speak English exclusively with most of the school personnel. Typically, these students are identified as F.E.P. (Fluent English Proficient) and speak Spanish in the home and in other community contexts. Many of the fluent English speakers in this group are found in the general or remedial classes but not in the E.S.L. or beginning reading courses. Many of the Spanish-surname students in the college prep track in the school are from this Mexican-oriented category. The most active and visible Mexican-descent students in the school are in this category, especially those active in the leadership of *Sociedad Bilingue*, considered to be the most active club of Mexican-descent students in the school. Their parents are Mexican-born immigrants, typically from the Mexican states of Jalisco, Michoacan, Guanajuato and San Luis Potosi.

Students in this group maintain a strong identity as Mexicanos although many have lived most of their lives in this country. They see themselves as being different from the recent Mexican immigrant, Mexican-American, Chicano and Cholo groups in the school. They usually cite pride in their Mexican heritage as a primary difference between themselves and the more *"agabachados"* (Americanized) students of Mexican descent in the school. They do not identify themselves as Mexican Americans or as Chicanos or Cholos. They view the ethnic labels Chicano and Cholo as derogatory and would not use them as self-descriptors; these labels are viewed as symbols of gang membership and a host of offensive qualities. Frequently, these students are Mexican born and have lived in the United States for at least five years, and usually longer. They have attended junior high and elementary school here, although some may have attended the first year or two of *primaria* in Mexico. Their manner of self-presentation, especially style of clothing and language usage, is considered more "American," but is not what is considered "quaddie" or "preppie" at the school.

Mexican American

Students in the "Mexican American" group are almost always U.S.-born English speakers. Students in this category can be further subdivided into various groupings: (a) some are Mexican in last name only, are very acculturated and do not manifest any of the overt ethnic symbols associated with other Mexican-descent students; (b) others, while acknowledging their Mexican parentage, see themselves as having moved away from a more traditional Mexican culture and as now being members of a contemporary, more advantaged American present; and (c) still others in the group can be labeled "cultural codeswitchers" or "cultural switch-hitters" for they function as Mexicanos at home and Anglos at school. As a category, the Mexican Americans are much more American-oriented than either of the two previously described student categories. They are likely to be described by the school personnel as "totally acculturated." They often do not speak Spanish well or, even if they do, prefer to speak in English at school. There is a range of oral Spanish-language proficiency within this group, depending on the extent to which the student must use Spanish in the home and community context.

Students in this category see differences between themselves and the recent Mexican immigrant and the Mexican-oriented students, as well as between themselves and the Chicano and Cholo groups. They view the label Chicano as an offensive one and consider it to be synonymous with other low-status labels, such as Cholo and Low Rider. Some of the active, most esteemed Mexican-descent students in the school can be identified as members of this category. They tend to participate more in the mainstream school clubs and activities than either of the Mexican-immigrant student groups do. They are members of clubs and activity efforts in which whites and Japanese American students participate. For the most part, they do not participate in the organizations and activities which are considered more Mexican, such as the *Sociedad Bilingue* or more Chicano such as M.A.T.A. (Mexican Americans Taking Action). With the exception of the "switch-hitters" in this category, the Mexican Americans appear more ambivalent, more uncommitted to ethnic labels than students in the other categories. They tend not to call attention to themselves in ethnically explicit ways observed among other groups of students. Additionally, they are not explicitly immigrant or nonimmigrant (as these terms are defined in this book), manifesting neither modal orientation.

Chicano

The term "Chicano" has been selected to differentiate another subgroup of Mexican-descent students from the above three categories. However, it must be understood that the term Chicano in this school community is not salient, nor does it carry the political connotations of the term as it is used in university settings or academic discourse. The term as it is used in this analysis serves to differentiate among the distinct groupings of Mexican-descent students in the school population. These students are typically English-speaking and are usually at least the second generation of their family in the United States. The Chicano category comprises students who are among the most alienated Mexican-descent students in the school. They tend not to participate in school activities, exhibit poor attendance and performance in class and are usually described by teachers and staff as being unsuccessful or uninterested in school. Not all students who could be considered members of this subgroup are unsuccessful students, but many of the Mexican-descent students who are considered to be unsuccessful by school-defined criteria emerge from this subgroup.

When asked, these students will first identify themselves as Mexican or Mexicano, but they do not find the term Chicano offensive or derogatory. Often they will call themselves "homeboys" or "homegirls." Academically successful Mexican-descent students— those who attend classes regularly, participate in mainstream activities and who generally conform to school expectations for academic achievement—they call "schoolboys" and "schoolgirls," especially those from the Mexican American category. These terms are used derisively. Another term used by Chicano students to ridicule the "schoolboys" and "schoolgirls" is "Wannabe," which is understood as meaning "wants to be white" or "wants to be Anglo." "Wannabe" was frequently used to describe Mexican-descent girls who dated Anglo boys or who associated almost exclusively with an Anglo peer group.

Many teachers describe these students as being more concerned with loyalty to the Chicano group and displaying an attitude and behavioral orientation that indicates apathy or outright defiance of the school culture. If Chicano students are active in any club or organization, it is the M.A.T.A. club, but club membership is small and the level of activity minimal. Students in this group may try to do well in school and often declare a desire to do well in school, but they behave in ways that are counterproductive to academic achievement: their characteristics include frequent absences, disruptive behavior, failure to bring books to class and to do homework and failure to pass enough classes each year to maintain their academic standing.

Cholo

The "Cholo" subgroup is by far the smallest of the five categories of Mexican-descent students at Field High School (almost to the point of disappearing from the school community at the time I conducted fieldwork), but it is the most distinguishable because of certain obvious stylistic cultural symbols which are readily identifiable to the entire school community. Particular kinds of pants, shirts, shoes, make-up styles and ways of walking are identified as distinctly Cholo. Visually, this particular style of dress stands out in the school community and identifies the wearer as Cholo/Chola. Students who affect the stylistic symbols of this category are frequently identified by others as "gang-oriented," "gang-bangers" or "gang-sympathizers." Not all students who manifest the sartorial symbols of the Cholo are members of gangs, but because they affect the Cholo style they are usually considered to be sympathetic to Cholos. The manner of the Cholo style is a distinct symbol of an identity which is definitely not "Mexican" or "American." Cholos are also often called "Low Riders," which is another term used to describe Mexican-descent youth who drive distinctively styled cars. Low Riders are not necessarily gang members or gang-affiliated, but are generally perceived as such by others. Chicanos and Cholos are held in low esteem by the other Mexican-descent students in the school, as well as by mainstream students, who often express fear or contempt of what they recognize as Cholo.

Differences among these categories of Mexican-descent students are sometimes quite explicit, as is the case between recently arrived Mexican immigrants and Mexican Americans, or blurred, as between Chicanos and Cholos. Additionally, within each group there are further refinements which can be discerned. However, in general, these five major groupings are the most obvious within which the majority of Mexican-descent students in this school can be placed.

School Failure among Mexican-Descent Students

There has been a virtual shift over a 13-year period in the relative proportions of white and Spanish-surname students enrolled at Field High School. In 1971, the Spanish-surname enrollment was 34 percent of the total school. By 1984, it composed 57 percent of the total. The white enrollment in 1971 was 60 percent and by 1984 it was reduced to 33 percent.

During this period of rapid increase in the Spanish-surname population, the proportion of students entering the ninth grade from one of the district's local junior high schools who were reading substantially below grade level increased. School documents reporting the reading levels of all entering ninth grade students from 1976 to 1982 indicate that 34 percent were reading at the sixth-grade level or below. In 1982, the percentage of students reading at the sixth-grade level or below had jumped to 50 percent of those entering as freshmen. While these data are not identified by ethnicity or language dominance, but rather as aggregate data for all students entering from the local feeder junior high schools in the district, it is important to remember that the school district and high school were both experiencing large increases in Mexican-descent students.

Perhaps a clearer indication of the patterns of school failure is reflected in the attrition rate in the class of 1985. When the class entered Field High School in 1981, 386 students, or 60 percent of the class (n=643), were Spanish-surname. Four years later, 232 of the original 386 Spanish-surname students entering as freshmen were identified as dropouts, reflecting a 60 percent attrition rate.

An analysis of the dropouts by place of birth indicates that the majority (61 percent) were born in the United States and, within this group, that 78 percent were born in the local county or an adjacent one (see Table 2). Most of the dropouts, moreover, had entered Field High School from one of the local junior high schools (see Table 3).

Table 2. Field High School, Class of 1985: Non-Continuing Spanish-Surname Students by Place of Birth (n=232)

Born in Santa Cruz County	91
Born in adjacent county	20
Born in California	20
Born out of state	11
Born in Mexico	90

Another indication of school failure is found in the list of ninth grade demotions. Regularly enrolled ninth grade students in the school are expected to earn at least 40 credits by the beginning of their sophomore year to qualify for sophomore standing. If they fail to earn enough credits at the end of their ninth grade year, they are demoted in standing. Such students will consider themselves sophomores, but in order to earn the credits to graduate with their class, they will need to pass enough classes in the next three years, as well as make up the credits they failed to earn as ninth graders. Students can do this by attending summer school and, if need be, by going to adult school when they turn seventeen.

Table 3. Non-Continuing Spanish-Surname Students, Field High School, in the Class of 1985 (n=232)

Category	Number of Drops
Entered from local junior high	184
Entered from school outside district	20
Entered from local parochial school	6
Entered from Mexico	20
Other	2

The school does not keep official records on those students who are demoted at the end of their ninth grade year, but unofficial tallies of ninth grade students demoted at the end of their freshman year in June 1985 indicate that there were a total of 105 such students. As of September 1985, there were 80 Spanish-surname demotees (76 percent of all demotees) while Spanish-surname students made up less than 60 percent of the class. Such students can be considered "at risk" for noncontinuation. They will have already begun to manifest other behaviors associated with poor school performance such as frequent absenteeism and poor performance in class. Once this pattern has been established, many students find it difficult to develop and maintain more successful responses to the demands of schooling. Many of these ninth grade demotees are located in the Chicano category.

School Success among Mexican-Descent Students

Many students of Mexican descent at Field School are successful in meeting the demands of the school program. In fact, there is considerable evidence indicating that some Mexican-descent students are very successful in school. Mexican-descent students are enrolled in college preparatory courses, are active in school activities, earn above-average grades, maintain regular attendance and go on to college—all school-defined measures of success.

An examination of the 1983–84 class lists for college-preparatory English, mathematics and science reveals that Spanish-surname students are represented in this higher-track curriculum. Most of these students could be identified as either Mexican-oriented or Mexican American; virtually no Chicanos or Cholos were found in college-preparatory courses.

One of the best indications of success among Mexican-descent students, especially among the Mexican-oriented, is reflected in the class rankings compiled at the end of the senior year. An examination of these rankings for the years 1983, 1984 and 1985 reveals that Spanish-surname students are represented in the top 10 percent of their graduating classes. In 1983, the top 10 percent of the graduating class was made up of 38 students of whom 26 percent (n=10) were Spanish-surname. Of these ten students, seven were girls and three were boys. Although 26 percent underrepresents the proportion of Spanish-surname students in the class (which was more than 50 percent), it does indicate that a not-insignificant proportion of these students were academically successful in their four years at the school.

The class of 1984 had 375 students in the graduating class, of whom 53 percent (n=197) were Spanish-surname. This class had 37 students in the top 10 percent, of whom 35 percent (n=13) were Spanish-surname. Moreover, there were 83 students in the entire class with a grade point of 3.0 (an average of "B") or above. Of these latter students, 42 percent (n=32) were Spanish-surname. Once again, somewhat more than two-thirds of the high-achieving Spanish-surname students were female: 22 girls and 10 boys.

In the class of 1985, there were 377 students who received diplomas, of whom 57 percent (n=214) were Spanish-surname. The top 10 percent of the graduating class was composed of 37 students, of whom 43 percent (n=16) were Spanish-surname. Of these 16 Spanish-surname students, 81 percent (n=13) were girls and 19 percent (n=3) were boys.

An examination of the Spanish-surname students in the top 10 percent of the classes of 1984 and 1985 indicates that these students had been regularly enrolled in college-prep courses during their four years in the school, had good attendance, were active in school activities and had plans to attend college upon graduation. In fact, many of these students received substantial scholarships to attend leading four-year institutions of higher education. They were considered by their teachers and counselors to be hard working, conscientious, motivated students. Virtually all of these students identified themselves as Mexicanos and could be described as students in the Mexican-oriented category. A few others could be categorized as Mexican Americans.

The above data clearly indicate that the Mexican-oriented girls consistently were more conspicuous in the rankings of the top 10 percent in at least three of the most recent graduating classes. These same girls were the ones who provided most of the leadership in the *Sociedad Bilingue* and were among the most visible, active and esteemed Mexican-descent students in the school. This apparent pattern raises important gender implications which warrant more careful scrutiny in any future studies of this kind.

What is clear from the data presented thus far is that academic persistence and success are much more likely to be found among the immigrant Mexican-oriented students and that poor performance is more likely to be found among the nonimmigrant Chicano/Cholo groups. This is not to suggest that the patterns of success and failure are restricted to these groups. However, the data do indicate that variations in patterns of school success and failure reflect a continuum in the variations in ethnic identities observed among the Mexican-descent students in the school and that these variations are broadly reflective of the differences between immigrant versus nonimmigrant accommodations to the demands of schooling. The one group that does not fit easily into either of these two modal patterns of success or failure is the group I have described as Mexican Americans. This group will be discussed later in the context of the research and policy issues they raise.

Staff Perceptions of Mexican-Descent Students

The problem of poor performance among many Mexican-descent students is one that is generally recognized by teachers, counselors, administrators and staff. Perceptions of what accounts for the poor performance, which vary greatly among the school personnel, include: migrancy and frequent travels back and forth to Mexico during the school year, lack of parental support and interest in school, lack of successful role models, poor school habits and a peer culture which rejects school achievement.

Many adults in the school community also recognize the heterogeneity within the large Mexican-descent student clientele and acknowledge that some of the schools' most visibly successful students are of Mexican descent. Teachers may identify a Spanish-surname student as the recipient of a scholarship to a prestigious Ivy League college or cite the recent accomplishments of a Spanish-surname student elected to a student body office as examples of Mexican-descent students who have been successful in school.

Many teachers describe the differences they have observed among the Mexican-descent students in general terms, distinguishing between those students who are "more acculturated to American culture" and those who are less so. Others describe the differences in terms of those who have been in the United States longer and who speak more English. Only a few of the school personnel link up the strong, positive Mexicano identity with the academically successful Mexican-descent students, but most identify the unsuccessful Mexican-descent students in terms of their perceived Chicano or "anti-school" orientations.

In general, the stereotypic view of the "more Mexican" students is that they are more polite and respectful, more serious about school, more eager to please, more motivated and much less sophisticated in ways to undermine school rules and practices than are "more Americanized" Mexican-descent students, especially Chicano/Cholo students. When asked to describe the differences between students more oriented to Mexico and Mexican culture and Chicano students, for example, many adults described Chicano students as "less interested in school," "more irresponsible," "more smart-mouth," "more street tough," and "less motivated" than students they perceive to be "more Mexican." As one teacher with more than 20 years in the school said:

> The "more Mexican" students in the school, the ones who are active in the *Sociedad Bilingue*, for example, are high achievement-oriented. They take leadership roles in the school, they get good grades, they follow the school rules, they are law abiding. We now have so many students like this that it is no longer a surprise among the staff that Mexican students can succeed in school. The typical Chicano students, on the other hand, are associated in the school with a "school isn't important"

attitude. Doing well in school among this group is not encouraged. In fact, it is derogatory to [be viewed as doing] well in school. To do well would mean running the risk of being called a "schoolboy." Among Chicanos, loyalty to the group is high. And this is a problem that sometimes leads to gang involvement.

Sociedad Bilingue is generally recognized among the staff as being the preeminent "Mexican" organization on the campus, serving as the most visible organizational symbol of Mexican students' involvement in the school. The club is active throughout the year, raising funds for scholarships which the group awards at the end of the year to students going on to college, organizing dances, sponsoring cultural events such as Semana de la Raza during the Cinco de Mayo week in May and planning field trips to university campuses to encourage student interest in college. The school staff is divided on the importance of this club on the campus. Some view the club as promoting "too much" Mexican culture and being "too activist-oriented." They think it should, instead, be promoting "acculturation into the campus mainstream." Those who hold this view tend to express the belief that rapid acquisition of English and acculturation into the "American mainstream" are the most important vehicles for school success. They see Sociedad Bilingue as "maintaining cultural separatism" between Mexican students and the mainstream students in the school. Another criticism is that the club is "too disruptive of the academic program in the school" by encouraging students to be "too active in the club's activities and not [active] enough in their school work." A few see the club as providing a valuable resource and sense of belonging for the Mexican students in the school and express the wish that other clubs would function as actively for other groups in the school.

Sociedad Bilingue was founded in the late 1970s by a group of recent Mexican immigrant and Mexican-oriented students in the school who wanted an organization to bridge the apparent social distance between themselves and the Anglos in the school. Hence, the name Sociedad Bilingue was coined. Initial efforts were aimed at having both "Anglos" and "Mexicans" in the club. However, the club's membership has been virtually exclusively "Mexican" and the club's activities attract the Mexican-descent students, particularly the Mexican-oriented students in the school. The organization is viewed by the general student body as the club for the Mexican students.

A teacher with more than eight years at Field School indicated that there are now so many Mexican-descent students in the school that the staff has been "forced" to make distinctions among this growing student population. The general image of Mexican-descent students, according to this teacher, has changed from a distinctly negative one to one that is now more positive or at least more "ambivalent":

> When I first got here the image was one that was very electrically charged. Now it is more one of we have our good Mexicans and we've got our bad ones. It was a time of militancy when I got here [early 1970s] and now in the Reagan era ethnic groups are less militant. Also, the passing of fashion of the Cholo and Pachuco image here in the school makes the Mexican presence in general much less threatening. Also, we have had some very successful Mexican students here. This has forced people here to look more closely at this population.

Many of the more "Mexican" students are perceived by the staff to have difficulty in school. However, these troubles are perceived differently from the difficulties attributed to Chicano/Cholo students who are unsuccessful in school. The unsuccessful "more Mexican" students are perceived to have difficulty in school because they do not have satisfactory English-language skills and/or because they lack competence in academic skills in Spanish and English and because they are perceived to come from a rural peasant Mexican background which has not prepared them to meet the demands of schooling in the United States. Despite such difficulties in school, these students are frequently described by the staff as "shy but unfailingly courteous," "cheerful," "grateful for what you can do for them" and "well-behaved."

Chicano and Cholo students who are unsuccessful, on the other hand, are perceived to be unsuccessful because they lack the "motivation, interest and respect for schooling." They are perceived to fail in school because they reject what the school has to offer. They are also viewed as more "apathetic," "sullen," "withdrawn," "mistrusting" and "discourteous" in general than are the "more Mexican" students. They are likely to be described as coming from families unsupportive or uninterested in the academic success of their children. Successful Mexican-descent students, on the other hand, are described as hard-working, goal-oriented, respectful, active, conscientious students who come from supportive, intact families. These students are typically not described with reference to their identity as "Mexicanos." Some adults appear to be keenly sensitive to differences that Mexican-descent people in the school see in themselves—differences which are often too subtle to be noticed or are overlooked by many in the school. Other adults appear to be less aware of these differences or describe them in terms of a continuum of "less," "more" and "totally acculturated."

There are differences, then, in the perceptions school personnel have of students who are easily identified as immigrants (the recent Mexican immigrant and the Mexican-oriented) and those who can be identified as nonimmigrants (the Chicanos and Cholos). The differences are marked. It could be that the very behaviors which are rewarded among the more "Mexican" students are those which do not violate the cultural expectations of the mainstream of appropriate "Mexican" behavior. That is, the cultural expectation in the school is that the "more Mexican" students are obedient, respectful, timid and appreciative. Mexican-descent students manifesting these behaviors are positively acknowledged. Other behaviors, such as being outspoken, assertive, critical and aggressive—behaviors which are often esteemed in Anglo students—are not associated with these Mexican students. The same behaviors, however, could be applied to the more Chicano-oriented students but with a different interpretation. That is, common staff perceptions are that Chicanos are "smart-mouth" (outspoken), "discourteous" (critical) and "resistant" (assertive), etc. It very well could be that these descriptors of student behavior are related to staff perceptions of what is appropriate behavior for "successful" and "unsuccessful" low-status Mexican-descent students in the school. Mexican-descent students succeed in school because they conform to what is considered the culturally appropriate behavior of the "successful" Mexican student: obedient, appreciative and docile. Chicanos fail in school because they, too, conform to what is considered the culturally appropriate behavior for them: defiant, disobedient, rude and lazy. Interestingly, the failure of the Mexican immigrant or "more Mexican" student is perceived to be the result of factors essentially beyond the student's control (migrancy, rural background, poverty, etc.) while the failure of Chicano students is perceived to be the result of characteristics in the individual students themselves.

Another interesting aspect of some of the staff's perceptions of differences in Mexican-descent students is their emphasis on "less acculturated" versus "more acculturated." The staff makes no discernible linkages between the various forms of Mexican identity systems present in the school and the various patterns of school performance and participation found in the Mexican-descent students. These kinds of staff perceptions were much more common among those who were less knowledgeable and sensitive to the subtleties and nuances of the ethnic peer cultures in the school. Such perceptions could be associated with conventional interpretations linking academic success and social mobility to assimilation and the "melting pot" ideology. The contradiction to these conventional explanations presented by the obvious success of the bilingual students with a strong identity as Mexicanos was not readily apparent to teachers and staff members.

Differences in Perceptions of the Future among Successful and Unsuccessful Students

Successful Mexican-Oriented Students

The more successful Mexican-descent students tend to emerge from the Mexican-oriented category; they are achievement-oriented and goal-oriented, even if they lack a specific career goal. They want to be successful. Moreover, they see a definite connection between their experiences in high school and their success as adults. Virtually all of these students express an interest in going on to college, although some indicate that family circumstances (e.g., return to Mexico, financial difficulties) may make this difficult or impossible. Many of these students look to adults in the school—Anglo as well as Mexican descent—as role models of success. They recognize a practical value in meeting the demands of high school and manifest a marked sense of purpose in doing well in school. They know generally which are the "right" courses to take in order to go on to college; they know that it is important for them to be active in school activities in order to go on to college and they have a generalized understanding that what they do today will serve them well later on in life.

Many of these students were born in Mexico and received their earliest schooling there. Others were born in the United States but traveled frequently back and forth to Mexico, typically having an extended family network on both sides of the border. They had received virtually all of their schooling in the California Central Coast region incorporating the Pajaro Valley. All were the sons and daughters of agricultural workers, cannery workers or laborers in some kind of low-skilled occupation.

For the successful Mexican-descent students, adult success is often defined in terms of "having a nice car, a nice house, a nice job," and enough "money that you don't have to worry about it anymore." A few of the students expressed a definite occupational choice, such as interior designer, engineer or lawyer. But for the most part, the students were no more specific than expressing an interest in working in "a big company," "in a large corporation," "with something in computers," or "for a bank." One student, a senior going on to a University of California campus, said: "I guess I want to hold a job that pays at least $10 an hour, a job where I can make at least more than my brother [a computer assembly line worker]."

Another, also a twelfth grader, said: "I would like to have a very good job where I could get good money and meet new people, like working in a bank or as an accountant." Another senior said: "I don't know exactly what. Probably working for a big company, like the telephone company."

When asked about their purpose in going to school, the successful Mexican-descent students expressed a strong belief in the linkage between doing well in school and being a successful adult, in "being someone" and "earning good money." As one eleventh grader expressed it: "*Es una preparación que te esta llevando a pasos mas grandes* [It is a preparation which is taking you to greater things]."

These students definitely feel motivated to do well in school so that they can have what they perceive to be greater opportunities for higher-paying, more satisfying jobs than their parents. Another eleventh grader commented:

> My mother keeps telling me, "*Ai mi hija, tienes que sacar buenas calificaciones en la high school para que no te estes chingando igual que yo* [You have to earn good grades in high school so you won't have to struggle the way I had to]." And you know, she has a point. I don't want to be doing that. I've

been in the cannery before. Like taking things to my uncle who works there with my mother. Just being there I can tell I wouldn't want to work there. I don't like it. I've got to do well in school so that I don't have to face this in my future.

Despite the fact that these students are remarkably achievement-oriented in school, they do not know people with the jobs they would like to have as adults and they do not have extensive knowledge of these kinds of jobs. They may know "a friend" or "my cousin's friend" who works in a bank or they may have visited a computer firm, but in general, they lack intimate knowledge or experience with adults who have the types of higher-status jobs and occupations they aspire to. Nonetheless, these students express a definite belief in the linkage between doing well in school and succeeding in what they perceive to be more rewarding, higher-status adult occupations. And "doing well in school," according to these students, means attending classes regularly, doing the homework, asking teachers for help when they do not understand, trying as "hard as you can" and getting along well with your teachers.

Most, but not all, of these successful Mexican-descent students indicated that one reason for their success in school was their parents' interest and support. Family encouragement stemmed from a strong parental desire that their children achieve more than they had been able to here or in Mexico. Some of the girls, however, indicated that their parents had not been particularly supportive and that their encouragement to do well in school had come from teachers and counselors. These same girls indicated that their parents feared their going on to a university or college setting where they would live away from home. They also thought that their parents would probably move back to Mexico rather than have them begin postsecondary schooling in the United States, a fact which disturbed some of these girls. As one said, "I think the real reason why my parents don't want me going away to college is that they are afraid I might get pregnant or something. That plus they want me to work in the restaurant like my older sister. And that is something I don't want to do."

Many of these girls feel torn between wanting to conform to their parents' expectations, on the one hand, and their desire to chart a different course for themselves, on the other. This dilemma is a source of confusion and difficulty. They have long been accorded recognition and praise for their scholastic achievement and yet, as they approach an important step in their academic careers, they are expected to suspend or terminate postsecondary education in order to pursue the perceived gender-appropriate roles as obedient daughter, prospective wife and mother. These gender role conflicts among the successful Mexican-descent girls raise important research questions, especially as they relate to the postsecondary academic persistence of such students.

Unsuccessful Mexican-Descent Students

Unsuccessful Mexican-descent students are among the most visible on campus. Their manner of dress, walk and speech frequently identify them as Chicanos or Cholos. Moreover, they congregate in specific places on campus which are considered their "turf." Just as the mainstream "quaddie" students "hang out" in the area between the main administration building and the swimming pool, the Chicano and Cholo students are most often found congregating further away from the center of the campus. The students perceived to be more gang-oriented tend to be even more exclusive in their choice of where to "hang out" since certain areas are considered the exclusive province of one of the two major gangs in the community.

Another marker of the visibility of the Chicano and Cholo students is the fact that they are frequently visible roaming the campus after the class bell has rung. They walk across the street to a fast-food stand, meet friends in the faculty parking lot or just "hang out" in the corridors of remote hallways. They are also quite visible in the "study center," which is located in the cafeteria during each class period. This "study center" is reserved for students who are late to class and are thus prevented from entering, or who have been permanently ejected from a class and have no other class in which to reenroll. As the semester progresses, there are more and more students assigned permanently to the "study center." It is monitored each period by an "attendance specialist" who makes sure the students do not leave the room. Although students are asked to bring books and materials, they rest their heads on the table, as if asleep.

Chicano- and Cholo-oriented students are much more likely to be enrolled than other students in the high school's S.W.A.S. ("school within a school") program. This is an alternative program established for students considered to have attendance problems and/or an inability to function effectively in the regular school program. Classes in the program are shorter and the curriculum is less structured or rigorous than in the regular program, although students are required to participate in reading, writing and discussion exercises in class. Other courses are less traditional and, in some cases, perceived to be "much easier" than the regular curriculum. For example, during one grading period in a class containing all boys, the main activity consisted of assembling model cars, many of them in the Low Rider style. The program is considered to be one for students who are unsuccessful and in danger of dropping out of school. Students enrolled in the program are keenly aware of this school-wide perception and of their precarious, unesteemed position in the school community. Hence, the content and structure of the program appear to reinforce the students' marginality and alienation in the school community.

Interviews with unsuccessful Chicano students indicate that some express high-status career aspirations and that others have no definite plans once they leave high school. Initially, these students espouse the conventional notions about going to school to get "good jobs," but in successive interviews, it becomes clearer that most of them anticipate having continuing difficulties in school, express uncertainty about their future and doubt about their chances of graduating from school. One of the students, for example, expresses a commonly shared sentiment: "I would like to graduate but I don't know if I will."

Unsuccessful Chicano students present a decidedly different set of perceptions, experiences and accommodations than successful immigrant Mexicano students. The form and substance of much of their schooling appear to reinforce their marginality and alienation, thus heightening their sense of being "different" from the dominant group and from Mexicanos. They tend to be concentrated in either the general or low-track classes and are not particularly active in student activities. They are much less goal-oriented or goal-specific than the Mexicano students.

The parents of these students I talked with were employed in marginal occupations such as seasonal cannery work, laborers, gardeners or were unemployed. The unsuccessful Chicano students frequently talked about wanting to work in an office or in some occupation which is less physically demanding or "more interesting" than the work their parents, siblings or relatives are engaged in, yet they frequently did not know how one goes about getting a job as a medical secretary, a bank teller or a disk jockey. Or, they were misinformed about securing a job with such companies. For example, unsuccessful Chicano students expressed interest in leaving school early to get a job in a local computer firm. When I asked them, "Do you think it is possible to get a job with such a firm if a person has not graduated from high school or can't read above the sixth-grade level?," some students indicated that they believed a computer firm would teach the person the skills they would need for the job "if the company decided to hire you."

With respect to perceptions about jobs and career paths open to them, these Chicano students are not that much different from the successful Mexican-immigrant students in that they have limited exposure to these occupations and to the cultural knowledge about how to successfully pursue these careers. Their individual family members, as well as their community role models, are typically engaged in low-status occupations.

This society places little, if any, social value on the labor of field hands or cannery workers. Consequently, a parent who raises seven or eight children from his or her labor in these occupations is not viewed as a model of adult success as defined by society. Furthermore, these parents, and others like them who serve as role models, are not in a position materially or structurally to expose the students to worlds and alternatives which they themselves do not know. The structural connection here is an obvious one: the job ceiling experienced by students' parents and other adult community role models also serves to create a ceiling on experiences from which to expose, instruct or inspire these students about a more-advantaged adult opportunity structure and the alternatives within it.

Where the successful Mexican-immigrant students differ is that they and their parents continue to believe in the future value of educational credentials in securing more advantaged futures regardless of present circumstances. The parents of unsuccessful Chicano students, on the other hand, were typically unsuccessful in school themselves or were forced to quit school very early and very possibly do not see school as important in their lives or in the kinds of jobs they or their children are likely to get. Very often these students indicated that "it would be okay" with their parents if they dropped out of school before graduation.

Many of the unsuccessful students also noted that they did not know what kind of job their parents or family would like them to pursue nor had they discussed this with them. Again, this appears to be a difference between the unsuccessful Chicano students and the successful immigrant Mexicano students. The latter were usually able to give ready examples of discussions they had with their parents about their futures and the kinds of jobs and careers they aspired to. Differences in parental aspirations for their children, as well as family ideology about preparing for the future and one's place in it, appear to be significant in the messages that are communicated to unsuccessful Chicano students and successful immigrant Mexicano students. Although extensive interviews with parents were not a part of this initial study and the data I refer to here are impressionistic, I recognize its critical importance. I underscore here the need to collect much more extensive data in this domain.

All students in the sub-sample were asked to describe successful and unsuccessful adults and to elaborate on the reasons for becoming successful or unsuccessful. Many of the Chicano students could not describe a successful Mexican-descent adult whom they knew well. They were more likely to describe an Anglo teacher or youth counselor. Of, if they could describe a Mexican-descent adult whom they considered to be successful, the adult was engaged in activities which would not be valued or would be considered unsuccessful by others. For example, one Chicano tenth grader carefully described his uncle as a "successful adult." The uncle was a leader in Northside (a local gang) and he was "smart with money." He became successful because of "being on the streets" and "knowing what's happening." Another tenth grade student described his grandmother as a successful adult: "She used to own several restaurants and bars in town but she isn't here no more because they kept closing her places down because of the gangs and stuff."

When asked to explain how people become unsuccessful adults, Chicano students articulate a range of responses, indicating the extent to which they may have internalized conventional notions which link success and failure to individual efforts. Typical responses were: "They are lazy and dropped out of school"; "they got too much into partying and doing drugs"; and "they are just lazy and before they realize it, they have messed up too much to start going right." Responses also suggested the extent to which students perceive structural discrimination and limitations: "They work in the fields and they never went to school"; "they got a rotten education"; "Mexicans don't have a chance to go on to college and make something of themselves"; "people like us face a lot of prejudice because there are a lot of people who don't like Mexicans"; and "there aren't enough good jobs to go around." Whether indicative of a conventional ideological interpretation or a perception of structural determination of adult failure, it was much easier for these students to elaborate on and give details of strategies for failure than on strategies for success.

Among this group of students there is a pervading sense that they really do not know what the future holds for them. Unlike the more successful students in the sub-sample, they have a difficult time articulating what they expect to be doing in 10 years. "Gee, I don't know. I hope I have a job, but I don't know," "I haven't really thought that far ahead but I hope I finish school," and "It's hard to think that far ahead" were characteristic responses. The unsuccessful Chicano students are much more likely to discuss at length their concerns and hopes for today, tomorrow or possibly the weekend. This focus on the present or immediate future is no doubt reflective of the daily struggles and constrained material realities these students and their families face. The uncertainties and stress of these conditions extract a certain psychological and emotional energy and must be understood as important contextual influences in the schooling experiences of these students and in the processes of negotiation through which their identities are established and affirmed.

Ethnicity as a Strategically Exploited Response to the Demands of Schooling and to Structured Inequality

The foregoing discussion presents us with an opportunity to reexamine our understanding of ethnicity and ethnic identity systems, especially as they relate to the variations in patterns of school performance of Mexican-descent students. The data I have presented here indicate that school success and failure among these students do not correlate with a "less acculturated/more acculturated" continuum of ethnic identity and, in fact, speak to a much more complex, interactive set of phenomena.

There are several different ways of defining ethnic groups. One approach is to define an ethnic group objectively in terms of observable traits, behavioral orientations or combinations of such traits and feelings. Another approach involves defining ethnic groups in terms of subjective criteria. Individuals either identify themselves as being different from others or as belonging to a different group, are identified as different by others, or both identify themselves and are identified by others as different.

These approaches to ethnicity and ethnic identity are limited in their usefulness in understanding the interactive nature of ethnicity or the situational context in which ethnic identity is employed—or not employed—as a specific strategy. Nor are these approaches particularly successful in making cross-cultural comparisons or in suggesting generalizations about ethnic identity.

A more useful approach to ethnicity is proposed by the Social Science Research Council (1973). The Council presents criteria which are useful in understanding what it means to be Chicano, Cholo, Mexicano and Mexican American at Field High School. The Council's criteria suggest that ethnic categories have different meanings in different social settings and for different individuals. So, for example, it means different things to be a Chicano or Mexicano at Field High School. It means one thing to be a Mexicano/a at home and something else to be Mexican American at school or in some other situational context. For some it might mean being a Pocho/a (person of Mexican-descent who speaks Spanish with an American "gringo" accent) at home among family members and something entirely different to be a Mexican American or Cholo/a outside the home. Similarly, it means one thing to be a Chicano (activist or politically sensitive) rather than a Mexican American ("*tapado*," "*vendido*" or "sell out") in a university or college setting.

Another of the Council's criteria deals with the emblematic character of ethnicity and addresses the symbolic nature of ethnic categories. The symbolic content of the identity has meaning for both members of the group and for analysts of ethnic phenomena. Hence, the ethnic labels Chicano, Mexicano, Cholo, Mexican American, Pachuco, etc., are by themselves powerful symbols around which the negotiation of identity takes place. Labels with negative implications, such as the term Chicano as it is used by many Mexicanos at Field High School, can be used to impose a sense of social distance from those perceived to be deviant or a sense of inferiority on other Mexican-descent people, or it may be used to define a dominant-subordinate relationship.

Groups concerned with changing the status or image of the group may change the label by which they are known or imbue an existing label with new meaning. For example, prior to the 1960s, Mexicans in the United States identified themselves primarily as Mexicans, Mexicanos or Mexican Americans, but with the evolution of the civil rights movement the more politically active, social activist members of the group preferred to identify themselves as Chicanos. Frequently, students who identified themselves as Mexicanos at Field High School found themselves in some university contexts preferring to be identified as Chicanos. This was in recognition of the Chicano label as a symbol of solidarity with the sociopolitical struggle of Mexican Americans against discrimination and domination.

A useful way to understand ethnicity is an interactionist approach—one that emphasizes interaction and contact with others who are different. Such an approach focuses on how contact with, as opposed to isolation from, others heightens the ethnic group's sense of identity. Such an approach is advanced by Spicer (1971), who maintains that opposition is an essential factor in the maintenance of a persistent ethnic identity system. Spicer persuades us that the development of a persistent ethnic identity in opposition to the dominant group has both historical and structural antecedents. Moreover, it is not a mere epiphenomenon or byproduct of the interethnic contact. Rather, Spicer views an oppositional process as the essential ingredient of an enduring, collectively developed identity.

Spicer's model of the persistent identity system and the oppositional process is particularly useful in understanding what it means to be a Chicano or Cholo at Field High School. Spicer's model suggests that involuntary minorities, as opposed to autonomous minorities (described in Ogbu and Matute-Bianchi, 1986:87), form a sense of peoplehood or collective social identity in opposition to the collective social identity of the dominant group. In response to the enduring system of structured inequality and domination that characterizes their life in the United States, some Mexican-descent people have developed a bonding, collective oppositional identity which is best understood as an adaptive strategy that enables them to endure their status as a stigmatized minority within a system of structured inequality.

I am not suggesting here that Chicanos and Cholos at Field High School are consciously aware of their history and the history of other Mexican-descent people as involuntarily enclaved subordinate minorities in the United States. They do not know their history nor have they been provided with the tools to learn that history. But they do have an explicit awareness of their lives in this community as a stigmatized, low-status group with decidedly fewer opportunities than the dominant group. They are keenly aware of the low status they have in the community, a status which is reflected back to them by the school personnel and by other students. To a large extent their world is restricted to this particular community; it is what they live each day. Their reality is one which teaches them that Mexicans mostly work in the fields or in the canneries or are unemployed, a reality which tells them that most people like themselves do not do very well in school, and a reality which imposes strict limits on their future. It matters little whether their grandparents were immigrants or long-term residents of the United States. What matters is that they understand their structural and social position in this community and they have some sense that "this is how it has always been for our race." This collective understanding is an essential part of their identity, which in turn is part of an oppositional process in which the identification with others who share their origins, traditions and experiences has been critical in developing feelings of efficacy and value in their own eyes.

The maintenance of a Mexicano identity at Field High represents a much different ethnic strategy. The immigrant Mexicanos and those who maintain a separate identity as the descendants of Mexicano immigrants are either optimistic about their chances of succeeding here in the United States or at least share a perception that there are more economic opportunities for them here than in Mexico. Although they are aware of discrimination and prejudice against Mexican people here, they perceive it differently than Chicanos. Either they see these barriers as hurdles to be overcome or as reasons for returning to Mexico. They see the obstacles as part of their reality here but they are optimistic about their chances of overcoming them and becoming successful adults in occupations that earn more money and have higher status than those of their parents. For them, hard work and belief in the future value of educational credentials are an explicit part of their response to the demands of schooling. Others see these barriers as the way life is here and if they are not successful in "making a go of it here," they can "always go back home to Mexico." For many of the recent immigrants, their material conditions in the United States are demonstrably better than what they knew in Mexico, and from their frame of reference life is in some ways much better than it was in Mexico even if there is discrimination and prejudice against Mexicanos. Chicanos, on the other hand, see no dramatic improvement in their standard of living for they have no basis for comparing one situation to another. Their only frame of reference is what they know in this coastal community. That reality has not improved.

For successful immigrant Mexicano students there is an expression of self-confidence about their futures or at least an extreme desire to try hard to be successful in that future. Hence, those students with a strong Mexicano identity reflect a different accommodation to the sociocultural context, an accommodation that is based on very different interpretations of their opportunities and very different frames of reference. This identity is frequently linked to relative optimism about the future and about their ability to direct that future.

The oppositional identity system of the nonimmigrant Chicanos is linked to futures that are seen as limited and unknowable, to life chances that are perceived as limited and to goals that are seen as unattainable. The identity is developed through collectively experienced and interpreted processes of exclusion and subordination which are an enduring part of their daily realities, including their lives in school.

Summary and Recommendations

The foregoing presentation indicates seven major findings:

(1) The Mexican-descent student clientele is indeed a heterogeneous one, broadly reflective of a range of strategies and accommodations to the schooling process. This heterogeneity can be delineated by a five-category typology of Mexican-descent students: recent Mexican immigrant, Mexican-oriented, Mexican American, Chicano and Cholo.

(2) School success is much more likely to be found among the Mexican-oriented students who maintain strong, positive identities as Mexicanos as well as immigrant perspectives about the value of educational credentials in achieving adult success.

(3) Patterns of school failure are more likely to be found in the nonimmigrant Chicano/Cholo students who have a sense of themselves as a stigmatized group with

       comparatively limited adult opportunities and with futures that do not require educational credentials.

(4)   The obvious scholastic success of bilingual students with a strong identity as Mexicanos contradicts the conventional wisdom—and educational policies based on this presumed wisdom—that academic success belongs to those who acculturate and are monolingual English speakers.

(5)   School success among Mexican-oriented girls is more pronounced than it is for any other category of Mexican-descent students, with the possible exception of Mexican American girls. This raises important questions for subsequent research and bears more careful study.

(6)   The choice of ethnic labels and symbols, as well as variations in ethnic consciousness among Mexican-descent students, reflects an interactive process between the perceptions Mexican-descent students have of themselves and the perceptions school personnel, other students in the school, and the larger community have of them.

(7)   There is a relationship between student perceptions of the job ceiling and adult opportunities that their families have experienced, their explanations of the opportunities and the strategies developed in response to them that accords with variations in patterns of school success and failure. In other words, these patterns are broadly reflective of differences in student perceptions of the adult opportunity structure, their chances of becoming a successful adult and the importance of school achievement in achieving adult success.

The one group in my study that defies easy description is the Mexican American. It does not fit easily into the immigrant versus nonimmigrant continuum. As indicated earlier, there are at least three subgroups in the Mexican American category: students who are "totally acculturated" so that all that remains of their Mexican roots is their last name; students who are "cultural switch hitters" who alternate easily between being Mexicano at home and "American" at school; and students who see themselves as neither "purely American" nor "purely Mexican" but as some combination of the two. With the exception of the "switch hitters," the students in this category are more ambivalent and uncommitted in their ethnic orientation. They do not manifest the behavioral symbols or styles of the Chicano/Cholo identities nor do they affect any of the overt symbols associated with the Mexicano identities. Some of these students are active and successful in school, but many appear to drift, to be disengaged and withdrawn from much of what the school offers. They can be found in all curriculum tracks in the school, but probably are more likely to be found in the general or low tracks. They are more likely to be seen and not heard. They do not really fit into any of the modal categories I have defined along the immigrant versus nonimmigrant continuum, nor do they fit any of the generalizations I have made about students in other categories.

That the Mexican Americans at Field High School do not neatly fit into these generalizations or into the immigrant versus nonimmigrant categories does not necessarily invalidate the theoretical foundation upon which I framed my study. Rather, I think the difficulty in categorization that the Mexican American group presents reflects the complexity and diversity of sociocultural adaptations that Mexican-descent students and their families have made and are making to an ever-changing context. We have only just begun to identify the heterogeneity of this large Mexican-descent population and to describe some of its internal differentiation. One of the next research questions should be to what extent this five-category classification of Mexican-descent students is found in other similar agricultural communities and to what extent it is reflective of Mexican-descent students in urban communities, especially those with nonwhite minorities (blacks, Koreans, Vietnamese, Filipinos) and other Latino groups (Central and South Americans). What other categories might we find? What refinements might be made? What other kinds of accommodations and adaptive strategies are being worked out?

The elusiveness that I have described among the more ambivalent and uncommitted Mexican American students raises another issue. Educational intervention programs and policies aimed at improving academic achievement among Mexican-descent students assume a cultural homogeneity that does not exist and typically focus on single-cause assessments and solutions to perceived problems. The students' failure to achieve in school has been explained by some in terms of their inability to speak English, their culturally impoverished homes and/or the mismatch between the language and culture of the home and school. Based on these perceived causes of school failure, simplistic educational solutions are proposed to fit stereotypic categories of students: ESL for the non-English speaker, multicultural education for the "culturally deprived," and special programs for the "at risk," the migrants and the learning-handicapped. The response has been to create categorical programs for categorical students, with the expectation if not fervent hope that we can change the students to fit the "regular" school program. The situation of the Mexican American students at Field High School indicates the high cost to those students who do not fit any of the single-cause assessments of school failure, who do not warrant special attention as either "at risk" or as "gifted and talented" and who are neither "gang bangers" nor *mojados* at either extreme. The students are ignored. They drift politely and quietly, remaining bored and unchallenged, and they spend the majority of their time in school just getting by.

I have developed the typology of the students I observed at this school for the purposes of making generalizations about a student population that has long been perceived as a homogeneous one. The typology presents a useful starting point in understanding the intragroup variability and diversity of adaptations that can be found within the group. The case I have presented of the ambivalent, uncommitted Mexican Americans, however, raises an important caution in the interpretation of this typology. It would be a gross misinterpretation of my study to develop specific interventions and programs to "fit" the modal characteristics of the students I have identified by the typology. A more appropriate response to these findings would be to stop creating special programs to fit stereotypic perceptions of students and their perceived problems and to begin changing the school climate, structure and practices to ones that are more broadly sensitive, responsive and challenging to this diverse student clientele.

This study documents variations in patterns of school performance among Mexican-descent students. It suggests a new way for educators to look at ethnic identity as an interactive process which includes all the participants in a social context, including the school. In particular, it calls upon educators to examine closely the relationship between a strong, positive Mexicano identity and academic achievement and to see such an identity system not as a liability but as a source of strength in helping students to succeed in school. The academic success of the Mexican-oriented students suggests that assimilation and acculturation are not necessarily the sine qua non of scholastic achievement. The success of these students, especially the support for academic achievement that is provided by their involvement in *Sociedad Bilingue*, suggests not only the role of ethnic pride in promoting school achievement but also the importance of the peer culture in legitimating academic success. *Sociedad Bilingue* functioned as an important source of ethnic pride and leadership development in the lives of many Mexicano students and as a decidedly positive influence in a school where the various peer cultures were often "anti-school" in orientation.

The study also indicates that the job ceiling constraining a student's future creates a ceiling on exposure to and experiences with alternative futures and opportunities. How can students aspire to something that they and their families do not know exists? In this regard, the school has an important role to play in providing these students with the exposure to careers and jobs in a world beyond what the students know as their daily reality, providing access to information and successful role models in esteemed occupations. Schools must become active partners with the larger community, with private industry and the business community and with service organizations in providing these students with mentors, internships, apprenticeships and other enhancements. The schools by themselves cannot be expected to provide the necessary exposure and access to information. The effort must involve the community beyond the school.

I have suggested here the crucial importance of ethnic identity and minority status for patterns of school performance within distinct groups of Mexican-descent high school students. Of issue in subsequent research is the process of recruitment into a particular identity system. My impression of these students is that the particular identity a student claims is made long before he/she reaches Field High School, and that the process of recruitment begins much earlier. Just as the high dropout rate among Mexican-descent students must be understood as a process which begins early in the elementary school grades, my hunch is that the recruitment into the Chicano/Cholo identity systems begin about this time, and that the particular identity is confirmed by the time the student reaches junior high, about the time when the peer groups begin to assume much greater influence in the lives of students. By the same token, I think students who enter the schools with a strong, positive identity as Mexicanos probably have different sets of experiences at home and in school that allow them to maintain this self-confident identity system. A fruitful venture for subsequent research would be to follow Mexican-descent students longitudinally through a particular school system, documenting the internal differentiation in ethnic identification as it begins to develop, identifying emerging patterns of school performance, documenting variations in schooling experiences and other school input factors, and relating these developments to family histories, ideologies and other sociocultural variables.

The variations in ethnic identities among the Mexican-descent students are inextricably linked to the development of their identities as students long before they reached Field High School. In a larger sense, their identity systems are anchored to broader historical and structural antecedents in a community that has undergone rapid, dramatic changes. The community's established interethnic structures of domination and subordination are changing, thus providing a complex, multifaceted, interactive context in which students learn the significance of what it means to be "Mexican" and thus "different" from others. This context exerts a powerful influence not only on what students learn but on what they do with that knowledge, on the opportunities they have to acquire and apply socially valued knowledge, on how they see themselves today and tomorrow and on the value they place on schooling in getting them from today into the future.

References

Achievement Council, The. 1984. *Excellence for Whom?* A report from the Planning Committee. Oakland, California.

Arias, B. 1986. "The Context of Education for Hispanic Students: An Overview." *American Journal of Education* 95(1):26–57.

Assembly Office of Research. 1986. "California 2000: A People in Transition. Major Issues Affecting Human Resources." A report prepared by the Assembly Office of Research. Sacramento, California.

Baca, R., and D. Bryan. 1980. *Citizenship Aspirations and Residency Preference: The Mexican Undocumented Worker in the Binational Community.* Compton, Calif.: SEPA-OPTION, Inc.

Bowman, C. 1981. "Between Cultures: Toward an Understanding of the Cultural Production of Chicanos." In *Socioeconomic Attainment and Ethnicity: Toward an Understanding of the Labor Market Experience of Chicanos*, ed. M. Tienda in collaboration with C. Bowman and C.M. Snipp. Springfield, Va.: National Technical Information Service.

Brown, G., et al. 1980. *The Condition of Education for Hispanic Americans*. National Center for Education Statistics. Washington, D.C.: U.S. Government Printing Office.

Browning, H., and R.O. de la Garza. 1986. *Mexican Immigrants and Mexican Americans: An Evolving Relation*. Austin, Tex.: CMAS Publications, University of Texas at Austin.

California Postsecondary Education Commission. 1982. *Equal Education Opportunity in California Education. Part IV*. Sacramento, California.

Cameron, J.W. 1976. "The History of Mexican Public Education in Los Angeles, 1910–1930." Ph.D. diss. University of Southern California.

Carter, T.P. 1970. *Mexican Americans in School: A Decade of Change*. New York: College Entrance Examination Board.

Carter, Thomas P., and Roberto D. Segura. 1979. *Mexican Americans in School: A Decade of Change*. New York: College Entrance Examination Board.

Coleman, J., et al. 1966. *Equality of Educational Opportunity*. Washington, D.C.: U.S. Government Printing Office.

Dinerman, I.R. 1982. *Migrants and Stay-at-Homes: A Comparative Study of Rural Migration from Michoacan, Mexico*. San Diego: Center for U.S. Mexican Studies, University of California, Monograph Series #5.

Donato, R. 1987. "Pajaro Valley Unified Schools: Bilingual Education and Desegregation." Ph.D. diss. Stanford University.

Keefe, S., and A. Padilla. 1987. *Chicano Ethnicity*. Albuquerque, N.M.: University of New Mexico Press.

Matute-Bianchi, M.E. 1986. "Ethnic Identities and Patterns of School Success and Failure Among Mexican-Descent and Japanese American Students in a California High School: An Ethnographic Analysis." *American Journal of Education* 95(1):233–55.

Mines, R. 1981. "Developing a Community Tradition of Migration: A Field Study in Rural Zacatecas, Mexico and California Settlement Areas." San Diego: Center for U.S. Mexican Studies, University of California, Monograph #3.

Ogbu, J. 1974. *The Next Generation: An Ethnography of an Urban Neighborhood*. New York: Academic Press.

———. 1978. *Minority Education and Caste: The American System in Cross-Cultural Perspective*. New York: Academic Press.

———. 1982. "Cultural Discontinuities and Schooling." *Anthropology and Education Quarterly* 13(4):290–307.

————. 1983. "Minority Status and Schooling in Plural Societies." *Comparative Education Review* 27(2):168–90.

Ogbu, J., and M.E. Matute-Bianchi. 1986. "Understanding Sociocultural Factors: Knowledge, Identity and School Adjustment." In *Beyond Language: Social and Cultural Factors in Schooling Language Minority Students*, pp. 73–142. Sacramento, Calif.: State Department of Education, Bilingual Education Office.

Orfield, G. 1986. "Hispanic Education: Challenges, Research and Policies." *American Journal of Education* 95(1):1–25.

Portes, A., and R.L. Bach. 1985. *Latin Journey*. Berkeley: University of California Press.

Rios-Bustamante, A.J. 1981. *Mexican Immigrant Workers in the United States*. Los Angeles: Los Angeles Chicano Research Center, University of California, Los Angeles.

Rodriguez, N., and R.T. Nunez. 1986. "An Exploration of Factors that Contribute to Differentiation Between Chicanos and Indocumentados." In *Mexican Immigrants and Mexican Americans: An Evolving Relation*, ed. H. Browning and R.O. de la Garza, pp. 138–155. Austin, Tex.: CMAS Publications, University of Texas at Austin.

Romo, H. 1984. "The Mexican Origin Populations' Differing Perceptions of Their Children's Schooling." *Social Science Quarterly* 65(2):635–50.

Social Science Research Council. 1974. "Comparative Research on Ethnicity: A Conference Report." *Items* 28:61–64.

Spicer, E. 1971. "Persistent Identity System." *Science* 4011:795–800.

Takash, P.C. 1988. Personal communication. June.

U.S. Commission on Civil Rights. 1971. *Mexican American Education Study*. *Reports* 1–4. Washington, D.C.: U.S. Government Printing Office.

Valverde, S. 1987. "A Comparative Study of Hispanic High School Dropouts and Graduates—Why Do Some Leave School Early and Some Finish?" *Education and Urban Society* 19(3):320–29.

Wollenberg, C. 1976. *With All Deliberate Speed: Segregation and Exclusion in California Schools, 1955–1975*. Berkeley: University of California Press.

Chapter Eight
Low School Performance as an Adaptation: The Case of Blacks in Stockton, California

John U. Ogbu
University of California, Berkeley

Introduction

This chapter is the result of an ethnographic study in Stockton, California from 1968 to 1970. Some data were collected in subsequent years during occasional visits. From the city's inception in 1848, Stockton's population has included American Indians, black Americans and Mexican Americans. Today it also includes Burmese, Chinese, Filipinos, Hawaiians, Indian Sikhs, Japanese, Koreans, Vietnamese and others (Litherland, 1978; Ogbu, 1974, 1977). There are significant differences between earlier involuntary minorities and later immigrant minorities in school experience and performance. Generally, the involuntary minorities are not doing well academically while the immigrants are doing relatively well. The present chapter focuses on the school experience and performance of black Americans, an involuntary minority group. It examines the reasons why black children are not doing well in school and why remedial programs have not worked effectively to improve their school performance.[1]

Blacks in Stockton

Black Americans were originally brought to the United States as slaves and thus are an involuntary minority group. California was not a slave state, so that the 31 black settlers in the city in 1850 had already achieved their freedom (Martin, 1959). But these and later black settlers were relegated to the status of a lower caste, as they have been throughout the history of the United States. The local black population remained small until World War II. It then increased through immigration from the American South. Increasing immigration reinforced the blacks' castelike status, which was symbolized by increased residential segregation and occupational restrictions. For their part, blacks began to form local chapters of national civil rights organizations to fight the discrimination and prejudice against them. They also developed an identity and cultural system to cope with their denigration and subordination.

Today, racial stratification in Stockton is more flexible than it was, say, in 1960. It is also considerably more flexible than in the Deep South. Nevertheless, it is this social system that largely determines the social relationship between blacks and whites, the nature of black participation in the social and economic life of the city and black access to education and its rewards, as well as black development and responses to education.

As in other parts of the United States, the racial stratification system in Stockton is based on skin color and its assumed innate differences. The black and white groups do not usually intermarry. When they do, the couples are not fully accepted by either group. The offspring of such marriages as well as offspring from other forms of interracial matings are defined as black by local rules of descent. This rule contrasts sharply with those for offspring of other interethnic matings. In other cases, the children may be affiliated with the ethnic group of one or the other parent. For example, the offspring from a mating between a black and a Chinese may belong to either the black or Chinese community or even both. The same is true of the offspring from a mating between a white person and a Mexican American or any of the other groups. But all offspring from matings between blacks and whites must affiliate with blacks.

Black Education: A Paradox of High Aspiration and Low Performance

Aspirations. Black parents interviewed in the course of this study said that they stress education for their children because the civil rights movement and affirmative action programs are broadening opportunities for blacks. Some parents not only urge their children to do well in school but also reward them for doing well. In one family, for example, a child gets two dollars for an A, a dollar for a B and 50 cents for a C. A child also gets punished for getting a D on a report card. Some other parents neither encourage nor reward their children for doing well.

Most parents I interviewed, however, want their children to have more education than they themselves had; they want them to graduate from high school and even to go on to college. One mother expressed the feelings of many parents when she said:

> I want [my children] to get as much education as they possibly can. If it takes me eating bread and beans for the rest of my life to see that they have education, that's what it'll take. That's how far I want them to go. I want them to have an adequate education so that they can get jobs that will—that they might be able to maintain a family on a not-luxury basis but maybe two or three steps above necessity, you know. Maybe that's not explaining it too good—I'd like them to have, maybe, more than four years [of college]. I don't know if I'll be as lucky as to have them go more than that. I might be pushing my luck too far. But I would love for them to have college education.

Lower-class black parents do not want their children to drop out of school because, as one mother put it, those who dropped out have suffered for it. Among the middle class, the desire for children to have a college education is very strong. One mother said that her children have no option but to go to college. These expressions of desire for good education contradict the belief among school officials that the parents do not value education and do not encourage their children to do well.

As for the children, they agree with their parents that good education or good school credentials are desirable for employment. They say that their parents encourage them to pursue education and to do well in school. Of the one hundred junior and senior high school students I surveyed, 99 percent want to graduate from high school, 53 percent want to earn a degree from a four-year college and 34 percent want more than a four-year college degree.

Low Academic Performance. In spite of blacks' desire for good school credentials in order to obtain jobs that pay well, black school performance in Stockton is relatively poor and has been that way for generations. Before 1900, when there were few blacks in the city's schools, their poor school performance was not regarded as a serious problem; but the influx of blacks during and after World War II brought their poor performance to the fore.

Differences in school performance between blacks and whites can be seen by comparing the results of standardized achievement tests administered at the elementary and senior high schools annually (see also Ogbu, 1974:97–101). The tests are given to children in grades one, three, six and ten. Table 1 shows the gap in the test scores between predominantly white schools and predominantly minority (especially black) schools, for the years 1960 to 1973.

For the purpose of this comparison of black and white school performance, the schools are divided into white schools (where whites constitute 50 percent or more of the student population), minority schools (where minorities make up 50 percent or more of the students) and black schools (where blacks are 25 percent or more of the students). As Table 1 shows, most white schools usually score at or above the school district average, while most minority schools, especially black schools, usually score below the district average. I might add that in a school-by-school comparison shown in Table 1, only one black school out of ten consistently scored at or above the district average on grade one reading tests for the five-year period of comparison. Five other black schools scored at or above the district average for two years, one black school scored above the district average for one year, and three black schools never reached the district average any year.

In contrast, nine of the 18 white schools scored at or above the district average for the entire five-year period of comparison, four white schools scored at the district average for three years, and three other schools for two years. Only two white schools never reached the district average.

Table 1. A Comparison of the Number of White, Minority, and Black Schools Scoring At or Above District Level in the State-Mandated Reading and Math Tests, 1968–69 to 1972–73 School Years (Figures in parentheses are the total number of schools in each group)

School	1st Grade Reading			3rd Grade Reading		
Year	White	Minority	Black	White	Minority	Black
68/69	10	3	2	12	1	1
	(18)	(14)	(10)	(18)	(14)	(10)
69/70	11	2	1	12	0	0
	(17)	(15)	(10)	(17)	(14)	(10)
70/71	13	8	4	14	0	0
	(17)	(15)	(10)	(17)	(14)	(10)
71/72	14	7	3	14	4	3
	(17)	(15)	(9)	(17)	(14)	(10)
72/73	13	7	4	13	2	2
	(16)	(14)	(8)	(16)	(13)	(8)

School	6th Grade Reading			6th Grade Mathematics		
Year	White	Minority	Black	White	Minority	Black
68/69	15	1	0	14	1	0
	(18)	(13)	(10)	(17)	(14)	(10)
69/70	14	0	0	14	1	0
	(17)	(14)	(10)	(17)	(14)	(10)
70/71	14	2	2	14	3	1
	(17)	(14)	(10)	(17)	(14)	(10)
71/72	13	2	0	12	2	1
	(17)	(14)	(10)	(17)	(14)	(10)
72/73	11	0	0	11	0	0
	(16)	(13)	(9)	(16)	(13)	(9)

Source: Stockton Unified School District, Research Department Reports on the State Testing Results 1969, 1970, 1971, 1972, 1973.

At grade three, the differences between black and white schools in reading achievement test scores widen. At grade six, the gap between black and white schools widens still further. The widest gap occurs at the senior high level. Here, the predominantly minority high school not only failed to score at or above the district average even once during the five-year period, but it also consistently had an average test score in both reading and "quantitative thinking" that was less than 50 percent of the average scores of the predominantly white high school.

Stockton schools are not entirely segregated by race and ethnicity. Consequently we can compare black and white performance within the same schools. Such a comparison shows that black students do not perform on a par with their white peers (Ogbu, 1974).

An examination of the course grades received by students in the same school shows a similar lag on the part of black students relative to white students and relative to immigrant minority students. Black students receive lower grades even though many are taking "remedial courses" in English and math.

A school dropout problem among blacks was evident during my research. Black students tend to leave school much earlier than whites. Proportionately fewer blacks complete high school or receive adequate academic preparation to go on to college. Stockton schools have a long history of school dropout problems involving all ethnic groups, but the dropout problem has long been recognized as more serious among blacks. The first systematic study of the problem was done in the 1940s when it was found that although blacks made up 7 percent of the school population at the seventh and eighth grades, their representation at the twelfth grade was less than 2 percent (Stockton Unified School District [SUSD], 1948a:2–3). Another study of the dropout problem for 1960 through 1962 also showed that the dropout problem was most serious in two predominantly minority high schools (SUSD, 1963).

Local Explanations of the School Performance Gap and Related Problems

In the course of my fieldwork I probed into the reasons for the lower school performance of black children. I interviewed representatives of various segments of the city's population, listened to views expressed at public and private meetings on local educational issues and read local documents. The information gathered from these sources does not indicate any general consensus. I have chosen to focus on the official explanations which are used to rationalize intervention programs intended to improve black school performance.

The most general explanation given by the school officials is that of social class differences. This is explicitly stated in annual reports of the state-required testing described earlier. The reports repeatedly state that there is a correlation between the average student test scores and the average income and median years of schooling completed by adults in the neighborhood where the school is located (SUSD, 1968a:11, 1970:8). The social class explanation implies that black test scores are lower than those of whites because they are lower class and their schools are located in lower-class neighborhoods.

Another explanation attributes the lower school performance to the rural background of black parents or black families. This theme is emphasized in the annual reports of school principals. For example, the annual report of the elementary school principal of the neighborhood I studied begins each year with the statement that blacks had "migrated from the Deep South, primarily Alabama and Arkansas" in the last 15 years and that they have "preserved their basic attitudes, and their children and adults consequently have a low aspiration level with many personal prejudices" (SUSD, 1967:1). A similar assessment is made by the report of the junior high school where the principal points out that "the greatest problems are low-level aspirations on the part of the students, with attendant implications in terms of poor attendance and low achievement" (SUSD, 1969b:14). The report goes on to say that parents are uninterested in their children's education or in communicating with the school (SUSD, 1969b:11).

A third reason given for the lower performance consists of a list of traits relating to the children's background, ranging from limited English proficiency to a poor home environment where there is a tradition of school failure. These factors, it is suggested, result in frequent absence from school, mobility from school to school and the like. Some even subscribe to a prevalent view in the white community: that blacks do not encourage their children to succeed in school because they prefer to remain on welfare.

Remedial Efforts

A number of official and unofficial programs have been initiated since the early 1960s to improve the school performance and discourage school dropouts among black and other minority children. There are volunteer programs for tutoring and other forms of assistance, programs to improve community-school relations and to increase the number of minority teachers and staff, to promote school integration and to bring the schools under community control. There are bilingual education programs, compensatory education programs and preschool programs. The effectiveness of some of these programs in improving the school performance of black children cannot be measured directly with standardized tests, but they are, nevertheless, intended to contribute to the overall improvement of the children's performance. I have described the remedial efforts in detail elsewhere (Ogbu, 1974, 1977); here, I will focus on compensatory education, which has operated longest and has as its stated goal the raising of the academic achievement of black and other "disadvantaged" students.

Compensatory education in Stockton dates back to 1963 when it began with state funds. However, the major thrust began in 1965 with Title 1 funds. Students are selected to participate in the program because they come from low-income families and are not doing well in school; this would include many blacks and Mexican Americans who normally constitute the majority. The primary purpose of the program is to raise the school performance eventually to the level of their white middle-class peers.

To what extent has compensatory education succeeded in raising the academic achievement of black children and in closing the school performance gap? Local evaluations and supporters of the program present no convincing evidence that the children's academic achievement is improving. Nevertheless, they assert that compensatory education is successful *because* it helps to improve students' attitudes toward school as well as improve their school attendance and self-esteem, *because* it provides nutritional and health services for children, empowers their parents and involves them in decision making, and *because* it provides inservice training for teachers to help them become more aware of the special needs of disadvantaged students.

But the key questions in the assessment remain: to what extent does compensatory education succeed in raising the academic achievement of black children and narrowing the gap between them and their white middle-class peers? Furthermore, to what extent do compensatory education students achieve more than other black students from similar backgrounds who do not receive compensatory education services?

Compensatory education in Stockton does not seem to have significantly improved the school performance of children in the schools that have the program relative to their white middle-class peers. The achievement test scores of all the elementary schools in the district for grades one, three, six and over a five-year period were discussed earlier. The results of these tests show no significant trend toward convergence in performance of the compensatory education schools and the predominantly white middle-class schools. Furthermore, when compared with other predominantly minority schools without compensatory education, the minority schools with compensatory education more frequently score below the district average (Ogbu, 1977).

The rest of the tests specifically given during the annual evaluation also reveal that compensatory education is relatively ineffective. The test scores for the years 1970, 1971 and 1972 testify to this, as can be seen in Table 2.

The Stockton school district has known for some time that the remedial compensatory education approach at the school level may not solve the problems of minority students from poor families. The explanation is that the programs are already too late. What is needed, the argument goes, is a preschool intervention program which begins almost at birth. Thus the school district designed a program in 1968 called Happy Birthday (SUSD, 1968b). Basically, the Happy Birthday project was intended to train black mothers and other disadvantaged parents to rear their children like white middle-class parents to enable them to succeed in school. These parents would be taught how to rear their children to develop the cognitive and motivational skills considered essential for academic success.

The Happy Birthday project differed from the ongoing Head Start and other preschool programs because the former is designed to train parents to rear their own children. In the existing programs, the

Table 2. Number of Predominantly Minority (Black) Title 1 Schools (N=5) and Number of Predominantly Minority (Black) Non-Title 1 Schools (N=5) Scoring At District Average in State-Required Tests from 1968–69 to 1972–73 School Years

No. of Times Schools Score at District Average	NO. OF TITLE 1 SCHOOLS			
	Reading			Math
	1st	3rd	6th	6th
0	1	4	5	4
1	3	1	-	1
2	1	-	-	-
3		-	-	-
4		-	-	-
5		-	-	
Total number of schools	5	5	5	5

No. of Times Schools Score at District Average	NO. OF NON-TITLE 1 SCHOOLS			
	Reading			Math
	1st	3rd	6th	6th
0	1	2	4	4
1	0	2	1	1
2	3	1	-	-
3	-	-	-	-
4	-	-	-	-
5	1	-	-	-
Total number of schools	5	5	5	5

Source: Stockton Unified School District, Research Department Reports on the State Testing Results, 1969c, 1970, 1971, 1972, 1973.

children are trained by experts, although parents may be encouraged to continue some of the training in the home.

No one will deny that compensatory education, preschool and other programs have some positive effects on black students. The elimination of tracking, for example, has shown that some lagging students do better if they are allowed to take more intellectually challenging courses (Ogbu, 1974). Nevertheless, the programs have not altered the basic patterns of black school performance. In fact, given the assumptions underlying the remedial programs, especially compensatory education, it is very doubtful that they can succeed in closing the black-white school performance gap. Compensatory education at both preschool and school-age levels not only ignores the structural basis of the lower black school performance, but also assumes that the lower school performance is caused by developmental deficits in essential skills that result from inadequate socialization in the family (Bloom, Davis and Hess, 1965). Compensatory education programs further assume that in order to improve black school performance, black children require some kind of personality change or rehabilitation. But the rehabilitation strategy does not work well in a system of racial castes. In spite of our wishes and dreams, it is not easy to eliminate an adaptation to a castelike stratification while the stratification itself and all that it means persist.

An Alternative Explanation of the Paradox

A prerequisite for understanding the paradox of high aspiration and low school performance of black students as well as for understanding the persisting black-white gap in school performance is to recognize the historical and structural roots of the phenomenon. The lower school performance of black children does not originate in the inadequacy of the black family environment, in the inadequacy of black parents as child-rearing agents, or in the autobiographies of individual black children. The problem originated in the involuntary incorporation of blacks into American society, in the subsequent subordination and discriminatory treatment of blacks and in the adaptive responses of blacks to their castelike status. All these resulted in a differential school experience for blacks, which produces the lower school performance.

I will first discuss four structural and cultural consequences of black status as an involuntary or castelike minority: namely, (1) differential status mobility, (2) cultural and intellectual derogation, (3) interracial conflicts and (4) the adaptive responses of blacks. Following this, I will indicate how the above structural and cultural forces shape black schooling to produce the lower school performance.

The Status Mobility System and Schooling

The concept of a status mobility system allows us to understand peoples' motives for responding to schooling the way they do. A status mobility system is the folk theory and method of getting ahead in a society or within a given population (LeVine, 1967). Members of a given population share a theory of getting ahead and a set of skills required to get ahead in their system. The status mobility system of a population "works" insofar as the actual experience of a large proportion of its members confirms the prevailing folk beliefs about getting ahead. And the status mobility system generally influences how members of the society structure their schooling and how they respond to that schooling (Ogbu, 1978).

Schooling in Stockton is structured on the common-sense idea of preparing young people in marketable skills and giving them credentials to enter the labor market. The relationship between schooling and the economy can be seen in the stages through which Stockton schools have evolved in response to changes in the local economy. High school and junior college programs were, for example, added and then expanded as the local occupational structure began to require more and more formal education. For example, in 1948, the school district reorganized its high school curriculum to permit the schools to train students more effectively for local jobs in response to a study of changes in the local occupational structure and educational requirements (SUSD, 1948b). A similar study at the county level in the 1960s resulted in the establishment of a vocational education school, the Regional Occupational Center, to serve the occupational needs of the county. Other changes have also been made to give some students more academic training and prepare them for higher education in order to meet the requirements of higher-level occupations.

A high school diploma symbolizes the attainment of adulthood and the qualification to participate in the local economic system. Local whites, especially the middle class, believe that a good school credential is essential for a person to get a good job, earn a good wage, live in a good neighborhood and hold important appointive and elective offices. The belief that formal education is important for achieving adult status and social mobility comes up whenever problems of schooling and employment are discussed. And when Stocktonians run for the school board or other elective offices their campaigns usually emphasize the need for more and better schooling for their community so that every child will have a chance at better jobs, higher wages, good neighborhoods and the civic responsibility of paying taxes.

The belief that a good school credential is a passport to a good job that pays well and to general self-betterment appears to be the basis of school support and the educational striving of families and individuals. I specifically asked Stocktonians why they supported their schools financially and in other ways, why they went to school or sent their children to school. I took notes at public meetings and private discussions where schooling and related issues were the subject; I read relevant documents from various sources and generally probed into the meaning of education for the people. Data from the diverse sources led me to conclude that Stocktonians—lower class as well as middle class, whites, blacks, Chinese, Mexican Americans and other groups—go to school to get an education to enable them to get a good job that pays well and to obtain other societal benefits believed to come from education.

Among whites, especially middle-class whites, there is no doubt that good education leads to good jobs and good wages and that it improves one's chances of living in a good neighborhood and having a good standard of living. Statistical data from predominantly white neighborhoods show that there is a positive correlation between median years of schooling completed by adults and median family income. White Stocktonians generalize their experience, however, to nonwhites, saying that this correlation is true of all Stocktonians. Whites further insist that in jobs, wages and place of residence, all Stocktonians are judged as individuals according to their training and ability, not as members of categories. But, as noted later, this generalization is not applicable to black Stocktonians.

Status Mobility System and Minority Status

In a plural society or community such as Stockton, which is stratified by racial castes, adult roles are not the same for members of the dominant and subordinate groups and the methods of attaining adult roles or getting ahead may not be the same. Therefore, the status mobility system tends to be different for the different strata. This has implications for the schooling provided to the subordinate minorities and how the latter perceive and respond to schooling.

Because blacks in Stockton are defined as an inferior racial caste, they have historically been given an inferior education to prepare them for their marginal roles. Moreover, when they complete their schooling, they are not permitted to compete freely for desirable jobs above the job ceiling and for other desirable positions. This situation affects the way blacks perceive and respond to schooling.

Cultural and Intellectual Derogation

White Stocktonians denigrate blacks culturally, socially and intellectually in a number of ways. The most prominent form of derogation historically and during the period of my study is the stereotype that low-income blacks (which includes most Stockton blacks) are "nontaxpayers" (Ogbu, 1974:49–57; 1977). Low-income blacks, like everyone else, of course, pay property tax (if they own homes) and income tax (if they work and earn wages) as well as sales tax, but they are often publicly referred to and treated as nontaxpayers. In the local white folk classification, a taxpayer is one who not only pays taxes (property, income, sales) but also is publicly acknowledged to be a taxpayer. And to be so recognized, a Stocktonian must live in a neighborhood (1) with few or no welfare recipients, particularly those receiving Aid to Families with Dependent Children (AFDC) or (2) with high assessed property value. The nontaxpayer is a person who lives in a neighborhood (1) with many welfare recipients, (2) with low assessed property value, or (3) is himself or herself a welfare recipient. Most blacks lived in such nontaxpayer neighborhoods and would, therefore, qualify as nontaxpayers. Generally, nontaxpayers are regarded and treated as incompetent and dependent people who make little or no useful contributions to the cost and responsibility of running city government and providing social services, such as education. Instead, taxpayers are thought to carry the financial burden and social responsibility. Since 1850, taxpayers in Stockton have from time to time protested against "high and unjust taxation" (Ogbu, 1974:51–52). There is elaborate news coverage of the interests and opinions of taxpayers in the local newspapers, on radio and television; news about nontaxpayers is also reported frequently but it is usually about "their problems," with particular emphasis on nontaxpayers' violations of the law, their family and other crises, and what taxpayers are doing to help or rehabilitate them.

Another characterization is that blacks as nontaxpayers "resist assimilation" into the "mainstream culture." That is, they are unwilling or unable (if left on their own) to adopt values that would transform them into taxpayers and more "useful citizens." A survey of churchgoing taxpayers found that 62 percent thought that nontaxpayers "are stupid, narrow in their view, intolerant, lacking in imagination, lacking in curiosity and lacking in ambition." Taxpayers also regarded them as "immoral and dirty," selfish and "not willing to improve their own situation" (Hutchinson, 1965:4).

Still another characterization worth mentioning is that nontaxpayers are caught in a "welfare cycle" (Ogbu, 1974:181–82, 1977:24). That is, white Stocktonians think that black parents on welfare are not able to rear their children to be self-supporting adults. As a result, their children also grow up to become welfare recipients who, in turn, rear their children to become welfare recipients. At the time of my initial study, taxpayers were considering various measures to break the welfare cycle. In one program already mentioned (the Happy Birthday program), the training of black mothers to rear their children as white middle-class parents do was viewed as a method to enable black children to succeed in school, get jobs as adults and stay off welfare (SUSD, 1968a, 1968b). In another program, an elementary school had white middle-class families "adopt" the families of its black and Mexican American students. According to the school, the white families would help their adopted children develop better attitudes about themselves and about their chances of succeeding in school and later adult life.

Interracial Conflicts

One prominent feature of black/white relationships in Stockton and the black/school relationships is conflict. Blacks and whites continually fight over education, jobs, crime and justice, housing and the like. Blacks boycott white businesses to protest discrimination and prejudice in employment and promotion; they also carry their complaints to federal and other government agencies from time to time. One example of these conflicts occurred in 1963 when black families for the first time moved into white neighborhoods; white neighbors threw garbage into the yards of the blacks. There are frequent conflicts over educational issues, dating back to the exclusion of blacks from the public schools from 1863 to 1879, and conflicts over school desegregation loomed large throughout the period of my research (Ogbu, 1974, 1977). These conflicts have generated a tremendous distrust of white people and the schools and other institutions they control.

Black Responses to their Treatment

How do blacks respond to the collective problems facing them: the limited opportunity structure, cultural and intellectual derogation, and hostility? In my ethnographic interviews and observations, black parents and other adults often express the wish that they could get ahead according to the conventional strategy of using school credentials, but they also know that they cannot because of a job ceiling and discrimination. Nor do they think, as do local Chinese and Japanese whom I also interviewed, that they can overcome barriers in employment by merely getting a good education or by going into business for themselves. Indeed, blacks in Stockton seem to have formulated their problems in the area of adult opportunity structure (i.e., employment, income, housing, etc.) in terms of institutionalized discrimination. That is, they seem to believe that they cannot succeed or get ahead in areas controlled by white Stocktonians by merely following rules of behavior that work for white people, such as by getting school credentials.

Although the situation is changing somewhat because of civil rights legislation, affirmative action programs and intensified collective struggle, there are many events in the city which seem to reinforce blacks' beliefs and claims that discrimination restricts their opportunity to get ahead.

As a consequence, Stockton blacks have developed several "survival" or alternative strategies for dealing with their economic and other problems. Some of the survival strategies, such as collective struggle or civil rights activities and Uncle Tomming or clientship, serve to break, raise or circumvent the job ceiling and related barriers and thus enable blacks to advance within the institutions controlled by whites. Other survival strategies, such as hustling, are used to exploit resources outside mainstream institutions. I will describe briefly, as representative examples, the use of collective struggle and hustling (see Ogbu, 1986, for other survival strategies).

An example of the use of collective struggle is the attempt by blacks to change employment rules made by whites that do not work for them. One way in which blacks try to change such rules is by boycotting white businesses and white-controlled public institutions. A number of such boycotts took place between 1967 and 1973. Briefly, in 1967 the Black Unity Council organized a boycott of major white businesses, including J.C. Penney. Following this the white businesses began to hire blacks as sales and clerical workers for the first time. In 1969, Ebony Young Men of Action, another black organization, threatened to boycott several white businesses that had hiring and promotion policies considered discriminatory by blacks and other minorities. In response, the businesses negotiated with the organization and subsequently hired about 390 blacks and other minorities in positions not open to minorities previously. I should add that "collective struggle" includes activities that increased the pool or resources for blacks but were not necessarily approved by the white majority. An example is the use of rioting in 1969 to increase the number of black school administrators, teachers and counselors.

Some blacks resort to hustling and pimping as coping mechanisms. Hustling is a technique for exploiting interpersonal relationships for material and nonmaterial benefits. It appears to be used primarily to exploit nonconventional resources to tap into the "street economy." Some informants consider hustling a "legitimate thing" for blacks, arguing that whites are against it because it is a "black thing." They admire hustlers partly because a hustler works for himself and not for white people. This attitude is reflected in the following excerpt from an interview with a high school student and his mother:

Student:	They say that the hustler is not good.
Mother:	But he's black.
Student:	This is good, you know; this is all he can survive. [This is the only way he can survive.] I am not going to say that this is all he can survive, but then, if he's got to survive somewhere, I mean, you know, the toughest way, he's going to do it. And this is what I'm saying. He uses his head—
Mother:	And not the *white man's head*.
Student:	See? And as far as I am concerned, this is good because he is doing his own thing. *He's not doing the white man's thing*.
Anthropologist:	All right. Would you recommend that many of us go into the pimp business? Or the hustling business? That is, black business?
Student:	Wait! If this is your own thing, do it.
Mother:	In other words, he is saying, if this is what you want to do, you do it, and *not do what the white man wants you to do*. Because this is the way it has been from generation to generation [i.e., the white man has been telling the black man what to do].

In summary, from individual and collective encounters with the job ceiling and other barriers, black Stocktonians have come to believe that the way to get ahead is not exactly the same for blacks and whites. Consequently, blacks have developed a folk theory of getting ahead that differs in some important respects from the white folk theory. Black folk theory includes survival strategies that are not necessarily approved by white Stocktonians. Yet, the difference in the folk theory is not always evident from verbal replies to direct questions about how a black person gets ahead because blacks tend to answer like whites that to get a good job one needs a good education or school credential. To learn what black Stocktonians really believe about getting ahead one has to listen to their public and private discussions of the problems they face when they try to get a job, to get promoted on the job, to get a loan to start a business or to buy a home in a white neighborhood. Further knowledge of their folk theory of getting ahead comes from observing their efforts to change the rules of employment and promotion established by whites and from observing their survival strategies.

In response to treatment by whites—discrimination in employment and housing, derogation and exclusion from true assimilation—black Stocktonians, like their counterparts everywhere else in the United States, have developed a kind of oppositional identity and cultural frame of reference. Some black informants say that blacks and whites live in mutually exclusive worlds. Culturally there is a white way and a black way. That is, some ways of behaving are acceptable and defended as black because they are not the way of whites; this is especially true if white people condemn such behaviors. For example, in the interview excerpt above, hustling is defended as "the black thing," which is condemned by white people.

Black people are expected to stick together against whites, especially in times of crisis or when a black runs for a public office against a white person. The latter was brought home to me in 1969 during the campaign for election to the County Board of Supervisors. I had taken my seventy-four-year-old landlord to a meeting of the Black Unity Council, not knowing that he was not welcome because he had campaigned for a white candidate opposing a black. His presence changed the orientation of the meeting as speaker after speaker condemned him for being "the white people's nigger." After half an hour of such uncomplimentary speeches, my landlord left. When I returned from the meeting, we had a long discussion about black-white relationships in Stockton and during the discussion he explained why he campaigned for the white candidate even though he was expected to support the black candidate.

The conflicts noted earlier between blacks and whites and between blacks and the schools have caused blacks to develop a deep distrust for white people and the institutions they control.

Differential Schooling

A differential status mobility system, intellectual and cultural derogation, and interracial conflicts not only influence the type of schooling provided to blacks by the wider community and how they are treated within the schools, they also influence how blacks perceive and respond to their schooling. The first part of this section will, therefore, deal with the way "the system" treats blacks through the educational policies of the community at large and within the schools and classrooms. The second part focuses on the perceptions and responses of black themselves (or what I call the second half of the problem).

"The System"

Differential Access. The problem of channelling blacks to inferior social and economic positions in adult life is partially solved through differential schooling. The latter ensures that most blacks do not perform well enough in school or go far enough to be able to compete with whites for high-status jobs and other desirable positions in the wider community. One aspect of the differential schooling is that blacks have had unequal access to quality education.

The racial stratification system has always had a direct restrictive influence on the education of Stockton blacks. For example, during the first 16 years of public school education (1863–79), blacks and American Indians were forbidden to attend schools with whites. Later increases in black population altered the pattern of black distribution in the public schools. Since blacks were denied the freedom to live in neighborhoods of their choice, they concentrated in a few neighborhoods. And because Stockton schools were neighborhood schools, they became racially segregated.

In 1974, the California Rural Legal Assistance Board sued the Stockton Unified School District, charging it with discrimination against minorities. Some informants and witnesses at the trial pointed to school policies and practices that might have contributed to the segregation. School officials denied this; they also denied employing discrimination mechanisms such as unequal funding, facilities and staffing of white and minority schools. I did not study these problems systematically but took note of several occasions when they were discussed at public meetings or mentioned during my ethnographic interviews. In addition, the superintendent admitted in a document on school desegregation prepared for the Board of Education that the district had established a policy of not hiring minorities in the past but that this had ended when it hired the first black teacher in 1947. He also noted that since 1965 the district had actively recruited minority teachers and deliberately placed them in 41 of its 43 schools (SUSD, 1969c).

Within-School Treatment. Although officially sanctioned discrimination no longer exists in Stockton and may be difficult to prove, there are some subtle ways in which the schools contribute to the lower school performance of black children. Among these are low teacher expectations and attitudes, clinical definitions of black academic problems, testing and tracking, biased curriculum and textbooks, and socializing into lower expectations and inferior jobs. I have described these features elsewhere and will focus here on some aspects of teacher attitudes and practices (Ogbu, 1974:164–69, 1977).

There are two ways in which teacher attitudes, expectations and practices affected the school performance of the children I studied. One has to do with the relationship between teachers and parents and the other is the manner in which teachers evaluate the academic work of their pupils.

Stereotypes, negative attitudes and expectations, as well as distrust, characterize the relationship between parents and teachers partly because of physical and social distance between teachers and parents. Few teachers live in black neighborhoods and most confine their contacts with blacks to school settings where the two groups interact as representatives of their respective racial groups. Interracial stereotypes, low expectations and distrust thus prevent them from using PTA meetings and parent-teacher conferences as opportunities to discuss candidly the academic problems of the children and the mutual efforts to help the children. When a discussion does take place between teachers and parents, the latter are skeptical of teachers' explanations of their children's academic problems partly because teachers tend to blame children's difficulties in school on "the home situation." Teachers, for their part, do not usually accept parents' diagnosis of their children's academic problems nor their suggestions for solving the problems because teachers do not believe that the parents are capable of understanding academic problems—not even those of their own children.

During my ethnographic interviews I found instances in which teachers' rejection of parents' opinions of their children's academic problems proved disastrous for the children's academic careers. This is illustrated by the case of one twelfth-grade youth. According to his parents, he was very "smart" in the early grades but later became increasingly uninterested in his schoolwork and began to receive low marks on his report cards. After talking to him, his parents concluded that he was bored because the class work was not challenging. They went to see his teacher and school principal, requesting that the boy be given "extra" work. But their diagnosis and request were rejected. Their son's problem grew worse and worse and at the time of my study he was receiving mostly Ds and Fs in the twelfth grade.

The way that teachers evaluate black students has some influence on the children's academic work orientation and performance. In general, when a teacher evaluates children's class work by assigning letter grades A, B, C, and so on or by using other symbol systems, he or she is not only rewarding pupils for their immediate efforts but also is teaching them important values and skills that are adaptive throughout their schooling and later in the wider community. Through this reward system, children learn that higher marks, say a B instead of a C, can be achieved through better work habits and persevering efforts. When elementary school children develop this attitude and its behavioral component—namely, good work habits and performance strategies—they thereby acquire an important learning tool or skill that will facilitate good performance in the higher grades. The same attitude and behavior patterns can be transferred later to postschool participation as adults in the wider community, which ideally rewards its members (in terms of jobs, wages, promotions, etc.) on the basis of achievement.

The experiences of black children in the elementary school I studied appear to be different. The marks they receive do not really differentiate them on the basis of achievement, that is, they do not reflect various levels of performance among the children. Most children complete grade one with the mark of C or D, which is locally called "the average grade." In subsequent years, teachers almost consistently give the same average grade, regardless of the student's performance. That actual performance may vary more widely among the pupils and for the same pupil from year to year is suggested by teachers' written comments on individual pupils. Yet, they give the child the same average mark as the previous year and the same average grade received by "less progressive" classmates. As an illustration, I will cite the case of 17 children (blacks and Mexican Americans) who received the average mark of C at the end of grade one in the 1964–65 school year. Sixteen of these children continued to receive the same average mark through grade six in 1969. The one exception received a C+ to B- in one year. This means that throughout their elementary school career, under several teachers, 94.12 percent of these children maintained the same level of achievement!

The fact that the children are not rewarded on the basis of their real performance or ability, or for their "progress" or "efforts" contributes to their school failure in a number of ways. First, the children fail to learn to associate earning higher marks with making greater efforts in their class work. Second, they do not learn to develop proper work habits and performance strategies that facilitate earning higher marks. Both weaknesses result in still poorer marks when the children enter junior high school and high school.

Why do elementary school teachers assign marks that do not properly differentiate black children by levels of performance? A part of the answer lies in the situation to be described in the next section: the reward system that blacks experience in the classroom is compatible with the reward system that adult blacks encounter in the wider Stockton community where, historically, they have not been hired, paid or promoted on the basis of education or ability. The school is, therefore, unconsciously preparing black children for their destined future experience in the adult opportunity structure.

Denial of Equal Rewards for Educational Accomplishment. There has been no systematic study of the extent to which Stockton rewards blacks and whites for their school credentials in terms of jobs, wages, promotion and so on. But my own ethnographic study shows that historically Stockton has not fully utilized black academic skills, nor has it rewarded blacks equitably for their educational efforts and accomplishments in terms of jobs, income, housing and social position. It appears to have been more difficult for blacks than for any other group in the city's history to advance socially and economically in terms of education and length of residence. The first black settlers worked as sailors, shopkeepers, cooks, carpenters and muleteers in the gold mines (State of California, 1972). For the next 100 years, blacks did not achieve much higher occupational status because of a job ceiling operating against them. Labor shortages during World War II resulted in many blacks, both old settlers and newcomers from the South, being absorbed into slightly higher occupations that whites had vacated so that they could go into more desirable jobs created by the war. (In the war period, Stockton was an important food-processing center for the support of American military efforts abroad.)

After the war blacks were able to retain some of their occupational gains, but further advances were difficult (U.S. Department of Justice, 1967). Thus a study of the school dropout problem by the Stockton school district found that blacks faced many employment barriers; the report went on to say that blacks are "at best greatly restricted in their fields of occupational endeavors, and are subject for the most part, to less desirable social environment" (SUSD, 1948b:7–8). The occupational status of blacks remained relatively low up to the time of my study in 1968–70, as can be seen in Table 3, which shows the under-representation and over-representation of blacks in various occupational categories in 1960 and 1970. An index of 100 would represent their proportional participation in a given category. The figures for 1970 include only blacks and thus more accurately reflect their occupational representation. In 1970 the average participation of blacks above the job ceiling had an index of only 53.53.

Blacks and whites disagree regarding the reasons for the limited participation of blacks in occupations above the job ceiling. Whites say that blacks are under-represented because they do not have the educational credentials for such jobs. Blacks see it differently, however, contending that many white businesses and white-controlled public agencies would not hire them even if they were qualified. One event during my fieldwork in 1969 clearly illustrates the divergent views by blacks and whites of the problem. This was a public debate over the purpose and fairness to minorities of the use of standardized tests for civil service employment (Ogbu, 1977).

When we compare blacks and the general population in 1960 and 1970 in terms of educational attainment and occupation status, we find

Table 3. Nonwhites (Blacks) as Percentage of All Employed Persons in Stockton in 1960 and 1970, and Index of Their Participation in the Same Years

Occupation Group	Percentage Black		Index of Black Participation	
	1960*	1970	1960*	1970
Professional, technical, and kindred workers	8.43	5.36	56.81	68.02
Managers, officials, and proprietors, except farm	11.05	2.07	74.46	26.27
Clerical and kindred workers	7.85	6.48	52.90	82.23
Sales	7.37	2.40	49.66	30.46
Craftsmen/foremen	6.59	4.78	44.41	60.66
Job Ceiling				
Operatives	16.14	12.00	108.76	152.28
Private Household workers	44.07	30.94	296.97	392.64
Service workers	22.52	10.80	151.75	137.06
Laborers, except farm	29.84	17.28	201.08	219.29
Farm laborers	?	5.08	?	64.47
Farmers	?	?	?	?
Total, all employed nonwhites/blacks	14.84	7.88		
Average participation				
(1) above the job ceiling			55.70	53.53
(2) below the job ceiling			189.64	193.15

Source: U.S. Department of Commerce, Bureau of Census. Stockton, Calif.: Standard Metropolitan Statistical Area. 1960, Tables p. 4, p. 45; 1970, Tables p. 6, p. 44.
*Figures for 1960 include other nonwhites.

that the educational gap is narrower than the occupational gap. Thus, Table 4 shows that in 1960, the median years of schooling completed by nonwhites was 8.3 or 79.91 percent of the median for the general population. Among persons twenty-five years and over completing at least one to three years of high school, the index of nonwhite educational attainment averaged 61.43, leaving a gap of 38.57. We may assume that the minimum educational attainment required for participation in the occupations above the job ceiling is some high school education (Norgren and Hill, 1964). The index of nonwhite participation above the job ceiling in 1960 was 35.70 (Table 3), which is lower than their educational attainment index and lower than would be expected from the gap in median school years completed. In 1970, when the figures are for blacks only, the discrepancy increases: the median years of schooling completed by blacks increased to 85 percent of the median for the general population, and their educational attainment index drops to 68.26, but the index of their participation above the job ceiling is only 53.53, which is even lower than the index of the nonwhite participation in 1960.

To summarize, before the passage of the civil rights laws of the 1960s and the institution of affirmative action programs, Stockton blacks had uncertain and limited access to the more desirable jobs requiring more education and providing a payoff to those who have the education. Even in the mid-1970s, blacks had not advanced significantly above the job ceiling, judging from local government employment statistics. For example, a report to the City Council on January 18, 1977, by the local National Association for the Advancement of Colored People (NAACP) showed that there were only 52 blacks among a total employee population of 1,102, i.e., blacks made up only 4.7 percent of the local government work force; this was down from 49 out of 918 or 5.3 percent of the work force in 1972 (Best, 1977:1).

Income. The restriction of blacks to unskilled labor means that blacks are subject to seasonal employment, underemployment and unemployment. Thus, the unemployment rates of black males, both in 1960 and 1970, were almost twice the rates for white males; the rates for black females were more than five times those for white females (Ogbu, 1974:49, South Stockton Parish, 1967). Unemployment and underemployment are the two major causes of low income and poverty among local blacks. In 1960, for instance, the median family income of

Table 4. Nonwhites (Blacks) as Percentage of All Persons in Stockton, 25 Years of Age and Over, Completing Specific Levels of Education in 1960 and 1970, and the Index of Nonwhite (Black) Representation at Each Level

Level of Education	Percentage Nonwhite/Black 1960*	Percentage Nonwhite/Black 1970	Index of Nonwhite/Black Attainment 1960*	Index of Nonwhite/Black Attainment 1970
Median school years completed by nonwhites/blacks	8.3	10.2	79.81	85.0
High School				
1 to 3 years	11.31	9.13	80.16	101.21
4 years	9.03	6.39	64.00	70.84
College				
1 to 3 years	7.79	5.21	55.21	57.76
4 years	6.54	4.26	46.35	47.23
Average attainment index			61.43	69.26
Total, all nonwhite/black 25 years and over	14.11	9.02		

Source: U.S. Department of Commerce, Bureau of Census. Stockton, Calif.: Standard Metropolitan Statistical Area. 1960, Tables p. 1, p. 13; 1970, Tables p. 4, p. 45.
*Figures for 1960 include other nonwhites.

blacks was only $4,279, compared to the median family income of $6,059 for the general population. In 1970, this income gap widened, with black median family income being $6,021 and the median family income of the general population standing at $9,533. Note that this increasing income gap occurred during a period of a significant narrowing of the educational gap.

Education. An equal amount of education does not lead to equal income for blacks and whites. For 13 of the census tracts in Stockton for which data are available by race for 1969, we find that in seven of ten tracts, blacks had higher median years of schooling completed but substantially lower median family income when compared to the general population (San Joaquin County, 1973). In three out of the ten tracts (tracts 19, 20 and 38) blacks had more median years of schooling than the general population and their income was slightly above the median for the city. Only in one out of the 13 tracts (#6) was the median family income of blacks higher than that of the general population although their median years of schooling were lower. The reason for this is that there is a concentration of black professionals in this tract who service the black community, such as morticians, builders and so on. These professionals have relatively little education, although they are engaged in lucrative businesses.

Housing. Just as most blacks are not able to obtain jobs or income similar to those of whites with similar school credentials, so also they are not able to move into neighborhoods of their choice by buying or renting homes. Figure 1 shows the concentration of nonwhite population in each of the five metropolitan districts in 1960 and 1970. The concentration of blacks in the least desirable district, D2, began during and after World War II. In 1950 about 75 percent of the nonwhites lived there; this rose to 88 percent in 1960 (Stockton City Planning Department, 1973). Although the nonwhite concentration decreased to 78 percent in 1970, the black concentration remained high, 89.02 percent in 1960 and 88.57 percent in 1970 (Stockton City Planning Department, 1973). Of all minority groups in the city, blacks made the least progress in moving into predominantly white neighborhoods in districts A and B between 1960 and 1970 (Stockton City Planning Department, 1973).

Local whites give two reasons why blacks do not live in white neighborhoods. One is that blacks are too poor to afford to buy or rent homes in white areas. However, poverty alone does not explain

Figure 1. Metropolitan Stockton Showing Distribution of Blacks in Various Districts as Percentage of Total Metropolitan Black Population

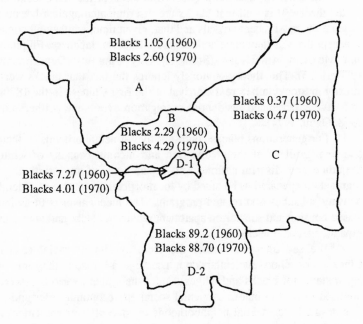

Adapted from Stockton City Planning Department Neighborhood Analysis Program, Profile No. 2, 1973: 212, 216

Stockton residential segregation. Consider that in 1963 the average cost of a home in districts A and B was about $16,500. At that time, many black couples were refused the right to buy homes in those districts even though the couples were professional workers (teachers, social workers, medical doctors) who could afford to buy there. Their average annual income was about $12,000 which was above the average annual income of many white families living there; the black couples were also more educated than many white couples (see Meer and Freedman, 1966; Ogbu, 1974).

The other explanation is couched in terms of the "race relations cycle" theory. It is said that blacks are discriminated against because they are the most recent arrivals and that, given time, whites will come to accept them as they have done with the Chinese, Japanese, Filipinos and Mexican Americans (Stockton City Planning Department, 1970:31–35). This theory obviously ignores the fact that blacks were already in Stockton before the arrival of the first Chinese in the 1870s and have experienced residential segregation ever since (Litherland, 1978; Ogbu, 1974).

For generations blacks could not live in neighborhoods of their choice regardless of their education and income because of white prejudice and discrimination. And at the time of my study their segregation appeared to be aided by local officials in charge of federal housing subsidies and related programs. The mechanism is to assign leased housing and subsidized apartment rentals to blacks and whites in separate parts of the city and county.

We see then that under the local system of racial castes, education or school credentials do not serve as a bridge to the same or equal status for blacks and whites. Under the system, various devices are used to restrict blacks to menial social and economic roles and to less desirable residential neighborhoods in spite of their education, a situation which undoubtedly discourages black investment of efforts in schooling, as I will show in the next section.

Blacks' Perceptions and Responses: The Second Half of the Problem

Good teaching and good school environment help black children learn and perform well academically. Barriers in education, such as those described above, make it difficult for them to learn and perform.

But also important in determining their school adjustment and performance is how black children and their parents as individuals and as members of a group consciously and unconsciously perceive, interpret and respond to schooling in the context of their understanding of their status mobility system, their relationship with white people who control the schools, and their sense of cultural identity and cultural frame of reference.

Thus, the way in which Stockton blacks perceive and respond to schooling because of their historical treatment at the hands of white Stocktonians is important in understanding their school performance and related problems. The situation is, however, paradoxical. As noted earlier, blacks appear to accept the assumption underlying the white status mobility system—namely, that recruitment into and remuneration and advancement in the job hierarchy should be based on educational credentials. On the basis of the long historical and collective struggle for equal education, it is clear that blacks see formal education as a good strategy to improve their status. Studies show, too, that at any given class level, blacks verbally express a desire for education as much as whites do.

In my interviews, both black parents and black children say that they desire education and school credentials for the same reasons that whites and others gave in my interviews with them: to get a good job with good pay. As blacks put it, they want a good education to "better" themselves. And their job preferences indicate that most desire jobs requiring good school credentials and where education pays off.

However, blacks do not match their wishes and aspirations with effort. This is clearly the case in Stockton, where I was impressed by the fact that the children tend to divert most of their efforts away from schoolwork into nonacademic activities. I suggest that the reasons for the inadequate effort lie in the pattern of black responses to their treatment by the Stockton community and its schools described previously. I will now discuss how some of these responses enter into and affect the schooling of black children.

My ethnographic interviews and observations suggest that black children, especially older ones, perceive that their chances of making it according to the mainstream strategy of using school credentials are not as good as those of their white peers and that this perception affects the way they look at schooling (Ogbu, 1974, 1977). The children learn about the job ceiling quite early in life, from observing their unemployed and underemployed parents, older siblings, relatives, family friends and other adults in their neighborhoods. They also learn about the job ceiling and other barriers from public demonstrations by blacks and their supporters for more jobs, better wages and housing, and from reports in the mass media about problems of black joblessness.

I have already noted that parents very much want their children to get a good education. What I should add is that the same parents do not seem to instill sufficiently in their children appropriate instrumental attitudes and behaviors to help them do well in school. Another factor further weakening parents' educational strategies is that they seem to teach their children contradictory or ambivalent messages about schooling without knowing it. On the one hand, they tell their children to get a good education and encourage them verbally to do well in school; those who can, of course, help their children with homework. On the other hand, the actual texture of the lives of these parents, in which job and other forms of discrimination and underemployment and unemployment figure strongly, reproduces a second message powerful enough to undercut their exhortation. The result is that the children increasingly become disillusioned about their ability to succeed in adult life through a mainstream strategy of gaining school credentials; they become doubtful about the real value of schooling (Hunter, 1980).

In this context, even very young black children begin to realize that for black people in Stockton the connection between school success and one's ability to get ahead is weak, or at least not as strong as the white's (Ogbu, 1974, 1977). As these children get older and experience personal disappointments and frustrations in looking for part-time or summer jobs, their unfavorable perceptions and interpretations of future prospects become even more crystallized and discouraging.

The survival strategies described earlier also contribute to the problem of lower school performance. Although they may increase black people's access to conventional or mainstream and other resources, they also may promote attitudes and behaviors that are not necessarily conducive to academic striving and success. Although I did not conduct a systematic study of the effects of the survival strategies on schooling, I will speculate on some possible contributions they make to the academic attitudes, lack of sufficient time devoted to schoolwork, lack of perseverance, and tendency toward disruptive school behavior.

Collective struggle, as noted earlier, increases the opportunity of blacks in mainstream jobs and institutions. It can thus be expected to increase the motivation of black youths to succeed in school to qualify for the new opportunities. But the success of collective struggle also appears to teach black youths that it is "the system" that causes high unemployment and related problems for black Stocktonians. Eventually the children learn to blame "the system," including the schools, for their own failures in seeking part-time jobs and in school. Some black youths use this to rationalize their low school performance when, in fact, they fail because they do not work hard.

Hustling and related strategies adversely influence black youths' academic endeavors in at least three ways. One is that the reverse work ethic of hustling insists that one should "make it without working," especially without working for white people. Something of this attitude is expressed in the excerpt from the interview with a high school youth and his mother. Others have reported that black children with a hustling orientation feel that doing schoolwork is "doing the white man thing" (Foster, 1974; Ogbu, 1977). Second, the assumption that every social interaction is an opportunity to manipulate other people for personal exploitation might also affect black youths' schoolwork. Youths who play the manipulative game with teachers or classmates cause disruptions detrimental to learning in the classroom. Finally, even though most black youths do not become hustlers or pimps (Perkins, 1975), for some youths hustling presents an attractive alternative strategy to schooling (for the possible effects of other survival strategies on black youths' schooling, see Ogbu, 1986).

The elements of opposition—identity and cultural frame of reference—lead more or less to an equation of school learning with the learning of a white cultural frame of reference which, to some black youths, is unacceptable. School curriculum is equated with white culture and doing schoolwork is interpreted by some as "doing the white man thing" or as obeying white people's orders. It is believed by some that school knowledge is white man's knowledge, not black people's knowledge, so that although it is necessary to learn school knowledge to get credentials for employment, black people cannot really identify with it.

I should point out that the apparent resistance to school learning is not merely because it is learning white people's knowledge or a white cultural frame of reference. Blacks appear to interpret the situation as obeying white people's orders, just as blacks did in the days of slavery. Even in interviews with parents and other adults, there is often a nonverbal feeling of anger and resentment that since slavery the white man has always been the one to tell the black what to do. The black man has never really been free to do what he chooses to do. Note that in the earlier interview excerpt about hustling, the black youngster and his mother expressed their admiration for the hustler because he "is doing his own thing, not the white man's thing."

Finally, the distrust which blacks have for white Stocktonians and the schools also adversely affects the academic orientation and efforts of black youths. Black children share with their parents and other members of their community the belief that one cannot trust white people and the public schools to do what is right for blacks. The children also know that even black school employees do not trust their white colleagues and "the system" in which they work because they are bitter and frustrated as a result of what they regard as prejudice and discrimination against them. In my ethnographic interviews and observations I found that blacks are generally skeptical that the schools can educate their children as well as they educate white children; to get a good education one must "fight" against the schools, not work with the schools. I also found that black children and their parents are generally skeptical about what schools teach them about the economy, the polity and history. Take, for example, an incident which took place at a public meeting following a high school riot in 1969. The hero of the occasion was a black youth who had been in and out of jail several times. He was holding a high school history textbook, *The Land of the Free*. As he strolled from one end of the platform to the other, he asked the teachers in the audience if they ever thought while teaching their classes what the title of that book meant to blacks and other minorities in those classes. The youth was cheered by students and parents alike as he repeated the question over and over. Apparently, not only did black and other minority students agree with the youth, but also black parents and other minority parents agreed that the school history textbook did not reflect their social reality as they experienced it.

I would suggest that because of the amount of distrust that blacks have for whites and the schools controlled by the latter, it is difficult for black parents to teach their children successfully to accept, internalize and follow school rules of behavior made by whites, and it is difficult for black children to accept, internalize and follow such rules of behavior for academic achievement.

Conclusion

The central thesis of this chapter is that the relatively poor school performance of blacks in Stockton, in spite of their wish to succeed, is rooted in their history of involuntary incorporation into American society and the subsequent discriminatory treatment of them in a system of racial castes. The economic and other positions assigned to blacks under this system did not require, promote or reward school success for many generations. The lower school performance adaptive to their position was encouraged by differential schooling. The latter was achieved through communitywide educational policies and practices, the treatment of blacks within the schools themselves and through denying blacks payoffs commensurate with their educational efforts and accomplishments. For their part, blacks contributed to the problem of lower school performance by the nature of their coping responses. They developed a folk theory of success in which school credentials play an ambiguous role, survival strategies compete with or detract from schooling, a cultural frame of reference and identity system make it difficult to cross cultural boundaries in school learning, and a deep distrust does not encourage school learning or following school norms.

Notes

1. Although written in ethnographic present, this chapter describes minority education in Stockton, California, as it was between 1968 and 1970.

References

Best, E. 1977. "NAACP Charges Bias by Stockton in Hiring." *Stockton Record*, 18 Jan.

Bloom, B.S., A. Davis, and R.D. Hess. 1965. *Compensatory Education for Cultural Deprivation*. New York: Holt.

California, State of. 1972. "City of Stockton: Affirmative Action Survey," Unpublished Manuscript. California Fair Employment Practices Commission. Sacramento, Calif.

Foster, H.L. 1974. *Ribbin', Jivin' and Playin' the Dozens: The Unrecognized Dilemma of Inner City Schools*. Cambridge, Mass.: Ballinger.

Hunter, D. 1980. "Ducks vs. Hard Rocks." *Newsweek*, 19 Aug., pp. 14–15.

Hutchinson, E.W. 1965. "Stockton Church Metropolitan Strategies, Parish Studies." Report 1: Appendix A: Characteristics of the Stockton Metropolitan Area. Mimeo.

LeVine, R.A. 1967. *Dreams and Deeds. Achievement Motivation in Nigeria*. Chicago: University of Chicago Press.

Litherland, R.H. 1978. "The Role of the Church in Educational Change: A Case History of a Feasible Strategy." Ph.D. diss. San Francisco Theological Seminary.

Martin, V.C. 1959. *Stockton Album Through the Years*. Stockton: Stockton Record.

Meer, B., and E. Freedman. 1966. "The Impact of Negro Neighbors on White Homeowners." *Social Forces* 45:11–19.

Norgren, P.H., and S.E. Hill. 1964. *Toward Fair Employment*. New York: Columbia University Press.

Ogbu, J.U. 1974. *The Next Generation: An Ethnography of Education in an Urban Neighborhood*. New York: Academic Press.

———. 1977. "Racial Stratification and Education: The Case of Stockton, California." *ICRD Bulletin* 12(3):1–26.

———. 1978. *Minority Education and Caste: The American System in Cross-Cultural Perspective*. New York: Academic Press.

——— 1985. "A Cultural Ecology of Competence Among Inner-City Blacks." In *Beginnings: Social and Affective Development of Black Children*, ed. M.B. Spencer, J. Brookins and W. Allen. Hillsdale, N.J.: Lawrence Erlbaum.

———. 1986. "Stockton, California, Revisited: Joining the Labor Force." In *Becoming a Worker*, ed. K.M. Borman and J. Reisman, pp. 29–56. Norwood, N.J.: ABLEX Publishing Corp.

Perkins, E. 1975. *Home is a Dirty Street: The Social Oppression of Black Children*. Chicago: Third World Press.

San Joaquin County. 1973. "Median Family Income, 1970: By Race and Census Tract." Stockton: Department of County Planning.

South Stockton Parish. 1967. "A Statistical Analysis of South and East Stockton." Unpublished manuscript. Stockton, California.

Stockton, City Planning Department. 1970. "Housing Plan: Elements of the General Plan." Unpublished Manuscript.

————. 1973. "Profile No. 5: Education Study." Unpublished Manuscript. Neighborhood Analysis Program.

Stockton Unified School District. 1948a. "Community Survey: In-School Youth." Unpublished Manuscript. Research Department.

————. 1948b. "Community Survey: Occupational Data." Unpublished Manuscript. Research Department.

————. 1963. "Dropout Rate, Stockton Unified School District." Unpublished Manuscript. Research Department.

————. 1967. "Annual Report." Unpublished Manuscript. Washington Elementary School.

————. 1968a. "Report on the State Testing Results." Unpublished Manuscript. Research Department.

————. 1968b. "Assisting Parents to Promote School Success: A Proposal." Unpublished Manuscript. Office of Compensatory Education.

————. 1969a. "Report on the State Testing Results." Unpublished Manuscript. Research Department.

————. 1969b. "Annual Report." Unpublished Manuscript. John Marshall Junior High School.

————. 1969c. "Superintendent's Statement on Equal Facilities," Minutes, 28 Jan., p. 4456. Board of Education.

————. 1970. "Report on the State Testing Results." Unpublished Manuscript. Research Department.

————. 1971a. "Report on the State Testing Results." Unpublished Manuscript. Research Department.

————. 1971b. "Evaluation of a Comprehensive Compensatory Education Program." Unpublished Manuscript. Office of Compensatory Education.

————. 1972. "Report on the State Testing Results." Unpublished Manuscript. Research Department.

————. 1973. "Report on the State Testing Results." Unpublished Manuscript. Research Department.

U.S. Department of Commerce, Bureau of Census. 1962. *U.S. Census of Population and Housing: Census Tracts Final Report*, PHD (1)153. Washington, D.C.: U.S. Government Printing Office.

U.S. Department of Justice. 1967. "Model Cities Correctional Project." Unpublished Manuscript. Stockton, California.

Chapter Nine
Education and American Indians:
The Experience of the Ute Indian Tribe

Betty Jo Kramer
Community and Senior Citizens Services
County of Los Angeles

> These Indians do not understand what you are
> talking about and you don't understand what they
> mean.
>
> Happy Jack, 1903

Introduction

For 100 years, the Utes have been exposed to the American educational
system through private, church-run or federally funded on-reservation
schools, boarding schools and the state public school system. The free
public education system of Utah has served Utes since 1952 but has
produced relatively few Ute high school graduates. Utes perceive the
school district and the schools as generally hostile to their children and
as a system which is nearly unassailable. This perception is based on a
history of long-standing grievances between Utes and neighboring non-
Indians, on the racist attitudes of many non-Indians, and on the
differing values and expectations held by Utes and the public schools.
Whether purposefully or inadvertently, the schools have served as
agents of assimilation. They are viewed, therefore, as a threatening
rather than a beneficial force in the lives of Ute children.

The findings reported in this chapter are drawn from participant observation as a resident on the Uintah and Ouray Reservation from 1979 to 1983. The Ute Indian Tribe employed me to direct its Head Start project and ancillary parent and staff development programs, and authorized me to conduct anthropological fieldwork. While I did not systematically study the relationship between the Ute Indian Tribe and the local school district, awareness of the district's influence on reservation life was unavoidable. The relationship between the tribe and schools was characterized by mutual distrust, misunderstanding and an atmosphere of prejudice. In order to represent local perspectives, I cite published and unpublished Ute sources, as well as the manuscripts of local educators.

The Ute Indian Tribe

Ute bands that settled onto the Uintah and Ouray Reservation in northeastern Utah are federally recognized as the Ute Indian Tribe and are also known as the Northern Ute. These bands were composed of individualistic extended family groups. Prior to the reservation period, there was only occasional cooperation between bands for hunting antelope or rabbit, for raids on other tribes and for the Bear Dance (Conetah, 1982:3–11). By creating this reservation, the federal government forced independent bands into an enduring relationship.

The Uintah and Ouray Reservation is composed of Utes with diverse histories, traditions, dialects and political interests. The Taviwach, now known as the Uncompahgre band, formerly lived in the high mountains of central Colorado. The Taviwach were settled onto the Uncompahgre Agency in Colorado in 1875 and were later removed to the Ouray Reservation. The Uintah band was named for the Uintah Agency, to which the Uinta-ats, Tumpanawach, Pah Vant and San Pitch Utes were removed from their homelands in eastern and central Utah. The Yamparika and Parianuche, who share features more in common with Plains Indian peoples than with other Utes, were placed on the White River Agency in Colorado and later moved to the Uintah Reservation. The Uintah and Ouray Reservation was formed by the consolidation of the Uintah Reservation which was established in 1865 and the Ouray Reservation which was established in 1882 (Conetah, 1982:77–118). Between 1954 and 1961, Ute "mixed bloods" (i.e., persons with 50 percent or less Ute ancestry) were terminated from tribal membership (Conetah, 1982:150–52; cf. Lang, 1961–62). The Ute Indian Tribe established the most stringent requirement for tribal membership of all federally recognized American Indian tribes. Only "full bloods" (i.e., persons for whom a five-eighths blood quantum can be demonstrated) were enrolled as tribal members. Enrolled tribal members continue to trace their band membership matrilaterally.

Traditionally, the extended family was an economic and political unit. The elder family members were responsible for educating and socializing Ute children. Grandparents taught appropriate skills to youngsters while their parents and other young adults provided the family's subsistence base. Elders have continued to counsel and preserve Ute customs and rituals although their teaching role has been attenuated. Each family considers its own traditions unique and inviolable. For non-family members to advise children or to instruct them on cultural issues is considered unwelcome interference.

History of the Relationship between Utes and Non-Indians

The Uncompahgre, White River and Uintah bands were removed from their homelands in order to facilitate mineral and ore extraction, ranching and farming. This process continued even after the Utes had been placed on reservations. Although in 1861 Mormon settlers considered the bleak Uintah Basin only good to "hold the world together" (Unterman and Unterman, 1972:16), by 1885 settlers began illegally to divert water for irrigation. Moreover, miners established gilsonite and gypsum claims and built access roads on the Uintah Reservation. In 1887, the federal government authorized a railroad line to transport minerals across the Uintah Reservation and in 1888 removed a 7,000 acre strip of gilsonite claims from the Uintah Reservation. It then opened the reservation to public domain (the Ouray Reservation in 1898, Uintah Reservation in 1905–06), extinguished the Uintah Reservation's title to Strawberry Valley in 1910 and allowed water and land rights to be ceded in 1914 (Conetah, 1982:118–29).

The relationship of the Utes with non-Indians was eloquently expressed by Happy Jack, a White River band leader, in a 1903 General Council:

> After the white people come in here they will say, "We took your lands, now we will take your water and your house, so you

get off this land, go to some other country and find some other
place!" That is the reason that we feel bad over this business.
The land where the white man's towns are belonged to us at one
time. These Indians do not understand what you are talking
about and you don't understand what they mean. You are just
like a storm from the mountains when the flood is coming down
the stream, and we can't help or stop it. (cited in Conetah,
1982:125)

Neither Happy Jack, who opposed the opening of the reservation to
public domain, nor the other Utes knew that the public domain act had
been passed by Congress before their council was convened and their
consent sought (Conetah, 1982:125).

The relationship changed little during the intervening 80 years.
Although Utes successfully sued to receive compensation for the
forcible ceding of resources in violation of their treaties, their resources
continued to be subject to negotiation. In 1982, Utes were urged by
their tribal council, lawyers and the Bureau of Indian Affairs to cede
additional water rights and to increase their participation in the Central
Utah Water Project. Many tribal members did not understand how they
would benefit from a new water compact and chose not to vote on this
issue. In fact, so few Ute voters turned out at the polls that there was no
legal quorum to decide this crucial issue. The Central Utah Project and
the state could ill afford to let the matter go unresolved. One business
committee member accused Utah Congressman James Hansen of tactics
to reduce Ute tribal control over what was said to be "more precious
than oil, money or even life" (*Ute Bulletin*, 1982a:4).

The relative wealth of Ute resources and the tribe's apparent
access to federal financial support was a continuing source of jealousy
for the adjacent non-Indian community. The bleak high desert basin,
good only to "hold the world together," turned out to be rich in oil and
minerals. In 1983, each tribal member's monthly dividend from oil
leases on tribal land was $350 and many Utes also received revenue
from oil leases on their individual land allotments. Although dividends
were to be held in trust for minors, their parents or guardians were able
to withdraw funds if they could show cause for needing that money. No
cause needed to be shown, however, to withdraw a quarterly allowance
for students. In addition, children's school supplies were paid according
to their need for assistance. Senior citizens received an additional $350
per month "golden age money," three-course luncheons Monday

through Friday, and free coal or wood. Seniors were also provided with group travel opportunities. The tribe distributed to all members large turkeys at Thanksgiving and produce from the tribally operated farm at harvests. Tribal members were eligible for noncompetitive jobs in the tribal organization, free health-care services through the Indian Health Service, low-cost housing through H.U.D. grants and loans through the American Indian National Bank.

Non-Indians living near the reservation frequently and mistakenly regarded these sources of unearned income as welfare. They accused Utes of being social parasites and blamed the dole for creating a tribe that burdens society. This sentiment was voiced as frequently among school-aged non-Indian children as adults. The same discontented non-Indians would not have denigrated the white rancher who received revenues from oil leases on his acreage and stock dividends from wise investments or who salted money into a retirement fund, inherited wealth, received medicare, received senior citizens' discounts from merchants, or whose grandchildren applied for Basic Educational Opportunity Grants to defray college expenses. Nevertheless, the relative difference in disposable income and perceived access to resources was a source of friction.

History of the Ute Involvement in American Educational Systems

The Government On-Reservation Schools

Fred A. Conetah (1982:130), the Ute Tribe historian, noted that "one issue that was particularly troublesome for the People was the efforts of federal officials to educate Ute children." Utes opposed and resented the notion of their children being taught "white ways," and most refused to send their children to school until the second decade of this century.

The first Uintah school was opened by the Indian Agent Critchlow in 1874. The agent's wife ran the school in her home and educated her own children along with 25 Ute boys who attended irregularly. Critchlow requested government funds to feed and board the Ute students, who traveled some distance to attend class, but his request was denied. The school closed for a year, then reopened in 1877 and by that time Critchlow had secured funding to hire a teacher. The first teacher resigned after eight months, and his successor lasted only seven months (Conetah, 1982:130).

A second school was opened under contract with the Presbyterian Church. This was in keeping with the federal policy of the time to assume responsibility for Indian education or to contract that responsibility to private organizations. The new school building opened its doors in January 1881. By March, not a single student remained. The following year, control of the school was transferred to the Indian service, which managed to operate it with only a few students attending. In 1885, Uintah and White River women held a council to express their opposition to sending children to the schools (Conetah, 1982).

The Indian Agent serving Uncompahgre fared no better in convincing parents to send their children to the Ouray school. Not only did parents object to the school's interference in traditional educational practices and its promulgation of non-Ute ways, but local tensions must have been high as the government established a new fort to better control Uncompahgre. The option of sending children to schools outside Utah was also rejected because parents feared that "Ute boy no understand white man houses, mebbe so die" (Commissioner of Indian Affairs, 1883:183). In 1883, the Ouray Indian Agency built a frame school house and hired a teacher. This school was closed after only two months. No educational effort was launched on the Ouray Agency until 1892 when a boarding school was built (Conetah, 1982).

That same year a boarding school was opened on the Uintah Agency. Attendance was low because Uintah and White River bands feared that "children always died when they went to school" (Commissioner of Indian Affairs, 1901:392). In 1901, their worst fears were realized when a measles epidemic swept through the Uintah Boarding School, and 26 percent of the 65 students died (Conetah, 1982:131).

General conditions at the Uintah Boarding School improved after 1910. Attendance increased especially after the students from the Ouray Boarding School were transferred there. The boarding school remained open until June 1952 when administrative responsibility for the education of Ute children was transferred to the public school system (Conetah, 1982).

Entry into the Public School System

The closing of the Uintah Boarding School represented a major shift away from federal responsibility for Indian education to state and local school responsibility. This shift reflected the federal policy of termination which aggressively promoted assimilation at the expense of the federal government's "unique" and "solemn obligation" to American Indian peoples. By eliminating "Indian education" the policy makers anticipated that American Indian students would be placed in the mainstream of "American education" and American life. Without the protective federal involvement to maintain their unique status as sovereign domestic nations (cf. the pivotal United States Supreme Court cases of *Cherokee Nation v. Georgia*, 30 U.S. [5 Pet.] 1 [1831] and *Worcester v. Georgia*, 31 U.S. [6 Pet.] 515 [1832]), American Indians were relegated to the same status as other American ethnic minorities.

The transfer of Indian Bureau functions to the tribes and to appropriate state and local agencies was costly but deemed necessary to promote assimilation. In order to accommodate the influx of Ute students into the public school system, Congress appropriated $250,000 to construct a new high school in Roosevelt, Utah. The contiguous school districts of Uintah and Duchesne counties each also contributed $250,000 to the construction and the new school was aptly named Union High School.

In line with the federal policy of assimilation, a high school education was made obligatory for all Utes. The entry of Utes into the public schools was not well received by the non-Indian population in Uintah and Duchesne counties. As the former principal of the Uintah Boarding School noted:

> Many whites objected strenuously to the recently introduced school ordinance which makes it necessary for Indian boys and girls to complete high school. This, of course, means they must go to the white high schools in the area. (Lang, 1953:52–53)

Many Utah educators were convinced that academic achievement correlated with race. One master's degree thesis in education surveyed a stratified sample of five full-blood Utes, five mixed bloods and five non-Indians attending Union High School. The study found that attendance, course grades and achievement on standardized tests were low for full bloods and high for whites, with

mixed bloods somewhere in between (Atkinson, 1955). Another
master's thesis in education compared Ute and non-Indian children's
standardized test results and found significant differences in both verbal
and nonverbal performance (Shuts, 1960). Shuts cautioned, however,
that the results of her study might be misleading, based on sample size
and cultural differences in testing situations. These differences, Shuts
indicated, might include culturally loaded test items, the predominantly
verbal and English-language content of the test, and Ute students' lack
of motivation in test taking, lack of concern with speed in timed test
taking, and difficulties in manipulating the separate answer sheet used
in tests.

The public school system failed to meet the needs of Ute
students, and when federal policy again shifted, this time toward self-
determination, encouraging Indian tribes to become responsible for
their children's schooling, the Ute Indian Tribe provided educational
alternatives to the public schools. These alternatives, financed with
federal funds, included off-reservation boarding schools, culturally
relevant instructional materials, and community educational programs.
Nevertheless, when the Ute Tribe's educational division compiled data
on academic achievement in 1981, there was clear evidence that Utes
were not benefiting from either free public education or from the
alternative and supplemental programs.

During the 1970s, the Ute dropout rate for the secondary school
years ranged from 64 percent to 94 percent; only one quarter of Ute
men over the age of twenty-five had completed high school (Ute Indian
Tribe, 1978). The high dropout rate was not unique to the Northern Ute.
In 1969, a U.S. Senate subcommittee on Indian Education reported that
American Indian dropout rates were twice the national average with
some school districts approaching 100 percent (U.S. Congress, Senate,
1969a:ix).

Contemporary Relationships with Public Schools

The once-pervasive fear that Utes would die in non-Indian
settings was seldom voiced in the 1980s. However, at the time of
fieldwork, many Ute parents clearly viewed the non-Indian educational
setting to be a pernicious influence on their children's lives. According
to testimony made before the Senate Subcommittee on Indian

Education, their perceptions were justified (U.S. Congress, Senate, 1969a).

The community in which Union High School was located expressed racial bias against American Indians in general and Utes in particular. When a U.S. Senatorial candidate campaigned at Union High in September 1982, a non-Indian student remarked that he would never get elected if he kept shaking hands with Indians. Strong prejudice against the Utes was also evident in the views of U.S. Congressman James Hansen. In a 1982 letter to then-Secretary of the Interior James Watt, Hansen observed:

> . . . when I was Speaker of the Utah House of Representatives, 1979–1980, I worked on the "Indian Complex" (sic) between the State of Utah and the Ute Indian Tribe. . . . In my opinion, they are the worse (sic) example of what a welfare state can do to individuals. Possibly it is because of my religious background, belief in work, self-sufficiency and belief that welfare without work is a grave sin, which brings me to these conclusions. (*Ute Bulletin*, 1982b:2)

A negative attitude toward American Indians has been pervasive throughout the West since the nineteenth century (Fritz, 1963). The U.S. Senate Subcommittee (1969a:24) found that non-Indians living near reservations had a stereotypic image of American Indians, believing them to be savage, lazy, dirty and drunken. Non-Indians believed, moreover, that Indians themselves were responsible for their condition. Educational materials used in the schools may have supported this image.

The Subcommittee also found that a climate of disrespect and discrimination was common in off-reservation towns which educate many American Indians in their public schools. Indians were despised, exploited and discriminated against, the Subcommittee reported, but always held in check by the white power structure so that their situation would not change.

These attitudes have been carried into the schools. James Coleman et al. (1966) found, for example, that in the mid-1960s fully one quarter of all public school teachers preferred not to teach American Indian children. Teachers' negative attitudes have often dominated the Indian child's school experience and hindered academic achievement (see Berry, 1969:34).

As Congressman Hansen's remarks (above) remind us, the social attitudes in many western states, and particularly in Utah, are strongly influenced by the Church of Jesus Christ of the Latter Day Saints (L.D.S.).[1] The L.D.S. Church, which developed on the American frontier, offers a doctrinal history and a prophesied future of American Indians. According to the Book of Mormon, Indians are a tribe of Israel that migrated to the New World before the Christian era. On this continent, one group fell into moral decay and was cursed by God with dark skins. These dark-skinned Lamanites annihilated the civilized, moral, and white remnant of the tribe. Contemporary Lamanites (American Indians) bear that ancient curse but will one day be redeemed, returned to greatness, and again be "white and delightsome."[2] The L.D.S. Church maintains a strong educational obligation, both secular and religious, to educate American Indians so that they can assume their special place in the Church's schema. The failure of Utes to embrace the L.D.S. religion and to fulfill spiritual, doctrinal and community obligations is frustrating to local church members. Given the religious imperative to proselytize, many school officials and teachers, themselves church members, give wholehearted support to L.D.S.-sponsored American Indian awareness programs and they ignore the indigenous local culture.

The frequently voiced sentiment that Americans Indians are themselves responsible for their substandard living conditions also has L.D.S. overtones. Mormons believe that every person has the power of Free Agency to choose good over evil, to be faithful or rebellious, to live an upstanding life or to degrade his or her own life. By that logic, the Indian bears the brunt of the responsibility for improving his or her lot.

During my tenure, one school principal openly expressed this belief at a meeting which proposed introducing a general health curriculum in the public schools. That meeting was convened by the Utah Department of Health, Center for Disease Control and the Ute Indian Tribe in an effort to reduce the incidence of adult-onset diabetes. The proposed curriculum would also have benefited the general population by promoting physical fitness and enhancing cardiovascular health. The school principal declared that health problems were not general but were limited to American Indians who would not exercise Free Agency to live a healthy life. Public health advocates quickly tried to mediate by arguing that exercise of Free Agency required information for making rational decisions and, therefore, that health information should be part of the school district's requirements, but it was too late for mediation. The damage was already done. Utes attending the meeting stiffened into an angry silence, and school administrators left the meeting. After their departure, Utes voiced both anger and feelings of helplessness. There was no way to respond to this baseless, racist allegation. Worse, in their interaction with the school infrastructure, there were no neutral subjects. Even health issues could not be discussed without reference either to the L.D.S. Church or to ethnicity.

According to Ute parents, educators continue to believe that there are racially determined performance capabilities. In response to the question, "Why do you think most Ute children do not do as well as non-Indian children in school?," Ute parents described a pernicious racist attitude that reduces the likelihood of Ute students receiving an equal education (Ute Indian Tribe, 1982:14, 41). I found many parents were reluctant to confront school officials with allegations of racism because they feared retaliatory treatment against their children. Despite the widely held belief that Ute children were subject to racial discrimination, the Ute Indian Tribe had not publicly established that racism existed in the public schools.

Cultural differences in reward systems were an ongoing cause of resentment. The school recognized students who made the honor roll, and it rewarded athletic teams that won the greatest number of games. Ute parents complained to me that they did not understand the underlying value. They believed that awards were deserved by those who tried the hardest in every class or in every game, regardless of the final grade or score. In the arts, the schools awarded prizes based on the abstract qualities of the finished artwork. According to Ute parents, prizes should have reflected the intensity and satisfaction of the creative process. Clearly, school values which promoted production and competition were at odds with values which encouraged process and personal commitment.

Education for its own sake was not promoted. Few Ute parents, public school teachers or administrators had high academic expectations of Ute children. Some community members recognized that there was a blatant lack of support for the educational system or for children's academic achievement (Ute Indian Tribe, 1982:13). Many parents insisted, when speaking with me, that their preschoolers be taught to recognize all the items on the elementary school's in-take screening. Their rationale was not to improve early academic achievement but to prevent having their children labeled as "slow learners." Several parents explained that they wanted their children to be successful in public school because state law obliged them to attend. These parents also felt that the non-Indian values promoted by the schools did not contribute to the emotional and spiritual development of their children.

The attitude that schooling was unimportant was reinforced through frequent reminders that some tribal council leaders had only a few years of elementary education. Tribal members with college degrees did little better in tribal employment than those who had not completed a secondary education. Because Ute society is essentially egalitarian, most tribal jobs are considered interchangeable, and most tribal employees can transfer from one administrative posting to another. Success within the Ute Indian Tribe has a political component based on family standing within the community, band positions on certain issues, and long-standing relationships of trust or enmity.

The tribe's education division tried to intervene in the schools through various programs, counseling and the development of materials on Ute culture and history, but the schools did not integrate these supportive opportunities into the curriculum. In 1983, Ute children were excused from regular classes for "Indian" programs, which were supplementary to the regular curriculum.

The schools had not taken an active lead in these areas, but neither had Ute parents. Many Ute parents were reluctant to support an elementary-level bilingual education program intended to facilitate the teaching of basic skills. When first proposed, the bilingual program was perceived as a threat to the unique and exclusive control of Ute knowledge. Parents feared that written Ute language materials might give any literate person, including non-Utes, access to esoteric dimensions of Ute culture. Overall resistance ebbed, however, because the program seemed to promote Ute identity and encourage self-esteem. Bilingual education as a strategy for promoting academic success and competency in the three Rs was not a major topic of discussion.[3]

Utes may not have been politically conscious of all the various forces operating within the public school system. For instance, rather than insist on fair treatment from non-Indian teachers, the Ute Tribe arranged for Utes to become certified as teachers. The tribe's education division contracted with the L.D.S.-sponsored Brigham Young University to carry out the teacher training and, thus, may have perpetuated a hidden curriculum. B.Y.U. certainly offered attractive options. While B.Y.U. promoted American Indian education through scholarships and courses on American Indian education and history and, in addition, agreed to provide freshman- and sophomore-level courses on the reservation rather than to immediately expose Ute students to the rigors and disappointments of campus life, the university also required all students to take courses in L.D.S. church history and the Book of Mormon. The objections of a few trainees that Mormonism was irrelevant to teacher training were not supported by the tribe's education division, which had contracted with B.Y.U. rather than with the nonsectarian state university that had an extension office just eight miles from the reservation.[4]

Utes were not politically organized to force the public school system to improve educational opportunities for their children. Neither the Ute Tribe, nor its education division, nor the education advisory committees tried to register Ute voters and mobilize support for crucial school issues. The presence of Ute children contributed to the school district's operating budgets; local public schools received funds to meet the needs of Ute children through public laws 81-874, 81-815, 92-318, the Johnson-O'Malley Act, and the Bilingual Education Act. The tribe did not use these federally funded programs for political leverage. Instead, each program was viewed as a stopgap measure to keep Ute children from failing. Moreover, these federal programs offered jobs to tribal personnel and were welcomed as employment opportunities.

It is not surprising that Utes did not enter into the local political arena. The social organization of loosely interrelated, independent families and interband rivalry did not facilitate an effective political bloc. More important, the Utes had little to gain by entering into local politics as a minority. The Utes' status, characterized by federal recognition but little local representation, isolated the tribe as a separate political entity. This was the crux of the issue. For the tribe, political success meant maintaining its own institutions, not integrating into the county, state and national systems.

Educational Curricula: Assimilation vs. Alienation

Neither Utes nor the local schools entered into their relationship by choice; it was imposed by federal policy which sought to assimilate the Utes. The policy was not particularly successful. Utes remained culturally distinct and largely uneducated by the Utah public school system.

The U.S. Senate Subcommittee on Indian Education (1969a) prefaced its report with the statement that the federal government had failed in its responsibility to provide American Indian tribes with good-quality, effective education. The report blamed this failure on coercive assimilation policies and on the alienation between American Indian and non-Indian communities. To alleviate the "dismal record of absenteeism, drop-outs, negative self-image, and low achievement" and to achieve educational excellence, the Senate Subcommittee called for adequate funding, American Indian parent involvement, civil rights investigation and the establishment of a Select Committee on Human Needs of American Indians (1969a).

The Subcommittee was clearly moved by the testimony presented at its hearings, and the strongest language was used to condemn past federal policies and their results. What the Subcommittee actually offered was an opportunity for American Indians and educators to voice discontent and to call for noncoercive assimilation through educational excellence.

But assimilation, whether coercive or benign, may be inimical to a tribe's preference to retain its own society and culture. As a Ponca Indian testified before the Senate Subcommittee, "School is the enemy!" By attempting to emancipate American Indian children from their families and tribes in order to "educate" them, schools have instead institutionalized alienation. The classroom becomes the battleground where American Indian children protect their integrity and identity by defeating the school system.

The federal policy, which imposed the relationship between American Indians and state public school systems, did not consider the setting into which the tribes would be thrust. The Utes and other tribes were forced to rely on antagonistic state governments to carry out educational policies. As recently as 1981, the U.S. Commission on Civil Rights (1981:41) found that the considerations of the Supreme Court in the 1886 case of *U.S. v. Kagama*, which addressed the tribal-state relationship, were still relevant: "They [tribes] owe no allegiance to the States and receive from them no protection. Because of local ill feeling, the people of the States where they are found are often their deadliest enemies."

Locally, the situation was no better a century later. Ute resources and special status continued to be sources of friction, used by non-Indians as justification for blatant racism. More subtle attitudes regarding the American Indians' place in the L.D.S. church also influenced daily interactions between the Indian and non-Indian communities. The relationship that developed was characterized by mutual distrust and prejudice.

Strategies of Integration vs. Separatism

If the issue were squarely faced, the problem is not actually education. The real issue is the use of schools to assimilate the Indian child into a non-Indian world. Yet, the dominant theme in contemporary interethnic relations has been cultural pluralism. Havinghurst proposed, for example, that the goals, problems and issues in American Indian education revolve around working out a viable position in the culturally pluralistic society that exists in America (Havinghurst, 1978). This begs critical questions in Indian affairs: is the unique and separate status of tribes recognized by American society and is the federal government committed to honoring this special relationship?

These issues were considered by the presidential-appointed National Advisory Council on Indian Education (National Advisory Council on Indian Education, 1982). The Council argued that American Indian education was a trust responsibility which Congress could safeguard by providing adequate funding. American Indian organizations such as the National Congress of American Indians and the National Indian Youth Council have promoted recognition and respect for enclave tribal communities, for traditional value systems and for indigenous languages and knowledge. They have expected American Indian children to perpetuate their respective Indian societies, not the American society at large.

American Indian tribes cannot be compared to other ethnic minorities. American Indians only stand to lose by integration into the larger society:

> Politically, other minorities started with nothing and attempted to obtain a voice in the existing economic and political structure. Indians started with everything and have gradually lost much of what they had to advancing alien civilization. . . . Indian tribes have always been separate political entities interested in maintaining their own institutions and beliefs. . . . So while other minorities have sought integration into the larger society, much of Indian society is motivated to retain its political and cultural separateness. (U.S. Commission on Civil Rights, 1981:32–33)

The most viable political and economic position for Indian tribes has been co-existence with American society, not entry into it.

As agents for a "melting pot" society, the educational role of schools is compromised (Medicine, 1976:290; Wax, Wax and Dumont, 1964:115; Wilkinson, 1982). Some Indian educators have advocated community control as a means of eliminating assimilation through the schools. Christensen and Demmert (1978:140) urged tribes to take legal and moral responsibility for their children's education by exercising control over school boards, approval of curricula and, if necessary, by establishing separate schools. The creation of separate tribally controlled school systems was also suggested by the National Association for the Advancement of Colored People (NAACP, 1971) as a way to ensure equal opportunity and to protect the rights of American Indian children. This approach was taken by Chippewa and Cree in establishing the Rocky Boy School District and by Navajo in establishing the Ramah School District and the Rough Rock Demonstration School.

Northern Utes had not set integration as one of their goals. The Ute Indian Tribe has maintained itself as a distinct political entity. Community solidarity was promoted by extending tribal privileges to those who remained on the reservation and most Utes did not leave. Those who did leave to attend off-reservation schools or to seek employment usually returned after a short absence. The reservation with its plainly marked signs, "This is Ute Indian land. No trespassing," was a clear physical reminder that Utes are a separate people.

The public school system did not encourage the goals or the solidarity of the Ute Tribe. The public school's insistence on individual achievement in non-Indian subjects, values, and environments was inimical to tribal identity and to tribal unity. There was no illusion of meaningful integration of American Indians into the educational policies, the general work force, the economy or the polity of the surrounding counties. The local job market was limited, and formal education provided little advantage. On the reservation, many tribal jobs have not in the past required high school diplomas, training certificates or college degrees.

The tribal strategy of short-term hiring of non-Indian consultants, experts, managers and professionals has actually promoted tribal solidarity. The outside expert was expected to solve a management or service problem and then was dismissed in order to restore tribal control. When operations depended on an outside expert who could not be easily replaced, gossip by community members and hostility by tribal authorities reduced the outsider's status. These extremely effective strategies created a secure impression that the tribe had control over its own destiny.

This type of accommodation brought the Ute Indian Tribe into a relationship with the larger American society through the mediation of educated outsiders. Whether the solution had long-term effects (e.g., maximizing returns from petroleum extraction) or short-term effects (e.g., policy for a one-year program of one-time funding) the Ute Tribe was the recipient of the benefits. Expertise, when needed for a specific tribal goal, remained a service which could always be purchased.

Educational Goals

In 1983, neither the Ute Tribe nor the non-Indian public extolled cultural relativism in the local schools. Education, whether formal or informal, whether Ute or non-Indian, was concerned with enculturation and with teaching culturally relevant information and values. Major cultural differences existed between Utes and non-Indians. They did not share the same concept of education, ethics, social productivity or "racial" differences. Even in an amiable atmosphere of understanding and open communication, these differences would be difficult to reconcile. Separateness was entrenched in the atmosphere that existed. "American Indians" was a unit subject usually taught in November to the general student body, while Ute Indian programs and Ute Indian teachers were available year-round to Ute Indian students, who were dismissed from other classes to participate in these "special" activities.

The public schools may have unintentionally promoted tribal separatism and solidarity. The schools maintained subtle policies of racism in teachers' attitudes, in staff predictions of success rates and in failure to integrate Ute culture into the curriculum. Students could defy the school's presumption of their inferiority by seeking higher education and off-reservation employment, by relocating and by separating themselves from tribal life. Students could also defy the educational system's goal of assimilation by failing in school and so reaffirm their tribal identity. The schools offered most students a painful, no-win situation.

Clearly, the public school system failed to provide a meaningful and effective education to Ute students. On the other hand, the Tribal Council had not actively promoted education as having purpose in peoples' lives. Nor had the Ute Indian Tribe's Education Division provided an answer to the question of purpose—at least, not when I was asking the question.

There was little basis for a formal dialogue. Neither the tribe nor the schools recognized their mutual need to educate Ute children, and so no truly integrated curriculum had been developed. Despite the high dropout rate, the tribal organization did employ tribal members who had earned a high school diploma, G.E.D. or university degree. The Ute Tribe's education division offered an adult education program which attracted middle-aged persons as well as young adults. Perhaps the adult educational option and the prospect of tribal employment will lend a more positive attitude toward academic education. Until tribal members and the tribal government reach a consensus that formal education can meet their real needs, there will be little incentive for the Ute student to succeed in a public educational system and schools will remain alien institutions. As long as the assimilation of the Ute child is the underlying purpose of the educational system, the goals of the public schools are likely to remain antithetical to the values and objectives of the Ute Indian Tribe and its members.

Notes

Acknowledgments: This chapter is a revised version of my article, "The Dismal Record Continues: the Ute Indian Tribe and the School System," which appeared in *Ethnic Groups* 5(3):151–72, 1983, and is reprinted here with the permission of the publisher.

1. Members of the Church of Jesus Christ of the Latter Day Saints (Mormons) pioneered parts of the Rocky Mountain West and established the theocratic state of Deseret (now, the state of Utah). Political, economic and social structures of Utah remain dominated by Mormons. U.S. federal courts have intervened in the church's intrusion into public education. The American Civil Liberties Union brought suit against the Utah State Board of Education for allowing L.D.S. religious training on public school time and granting public school accreditation for these classes. Since all federal judges in Utah were Mormon, the case was transferred to a federal district court in Wyoming which found for the plaintiff that the Utah practice was in violation of First Amendment rights (*Education Week*, 1982:3).

2. In 1981, the Church of Jesus Christ of the Latter Day Saints revised "white and delightsome" to "pure and delightsome," explaining that this is a more appropriate interpretation of the nineteenth century use of the term "white." This distinction is not yet completely accepted and many await the physical whitening of American Indians (cf. Jorgensen, 1972:2).

3. Since the original publication of this article, a long-term bilingual education program has been operated by the Ute Indian Tribe to supplement the elementary public school curriculum. The program and its impact on language renewal have been reported elsewhere by William Leap (1991).

4. The local option was feasible. Utah State University provided attractive on-reservation and local options to other tribal programs. For example, the tribe's Head Start Project had a reasonably priced contract with that campus and was successfully graduating credentialed teachers and other B.A. and B.S. degree holders.

References

Atkinson, D. 1955. "Educational Adjustment of the Ute Indians as Compared to Mixed Bloods and Native Whites at Union High School, Roosevelt, Utah." M.A. thesis. Utah State University.

Berry, B. 1969. "The Education of American Indians, a Survey of the Literature." Prepared for the Special Subcommittee on Indian Education, 91st Congress, 1st Session.

Christensen, R., and W. Demmert. 1978. "The Education of Indians and the Mandate of Indians." In *The Schooling of Native America*, ed. T. Thompson, pp. 139–52. American Association of Colleges for Teacher Education in collaboration with the Teacher Corps. Washington, D.C.: U.S. Government Printing Office.

Coleman, J., et al. 1966. *Equality of Educational Opportunity*. Washington, D.C.: U.S. Government Printing Office.

Commissioner of Indian Affairs. 1883. *Annual Report*.

————. 1901. *Annual Report*.

Conetah, F.A. 1982. *A History of the Northern Ute People*, ed. K. MacKay and F. O'Neil. University of Utah Printing Service, Salt Lake City: Uintah-Ouray Ute Tribe.

Education Week. 1982. "Utah Board Liable for Some Legal Fees in Religious Dispute." 27 Oct., p. 3.

Fritz, H.E. 1963. *The Movement for Indian Assimilation, 1860–1890*. Philadelphia: University of Pennsylvania Press.

Havinghurst, R.H. 1978. "Indian Education since 1960." *Annals of the American Academy of Political and Social Sciences* 436:13–26.

Jorgensen, J. 1972. *Sun Dance Religion*. Chicago: University of Chicago Press.

Lang, G. 1953. "A Study of Culture Contact and Culture Change: The White Rocks Utes in Transition." *Anthropological Papers*. Department of Anthropology, University of Utah, no. 15.

————. 1961–62. "Economic Development and Self-Determination: The Northern Ute." *Human Organization* 20:164–71.

Leap, W.L. 1991. "Pathways and Barriers to Indian Language Literacy-building on the Northern Ute Reservation." *Anthropology and Education Quarterly* 22(1):21–41.

Medicine, B. 1976. "The Schooling Process: Some Lakota (Sioux) Views." In *The Anthropological Study of Education*, ed. C. Calhoun and F. Ianni, pp. 182–29. The Hague: Mouton.

National Advisory Council on Indian Education. 1982. "Indian Education: America's Unpaid Debt." The 8th Annual Report to the Congress of the United States, June. Washington, D.C.

National Association for the Advancement of Colored People, Legal Defense and Education Fund. 1971. *An Even Chance.* New York: NAACP with the Center for Law and Education, Harvard University.

Shuts, E.S. 1960. "A Comparison of Performance of Ute Indian and White Children on Verbal and Nonverbal Tests." M.A. thesis. University of Utah.

United States Commission on Civil Rights. 1981. *Indian Tribes: A Continuing Quest for Survival.* Washington, D.C.: U.S. Government Printing Office.

United States Congress, Senate. 1969a. *Indian Education: A National Tragedy, A National Challenge.* 91st Congress, 1st Session, Report no. 501.

————. 1969b. *Testimony on Indian Education.* Hearings by the Senate Subcommittee on Indian Education, 91st Congress, 1st Session, 5 volumes.

Unterman, G.E., and B.R. Unterman. 1972. *Guide to Dinosaur Land and the Unique History of Uintah County.* Vernal, Utah.

Ute Bulletin. 1982a. "Councilmen Air Their Views." Vol. 16(11):4.

————. 1982b. "Text of Hansen's Treaty Letter." Vol. 16(4):2.

Ute Indian Tribe. 1978. "Ute Comprehensive Education Needs Assessment." Unpublished report, Education Division.

————. 1982. "Community Needs Assessment." Unpublished report, Education Division.

Wax, M.L., R.H. Wax, and R.V. Dumont, Jr. 1964. *Formal Education in an American Indian Community.* Atlanta: Emory University.

Wilkinson, G. 1982. "Educational Problems in the Indian Community, a Comment on Learning as Colonialism." *Integrated Education* XIX(1–2):42–50.

Chapter Ten
The New Zealand Experience: Maoris

John M. Barrington
Victoria University of Wellington

This paper examines the complex interaction of historical and cultural factors, including aspects of Maori-European interaction and education policy, and their implications for the school performance of Maori children. It demonstrates that the wars of the 1860s and subsequent land confiscations left a legacy of bitterness among some tribes which led them for many years to reject European institutions such as schools. Policies designed to secure the position of the Maori as a rural, land-based people often led to an adaptationist concept of education that was narrow and limited in scope in terms of fully utilizing Maori capacities. The paper also examines the effects of rapid urbanization after World War II, the various attempts to explain continuing disparities in the school performance of Maori and European (*Pakeha*) children and policies designed to close the gap which have achieved only limited success. The focus of attention is now on greater efforts by Maori communities themselves to promote Maori language learning at the preschool level and other examples of "grass roots" or self-help initiatives designed to foster greater educational achievement and economic development. Much greater prominence is also now being given to the Treaty of Waitangi, signed in 1840 between the crown and Maori tribes as a basis for the resolution of land claims and as a symbol of the move for greater acknowledgment of the rights of the Maori partner in all areas of New Zealand life including schooling.

Historical Background

Abel Tasman's arrival in New Zealand with two ships in 1642 heralded the first contact between Europeans and the indigenous Maori population. Tasman was followed in 1769 by Captain Cook, and in the 1790s by sealers and deep-sea whalers who set up camps and exchanged blankets, tools and guns for potatoes, pork and labor. Relations between Maoris and European visitors thereafter deteriorated and Europeans avoided New Zealand's shores for some years.

However, Christian missionaries were not deterred for long. In 1814, the Reverend Samuel Marsden founded a mission for the Church Missionary Society, and he was soon followed by clergy from other denominations and by traders. Mission schools were established and proved enormously popular. Instruction was provided in the Maori language, and although it is impossible to be precise about literacy figures, a cautious estimate would be that by the early 1840s a little over half the adult population of 90,000 could read or write a little in their own language (Barrington and Beaglehole, 1974). These were years when the Maoris easily dominated the European population, which had grown to 2,000 by 1840.

The Treaty of Waitangi heralded the beginning of a period of acculturation which was to last, virtually uninterrupted, for two decades as the Maoris enthusiastically adopted European ways. They planted acres of wheat, maize and potatoes, bought horses, pigs and cattle, operated flour mills and coastal schooners, and entered paid employment as laborers, carpenters, sawyers and blacksmiths (Metge, 1976).

These activities benefited the European settlements and were generally encouraged by the government, but disputes over land rights soon began to disrupt what had up until then been relatively harmonious relations between the races. By 1850, Europeans had obtained most of the land in the South Island and large areas in the North. Their population overtook the Maori in 1858 and as their hunger for more land continued unabated, Maori resistance stiffened. The Land Wars, which finally broke out in 1860, proved disastrous for many Maori tribes, leading to inevitable defeat in the face of superior European forces assisted by "friendly" Maori tribes. The Maori King (Tawhiao) retired into an area of steep hill country and the government confiscated further Maori lands.

The period from the Land Wars of the 1860s to the turn of the century has often been described in terms of Maori withdrawal and decline because Maori tribes, bitter and disillusioned from their experience of war and land confiscation, refused to cooperate with government agencies, including schools. However, this is now viewed as a far too general view of what was essentially a complex racial situation, with different patterns in different parts of the country (Sorrenson, 1956). Neutral and "friendly" Maori tribes (in Northland, the East Coast and the South Island) continued to seek close interaction with the Pakeha, and often suffered continuing loss of land and population decline as a result. Defeated tribes such as the Waikato and Maiapoto, who withdrew into the King Country, maintained their own way of life and a stable population, while still borrowing and adapting European tools and techniques. In Taranaki, such leaders as Te Whiti and Tohu attempted to maintain traditional social organization while demonstrating non-violent resistance to the government. This complex pattern of race relations had important implications for the way different Maori communities reacted to the government's subsequent efforts to develop a system of state Maori primary schools in rural areas.

During the early 1880s, the Waikato and Maiapoto tribes began to emerge from isolation, while other tribes continued their almost uninterrupted adjustment to European ways. By 1890, growing numbers of Maoris throughout the country were in paid employment, usually of an unskilled nature, building roads and railways, working in the bush, shearing sheep and digging for kauri gum, while those who had retained land continued efforts to make it commercially viable by growing grain, sheep-farming and dairying (Metge, 1976). The Maori population recovered, and in 1928 its rate of natural increase passed the European rate. The lifting of economic depression, combined with the election of a labor government in 1935, which was more sympathetic to Maori aspirations, gave fresh encouragement to Maoris in some areas, including greater practical assistance with land development schemes and increased spending on Maori education, housing and welfare.

World War II saw large numbers of young Maoris enter the Armed Services; the Maori Battalion suffered heavy casualties in the Middle East, where many of its members served with great distinction (Metge, 1976). After the war, limited opportunities in rural areas for the growing population and a Maori Affairs policy of encouraging Maoris to migrate to urban areas led to a rapid increase in the Maori urban population, which rose from 15 percent of the total in 1936 to 70 percent by 1971 (Metge, 1976). This population was also extremely youthful (50 percent of all Maoris are under the age of fifteen compared with only 25 percent of non-Maoris) and concentrated in particular cities. In 1945, only one of every 20 Maoris lived in the Auckland urban area. By 1976, nearly one in four (22.3 percent) of the Maori population was living in Auckland (Metge, 1976).

There has always been a strong assumption among European New Zealanders that the society is based on equality of opportunity and "classlessness" and has the "best race relations in the world." However, this sense of complacency has been questioned increasingly. Ausubel (1961) thought New Zealanders' attitude to race relations was unwarrantable, sanguine and complacent. Many New Zealanders, both Maori and European, are currently reexamining this situation. Nash (1983) argues that visitors from Britain and the United States, looking at New Zealand's northern cities, see an all-too-familiar sight: an ethnic division of labor, with its social and economic consequences; segregated housing areas; high levels of unemployment and high levels of involvement in crime. Metge (1976:292) commented:

> Most Pakehas [Europeans] deny believing in the innate superiority of a white skin, but their conversation and behaviour seem frequently to be based on the assumption that Pakeha ways are superior and Pakehas as a group and as individuals [are] more likely to behave acceptably by their standards. . . . Because the majority of Maoris are employed in un- and semi-skilled occupations and fall below the national average in living standards (measured in terms of income and possessions), housing and education, Pakehas tend to see "Maori ways" as causally connected and practically synonymous with lower socio-economic status.

Stereotyped attitudes about Maoris are undoubtedly held by many Europeans who see them as happy-go-lucky, well suited to manual jobs, good sportspersons, and having a different concept of the law from the European. Discrimination against the employment of Maoris has undoubtedly existed in some occupations (banks, shops, law enforcement). But as Metge also points out, there are important regional differences in Maori-Pakeha relations, depending on such factors as history of contact, population ratio and land ownership (Metge, 1976).

Maoris make up 9 percent of the New Zealand population. Unemployment, health (including infant mortality), income and education statistics demonstrate that they remain at a distinct disadvantage compared with Europeans in all of these areas. Young Maoris who leave school today are less well qualified than non-Maoris: over 50 percent of non-Maori pupils achieve sixth form certificates or better, compared with just over 20 percent of Maori pupils (New Zealand Planning Council, 1989). It is this kind of disparity which fuels the criticism made currently by many Maoris about the education system.

The Links to Schooling

What links did the interaction of historical, geographic and racial factors that affected the establishment of schools and the major policies governing their operation have with this situation? The Land Wars of the 1860s effectively shut down the missionary and government-aided efforts which had up to that time provided formal schooling of a European kind for Maori children. However, in 1867, with the worst of the fighting over, the government introduced a Native School Act to establish a national state system of Maori elementary schools in the rural areas where most Maoris lived. The pupils would receive instruction in English and the ordinary subjects of the primary school curriculum. The act had a strong self-help component; schools would only be built when a request was received from a Maori community and the communities would be expected to contribute land for a site and a share of the costs. The policy underlying this act, and Maori education policy generally, was clearly assimilationist in purpose. According to Walker (1984), the establishment of the Maori schools carried the goal of assimilation (and the attack on Maori culture) right into the heart of the Maori tribal areas. However, opinions differ regarding the broad motives of the settlers in their dealings with the Maoris. Ward (1973:308) views the colonization of New Zealand as "substantially an imperial subjugation of a native people, for the benefit of the conquering race." But Williams (1969:146) comments:

> The Maori people . . . were never simply shoved aside without the benefit of legal protection, like the civilized Indian tribes of the American Southeast. . . . They were never exploited in the

high-handed and arrogant fashion used by the white settlers of
East and Central Africa.

Nash (1983:42) sees European attitudes toward the Maoris as
paternalistic, but this was a "lot better than the genocidal practices of
the Australian settlers" toward Aborigines. The assimilationist policy
followed is viewed negatively today, but in the nineteenth century
context it could be regarded as relatively liberal because it "assumed, at
least in theory, that Maoris had the intelligence and the ability to make
the transition to a more 'advanced' cultural level, and that culture not
colour was the criteria of acceptability" (Metge, 1976:304).

The slow development of the Maori schools after 1867 reflected
the complex racial situation. Most early requests for schools came from
areas where tribes had remained neutral during the wars and had not
suffered land confiscation. Tribes defeated in war, who withdrew from
Pakeha contact, showed little inclination to enroll their children in
schools or have contact with other European institutions.

In 1879, the Maori schools (then 57 in number) were transferred
from the Native Department to the central Education Department,
where they were administered as a separate division with a national
uniform Maori school policy for the next 87 years. The Maori school
system had some parallels with the federal system of American Indian
schools and the broad policies followed in both systems also
demonstrated some remarkable similarities at particular periods of their
history (Barrington and Beaglehole, 1974; Szasz, 1974).

New policies introduced in 1880 continued to reflect the official
policy of assimilation based on the assumption of European cultural
superiority (Barrington and Beaglehole, 1974). A primary role of
education was to lift Maoris from a "lower" to a "higher" plane of
civilization, with their own culture regarded as impeding the process of
Europeanization.

The ultimate aim of assimilation was also reflected in the policy
that each Maori school would be transferred to an Education Board as
soon as the pupils' level of attainment in English had reached a
satisfactory standard. Through this process, the separate Maori school
system would eventually cease to exist and there would be one unified
national public school system catering to both Maori and Pakeha
children. However, it should be noted that European children living in
the vicinity of Maori schools often attended them, just as Maori
children living close to Education Board-administered schools attended

those. McKenzie (1982) has commented that in a nineteenth century context, the principle that both races should be educated in a common school was noteworthy and stood in marked contrast to the rigid educational separation of races which characterized many societies at this time.

As this system developed, the curriculum of the Maori schools steadily came to more closely resemble that of the ordinary board schools although greater attention was given to practical activities including basic agriculture, trade training and health. However, the academic achievements of the schools, when measured against national standards, remained abysmally low, and the year 1906 can be taken as an illustration of this. A pass in the proficiency examination marked the successful completion of the New Zealand elementary school standards, and in 1906 26 proficiency certificates were awarded to pupils in the native schools out of a total enrollment of 4,174. The majority of these successful candidates were not Maori pupils but Europeans enrolled in Maori schools.

Among factors impeding the academic progress of Maori children was the policy of assimilation, which made little allowance for cultural difference. The Maori language was permitted in the junior classes as an aid to learning English, a practice that must at least have eased the transition to school for some children, and an innovative inspector of Maori schools between 1880 and 1904 (James Pope) wrote several bilingual texts for use in reading, spelling and health instruction. But a new policy introduced in 1905 saw Maori excluded altogether on the grounds that the use of the language hindered the learning of English, with the teaching of English being viewed as the schools' primary task. Many Maoris complain today, with understandable bitterness, of being punished for speaking Maori at school.

In the society at large Maoris often depended on migrant seasonal labor for their livelihood and children's schooling was inevitably affected. When harsh economic times came, as in the 1880s, Maori families including children became preoccupied with the fight for survival. The effects of introduced diseases ravaged many Maori communities throughout the nineteenth century, killing children and regularly interrupting Maori schooling. Schooling was also affected by the circumstances typical of many isolated rural schools of the day— extremely long distances to travel on roads and rivers which could only be traversed in favorable weather conditions.

However, from 1880 on, the government provided scholarships to assist the most able graduates from the Maori primary schools to enroll in Maori denominational boarding colleges. The leading one of these, Te Aute, provided an education by the 1890s which was regarded as equal to that of the best secondary schools in the country. The principal (John Thornton) stated that Maori society would require doctors, lawyers and teachers, and he encouraged and assisted a small number of Maori youths to enter universities. Several of the most prominent Te Aute graduates (including Apirana Ngata, Maui Pomare and Peter Buck) later gained eminence in New Zealand or abroad in the fields of law, politics, medicine and anthropology. They also took a keen interest in Maori society and development, although they were not always unanimous regarding the most desirable path future developments should take. A debate occurred that was somewhat similar to that between Booker T. Washington and W.E.B. Du Bois regarding the future of blacks in the southern United States.

Ngata advocated an education that prepared Maoris for the full range of occupations, including the professions, but Pomare, influenced by his experience as the first Maori Officer of Health, favored a more practical education, with instruction in health care and agriculture. Pomare's view tended to be most influential and arguments of the kind he put forward proved to be those most acceptable to the Department of Education, thereby reinforcing an overemphasis upon "practical" education which was to persist at least until World War II. The prevailing attitude was most cogently expressed by the Director of Education in 1929 when he said "I want a form of education devised which will enable every Maori boy to be a farmer and every Maori girl to be a farmer's wife" (Barrington and Beaglehole, 1974:210).

Notions of "cultural adaptation" which sought to modify the prevailing policy of assimilation by catering to the background of Maori pupils "where they are" in rural areas further influenced this trend after 1930 (Barrington, 1976). An emphasis on practical training continued and aspects of Maori culture (songs and arts and crafts) were introduced into the curriculum in a limited form for the first time, although the Maori language continued to be excluded. Varied and sometimes apparently conflicting influences contributed to the new approach, including ongoing attempts by Maoris to revive or maintain aspects of their own culture and progressive education with its emphasis on making school relevant to the "real world" of the child.

The failure of assimilation policies to produce acceptable academic achievement levels among Maori pupils was another reason given for the policy change. Seen by their European proponents as a "liberal" development, adaptationist ideas were often viewed less favorably by many Maoris and other indigenous people because they emphasized policies which, if carried to their logical conclusion, could result in their leading second-rate lives, tied up cocoon-like in predominantly rural areas with only limited opportunity for participation in the political and economic mainstream (Foster, 1965; Barrington, 1983a).

The rural residence of most Maoris, their poverty and the absence of state high schools in the main areas of Maori population meant that opportunities for further education beyond the primary school stage remained extremely limited. When plans for the first Maori district high schools were announced toward the end of the 1930s, they reflected the preoccupation with a land-based future which had dominated official thinking. The core curriculum of the new schools did not include subjects leading on to the school certificate and university entrance examinations but emphasized:

> education of a practical nature only . . . including building
> construction, furniture making, metal work and some gardening
> for the boys and home management for the girls. The aim is to
> teach the skills and develop the tastes that make the house not
> merely a place of habitation but a home in the best sense of the
> word. (Barrington and Beaglehole, 1974:208)

After 1940, Maori primary schools were affected in several ways by rapid urbanization. The main focus of Maori education policy began to shift to the needs of the rapidly increasing numbers of Maori pupils in board-administered schools in urban areas. Arguments were put forward for abolishing the Maori primary schools altogether because of a steady decline in enrollment and a desire to rationalize the national system of administration of primary schools. Sensitivities within the Department of Education and the country generally about race relations were pricked when a visiting American scholar criticized the separate Maori school system and described it, somewhat inaccurately, as similar to the system of segregated black schools in the American South prior to the Supreme Court decision of 1954 (Ausubel, 1961).

After 1955 provision was made for Maori schools to transfer to education boards if a majority of parents favored integration, but the rate of transfers was slow. Many Maori communities had become very

attached to what they saw as "their" school, built on Maori land and
with a history sometimes going back 100 years. The issue of
educational achievement was also relevant here. Many parents had by
now come to feel that an environment had been created in the schools
which was more favorable to the educational advancement of their
children because of their majority status, the greater emphasis on Maori
culture and generally supportive teachers. When the government
announced that all remaining Maori schools would be transferred to
boards in 1968, opinion on the issue remained divided. A lecturer at
Auckland University (Dr. Pat Hohepa) produced research which
showed that the majority of Maoris who had graduated from the
university had received their primary schooling in a Maori primary
school, although for many years (since 1909) the majority of Maori
children had been educated in board schools. He suggested that further
investigation needed to be done into the relative merits of Maori versus
board schools before Maori schools were integrated. There were,
however, other Maoris, including the influential Maori queen, who
supported integration on the grounds that Maoris and Europeans should
be educated together in a common public school for the sake of race
relations, and when full integration did finally occur in 1969, it did so
with relatively little public dissension.

Underachievement

Maori children remain disadvantaged in terms of overall
educational achievement compared with Europeans, but there is little
consensus about the factors which contribute to this disparity, although
there has been a large amount of theorizing, speculation and debate
about the various factors involved, in addition to the historical
influences I have already discussed (Fergusson, Horwood and Shannon,
1982).

In the 1960s and 1970s, explanations of underachievement were
closely modeled upon American or English theories: the problem was
seen as being located in the personality and home experience of Maori
children—that is, outside schools. An American psychologist, D.P.
Ausubel, was influential in introducing the notion of cultural
deprivation to New Zealand during the early 1960s (Nash, 1983).
Compensatory education for preschool children became, as in the

United States, a major thrust of official policy to correct what was viewed as the negative effect on achievement of the "culturally deprived" or "intellectually impoverished" background of the Maori child's home environment.

The idea of a "restricted language" code developed by the British sociologist Basil Bernstein was also current at about the same time and was officially adopted by the New Zealand Department of Education. A widely circulated official report stated that:

> The language used in many Maori homes is a dialect form of English, in which some of the non-standard usages are due to the influence of the Maori language. . . . Bernstein has developed a theory that has some relevance to this discussion. . . . Learning at school requires some thought processes which cannot be achieved by a child whose only language is a restricted code. (Department of Education, 1971:21)

Numerous other explanations have been put forward for Maori academic underachievement in comparison with Europeans. They have included a low level of parents' education (Ausubel, 1961; Ritchie, 1963), lack of school and career knowledge by parents (Watson, 1967), overcrowded and substandard housing making study difficult (Ritchie, 1963), low self-esteem (Lovegrove, 1966), large families (Butterworth, 1967), lower-class status (Smith, 1956), racial prejudice (Ausubel, 1961), absenteeism and later school starting age (McQueen, 1945), different cultural background (Schwimmer, 1964), different cognitive patterns (Watson, 1967) and academic achievement not highly prized (Ausubel, 1961). Most of these explanations, which predominated in the 1950s and 1960s, focus on aspects of Maori language, culture, family structure and homes as "the problem." In more recent years, there has been a shift away from this "blaming the victim" approach to a much closer look at what is happening in schools and classrooms. Factors identified here as likely to impede the progress of Maori children include inadequate provision of the Maori language in schools (Benton, 1987), use of unsuitable tests and assessment methods (Nash, 1983; McDonald, 1987), low expectations by teachers (St. George, 1978; Simon, 1982), curriculum content and organization which is inadequate or inappropriate (Harker, 1980), school climate and teaching styles (Walker, 1984) and monocultural European teachers (Nightingale, 1977).

Miscommunication between Maoris and other ethnic groups, because the parties interpret each others' words and actions in terms of their own cultural understandings, has been studied by anthropologists Patricia Kinloch and Joan Metge (1979). Such misunderstandings can lead, Kinloch and Metge suggest, to the different groups "talking past each other," misreading each other's activities, responding inappropriately and judging each other as stupid, odd or rude in the light of their own cultural standards. School examples cited include misinterpretations arising over different ways of responding "yes" and "no," expressing approval and disapproval or expressing sincerity. European children "are explicitly instructed to 'look at' anyone they are talking to and to look superiors in particular 'in the eye.' . . . Maoris and Samoans on the other hand consider it actually impolite to look directly at others when talking to them" (Kinloch and Metge, 1979:13). Work of this kind, which also examines different cultural attitudes regarding such matters as the appropriateness of standing and sitting, asking and answering questions, and interpreting and reacting to silence, has been welcomed as a positive contribution to better understanding.

It was suggested by Harker (1979) that many Maoris still place a higher value upon such attributes as seniority of descent, knowledge of traditions and reputations on the *marae* (meeting ground) than on material or educational success in a European context. Research has also revealed that when young Maoris achieve highly on entrance tests for high school and are placed in high academic streams as a result, the subsequent separation from primary school peers can sometimes produce an effect so upsetting that they ask school principals and teachers to return them to lower streams with their friends (Barrington, 1983b).

Apart from the work of Kinloch and Metge, there has been little research of an ethnographic nature into the influences and effects of schooling. Harker (1979) views this approach as having the greatest potential for producing increased understanding of the school factors involved in underachievement because finding out what actually happens in classrooms, how people actually treat each other and what they actually think about each other is best revealed by observing them in real classrooms and in real schools. Harker is also critical of what he sees as a failure by researchers to take sufficient note of Maori views, with too few attempting to get outside their own cultural milieu to view the situation from the viewpoint of those being researched or to consult with them directly.

There has, therefore, never been any single or simple explanation for academic underachievement by Maoris in relation to Europeans. My own view is that historical factors have been very influential and often underestimated. These include the long-term persistence of attitudes resulting from the Land Wars, antipathy to European institutions including schools, assimilation policies that excluded the Maori language, "adaptationist" policies that overemphasized educating for rural life, poverty, limited opportunities for schooling, particularly at the high school level, and the disruptive effects of rapid urbanization. On top of these have come the postwar explanations, often based on social science research. Some consensus has now developed among policy makers and certainly among many Maoris that the focus of attention in the past has too often been on so-called "Maori problems," on "blaming the victim," with not enough attention being paid to educational environments, school climate, language and curriculum policies, and teacher attitudes. This consensus has been reflected in a variety of policy measures which are discussed below.

School Policies

Greater recognition of the importance of Maori language in schools had been a feature of curriculum change and is seen by many as likely to have a positive effect on self-concept and achievement. There are now eleven official bilingual schools and over 100 primary schools with bilingual classes (New Zealand Planning Council, 1989). Experience has shown that while many initial difficulties must often be overcome in establishing such programs, the results can be extremely positive. Teachers in one of the bilingual schools report that the children have greater self-esteem, their spoken and written Maori and English and their reading in both languages have improved, they are enthusiastic about being taught in Maori, and the school now has a better spirit (Department of Education, 1984).

Maori *marae* (meeting grounds) have also become increasingly important in the educational and cultural life of the education system. In recent years, the Education Department has arranged *marae* courses at which over 1000 principals, teachers, lecturers, advisers and school inspectors have often had their first real and immediate experience of contemporary Maori culture and have then considered ways in which aspects of it can be incorporated into school curriculum and organization to improve school climate for Maori pupils.

One approach has been to develop *whanaus* (small "schools within schools") which provide students with greater opportunities for close interaction and the growth of a "caring family feeling." Maori language and culture courses are now taught in all teachers' training colleges and multicultural courses are compulsory for all primary teacher trainees. The Department of Maori Affairs has also been active with schemes to assist Maori youth, promoting the *Tu Tangata* (stand tall) program. This program is designed to encourage ethnic pride and confidence through school visits by prominent Maoris and through visits to rural *maraes* by young Maoris in urban areas to acquaint them with traditional values and practices.

As we saw earlier, a separate Maori primary school system existed until 1969 as part of the national system. The Maori denominational boarding colleges have continued to play an important role in providing secondary education for Maoris. A high proportion of Maori leaders, at both local and national levels, graduated from these schools and the schools' pupils have had a significantly better record of passes in national examinations for Maoris than state schools. A major reason for the success of these schools has been the emphasis they place on Maori language and culture and on their being "Maori" institutions (Cleaver, 1976).

In recent years, there has been a strong grass-roots movement by Maori communities in both rural and urban areas to develop their own educational initiatives outside the formal school system. The *Te Kohango Reo* (language nest) program is an example of this trend and is viewed as being of major significance. Its purpose is to halt the decline of Maori language and culture among the young by involving Maori parents and creating Maori language nurseries for preschoolers. Only begun in 1982, the scheme has expanded rapidly and now receives official support from the Maori Affairs Department which assists with initial establishment of the program and support of Maori language instructors. Voluntary helpers from local communities remain an essential program component. The language nests are located on *maraes*, in church halls, community centers and private homes.

There have also been some extended affirmative action programs at the tertiary level. The medical schools have entry preference schemes for Polynesians and the Education Department has set a target of reserving 10 percent of all teacher training quotas for Maori and other Polynesian applicants. Auckland University has a program designed to boost the enrollment of Maori students by liaison with Maori communities and the provision of support services once students are enrolled. Several universities have also established *marae* for Maori students.

At a national *hui* (meeting) to discuss Maori education in 1981 one speaker argued that Maoris must now turn the education system around by setting up schools that will "work for them" (Benton, 1981). The Generation 2000 project provides one prominent example of a Maori tribe setting out to prepare a coordinated educational and economic development plan for a tribal area, including increasing representation in the professions, and the first Maoris recently graduated from a tribal university which is part of this scheme. Developments of this kind are part of a new drive by Maori communities themselves to promote improved educational achievement among their young people. Many Europeans support these developments, acknowledging that over 100 years of a largely monocultural European school system seems to have too often impeded rather than facilitated Maori academic achievement in school settings. However, there are other Europeans (and some Maoris) who criticize such developments as "separatist" and not likely to promote the kind of harmonious New Zealand society which they see as desirable.

During 1989, there was a major restructuring of the administration of the national education system. It included a greater emphasis on decentralization, a strong equity thrust with greater emphasis on targeting financial assistance to schools with large numbers of Maori students in order to assist with the teaching of Maori, and provision for up to 21 parents to withdraw from existing educational arrangements and set up their own institution provided they meet national guidelines for education (Office of the Minister of Education, 1988). The Task Force on the Reform of Educational Administration which originally made this recommendation did so with Maori parents very much in mind.

Despite such measures, however, many Maoris share a high level of dissatisfaction about present official policies and are skeptical that they will be any more successful than former policies in closing the educational gap between Maoris and Europeans. When a new bilingual school was opened at Ruatoki, the director of the Maori division of the Education Department was told: "Your department 10 to 20 years ago told us not to speak Maori in schools. Now you say our kids can do well by speaking Maori. Is this another trick being played?" (Ussher, 1981). Nash has commented that New Zealand has:

> some way to go before its level of commitment and support to its indigenous minority matches that of many other countries. The position of New Zealand Maoris compares unfavorably in this respect, for example, with the Swedish and Norwegian Lapps and the Romansch in Switzerland. . . . In comparison with the support being given to bilingual education at all levels in Wales, and more recently in the Gaelic-speaking areas of Scotland, Maoris come off badly. In all of these instances the schools have assumed major importance in the continued transmission of the central values of the culture. It is ironic that New Zealand forced through the transfer of Maori schools to Board control in the late 1960s at exactly the time when they might have developed along the lines of *Ysgolion Cymraeg* in Wales, the Lappish High School in Sweden and the Gaelic College in Skye, as a force for cultural regeneration. (Nash 1983:61)

Benton has commented that in a climate where education tends to be "subservient to the needs of a depressed economy, . . . debates about multiculturalism and education make little sense without giving major consideration to the issue of power, and specifically, the power of minority groups to make and carry through decisions within the institutional structure of society." As Benton notes, "the critical area for New Zealand is in those urban schools where there are a majority of Polynesian students, many of whom are going to leave school without any or adequate academic qualifications, with the obvious implication this has for labour market participation" (Benton, 1981:13).

Of major continuing concern to many Maoris is the fact that children who have been enrolled in Maori language preschools enter primary schools that have no teaching in the Maori language. They are also concerned about the need for greater resources for the teaching of Maori at all levels and the need for acknowledgment in education of the concept and spirit of partnership embodied in the Treaty of Waitangi (Royal Commission on Social Policy, 1988).

References

Ausubel, David. 1961. *Maori Youth.* Wellington: Price Milburn.

Barrington, John M. 1976. "Cultural Adaptation and Maori Education: The African Connection." *Comparative Education Review* 20(1):1–10.

―――. 1983a. *The Ngarimu Board and its Awards.* Wellington: Department of Education.

―――. 1983b. "The Transfer of Educational Ideas: Notions of Adaptation." *Compare* 13(1):61–68.

Barrington, John M., and T.H. Beaglehole. 1974. *Maori Schools in a Changing Society.* Wellington, New Zealand Council for Educational Research.

Benton, Richard. 1981. "Terong Pipit Goes to School." Unpublished paper.

―――. 1987. *How Fair Is New Zealand Education? Part 2. Fairness in Maori Education.* Wellington: New Zealand Council for Educational Research.

Butterworth, Graeme V. 1967. *The Maori in the New Zealand Economy.* Wellington: Department of Industries and Commerce.

Cleaver, P.J. 1976. "St. Stephen's School 1972–4: The Traditions, Society and Everyday World of the Predominantly Maori Boarding School." Master's thesis. Auckland University.

Department of Education. 1971. *Maori Children and the Teacher.* Wellington, New Zealand.

―――. 1984. *Annual Report.*

―――. 1988. *Administering for Excellence: Report of the Task Force to Review Education Administration* (The Picot Report). Wellington: Government Printer.

Fergusson, David, L.J. Horwood, and F.T. Shannon. 1982. "Family Ethnic Composition, Socio-Economic Factors and Childhood Disadvantage." *New Zealand Journal of Educational Studies* 17(2):171–79.

Foster, Philip. 1965. *Education and Social Change in Ghana.* London: Routledge and Kegan Paul.

Harker, Richard K. 1979. *Research on the Education of Maori Children: The State of the Art.* Wellington: NZARE Conference.

―――. 1980. "Culture and Knowledge in the New Zealand School Curriculum." *Delta* 27.

Kinloch, Patricia, and Joan Metge. 1979. *Talking Past Each Other.* Wellington: Victoria University Press.

Lovegrove, M.N. 1966. "The Scholastic Achievements of European and Maori Children." *New Zealand Journal of Educational Studies* 1(1):15–39.

McDonald, G. 1987. *You're a Year Behind: Promotion Out of the New Zealand Junior School.* Wellington: New Zealand Council for Educational Research.

McKenzie, D. 1982. "More Than a Show of Justice? The Enrollment of Maoris in European Schools Prior to 1900." *New Zealand Journal of Educational Studies* 17(1):1–20.

McQueen, Henry C. 1945. *Vocations for Maori Youth.* Wellington: New Zealand Council for Educational Research.

Metge, J. 1976. *The Maoris of New Zealand.* London: Routledge and Kegan Paul.

Nash, Roy. 1983. *Schools Can't Make Jobs.* Palmerston North: Dunmore.

New Zealand Planning Council. 1989. *From Birth to Death II.* Wellington: New Zealand Planning Council.

Nightingale, M.D. 1977. "Maoritanga: A Study of Teacher Sensitivity." Master's thesis. Massey University.

Office of the Minister of Education. 1988. *Tomorrow's Schools (The Reform of Education Administration in New Zealand).* Wellington: Government Printer.

Ritchie, J. 1963. *The Making of a Maori.* Wellington: Reed.

The Royal Commission on Social Policy. 1988. *Social Perspectives,* Vol. 4. Wellington: Government Printer.

St. George, A. 1978. "Perceptions, Expectations and Interactions." Ph.D. diss. University of Waikato.

Schwimmer, Eric G. 1964. *The Sense of Belonging in the Currie Report: A Critique.* Wellington: Association for the Study of Childhood.

Simon, J. 1982. "Ideology and Practice: Implications of the Views of Primary School Teachers of Maori Children." Master's thesis. University of Auckland.

Smith, Leone. 1956. "Educational Assessments of Maori Children." M.A. thesis. University of Auckland.

Sorrenson, M.P.K. 1956. "Land Purchase Methods and their Effect on the Maori Population 1865–1901." *Journal of the Polynesian Society* 65(3):17–31.

Szasz, Margaret. 1974. *Education and the American Indian: The Road to Self-Determination 1928–1973.* Albuquerque: University of New Mexico.

Ussher, J. 1981. "The Ruatoki Experiment." *New Zealand Listener,* 26 July.

Walker, R. 1984. "Address to New Zealand Association for Research in Education Conference." Dunedin.

Ward, I. 1973. *A Show of Justice.* Auckland: Auckland University Press.

Watson, J.E. 1967. *Horizons of Unknown Power.* Wellington: New Zealand Council for Educational Research.

Williams, J.A. 1969. *Politics of the New Zealand Maori: Protest and Cooperation 1891–1909.* Auckland: Oxford University Press.

Chapter Eleven
Social Mobility and Education:
Burakumin in Japan

Nobuo K. Shimahara
Rutgers University
With the Assistance of
Toshihiko Konno
Mie University, Japan

Introduction

In this chapter I shall discuss the Burakumin, a Japanese minority group that has, during the past 15 years, dramatically improved its social mobility and educational attainment. The improvement is especially dramatic and noteworthy because Japanese culture stresses homogeneity and uniformity and tends to repel intergroup pluralism (Shimahara, 1980).

The Burakumin's recent social mobility calls into question two prevailing theories. One is the theory of social mobility articulated by Banfield (1974) and McClelland (1961), which attributes mobility to factors of individual psychological orientation. Its explanatory mode is both ahistorical and astructural. The other is the caste theory, which focuses on cultural ascription as the major barrier to the mobility of a minority group. De Vos and Wagatsuma (1966a), for example, who have developed the most comprehensive analysis of the minority group available in English to date, have advanced this theory. These two theories fail to account for the Burakumin's recent mobility, which derives directly from their political and economic mobilization, a mobilization that has occurred under specific circumstances and has demanded greater social integration of the Burakumin into society.

The Burakumin have interested American anthropologists for the past two decades (Brameld, 1968; Cornell, 1961; De Vos and Wagatsuma, 1966a; Donoghue, 1957, 1977; Ogbu, 1978; Price, 1966; Shimahara, 1971; Totten and Wagatsuma, 1966). Recently they have also attracted the attention of a few political scientists and comparative educators (Hah and Lapp, 1978; Hawkins, 1983). Ironically, few Japanese scholars, except those affiliated with Burakumin organizations, study this minority group, considering the subject too sensitive and difficult. For the same reason, official surveys of Burakumin are sporadic and lack uniformity.

Central to this chapter is an analysis of the historical development that has led to the Burakumin's present enhanced condition. To shed contextual light upon this development, I will contrast the major characteristics of the Burakumin's socioeconomic conditions and education in the early 1960s with those in the late 1970s and early 1980s, based on my survey of accessible Burakumin literature and my ethnographic research. Thereafter, I will discuss the theoretical implications of the Burakumin's mobility.

The ethnographic research was conducted for one year from the fall of 1963 to the fall of 1964. Theodore Brameld, who supervised my research, and I established our residence near a Burakumin community named Junan in Kagawa Prefecture, to maintain maximum communication with its residents and the two schools (elementary and middle) that Burakumin children attended. The major research methods used were intensive interviews and participant observation conducted in the community and the schools. Additionally, the following methods were employed in order to obtain relevant data and access to the life of Burakumin and the process of the schools: a sociological survey of Burakumin families, informal visits to homes, meetings and festivities, and the study of documents and literature.

Among the few recognizable minorities extant in Japan, the Burakumin constitute the largest group. According to the latest official survey, conducted in 1975, 1,150,083 Burakumin live in 4,542 segregated communities throughout Japan (Isomura, 1982:270).

According to informed estimates, the totals would be much higher if they included all those who have passed into majority neighborhoods. The Burakumin group meets four of the five criteria used by Wagley and Harris to define minorities (1958:4–11): it occupies a subordinate position in a complex society and suffers from such social disabilities as prejudice, discrimination and segregation. This minority is in large part a self-conscious social unit based on in-group feeling and an intragroup solidarity that derives from sharing the common traits of social disability. Membership is transmitted by a rule of descent capable of affiliating succeeding generations. To reinforce this last criterion, endogamy is the predominant form of marriage among Burakumin. Though the Burakumin qualify as a minority through these characteristics, they do not meet the last criterion suggested by Wagley and Harris: that is, they do not have the special cultural and physical traits that distinguish a minority from a majority. The Burakumin have no distinct cultural and physical attributes that separate them from majority Japanese. Both Burakumin and the majority Japanese display commonality in language, culture and race.

The literal translation of Burakumin is "village (Burakuku) people (min)," a term that is commonly accepted and used. The term "outcaste," however, is frequently, though loosely, employed by De Vos and other anthropologists to designate this minority (De Vos and Wagatsuma, 1966a). This loose application of "outcaste" is unfortunate, because the term not only fails to describe and explain the present status of Burakumin adequately, but it obscures that status.

The existence of outcaste is predicated upon the existence of a caste society, but the social structure of contemporary Japan does not conform to caste criteria. De Vos speaks of two "prerequisites of caste": a fixed hierarchy and exclusive occupational specialization (1966:332–38). Evidence to be presented later indicates that these prerequisites cannot be cogently applied to this minority group. Berreman suggests that "to view caste in true perspective we must use three dimensions: [ascriptive] stratification, [cultural] pluralism, [segregated] interaction" (1967:47). As noted earlier, Burakumin have no distinctive culture. This fact lends little support to the claim that Burakumin are outcastes.

However, it is profitable, in my view, to study this Japanese minority group within the context of a continuum of stratification that has, at one pole, class organizations allowing for achieved status and, at the other pole, caste organizations with stress on ascribed status

(Berreman, 1967:56; 1981:12–17). With the application of this continuum, one can argue that Burakumin exist in a castelike society where both achievement and ascription influence the Burakumin's status.

History of Burakumin

The Tokugawa Period (1603–1868) laid a rigid and lasting foundation for the social structure of the present-day Burakumin. This period stabilized central feudalism and rigidified the social structure in which individual status, occupation and residence were ascribed and proclaimed as permanently unchangeable. The Tokugawa status stratification consisted of aristocrats, farmers, artisans, merchants and pariahs called Eta-Hinin. The majority of what had been known earlier as Senmin, "lowly people," were placed in the lowest stratum as untouchables. Eta literally means "defilement abundant" and Hinin, "nonhuman." Burakumin are direct descendants of these Eta-Hinin.

The pariahs' main occupations were leather work, bamboo craft, itinerant entertainment, peddling, gardening and unskilled labor, such as animal slaughter and removing sewage. Work dealing with animals was considered not only lowly but extremely defiling. Undoubtedly the influence of Shintoism and Buddhism were important in attributing defilement and pollution to Senmin for their work with animals. Sumptuary laws were imposed upon the pariahs to distinguish them from the commoners. They were required to wear designated clothing and slippers, to avoid ordinary hair styles, to stay out of the households of commoners and to stay in their own hovels at night.

Nevertheless, when the Tokugawa feudal system was finally repudiated by internal and external political forces, the Meiji Restoration of 1868 ushered in the era known as modern Japan. Four years later, the government proclaimed the emancipation of Eta-Hinin, and they were then called Shin-Heimin, "new commoners." However, this emancipation was nothing more than nominal; although the previous status-stratification structure was abolished, the Burakumin's place in society remained unchanged.

Japan's contact with Western civilization generated an intense movement toward modernization and began to create a social climate leading to public discussion of discrimination against Burakumin by some liberals and by Burakumin themselves. Meanwhile, the Burakumin's deep-seated anger and frustration with perpetual oppression and exploitation surfaced and led to intermittent riots throughout the Meiji Period (1868–1913). They no longer acquiesced to the unquestioned discrimination against them, and their struggles for emancipation began at last. Spontaneous protest movements erupted, pitting the Burakumin against the discriminators and governmental neglect. Initiated by victims of discriminatory incidents who had been incited to personal outrage, these movements exerted only limited influence, if any, and fellow Burakumin failed to unite against discrimination.

The minority group's protests culminated in the formation of Suiheisha, the Levelers Association, in 1922. This was the first national Burakumin organization influenced by a socialist orientation that was aimed at liberating the oppressed Japanese. The development of socialism and its subsequent impact upon Burakumin appeared to be significant in the evolution of the protest movement. Socialists stressed that Burakumin emancipation must be achieved through the class struggles of Burakumin themselves first, ultimately leading to a broadly based socialist revolution (Shimahara, 1980:29). However, the levelers' tactics emphasized "thorough denunciation," an eye-for-an-eye retaliation against the discriminating majority, which involved formal apology and repentance by discriminators. The Burakumin's resolute demand for apology in public led to numerous incidents accompanied by bloodshed. Once the new movement gained momentum in the 1920s it generated visible but token responses from majority Japanese and local governments. On the one hand, conciliatory government reactions were typical, and, on the other, majority Japanese avoided fearful, militant and vengeful Burakumin (Shimahara, 1980:30). This image of Burakumin prevails among government officials, teachers and other majority Japanese to the present day.

Suiheisha was disbanded in 1940 under military dictatorship. Shortly after the war, Jiichiro Matsumoto and his associates, who had played a central role in Suiheisha, organized the National Committee for Burakumin Liberation (NCBL). It deemphasized personal denunciation, although this remained an instrumental tactic, and called instead for struggles to improve living conditions (Shimahara, 1980:32). This tactical shift from individual retaliation to attack on the broader issues of social and economic inequality was very significant for the development of the later protest movement.

In 1955, NCBL changed to the so-called Kaihodomei, the Burakumin Emancipation League, to further expand the organizational network of the emancipation movement, which rank-and-file Burakumin had flocked to join. The Kaihodomei also broadened its political base by allying with the Japanese Communist Party and the Japanese Socialist Party, of which Matsumoto was an influential member. Since 1955, Kaihodomei has been the central force of social change in the Burakumin's struggle for equality.

As Kaihodomei gained strength and wider political support, it adopted the approach of linking incidents of discrimination at the individual level to local and prefectural legislative and administrative demands, which came to be known as "administrative struggle." Obviously, the focus of attention had changed from local short-range issues to broader, long-range ones. These organized efforts led to the first postwar legislation for minority groups. Its passage, in 1959, suggested an increasing concern with minority problems by the ruling Liberal Democratic Party and put into effect a 10-year plan to improve Burakumin communities and education facilities and to provide scholarships.

Having succeeded in calling national attention to the Burakumin plight, Kaihodomei increasingly concentrated on the national arena. In 1960, it actively mobilized Burakumin to participate with the Socialist and Communist parties in protest against Japan's security treaty with the United States. This effort was not directly related to Burakumin administrative struggles, but the issue served to provide a necessary focus for their activities.

In the following year, Kaihodomei sponsored the Grand March from Kyushu to Tokyo with the cooperation of labor unions and the allied political parties (Hah and Lapp, 1978). It was a massive mobilization of Burakumin to publicize their needs and plight. At the same time, Burakumin also launched a petition drive for the greater participation of prefectural governments in alleviating the minority problems.

The Grand March became instrumental in a nationwide petition campaign that demanded the national government's greater commitment to a comprehensive national policy to eliminate all inequities. This campaign resulted in the establishment of the Council on Burakumin Assimilation Policy in 1961. Composed of vice ministers of the relevant ministries, Burakumin leaders, intellectuals and journalists, the council conducted an extensive investigation into the Burakumin problem and submitted its findings and recommendations to the prime minister in 1965.

Despite its successes in the early 1960s, Kaihodomei grew ideologically moderate and more pragmatic in its approach to the problem. Instead of advocating revolutionary change in society and instead of fearing the pacifying effect of the government's intervention, Kaihodomei's new leadership in the late 1960s demanded greater entry of Burakumin into government bureaus, more input into government policy, occupational equality and better housing. In other words, Kaihodomei shifted from demanding sweeping changes to pursuing special interests with ideological moderation and pragmatic militancy, According to Hah and Lapp (1978), Kaihodomei's special-interest approach was even appealing to the ruling conservative party. It was in this political context that the organization's pragmatism played a vital role in 1968 when the historic Special Measures Law for Assimilation Projects was drafted—legislation that received unprecedented support from all political parties in the Diet. The council's recommendations served as the basis on which this legislation was drafted. It was a historic moment for all Burakumin when it finally became effective in 1969.

The Burakumin's pressure on the national government for equal rights also resulted in the closing of the Meiji family registries, Jinshin Koseki, in 1968, which had previously been used to identify Burakumin. I will explore the effects of the law on Burakumin in the next section.

Changes in Economic and Social Conditions

The organized administrative struggles of the 1950s and early 1960s did not substantially improve ghetto life, which was rife with castelike discrimination in employment and marriage, poverty, deteriorated and segregated housing, and foul living conditions. To shed some light upon these social disabilities of the minority group I shall draw upon my ethnographic research (1971).

Junan, the Burakumin community I studied, was located by a river, as are many other Burakumin ghettos. About 650 people, constituting 150 households, had their homes in a rectangular strip 2,000 feet long and 800 feet wide. It was separated from majority settlements by a 150-foot-wide river, on the one side, and rice paddies of nearby farming communities, on the other. Junan was founded as a village late in the Tokugawa Period, and it specialized in leather artisanship, such as tanning and drum-making.

A quick sketch of the sources of income upon which the Burakumin in Junan depended for their living may help one understand this minority community. In 1964, approximately 70 percent of the households received public welfare, an increase of 35 percent since 1960 (Shimahara, 1971). Sixty people were on the Shittai program, a government program for the unemployed that provided various types of unskilled labor on public projects. There were two junk dealers for whom 15 men worked and eight people engaged in leather work. Three people ran small food stores, and four people were specialized peddlers. Fifteen women were employed as pieceworkers in a small factory established by the municipal government within Junan to reduce unemployment. There were also one truck driver and two part-time farmers. One person held a public service position in a nearby agricultural cooperative and another was an elected city councilman. The latter was the most influential individual in Junan, ranking ahead of the two junk dealers. The economic situation of this community had deteriorated fast and steadily since about 1959, as junk collection, leather work and itinerant peddling sharply fell off. The decline in these occupations drastically increased the number of welfare recipients and Shittai employees.

A striking disparity between Junan and majority communities in the city, which includes Junan, was symbolized by the high incidence of Burakumin on public welfare—70 percent, contrasted with less than 6 percent of the majority population. A further marked contrast concerned housing. Nearly 50 percent of the houses in Junan had only two small rooms, in comparison with four to five rooms in an average house in the city. Furthermore, Burakumin houses were by and large shabby and dilapidated. Roads were very narrow, unpaved and adjacent to open ditches that carried sewage from each house. Not until about 1960 did running water come to the residents. In addition, Junan's extremely limited geographical area included a cemetery, a crematory and a junkyard, facilities not seen in majority residential areas.

My Burakumin informants rated Junan below average among the Burakumin communities in Kagawa Prefecture. However, the other Burakumin communities I visited in Kagawa and Kyoto displayed some of the same characteristics regarding housing, unemployment, the decline of traditional Burakumin occupations and the level of poverty. Furthermore, according to other research, the indices of ghetto life characteristic of Junan were relatively common in communities in other parts of Japan (Ohashi, 1962; Wagatsuma and De Vos, 1966:125–26). Ohashi found the disparity in income striking. The monthly average household income in one Osaka Buraku community, for example, was under 24,000 yen in 1959, whereas the monthly average working-class household income was 31,000 yen. In another Buraku in Kyoto, 20.2 percent of the population was on welfare in 1955 (Mahara 1960:127). Similarly, based on data gathered around 1960, Wagatsuma and De Vos (1966) pointed out Burakumin's heavy reliance on welfare and the Shittai program in various Burakumin communities in Japan.

That poverty among Burakumin was perpetuating and extensive around 1960 is evident from my terse description of Burakumin life. Burakumin in Junan were concerned with discrimination against them, particularly in employment and intermarriage. Without exception, my Burakumin informants reported encountering various degrees of job discrimination. Although they agreed that it was pervasive, they felt that it became less obvious and more subtle because of the Burakumin's belligerent protest against it and their continued denunciation of people who discriminated. Yet such discrimination was not only persistent but also more pronounced in certain sectors of private industry. For example, an executive of the largest bank in Kagawa Prefecture admitted that his bank refused to employ any Burakumin applicant regardless of ability. In his view, had his bank employed a Burakumin, his employees and customers would have protested.

Similarly, people in Junan encountered overt and covert sanctions against intermarriage. Nevertheless, they considered intermarriage desirable, although it was generally abhorred by the majority Japanese. The ultimate elimination of discrimination against the Japanese minority, said one Burakumin, would require free intermarriage. However, strict endogamy was breaking down among younger people in Junan as elsewhere.

Unprecedented improvement in the lives of Burakumin first became manifest in the late 1960s, when the national government assumed the major responsibility for alleviating the plight of more than one million Burakumin. Under the Special Measures Law for Assimilation Projects passed in 1969, the national government spent more than $6 billion between 1969 and 1981, and $5 billion between 1976 and 1981 to implement assimilation projects. Under the law, prefectural and municipal governments are required not only to implement these projects sponsored by the national government but also to match funding for many of the projects. Aimed at upgrading the social and economic status of this minority group, the Special Measures Law covers projects in six principal areas: (1) improving living conditions, such as housing, roads, sewage systems, recreational facilities and the environment; (2) upgrading welfare and health insurance programs; (3) ameliorating Burakumin industry at the primary, secondary and tertiary levels; (4) improving occupational opportunities; (5) enhancing educational opportunities; and (6) protecting human rights.

Not since the Meiji Restoration has the national government made such a broad and sustained commitment to the equality of Burakumin. In the past, all government programs launched on behalf of the minority group were economically nominal and could be viewed as political pacification to quiet the Burakumin's demands and protests. It is evident that such programs could not uplift those who were discriminated against. The timing of the assimilation projects required by the Special Measures Law was particularly significant in producing tangible effects on the minority group. Japanese per capita income tripled in the 1960s and 1970s as a result of the continuous and unparalleled economic and industrial growth of the nation. The continuous labor shortage during the industrial expansion was so pronounced that industry aggressively sought labor, even among middle-school graduates and married women. The economic growth in the two decades had a positive effect on Burakumin's employment and gains in personal income as will be discussed later, though measuring the precise relative consequences for the minority vis-à-vis the majority Japanese is difficult.

Meanwhile, the passage of the Special Measures Law in 1969 injected a momentum into the enhancement of Burakumin human rights. As mentioned earlier, Jinshin Koseki, the Meiji family registry originated in 1874 that identified Burakumin as "new commoners," was finally closed by the government in 1969, its predominant application having been to foster discrimination in marriage and employment. In addition, in 1976 the government issued a decree prohibiting inspections of current family registries without authorization, even though they do not identify Burakumin by particular designation. The law also led to another significantly modified employment practice: job application forms no longer required specific birthplaces but only the prefecture. Keeping in mind the background of the 1960s and 1970s, during which the Burakumin's organized struggles for equality won the most important legislative victory in history and support of local governments and private institutions, we can now appreciate the current social mobility of that minority group.

The latest data on the economic status of Burakumin in Osaka come from a consortium of Burakumin associations, which conducted an extensive survey in 1982 (Osaka Buraku Jittai Chosa Suishin Iinkai [OBJCSI], 1983:14–58). Because Osaka has the second largest Burakumin population, after Hyogo Prefecture, we can consider these data to be an index of the economic status of Burakumin nationally. In general, the data show that the gaps between the minority and majority populations in income and employment have narrowed, but that economic inequality has persisted. The following brief analysis is based on the data provided by the consortium.

Overall, more Burakumin are currently in the work force than before. Fifty-eight percent of the Burakumin in Osaka are now working, the same percentage as the majority population. There is a significant gap, however, between the two groups in employment patterns. Fifty-four percent of the Burakumin and 66 percent of the majority Japanese are permanently employed. Shittai employees and day workers among the Burakumin constitute, respectively, only 0.3 and 3.5 percent, representing a notable improvement. Similarly, Burakumin laborers have decreased from 20 percent in 1973 to 16 percent in 1982.

Salaried Burakumin employees have increased from 42 percent in 1973 to 54 percent in 1982. The increase of Burakumin professionals to more than 13 percent in 1982 from less than 4 percent 10 years ago is no less than dramatic. The national percentage of professionals in the work force is currently 15.6 (1979). Table 1 shows major categories of Burakumin occupations.

Table 1. Comparison of Occupational Patterns

Occupational Categories	Burakumin in Osaka 1982, %	Burakumin in Osaka 1973, %	All Japanese 1979, %
Professionals	13.3	3.9	15.6
Clerical Work	13.7	14.7	22.4
Retail Sales	7.5	6.1	11.8
Skilled Workers	20.1	31.8	30.7
Agricultural and Fishing Workers	0.6	0.4	1.1
Mining Workers	0.2	0.0	0.1
Semiskilled Workers	7.0	7.6	5.9
Unskilled Workers	16.1	19.7	3.9
Security Workers	1.4	0.3	1.5
Service Workers	11.9	5.4	6.9
Others	7.2	0.2	0.0
Unknown	1.1	9.9	---
Total	100.0	100.0	100.0

Source: Osaka Buraku Jittai Chosa Suishin Iinkau, 1983, *Buraku Kaiho,* Volume 202, p. 40.

According to the evidence, income differentials between Burakumin and the majority Osaka population are no longer very large. The annual average income of employed Burakumin is a little more than two million yen (computed with the inclusion of taxes), which compares more favorably now than ever with the median income range for the majority Osaka population (to two and a half million yen).

Though the Burakumin's average income has noticeably improved in a historical perspective, the data indicate that 10.5 percent of the Burakumin are receiving welfare aid, whereas, in contrast, only 1.6 and 1.2 percent, respectively, of the Osaka and national populations receive welfare. (The average for all minority communities was 5.4 percent in 1978.) As the welfare statistics attest, the proportion of Burakumin at the lowest economic stratum is much greater than that of majority people.

Turning briefly to Burakumin housing at the national level, grants offered through the assimilation projects programs have improved housing. New houses and apartments replaced extremely dilapidated homes in Burakumin communities in the 1960s. For example, dilapidated houses in Wakayama Prefecture were reduced to 3.9 percent in 1981 from 33.6 percent in 1971 (Wakayama-ken [WK], 1982:9).

Another significant change is in the patterns of settlement and intermarriage. Defining mixed settlement of minority and majority people as the percentage of Burakumin residents in a Burakumin community, we find that the national average of mixed settlement was 61 percent in 1975 (Isomura, 1982:271). This figure confirms that majority and minority people are not extensively mixed in Burakumin settlements. Interesting, too, is the steadily increasing rate of intermarriage. According to statistics compiled by Suginohara (1982:47), intermarriage in sampled Burakumin communities increased from 7.2 percent in 1951 to 24.9 percent in 1977; 52 percent of those under the age of twenty-nine are intermarried, and for those between thirty and thirty-nine the incidence is 35.5 percent. The rate decreases progressively among older people.

Burakumin's Education

Burakumin's Education in the Early 1960s

Since the establishment of universal education early in the Meiji Period, formal education has been considered essential for social and economic advancement. In the late nineteenth and early twentieth centuries, formal education became not only a central institutionalized mechanism for promoting the social mobility of individuals but also a powerful sorting system that allocated people to differential work roles in society. As Japanese society grew ever more industrialized and differentiated, the importance of education as a sorting system kept pace; but Burakumin received only minimum schooling and had no social mobility at all. This minority group's persistent social disabilities assured that its children's education would be as poor in the postwar period as in the prewar period. As late as the early 1960s, Burakumin children were notorious for poor academic performance and high rates of school dropouts, truancy and delinquency.

However, overt discrimination and prejudice against Burakumin children in school diminished considerably. My research and other studies conducted around 1960 support this generalization.

In both the elementary and the middle school where Burakumin from Junan were enrolled, majority parents, school administrators, teachers and other school staff concertedly denied the existence of explicit prejudice and discrimination against minority students.[1] An elementary school teacher pointed out that most majority students were actually unaware that the Junan students were Burakumin. Similarly, only one of my middle-school student informants knew of the existence of Burakumin. A comprehensive survey conducted by Wakayama Prefecture in 1978 confirmed the school staff's perception of the majority children's lack of knowledge about Burakumin. More than 28 percent of the sample learned about them between the ages of thirteen and fifteen whereas 36 percent of the subjects came to know about the minority group after the age of sixteen (Wakamaya-ken Dowa Iinkai [WDI], 1980:15). Most Burakumin children, however, according to elementary school informants, tended to become conscious of their minority status in the fifth and sixth grades (at eleven and twelve years of age).

In contrast, Miyazaki Prefecture's survey, conducted in 1982, revealed that 32 percent of the sample Burakumin subjects admitted that they became aware of their minority status during elementary-school years; 31 and 6 percent during, respectively, middle school and high school; 19 percent after high school (Miyazaki-ken [MK], 1980:8).

Majority students and youths learn the identity of Burakumin more often than not in subtle ways from a variety of sources including friends, neighbors and parents. For example, when parents who are conscious of Burakumin characteristics suggest to their children that they avoid close association with minority children, such a suggestion often leads to children's inquiries about Burakumin. Similarly, older adolescents frequently inform younger adolescents of the minority group, particularly when they become sensitive to interpersonal relations.

Majority students at both the schools I studied were keenly aware that Burakumin students were often aggressive, intimidating, temperamental, violent and vengeful. Yet, these same minority students, according to their teachers, were anxious, insecure, suspicious and apprehensive about majority children. In fact, most incidents of violence, minor fights and stealing that occurred at the schools involved Burakumin. Majority parents more often than not instructed their children to avoid militant minority children and to be cautious around them. Indeed, more than 50 majority students originally enrolled in the middle school where just about the same number of Burakumin were enrolled transferred to other school districts every year. Similarly, in PTA meetings at both schools, majority parents avoided direct conflict with Burakumin, often being intimidated by a small group of militant minority parents who dominated these meetings.

The Burakumin's poor academic performance was a tenacious problem at both schools. Recurrent themes that emerged from teachers' comments on Burakumin's performance included slow comprehension, lack of concentration, low motivation and lack of parental encouragement. The elementary school tried to promote the minority children's motivation for academic work under the assimilation education program. No such efforts were even initiated at the middle school, however. Instead, most Burakumin students were given relatively little attention by their teachers, on the assumption that the Burakumin were bound to seek employment at the end of their compulsory education.

Typically, after compulsory education, the Burakumin entered the work force in the shoe industry, automobile repair factories, general machine repair factories, ironworks, food stores, meat shops and the textile industry. Some Junan graduates stayed in their community without employment. While 85 percent of the majority students advanced to high school, only 20 percent of Burakumin did. Furthermore, 38 percent of the high school graduates continued education in college in Kagawa Prefecture, in which Junan is located, but college was seldom available to Burakumin: only one person from Junan was attending college. Students seeking admission to high school devoted one to two extra hours every day at school to preparatory drilling for high school entrance examinations at the third-year level. Minority students, once again, not only received meager attention from their teachers and classmates, but as the teachers admitted, were also bored and frustrated. These minority students walked out during class hours and often defied their teachers, who in turn tried to ignore their defiance. Truancy among these students proliferated. Furthermore, 50 percent of the students in special education classes consisted of Burakumin, although the minority students constituted 30 and 5 percent of the total enrollments of, respectively, the elementary and the middle schools.[2]

My interviews with teachers and school administrators in Kyoto in 1964 also revealed that one of the deep-rooted problems of the Burakumin children in the city was their lack of cognitive ability in such intellectual exercises as reading, writing and mathematics (Shimahara, 1980:17). Hence, a systematic tutoring program has been offered since 1952.

More to the point, Tojo (1960) reported a significant gap in IQ scores between minority and majority students. Mahara (1960) also pointed out a substantial disparity in standard achievement test scores between the two groups of students.

The low levels of minority children's motivation and school performance reflect parental ambivalence toward achievement. As pointed out by the teacher who organized the assimilation education program at the elementary school enrolling students in Junan, most Burakumin parents failed to encourage their children to study at home and failed to develop the children's disciplined attitudes toward school work. In his words, they did not consider *doryoku* ("effort") as critically important in determining their children's future. They expected their children to seek employment when they completed only compulsory education. There were, however, some exceptions to those parental expectations. The principal of the middle school, for example, often referred to a diligent, bright Burakumin student who, in his view, was a model for both Burakumin and non-Burakumin students at the school. His parents, according to the principal, pressed their son to study conscientiously and also always cooperated with the school. Eventually, he won admission to a competitive high school. But interviews with Burakumin parents and teachers revealed that Burakumin parents and children did not generally expect schooling to have positive effects upon their future.[3]

To summarize, the continuous structural exclusion of Burakumin parents is crucial in determining their children's low academic performance and the inequality of schooling they receive. One of the serious consequences resulting from the inequality of schooling is limited access to culturally defined skills, knowledge and symbols, as a result of which Burakumin children could not gain employment that would enable them to move to higher social strata. The low level of Burakumin's motivation may well be explained as a consequence of what De Vos and Wagatsuma refer to as "role expectancy" (1966c:244). Parental ambivalence toward achievement in the majority society may have played an important role in the development of children's perception of the utility of schooling in social mobility.

Economic Improvement and School Attainment

The improved economic conditions of Burakumin life in the 1960s and 1970s discussed earlier and the scholarships made available to Burakumin through the assimilation projects program immensely increased minority high school and college enrollments. Prefectural surveys indicate a great change in enrollment patterns across the nation, suggesting that the gap in educational attainment at the high school and college levels between Burakumin and majority youth is not as large as it once was. In Shiga Prefecture, for example, Burakumin enrollment at the high school level increased from 9.3 percent in 1965 to 89 percent in 1975 (Ito and Hanaki, 1983:350); in Nagano Prefecture it reached as high as 95.7 percent in 1980 (Nagano-ken Dowa Kyoiku Suishin Kyogikai [NDKSK], 1980:46); in Wakayama Prefecture and Osaka, respectively, 84.5 percent in 1978 and 86.6 percent in 1980 attended high school (Wakayama-ken Kyoiku Iinkai [WKI], 1979:162; Zenkoku Dowa Kyoiku Kenkyu Kyogikai [ZDKKK], 1982:4). In contrast, the current enrollment at the national level is as high as 94 percent (*Asahi Shimbun* [*AS*], 1983). Hence, the difference in high school enrollment between the eligible minority and majority populations has narrowed to less than 10 percentage points.

Meanwhile, the dropout rates of the minority and majority populations vary from one prefecture to another. For Burakumin the highest dropout rate, in the late 1970s and early 1980s, was 5.4 percent, as reported in Okayama Prefecture and the lowest rate was 1.6 percent in Nagano (NDKSK, 1980:43). By comparison, 2.7 percent is the highest dropout rate for majority students reported in Kochi.

With respect to college enrollments, 27.3 percent of the Burakumin in Wakayama Prefecture entered college in 1978, and 37.2 percent of eligible youth at the prefectural level went to college in the same year (WKI, 1979:162); 34.2 percent of Burakumin and 43.6

percent of eligible youths in Nara Prefecture went to college in 1974 (ZDKKK, 1982:4). In Nagano, 23.6 percent and 28.1 percent of, respectively, Burakumin and all high school graduates were admitted to colleges in 1977 (NDKSK, 1982:46). In Nara Prefecture, in 1967, freshman Burakumin enrollments in colleges were only 11.0 percent and in Nagano Prefecture they were 14.4 percent in 1972.

At the national level, 35 percent of all eligible youths are currently enrolled in colleges (*AS*, 1983). Hence, there is still a significant difference between Burakumin and majority youths in educational attainment at the postsecondary level, but the gap has been diminishing, as noted above.

The Burakumin showed an impressive gain in high school and college enrollments, but their academic performance was not equally significant during the 1970s, according to various surveys. I will discuss the results of three surveys, among others available, to illustrate a general pattern of Burakumin's school performance.

A survey conducted by Nagano Prefecture in 1978 reports that Burakumin children's performance, as indicated by students' grades in the Takamura community, is generally much lower than that of majority children at the first-, second- and third-grade levels. But the difference in performance is reduced in the higher grades of the elementary school and further reduced in the middle school. Nevertheless, it is evident that a difference in academic performance between the two groups persists throughout compulsory schooling. However, the profile of Burakumin's IQ scores generally reflects the normal distribution of scores (NDKSK, 1980:9–11). Table 2 shows a distribution of grades for seven required subjects.

In sharp contrast, a comparison of test results in Hino City, Shiga prefecture, reveals a large gap in school performance between Burakumin and majority students (Ito and Hanaki, 1983:28–31). For example, only 10 percent of former students in the ninth grade earned high grades (grades four and five) in math in 1978, though 30 percent of the majority students did. To look at it another way, 60 percent of Burakumin students earned low grades (grades one and two), in contrast to 23 percent of the majority students.

Table 2. Grade Distribution at Takamura (1978)

Grades	Level 1–3 Minority %	Majority %	Level 4–6 Minority %	Majority %	Middle School Minority %	Majority %
High (5 & 4)	18.6	36.0	20.3	32.4	29.1	31.8
Average (3)	53.6	52.8	42.0	42.5	34.7	49.8
Low (2 & 1)	27.6	11.2	37.2	20.1	27.2	18.8

Source: Nagano-ken Dowa Kyoiku Suishin Kyogikai, 1980, *Dowa Kyoiku Hakusho*, p. 23.

Wakayama Prefecture also conducted a large survey in 1978 involving fourth-grade students and eighth-grade students (WKI, 1979). Fourth graders were given tests in Japanese and math, and eighth-graders were tested on these two subjects and English. As in Shiga Prefecture, there is a large disparity in test scores between the two groups of students in Wakayama Prefecture (Table 3). Though the difference at the fourth grade level is within 5.5 percentage points, it widens to 9.1 percentage points in math and English at the eighth-grade level.

Table 3. Test Results in Wakayama, 1978

	Correct Answers: 4th Grade Minority Students %	All Students %	Correct Answers: 8th Grade Minority Students %	All Students %
Japanese	65.7	71.2	62.3	66.8
Math	76.4	81.6	63.4	72.5
English	---	---	45.3	54.4

Source: WKI, 1979, *Dowa Kyoiku no Genjo to Kadai*, p. 213.

Finally, a brief look at what is known as assimilation education: this is an inclusive term encompassing a wide range of school-related activities aimed at enhancing equality for Burakumin. Despite persistent prejudice and discrimination against the minority group, assimilation education was initiated by individual schools in the early 1950s. Unlike programs established by the ministry of education, assimilation education evolved as a voluntary program organized at the local level through the 1960s, responding to Burakumin's demands for equal education.

The recommendations made in 1965 by the Council on Burakumin Assimilation Policy and the Special Measures Law of 1969 were pivotal in promoting assimilation education at the national level. The council delineated the conceptual framework of assimilation education policy (Dowa Taisaku Shingikai [DTS], 1983). The recommendations included counseling and teaching on discrimination and prejudice, improving academic performance, enhancing opportunities for high school and higher education, and offering financial aid for Burakumin's postcompulsory education and equal opportunities for minority youths' employment. In addition, the council included specific policy recommendations for teacher training, financial incentives for teachers and administrators in school districts including Burakumin, and recommended improving educational facilities.

Accordingly, the prefectures having Burakumin residents developed policies and specific measures for assimilation education. Substantial national and local funds have been granted to implement the assimilation education programs. As Cummings observes, "The programs are so intensive that expenditures per student for outcaste children (Burakumin) are three times as great as the expenditures for the other children" (1980:9). As part of assimilation education, the majority of the Burakumin enrolled in high schools and colleges receive scholarships covering about one-third of their total expenses.

Although it is difficult to determine the precise effects of assimilation education, it is evident that it has in fact contributed to raising Burakumin's educational attainments. Nevertheless, from the foregoing analysis of Burakumin's school performance, one can infer that assimilation education has not significantly improved their academic achievement thus far.

To conclude, the educational attainment of Burakumin children has risen phenomenally in the 1970s. This reflects the improvement of Burakumin's economic life and greater educational opportunities created by the assimilation projects and the national economic growth.

Also, the increased educational attainment by minority students may be judged a consequence of the perception of these students and their parents that education is vital for social mobility. This perception was not present around 1960. On the debit side, I noted a large gap in school performance between Burakumin and majority students. It appears that upgrading the cognitive competence of the minority to the level of the majority needs much more time. After all, Burakumin have just begun to enjoy enhanced economic and educational opportunities.

Theoretical Implications

The preceding discussion has made it clear that the self-directed political mobilization of Burakumin is central to their attaining a significant measure of economic and educational equality. They learned that to protest effectively they must first translate personal enmity, resentment and hostility into collective action against acts of discrimination and segregation. Burakumin further transformed nonpolitical collective behavior, typical in the denunciations of discriminators most prevalent in the 1920s and 1930s, into political action and administrative struggle. The role of Kaihodomei in the postwar era has been most vital in mobilizing the rank-and-file Burakumin for administrative struggles both locally and nationally. These struggles culminated in major historic events in the 1960s: the establishment of the Council on Burakumin Assimilation Policy and the Special Measures Law. The political mobilization of Burakumin by organizational leaders was cardinal in the passage of the government's legislative measures and the minority's economic mobility. In addition, Japan's economic growth is a significant element. It produced more jobs, more educational opportunities and an improved material life for both minority and majority Japanese.

The Burakumin's mobility entails important theoretical implications. First, given the changes in economic conditions and political orientation toward the minority, Burakumin were able to gain achieved status to a measurable degree, an indication of mobility along the continuum of caste-and-class organizations referred to at the outset of this paper. Hence, generating political and economic conditions conducive to bettering the castelike minority was an essential variable in gaining achieved status.

Secondly, the minority's mobility was not so much a function of relaxation of the ascriptive cultural constraints imposed upon the group as a function of political and economic factors. The fact that the majority of children and early adolescents were unaware of the existence of the minority in the past two decades is attributable to their socialization, in which reference to Burakumin by parents and the general public was deliberately avoided for fear of personal denunciation and other forms of injury. Hence, this fact does not necessarily suggest a decline in the majority Japanese's covert and culturally inherent prejudice against the minority. Indeed, the occupational and social mobility that Burakumin have gained has itself contributed, in my view, to increased intermarriages and possibly some erosion of the traditional prejudice. I contend that the caste theory held by De Vos and Wagatsuma cannot sufficiently account for the Burakumin's politically initiated mobility.

Third, the Burakumin case clearly demonstrates close associations between the minority's attitudes toward work and the structure of job opportunities and between its orientation toward education and mobility. Majority Japanese have long believed Burakumin to be wasteful, parasitic, negligent, irresponsible and less assiduous (Shimahara, 1971:37; Brameld, 1968:132–33)—attributes common among lower-class people who suffer from poverty and social pathology. My analysis of the Osaka survey data suggests, however, that Burakumin are actively working. Moreover, the majority of employed Burakumin have stable employment. And public welfare recipients among Burakumin nationally have been reduced to 5.4 percent.

Foster, in his anthropological study of peasant society, contends that its opportunity structure determines individual cognitive orientation and that cognitive orientation is modified by "changing access to opportunity" (1965:310). His thesis is further supported by Silverman's research on Italian peasants (1968). Foster's thesis can be applied to Burakumin. When they gained more access to economic opportunities, their dependent attitudes diminished. Burakumin students' enrollments in high school and college rose dramatically. This suggests that Burakumin began to regard formal education as vitally instrumental to better employment. As their job opportunities have increased, Burakumin have sought more opportunities for training beyond the years of schooling that are compulsory; this training has led to better employment and social mobility. Ogbu's "job ceiling" hypothesis, that minority groups' educational attainment and performance are functions of limits placed upon their mobility, explains Burakumin's greater participation in education (1974:81–101; 1978:177–215). To put it differently, without occupational mobility for minority groups, one cannot expect their high motivation toward schooling or their increased participation in postcompulsory education. This contention is well supported by Willis's ethnographic study (1981), though he focused upon British working-class students, not a minority group per se.

The theses advanced by Foster and my study reject McClelland's contention (1961) that the presence of human motivation is a causative factor antecedent to economic growth and, by implication, antecedent to structural conditions leading to the social mobility about which this paper is concerned. In McClelland's view, it is "a change in the minds of men which produced economic growth rather than being produced by it" (1963:81). But, as Foster suggests, "the brakes on change are less psychological than social" (1965:310). It is "social" opportunities that have helped to develop Burakumin's motivation for mobility and higher educational attainment.

Similarly, Banfield's argument (1974) that psychological orientation determines access to opportunities is also rejected. The arguments promoted by McClelland and Banfield cannot explain the social changes of Burakumin, just as they fail to explain the placement of blacks in the structure of American society.

In conclusion, the Burakumin's further progress toward social and educational equality remains to be seen. They are still living in segregated communities and their membership in a minority group is transmitted through endogamous marriages. There are frequent reports in Burakumin literature that they encounter job discrimination. Nevertheless, their recent economic and educational advancement deserves the careful attention of scholars and policy makers in nations with minority problems.

Notes

Acknowledgements: This chapter is reprinted with minor changes from my article, "Toward the Equality of a Japanese Minority: The Case of Burakumin," which appeared in *Comparative Education*, Vol. 20, No. 3, 1984. Permission to reprint the article was granted by the publisher of *Comparative Education*. The article was originally based on my paper presented at the annual meetings of the American Anthropological Association in Chicago, 1983.

1. The Japanese educational system consists of elementary school for six years, middle school for three years, and high school for three years. Schooling at the elementary and middle levels is compulsory and begins at the age of six.
2. Graduates of five elementary schools attend the middle school.
3. Burakumin's low expectations toward schooling were closely related to what De Vos and Wagatsuma call "Burakumin's conscious self-concepts." These self-concepts consist of several elements including "a sense of personal inferiority," leading to resignation and passive resentment, and "a sense of economic handicap" and "injustice" (De Vos and Wagatsuma, 1966b:228–45).

References

Asahi Shimbun (Asahi Daily Newspaper). 1983. 12 Aug.

Banfield, Edward. 1974. *The Unheavenly City Revisited*. Boston: Little, Brown.

Berreman, Gerald D. 1967. "Stratification, Pluralism and Interaction: A Comparative Analysis of Caste." In *Caste and Race: Comparative Approaches*, ed. Anthony Reuck and Julie Knight, pp. 45–73. Boston: Little, Brown.

———. 1981. "Social Inequality: Cross-cultural Analysis." In *Social Inequality: Comparative and Developmental Approaches,* ed. Gerald Berreman, pp. 3–40. New York: Academic Press.

Brameld, Theodore. 1968. *Japan: Culture, Education and Change in Two Communities*. New York: Holt.

Cornell, John. 1961. "Outcaste Relations in a Japanese Village." *American Anthropologist* 63:282–96.

Cummings, William. 1980. *Equality and Education in Japan.* Princeton: Princeton University Press.

De Vos, George. 1966. "Essential Elements of Caste: Psychological Determinants in Structural Theory." In *Japan's Invisible Race,* ed. G. De Vos and H. Wagatsuma, pp. 332–52. Berkeley: University of California Press.

De Vos, George, and Hiroshi Wagatsuma. 1966a. *Japan's Invisible Race.* Berkeley: University of California Press.

———. 1966b. "Socialization, Self-Perception, and Burakumin Status." In *Japan's Invisible Race,* ed. G. De Vos and H. Wagatsuma, pp. 228–40. Berkeley: University of California Press.

———. 1966c. "Group Solidarity and Individual Mobility." In *Japan's Invisible Race,* ed. G. De Vos and H. Wagatsuma, pp. 241–53. Berkeley: University of California Press.

Donoghue, John D. 1957. "An Eta Community in Japan: The Social Persistence of Outcaste Groups." *American Anthropologist* 59:1000–17.

———. 1977. *Pariah Persistence in Changing Japan: A Case Study.* Washington, D.C.: University Press of America.

Dowa Taisaku Shingikai (The Council on Burakumin Assimilation Policy). 1983. "Dowa Taisaku Shingikai Toshin" (The Report of the Council on Burakumin Assimilation Policy). In *Tokyo Koho* (The Tokyo Bulletin), ed. Tokyo Seikatsu Bunka Kyoiku Kohobu, pp. 24–42. Tokyo: Tokyo-to.

Foster, George. 1965. "Peasant Society and the Image of Limited Good." *American Anthropologist* 67(2):293–315.

Hah, Chong-do, and Christopher C. Lapp. 1978. "Japanese Politics of Equality in Transition: The Case of the Burakumin." *Asian Survey* 18:487–504.

Hawkins, John. 1983. "Educational Demands and Institutional Response: Dowa Education in Japan." *Comparative Education Review* 27:204–26.

Isomura, Eiichi. 1982. *Dowa Mondai to Dowa Taisaku* (Assimilation Problems and Assimilation Measures). Osaka: Kaiho Shuppansha.

Ito, Kazuji, and Satoru Hanaki. 1983. "Seikatsu to Gakuryoku o Takameru Chiiki Gurumi no Torikumi" (Community-based Cooperation to Elevate Life and Academic Competence). *Dowa Kyoiku Undo* (Assimilation Education Movement) 20:27–43.

McClelland, David. 1961. *The Achieving Society.* New York: Free Press.

———. 1963. "The Achieving Motive in Economic Growth." In *Industrialization and Society,* ed. B.F. Hoselitz and Wilbert E. Moor, pp. 74–95. Mouton: UNESCO.

Mahara, Tetsuo. 1960. "Buraku no Sangyo to Shigoto" (Industry and Work in Buraku). In *Buraku no Genjo* (Present Situations in Buraku), ed. Buraku Mondai Kenkyusho, pp. 250–80. Tokyo: Sanitsu Shobo.

Miyazaki-ken (Miyazaki Prefecture). 1980. *Dowa Mondai Jittai Chose Hokoku* (Survey Report on Assimilation Problems). Miyazaki-shi: Miyazaki-ken.

Nagano-ken Dowa Kyoiku Suishin Kyogikai (Nagano Prefectural Association for the Improvement of Assimilation Education). 1980. *Dowa Kyoiku Hakusho* (White Paper on Assimilation Education). Nagano-shi: Nagano-ken Dowa Kyoiku Suishin Kyogikai.

Ogbu, John. 1974. *The Next Generation*. New York: Academic Press.

————. 1978. *Minority Education and Caste*. New York: Academic Press.

Ohashi, Kaoru. 1962. *Toshi no Kaso Shakai* (Urban Lower-Class Society). Tokyo: Seishin Shobo.

Osaka Buraku Jittai Chosa Suishin Iinkai (The Committee for the Study of Buraku Situations in Osaka). 1983. "Konnichi ni Okeru Osaka no Buraku no Jittai" (I) (Today's Situation of Osaka Buraku). *Buraku Kaiho* (Buraku Emancipation) 202:14–58.

Price, John. 1966. "A History of the Outcaste: Untouchability in Japan." In *Japan's Invisible Race*, ed. by G. De Vos and H. Wagatsuma, pp. 6–30. Berkeley: University of California Press.

Shimahara, Nobuo. 1971. *Burakumin: A Japanese Minority and Education*. The Hague: Martinus Nijhoff.

————. 1979. *Adaptation and Education in Japan*. New York: Praeger.

————. 1980. *Oppressed Japanese: Burakumin*. Tokyo: Yachiyo.

Silverman, Sydel F. 1968. "Agricultural Organization, Social Structure, and Values in Italy: Amoral Familism Reconsidered." *American Anthropologist* 71:1–20.

Suginohara, Suichi. 1982. *Gendaino Buraku Sabetsu: Jittai to Henka* (Present-day Buraku Discrimination: Reality and Change). Kobe: Hyogo Buraku Mondai Kenkyusho.

Tojo, Takashi. 1960. "Sengo no Dowa Kyoiku" (Postwar Education for Assimilation). In *Dowa Kyoiku* (Assimilation Education), ed. Buraku Mondai Kenkyusho, pp. 49–98. Tokyo: Sanitsu Shobo.

Totten, George O., and Hiroshi Wagatsuma. 1966. "Emancipation: Growth and Transformation of a Political Movement." In *Japan's Invisible Race*, ed. G. De Vos and H. Wagatsuma, pp. 33–63. Berkeley: University of California Press.

Wagatsuma, Hiroshi, and George De Vos. 1966. "The Ecology of Special Buraku." In *Japan's Invisible Race*, ed. G. De Vos and H. Wagatsuma, pp. 112–29. Berkeley: University of California Press.

Wagley, Charles, and Marvin Harris. 1958. *Minorities in the New World*. New York: Columbia University Press.

Wakayama-ken (Wakayama Prefecture). 1982. *Dowa Taisaku no Sieka to Kadai* (The Results of Assimilation Measures and Problems). Wakayama-shi: Wakayama-ken.

Wakayama-ken Dowa Iinkai (Wakayama Prefectural Committee for Assimilation). 1980. *Dowa Mondai ni Kansuru Wakayama Kenmin no Ishiki to Gakushu Sanka no Jittai* (Citizens' Awareness of Assimilation Problems in Wakayama and Participation in Learning Opportunities). Wakayama-shi: Wakayama-ken Dowa Iinkai.

Wakayama-ken Kyoiku Iinkai (Wakayama Prefectural Board of Education). 1979. *Dowa Kyoiku no Genjo to Kadai* (The Present Situation and Problem of Assimilation Education). Wakayama-shi: Wakayama-ken Kyoiku Iinkai.

Willis, Paul. 1981. *Learning to Labor*. New York: Columbia University Press.

Zenkoku Dowa Kyoiku Kenkyu Kyogikai (National Studies Association for Assimilation Education). 1982. *Dowa Kyoiku* (Assimilation Education), Number 6 (Newsletter).

Part III
Conclusion

Chapter Twelve
Minorities and Schooling:
Some Implications

Margaret A. Gibson
University of California, Santa Cruz

The ten case studies presented in this volume focus on the school performance of minority youths. As the individual cases make clear, there is much variability among groups and within groups. Students vary in their perceptions of and responses to schooling and in their academic achievement and persistence. Minority status has long been associated with unequal educational opportunities and with a high degree of school failure, but, as these studies show, many minority students are comparatively successful in school. All minority students face substantial barriers in school, however, relating most notably to the prejudiced attitudes of the majority or dominant group toward minorities, unequal access to jobs and a job ceiling that limits advancement, and home-school cultural discontinuities. Many minority students also suffer from the problems of poverty and assignment to schools of a quality far inferior to those attended by middle-class, majority-group agemates. What is surprising is not that so many minority youngsters do poorly in school or drop out at an early age but that so many in fact persevere and excel in spite of the obstacles (cf. Suarez-Orozco, 1989).

One of the major objectives of this collection of essays has been to look at the school-adaptation strategies of those minority groups who are successful in spite of the odds. A second objective has been to explore why it is that some minority groups are able to transcend the cultural, linguistic, and structural barriers that impede their progress more readily than others. A closely related issue is whether or not the barriers are in fact the same for the "more successful" and "less successful" groups of minority students.

The international and comparative literature on minority school performance shows clearly that minority youngsters of immigrant origin remain in school longer and meet with a greater degree of academic success than involuntary or nonimmigrant minority youths of similar social-class backgrounds. In quite a few instances, moreover, the school performance of the immigrant minority surpasses that of the majority (Gibson, 1987a). This volume has sought to explore variability in minority school performance in a comparative fashion and through the mode of ethnographic analysis.

The term *minority*, as used herein, refers to a group occupying a subordinate position in a multiethnic society, suffering from the disabilities of prejudice and discrimination, and maintaining a separate group identity. Even though individual members of the group may improve their social status, the group itself remains in a subordinate position in terms of its power to shape the dominant value system of the society or to share fully in its rewards (Schermerhorn, 1970; Wagley and Harris, 1958).

Nonimmigrant minority refers not simply to those who are native-born, but to groups incorporated into the host society *involuntarily*, most frequently by means of colonization, conquest, or slavery, and assigned a subordinate position within it. This volume includes examples of indigenous peoples whose lands were conquered by Europeans as well as those who were enslaved and colonized. It also includes the example of the Burakumin, a minority group that historically had no cultural or physical traits distinguishing it from the Japanese majority but that during the time of the Tokugawa feudal system was assigned a "permanently unchangeable" subordinate position.

Immigrant minority refers not only to those who are actual immigrants but also to those whose ancestors were immigrants and who continue to maintain a separate minority-group identity. Immigrant minorities, like involuntary minorities, are assigned a subordinate position by the dominant group and suffer the consequences of prejudice and discrimination. In the context of this book, immigrant minority refers chiefly to those who are linguistically, culturally and physically distinct from the majority population and who have migrated to the new country voluntarily and in search of economic opportunities. The West Indian case provides, however, an example of a group of immigrants who are similar culturally and physically to the native group. Their major distinguishing characteristic is their status as immigrants. This volume also includes examples of political refugees, guest workers and illegal aliens, whose situations differ significantly from those of voluntary immigrants with permanent-resident status. The similarities and differences in school adaptation among these several types of immigrants merit further comparative analysis.

Data from the 1980 United States population census help to illustrate the differing school-persistence patterns of immigrant and involuntary minorities and of majority-group young people. As shown in Table 1, children of Chinese, Japanese, Korean, Asian Indian, Vietnamese, Cuban, and Filipino ancestry remain in school longer than non-Hispanic white youths. White youths, on the other hand, persist in school longer than black Americans, Hawaiians, Puerto Ricans, Mexican Americans, and American Indians.

Articles in this volume provide additional examples of the disparities in school performance between immigrant and involuntary minorities. The very high dropout rates and low levels of academic achievement of some involuntary minorities are cause for national alarm, but remedial programs and more general efforts at educational reform have all too often proved ineffective in meeting the special needs of involuntary minorities or in bringing their performance levels into line with national norms. On the other hand, the comparatively high achievement of some immigrant groups has obscured the substantial problems that they, as minorities, encounter in school and has led, in some instances, to their being declassified as "legitimate minorities" (Wong, 1985:65).

It is the contrast between the school performance patterns of immigrant and nonimmigrant that provided the impetus for this volume and the central framework for our analysis. In the discussion that follows, I highlight a number of themes that run through the individual chapters and suggest, in summary form, some of the implications of our comparative analysis for the improvement of educational opportunities for minority students.

Table 1. School Persistence by Age, Race and Spanish Origin: Percentage Enrolled in School in the United States, 1980.

| | Years Old | | | |
	18–19	20–21	22–24	25–34
Chinese	83.9	74.0	50.7	21.9
Japanese	77.0	61.6	38.9	14.6
Korean	77.7	54.8	30.5	13.2
Asian Indian	72.0	54.3	39.2	14.8
Vietnamese	66.6	47.5	37.8	22.4
Cuban	65.1	44.8	28.5	12.7
Filipino	62.7	38.3	20.2	9.6
*White	53.1	33.6	17.4	8.5
Black	51.7	28.4	15.9	9.6
Hawaiian	42.2	21.7	13.5	7.3
Puerto Rican	41.8	21.7	13.1	8.0
·Mexican	39.2	18.9	11.6	7.2
American Indian	38.2	19.3	12.7	8.8

Source: Gibson, 1989:127 (compiled from U.S. Bureau of the Census, 1983, Tables 123, 160 and 166).
Note: *White, non-Spanish origin.

Immigrant Minority School-Adaptation Patterns

The case studies in this volume that look at immigrant minorities range from Turks in Australia to South Asians in Britain, West Indians in the American Virgin Islands, and Mexicans, Central Americans, East Asians and South Asians in the United States. On the whole, parents in these groups have very high educational and vocational expectations for their young. Immigrant minorities invest in schooling even when they know that discrimination will impede them from obtaining jobs commensurate with their education. Lee highlights this drive for education in her discussion of early Korean migrants to the United

States. In 1938, one in 10 Koreans residing in the United States attended an institution of higher education, compared to a rate of only one in 100 for the population at large. Suarez-Orozco's chapter on recent Central American immigrants demonstrates vividly this same drive to excel in school whatever the odds.

Immigrant parents believe, typically, not only that educational credentials and a strong command of the dominant language are essential to their children's future success but also that schools are one arena where minorities have the opportunity to compete on a more or less equal footing with members of the majority group regardless of family background. Although school credentials may not enable their young to get the same jobs as whites or members of the dominant group, a good education from their perspective will certainly enable their young people to get better jobs than would be possible without an education. Many immigrant parents themselves suffer from lack of schooling and have no choice but to accept menial, low-wage work. They believe that better opportunities will be available to their children if they have a good education.

In addition to what they perceive to be the instrumental value of schooling in terms of educational credentials, many immigrant minority parents also see schooling as providing their children with much-needed skills in the dominant language and culture. They view such proficiency as essential to their children's successful participation in the larger society.

At the same time, most immigrant parents want their young to maintain their minority cultures and identities. Parents recognize the difficulties their children face in upholding home values while also adapting themselves to the requirements of the school environment, and they worry about the conformist pressures placed on their children in school. These difficulties are viewed as obstacles to be overcome, however, rather than as insurmountable barriers. Even when children experience serious difficulties socially or academically, or as the result of classmates' outright racist attitudes, immigrant minority parents rarely blame the schools. In the face of such difficulties, parents generally counsel their children to accommodate themselves as best they can to the situation and to avoid being labeled a troublemaker. They fear that if their child gets into a fight at school, it will reflect poorly on the child and quite possibly jeopardize his or her educational opportunities. Parents also feel that confrontation with school authorities will distract the student from his or her studies (Gibson, 1988).

The parents, especially if they themselves have little formal education and lack proficiency in the dominant language, are hesitant to intervene in school affairs. Those more familiar with the system are more likely to get involved, but, so long as members of their group are not blocked from progressing through the educational system, they maintain their generally supportive attitudes toward the schools.

Many immigrant parents, most notably those who have migrated in search of economic betterment, share a sense of relative satisfaction with the opportunities available to them and their offspring. Even if they must struggle to make ends meet, they view themselves as better off than would be the case were they back in their countries of origin. Judged through their comparative lens, moreover, formal education in the host country is more accessible, less expensive, and of a higher quality than that available to members of their social class in the old country.

Immigrant minority youths, for their part, generally like school and have positive attitudes about their teachers. On the whole, they have better attendance records and fewer discipline problems than involuntary minority classmates. They also spend more time on homework and, given the chance, elect more demanding classes in high school. Like their parents, they see schooling as enhancing their life's chances. Most recognize that as members of a minority group they will encounter discrimination in the job market, but educational credentials, from their perspective, are their best hedge against discrimination.

Teachers, by and large, like teaching immigrant students because they have a sense of purpose and direction. Immigrant children also tend to hold teachers in high regard, cause few difficulties in class and abide by the rules set forth by those in authority. Immigrants' deference, combined with diligence, appears to give them an advantage in the classroom. Teachers respond positively to those who seem eager to learn. Students who have been socialized to respect teachers may also have an advantage because it is easier to learn from those one respects. Conversely, if students do not respect their teachers, they may have a difficult time respecting the knowledge their teachers seek to impart (Sung, 1979).

Variation in Immigrant Performance

By no means do all immigrant minority students do well in school, nor do all fit the modal pattern of response described above. Bangladeshi and Turkish students in Britain do far less well on national exams than Pakistani and Indian students (Inner London Education Authority [ILEA], 1987). In Germany, Turkish and Greek students encounter significantly more educational and social problems than Yugoslavian children (Malhotra, 1985). In America, in the early part of this century, Italian children did significantly less well in school than children of Jewish immigrants (Cohen, 1970).

Several of the case studies point to the sometimes serious academic problems encountered by recently arrived immigrants and to the disparities between their school performance and that of co-ethnics raised from early childhood in the new country (Inglis and Manderson; Matute-Bianchi; Suarez-Orozco; Gibson and Bhachu). Comparative research indicates that newer arrivals, particularly those who transfer into the schools of the host country after first or second grade *and* who lack proficiency in the dominant language, are at risk. Many remain behind native-born classmates throughout their school careers (Gibson, 1988). These children must cope not only with discontinuity and at times conflict between home and school cultures, with a curriculum for which they are unprepared, and with the many problems their families face while struggling to survive financially and adjust to demands of life in a new country, but also—and this is a widespread pattern—with the racist attitudes and actions of majority classmates. The newest arrivals—those who are least equipped to defend themselves—are preyed upon the most by prejudiced peers (Gibson, 1988).

The school experiences and special needs of immigrant minorities have received a great deal of attention in Western Europe in recent years, where by the year 2000 approximately one third of the urban population under age thirty-five will be of immigrant background (Tosi, 1984; see also Documentation Section, 1981; Eldering and Kloprogge, 1989; Fourth Seminar, 1979; Husen and Opper, 1983; Rothermund and Simon, 1986; Suarez-Orozco, 1991; Swann Report, 1985). The post-1965 influx of immigrants and refugees to America, mainly Latin and Asian peoples, has begun to bring similar attention to the problems faced by immigrant youths in U.S. schools (for example,

First and Carrera, 1988; Moore, 1987; Olsen, 1988, 1989; Trueba, Jacobs, and Kirton, 1990; Walker, 1989).

While much of the variability in immigrant school performance relates to students' length of residence in the new country, their age on arrival and their command of the dominant language, other factors come into play as well. Some immigrant groups and subgroups, such as the Bhattra Sikhs, view schools as a threat to their way of life and to their very identity as a separate people (Ghuman, 1980). The Bhattra response to schooling seems more closely to resemble the pattern we have described for involuntary minorities than that for voluntary immigrants. Their history as a low-caste and disparaged group within Indian society and the perpetuation of their stigmatized identity even within overseas Indian communities would appear to have had direct bearing on their success theories and the educational strategies which derive from them.

Other studies point to immigrant minority youths who, like nonimmigrant minority counterparts, actively resist instruction and deliberately seek to disrupt the classroom. Italians, in Germany today and in America earlier in this century, males in particular, provide one such example (Malhotra 1985; Ware 1935). In the American setting, the schools' assimilation policies were a primary source of the Italian boy's classroom misbehavior and his sometimes bitter opposition to his teachers. By condemning the boy's home culture and attempting to replace it with that of the larger American community, the schools succeeded instead, in the view of one observer, to drive the boy from the security of his ethnic group, yet, at the same time, to fail to draw him into a sense of belonging in the wider society. The net result for the Italian boy was neither a good education nor a good job but "maladjustment" to both the culture of his upbringing and that of the larger society (Bromsen, 1935:460–61).

As these and other examples of poor academic performance among immigrant minorities suggest, immigrant status is only one of many factors that influence the school-adaptation patterns of immigrant minorities (Becker, 1991; Smith-Hefner, 1990). The group's history prior to emigration, its culture, the circumstances that prompted migration, the opportunity structure and social stratification system of the host society, and the group's situation within the new society all work together to influence school achievement. So, too, do the school's policies with respect to cultural differences.

Involuntary Minority School-Adaptation Patterns

The case studies on involuntary or nonimmigrant minorities include Maoris in New Zealand, Burakumin and Koreans in Japan, Crucians in the American Virgin Islands, and blacks, Chicanos, and Ute Indians in the continental United States. Both among and within these groups there is a great diversity of school experience, with some groups and subgroups far more successful than others. Common to all, however, is the fact that they were brought involuntarily into a subordinate relationship with the dominant group of their present societies and subsequently treated to a history of denigration, exclusion and unequal educational and economic opportunities. This history has had direct bearing on the perceptions, interpretations and responses to schooling of involuntary minority students and their families.

On the whole, nonimmigrant minority parents have lower expectations for their children's success in school than immigrant parents. Although most (there is diversity here, as the Ute case shows us) desire formal education for their children and believe that educational credentials are a prerequisite to decent employment, they tend also to be skeptical that their children will actually have the opportunity to become well educated. A history of inferior schools for minority children, coupled with inappropriate curricula, poor teachers and all too often a teaching environment permeated by racial prejudice has led nonimmigrant minorities to lower their expectations for their children's school achievements. They recognize, moreover, that even with educational credentials minorities have not had equal access to good jobs or equal opportunities for promotion once hired. They are less optimistic than immigrant minority parents that time and effort invested in school work will yield a satisfactory return. Based on experience, they have come to believe that the system works for the dominant group but not for them. Their folk theories of success and strategies for getting ahead, including educational strategies, stem from this reality (Ogbu, in this volume).

Nonimmigrant minority youths adjust their school behaviors to fit the perceived realities of their situations. Those who have adopted what may be termed an *involuntary minority orientation* toward school tend, like their parents, to have lower educational and occupational expectations than students with an *immigrant minority orientation*. Although nonimmigrant minority youths may have high vocational aspirations, as high as immigrant minorities, they differ from the immigrants in that they may not actually expect ever to obtain the jobs they desire. Their school behavior reflects this lack of hope.

On average, nonimmigrant minority students spend less time on homework, have higher truancy rates, and run into far more trouble with their teachers and other school authorities than minority students of immigrant origin. The nonimmigrant students, and their parents, tend also to assume that the problems they encounter in school are a result of racial prejudice and discrimination rather than, as in the immigrant case, their own lack of diligence and persistence. Nonimmigrant minorities are less likely than immigrants to hold teachers in high regard. Teachers, moreover, are less likely to have positive attitudes about nonimmigrant minority youths than immigrant youths. Thus, in many cases, the relationship between nonimmigrant minorities and their teachers is characterized by negative attitudes of each for the other. So intense is this negative feeling on the part of some nonimmigrant minority youths that they actively and deliberately resist instruction.

The lack of effort invested in schooling by nonimmigrant minority youths relates not only to their belief that their labors will not be properly rewarded in terms of jobs and social recognition but also to their belief that school learning and the acquisition of proficiency in the dominant language and culture symbolize behaving like those who historically have oppressed them. Given their relationship of conflict with the dominant group and the institutions it controls, nonimmigrant minorities may have a difficult time respecting their teachers and learning from them. The minority peer group, moreover, may place pressure on its members to reject or even resist school learning. Black American and West Indian students who accept school authority may be accused of obeying white orders and working for whites rather than themselves, just as in the days of slavery (Ogbu, this volume; Gibson, this volume). Matute-Bianchi (this volume) points to a similar peer pressure among Chicano students, who use the term "Wannabe" ("wants to be white") to ridicule Mexican-descent classmates who conform to school expectations. Barrington (this volume) notes, as well, that top performing Maori students sometimes experience such extreme discomfort when placed in high academic "streams" (tracks) away from their Maori peers that they ask school officials to return them to lower streams.

Involuntary minority students who break with the group and seek to do well academically risk being teased or even cut off by their peers. On the other hand, those who resist school authority and stick together against whites (or the dominant group) may gain peer respect. Unwilling to be ridiculed or even made to feel outcast, involuntary minority youths may simply reduce their school effort.

Put another way, some involuntary minorities see the acquisition of academic learning and skills in the majority culture not as an additional set of skills to be drawn upon as appropriate, as is the case for many immigrants, but rather as a symbol of acquiescence to the dominant group and its values. They view acculturation—the process of culture change and adaptation which results when groups with different cultures come into contact—as a subtraction process leading to the replacement or even rejection of their ethnic cultures and identities (Gibson, 1987b:273–74). This view of acculturation, it must be noted, is the one held by many members of the dominant group. They, too, tend by and large to see acculturation as a one-way process in which the minority changes and only rarely as a two-way process in which members of the dominant group are also changed.

Immigrant and involuntary minorities alike are disturbed by conformist pressures in school, by the disparagement of their home cultures and by the job ceiling that inhibits their economic advancement. Unlike involuntary minorities, however, immigrants do not generally feel that they must choose between school success on the one hand, and group loyalty on the other. Immigrant minorities or those with an immigrant orientation have an easier time excelling in school than those with an involuntary minority orientation not only because they have greater optimism about their life chances and about the instrumental value of schooling, but also because they see acculturation in an *additive* rather than a *subtractive* light (Gibson, 1988:18–91; 1989:130–31). They do not assume that school learning will lead to an erosion of their identities and cultures but rather will enhance their ability to participate in both the larger society and their ethnic communities.

Minority Status, Gender and Social Class

Although the full set of case studies takes as the primary analytic framework the disparities in school performance between immigrant and involuntary minorities, it indicates as well the necessity of looking more closely at the interactive influence of minority status, gender and social class. To focus on only one status or another leads to an oversimplification of the forces that promote and impede success in school. It weakens efforts to remove educational inequities and strengthen educational programs for minority students.

Four of the studies point to the influence of gender on school performance and suggest that the forces impeding school success for minority students are sometimes gender specific. All of these studies, it may be noted, are the work of women (Bhachu, Gibson, Inglis, Manderson, and Matute-Bianchi), a fact that leads me to urge our male colleagues to attend also to gender differences. The West Indian case develops this theme most fully. In this example, males—Crucians in particular—have a far more difficult time than females in accommodating themselves to school rules while at the same time securing and maintaining their place within peer networks. By their late primary school years, West Indian males begin openly to resist instruction. Those who accept school authority and apply themselves to their studies do so at the risk of being cut off by peers. The girls are less influenced by a culture of opposition than the boys and, thus, find it easier to accept school authority. Unlike their brothers, these West Indian girls do not view school success as acting white, separating themselves from their black identity or acquiescing to the power of the dominant group.

Signithia Fordham's (1988) research in the United States suggests that high-achieving black female students may feel more pressure than their West Indian counterparts (in Britain or the Virgin Islands) to disassociate themselves from the black community. Fordham also finds, however, that males are more likely than females to associate the acquisition of schooling learning with forsaking black values and beliefs. Black female students appear to have a more additive view of acculturation than black males and, thus, may have an easier time than males in acquiring the knowledge and values their teachers seek to impart.

Matute-Bianchi's investigation of Mexican-descent students also points to a higher rate of academic success for females than males. As labor statistics show, however, girls' superior academic performance during high school provides no assurance of equal, much less superior, economic rewards. Beyond the inequities of the job market, females are handicapped by family and community role expectations. In Matute-Bianchi's study, at least some of the girls' parents saw less reason for females to pursue post-secondary education than males. Similarly, the Sikh case study shows how role expectations handicap the girls in terms of their educational and occupational goals, although this was much less the case in the British setting than the American. Inglis's and Manderson's interviews with Turkish women also indicate that at least some of the Turkish girls will be hindered by parental role expectations, although, as in the Sikh example, length of settlement will undoubtedly prove an important variable.

The labor-force participation rate of women in a particular ethnic group exerts strong influence on the school performance and persistence of girls from that group. In those groups where women are expected to become economically active, girls are likely to persist in school and to see a close relationship between their levels of schooling and their employment opportunities. On the other hand, in those groups where there is no tradition for women working outside the home or where there may be strong sanctions against doing so, girls may attend school for only a few years or until they reach the legal age for leaving school. For example, research on ethnicity, gender and school persistence in Hawaii shows that Puerto Rican and Portuguese females are far less likely to complete high school than Filipino females. Puerto Rican and Portuguese women also are far less active in the Hawaiian labor force than Filipino women (Wright and Gardner, 1983). A similar situation exists in St. Croix where Puerto Rican females have a low labor-force participation rate and a high school-dropout rate, much higher than is the case for Crucian females (Gibson, 1982). Among the women in my research sample, the Crucian women were twice as likely as the Puerto Rican women to be economically active (Gibson, 1976).

Like gender, social class has important bearing on educational and occupational expectations and attainments, but class alone cannot explain the disparities between immigrant and nonimmigrant school outcomes. Lee (in this volume) notes that social class differences distinguish the Koreans in Japan from the Koreans in America and that class background influences the Korean students' perspectives on schooling. Lee also indicates that the different social structures of the two societies and the Koreans' status as an involuntary minority in Japan versus an immigrant minority in the United States are equally if not more compelling reasons for the differences in student performance.

As Inglis and Manderson note, class status and employment experiences prior to migration serve as important resources to immigrants in their new homeland. Many of the families in the Inglis and Manderson study had worked as independent entrepreneurs in Turkey, and this fact, they suggest, helps to explain the parents' high expectations for their children's achievements. The same case may be made for the Sikhs, many of whom owned their own farms in their native Punjab. But socioeconomic status cannot explain the school achievement patterns of the Central American, Mexican or West Indian children described herein. Children from each of these groups do far better in school than can be predicted based on the educational, economic or social status of their families prior to migration. They do far better also than their parents' socioeconomic condition in their new country would seem to justify. So successful are these and many other immigrant children of working-class background in using schooling as an avenue to middle-class status that we must question the applicability of social and cultural reproduction theories to immigrant minorities.

Although for involuntary minority groups there is a far stronger relationship between social class and school performance, research indicates that class is only one of the statuses influencing school performance and not always the most important one. Ogbu speaks to this directly in the introductory chapter where he notes that black students' success in school is not strongly correlated with their parents' class status. In the West Indian study, furthermore, we have seen that girls do far better in school than boys and immigrants do better than natives even though all the students are of a similar, lower-class background.

The Dynamic Nature of Minority Adaptations

The cultural models and educational strategies of minority communities are in a constant process of renegotiation. Mobility strategies change as the societal context changes and as the minority group's situation within a given society itself changes. In turn, as we have seen in a number of the studies, role expectancies and folk theories of success themselves are modified.

Shimahara (in this volume) shows us how improved social and economic opportunities for the Burakumin have led to rapid improvements in the educational attainment levels among Burakumin children. Changes such as those described by Shimahara generally occur only when the government takes explicit steps to improve the situation of the minority group. The system rarely reforms itself, however, without outside pressure. In the Burakumin, Maori and black American examples, it is the collective struggles and civil-rights activities of the minority groups themselves that have provided the impetus for economic and educational reform.

Educational institutions have become more responsive to the needs of minorities because the minorities themselves have refused to accept the status quo and have demanded that the system uphold their rights and address their needs. In the Burakumin case this has entailed, among other things, an educational policy of assimilation, while in the Maori example the shift has been away from assimilation toward multiculturalism. In both cases there have been dramatic changes in school performance within a relatively short time frame. As Barrington (in this volume) suggests, however, a policy of multiculturalism may be little more than an empty slogan if it is not also accompanied by a real sharing of power with minorities in the running of the schools.

Ogbu (in this volume) cautions, furthermore, that there is inevitably a time lag between the lifting of the job ceiling for minorities and modification in a minority group's perceptions of and responses to schooling. It would appear, moreover, from the evidence of this volume, that in those cases where the minority has developed an oppositional relationship with the dominant group a lifting of the job ceiling must be accompanied by demonstrable change in the school's assimilation policies.

Migration from one society to another can also be the stimulus for rapid change in a group's educational strategies and its perspectives on the value of formal education. Lee (in this volume) shows us how Koreans in Japan, in spite of their traditional respect for education, have reduced their educational effort to fit their situation as a low-status, colonized minority with extremely limited job opportunities. Yet when Koreans migrate to the United States, where their situation is that of an immigrant minority and where opportunities for employment expand in proportion to the amount of one's education, they encourage their children to pursue education as far as their abilities and resources allow.

In the Sikh case, we have seen how women of rural origin, little education, and no previous experience in working outside their homes found in America and Britain the opportunity to become economically active. In both America and Britain, Sikh women have joined the labor force in large numbers and their earnings have become an essential part of the family income. This shift has produced new attitudes about the value of formal education for women; families that only a generation ago discouraged their daughters from pursuing schooling beyond the primary level, now actively support not only secondary but tertiary training for all their children (Gibson and Bhachu, this volume).

Migration may also lead to changed relationships between subordinate and superordinate groups and, in consequence, to new school-response patterns. We can see this in the St. Croix study where migration helped free West Indian males from their oppositional relationship with the dominant classes. In turn, this appears to have eased their accommodation to school rules. Even though the immigrant West Indians were the object of much Crucian animosity toward "aliens," the immigrant males were willing to accept Crucian (and white) authority in the classroom (Gibson, this volume). This was the case even though these boys knew they would face discrimination in the job market. They knew, too, that they, as immigrants and outsiders, would have little power to demand fair treatment or to protect their civil rights. Still they persisted, guided by their immigrant minority perspective.

Changing the Rules

Elsewhere I have noted that immigrant minorities are more willing than involuntary minorities to accommodate themselves to school rules. This is the case even when immigrants experience discomfort from the rules and believe that the rules work to their disadvantage (Gibson, 1987a). A strategy of accommodation, together with strong family support for education and an additive view of acculturation, helps immigrant minority students to transcend some of the barriers to their success in school. It does little, however, to alter basic inequalities within the educational system or within the larger society. It does little to break down the barriers of prejudice and discrimination. It does little to improve the quality of instruction that minority students receive. It does little to change an educational policy of imposed assimilation.

Although individual minority group members may get ahead in school and in the larger society by adhering to the rules of the majority or dominant group, the minority itself remains in a subordinate position vis-à-vis the majority. Involuntary minorities, in particular, recognize only too well that their past accommodations have led neither to equal educational opportunities nor, following school, to full and equal membership in the mainstream of their societies. They know, based on bitter historical experience, that even when they play by the rules they have much less than an equal chance of winning. And, as Michael Banton reminds us, when "the rules allow one team to build up an unassailable lead, members of the other teams may lose interest and refuse to continue the competition unless the rules are revised to give them a better chance" (1983:391). Thus, unless the rules themselves are changed, current educational reform efforts, especially those that seek to raise educational standards at the junior and senior high levels, may simply increase the gap between the rules players and the rules resisters. The rules resisters are likely to feel that the tougher standards simply increase the advantage of those students who already fit the system's expectations for appropriate behavior. Unless school structures and programs are changed to fit the needs and interests of a multiethnic clientele, it may be anticipated that many minority students will continue to do poorly in school.

Multiculturalism versus Assimilation

A major theme of this volume is that schools, albeit unintentionally, contribute to the educational problems of minority students by pressing for cultural assimilation against the wishes of minorities themselves. For the individual minority student assimilation implies loss of identification with his or her former group and incorporation at least on a cultural level into the majority group. Although minorities, no less than the majority, wish their fair share of the rewards which the larger society has to allocate, they may not

accept and may actively oppose the notion that full participation in the
larger society means giving up their distinctive identities and cultures.

In situations where the dominant group presses for assimilation,
or conformity to the dominant culture, but the subordinate group views
assimilation as inimical to its interests, we may anticipate intergroup
conflict (Schermerhorn, 1970). Such a situation is described by Kramer
(this volume) in her study of Ute Indians. The American educational
system, by attempting to "emancipate" American Indian children from
their cultures and their communities, has succeeded instead, Kramer
writes, in alienating Indian pupils and their families from the schools.
Many Indian students see schooling not as an avenue to a better life but
as an instrument of their ongoing oppression by the dominant group.
Rather than acquiesce to the school's assimilation agendas, many
Indian children opt instead to fail in school. It is for many Indian
children a "painful, no-win situation," a forced choice between, on the
one hand, success in school and separation from tribal life and, on the
other hand, failure in school and reaffirmation of tribal identity
(Kramer, this volume).

The history of American Indian education is, as Barrington (this
volume) notes, similar in a number of important respects to that of the
Maoris. During the early 1800s, when Maoris were the majority
population in New Zealand and when they still maintained control of
their lands, they welcomed mission schools and proved themselves
receptive pupils. By the early 1840s, over half of all Maori adults had
learned to read or write in their own language. Attitudes toward
Europeans and their institutions changed radically once the Maoris
were stripped of their land, reduced in numbers by war and disease, and
forced into the status of an involuntary minority. The Maori response to
the European's assimilation educational policies became one of
withdrawal and resistance.

An educational policy of assimilation, whether explicit or
implicit, coercive or benign, stems in part at least from the assumption
that minority students need to change their ways if they wish to be
successful in school. Such an assumption, as the evidence of this
volume makes patently clear, is unfounded. An assimilation policy may
also undermine just those qualities that enable many minority children
to excel in school in spite of the odds. The Mexican, Salvadoran,
Korean, Turkish, Sikh and West Indian immigrant students described
herein succeed in school *not* because they have assimilated but because

they have strong home cultures and a strong and positive sense of their ethnic identities. The same undoubtedly may be said for many of the involuntary minority children who excel in school, and we need a great many more studies that investigate and document the forces underlying their success. Similarly, we need more studies that examine the forces that inhibit school success for immigrant minority youths. Such studies can help explain why the schools' assimilation agendas appear, in some instances, to have as injurious an effect on the school careers of immigrant minorities as on those of nonimmigrant. The Bhattra Sikh and Italian schoolboy cases provide two such examples.

Assimilation is no prerequisite to minority success in school. Quite the reverse. The minority cultures and identities are themselves a strong source of capital and a resource that schools would do well to recognize and support. Thus, a more viable educational policy is one that sustains and promotes multiculturalism. Such a policy would encourage accommodation and acculturation but not assimilation (Gibson, 1988). Such a policy, if embraced by the schools, could help minority students to view the acquisition of academic learning and proficiency in the dominant language and culture as additional sets of skills that would lead not to a replacement of their minority cultures but to successful participation in both mainstream and minority worlds. A policy of *additive acculturation* would help students distinguish the acquisition of academic skills and proficiency in the ways of the wider society from their own social identification with a particular ethnic group.

A strong policy of multiculturalism would also help minority students apply themselves to their studies without having to choose between academic success and the maintenance of their ethnic identities, and this plainly is a choice no student should be forced to make (cf. Jordan, Tharp, and Vogt, 1986). Rather than communicating to minority students that they need to change their cultures or labeling as troublemakers those who resist assimilation, schools need to encourage minority students to maintain a strong anchor within their families and communities. Community forces play an essential role in the school adaptations of minority children, and schools must give greater attention to building strong, collaborative relations with minority communities.

Toward this end, teachers and administrators need to demonstrate that they view accommodation and acculturation as mutual processes of culture change and adaptation and that it is not only the minority child who is being asked to adapt. Teachers need to show themselves receptive to learning from the diverse cultures in their midst and they need also to teach majority-group students the value of interethnic reciprocal learning. Minority students are frequently asked to be more accommodating than majority students and yet for a policy of accommodation and acculturation to be successful it must be a shared process. Teachers need, furthermore, to send an unequivocal message to all their students that the mainstream society encompasses multiple cultures and that all students have much to gain through contact with students of diverse backgrounds.

An educational policy of multiculturalism offers no panacea for the problems facing minority youngsters in school, but it is an important step toward creating a school climate responsive to the needs of a multiethnic society. A school environment that genuinely supports ethnic diversity and encourages students to learn from one another culturally can be anticipated not only to improve interethnic relations but also to foster greater academic effort on the part of students who currently feel alienated.

Other Changes

A number of other themes emerge from the studies in this volume that have implications for educational improvement. Let me summarize these briefly.

Teachers need to convey a sense of positive expectation for individual and group achievement. This is especially important for those students whose lives have been surrounded by failure and whose families have conveyed to them little hope for their success in school. Immigrant minorities appear to be less affected than involuntary minorities by teachers' attitudes and expectations. If this is true, it must stem in part from the high expectations for their school achievement imparted to immigrant students by their families and communities.

Beginning in the early elementary grades, schools need to identify those students who have low expectations for their own academic achievement and who are little motivated to succeed in school. These students in particular need teachers with high, not low, expectations for their school success. Teachers, moreover, need to help underachieving minority students distinguish education from assimilation.

Schools alone cannot change the stratified nature of society or increase the jobs available to young people, but they can raise expectations and they can increase knowledge about the options young people have available to them if they persist with their schooling. Students need to understand the relationships that exist between educational effort and educational outcomes, between courses taken and future opportunities, between educational credentials and both jobs and income. Many minority students have limited role models and limited knowledge of the roles available to them. Schools need to give much greater attention to job counseling which needs to occur as an integrated part of the curriculum from the primary years onward.

Some students receive this sort of knowledge through their families and communities. If they do, they need not receive it through the school. Schools, of course, in many instances, already attempt to raise expectations and to counsel students about educational and occupational goals, but, in general, far more attention must be given these matters and at an earlier age.

Many minority students are reluctant to excel academically if it appears that they are leaving their peers behind. These students frequently place higher priority on advancing the interests of their group than on their personal academic achievement. Educators may wish therefore to give increased attention to educational methods that promote cooperative learning and group rather than individual achievement (Kagan, 1986).

Newly arrived immigrants in particular need strong educational programs, but, all too often, they are placed into ESL, remedial and lower-level bilingual classes with inadequately trained teachers and a watered-down curriculum. "Powerless immigrant children," as Suarez-Orozco reports (in this volume) are "not a priority," and this must change.

Racial prejudice, as Ogbu points out in the introductory chapter, is a major problem for both immigrant and involuntary minority students. Although long-established minorities have a heightened sensitivity to racism and are far less willing to turn the other cheek to prejudiced attitudes and actions when they encounter them, newcomers are more frequently the victims of outright and direct racial hostilities. In school, immigrant youths, particularly those more recently arrived, attempt to "ignore" the problems, and school administrators may even encourage them to do so, explaining that they must be "understanding" of their majority classmates' ignorance. Teachers and administrators, moreover, are themselves all too often unaware of their own prejudiced attitudes and how these attitudes impact upon their students (Gibson, 1988). Schools, together with teacher-training institutions, must take a leadership role in attacking racist attitudes wherever they exist.

In closing, I wish to reiterate a point raised by Matute-Bianchi in her chapter. It would be a gross misinterpretation of the goals of this volume if individual students were, for any kind of diagnostic or instructional purposes, to be classified according to the immigrant and involuntary minority typology. Programs designed to fit stereotypic perceptions of students will inevitably harm those they seek to help. A more appropriate response, as Matute-Bianchi suggests, is for schools to create learning environments that are "broadly sensitive, responsive and challenging to [a] diverse student clientele."

References

Banton, Michael. 1983. *Racial and Ethnic Competition*. New York: Cambridge University Press.

Becker, Adeline. 1991. "Responsibilities and Expectations: Interactive Home/School Factors in Literacy Development Among Portuguese First Graders." In *Literacy as Praxis: Culture, Language, and Pedagogy*, ed. Catherine E. Walsh, pp. 68–85. Norwood, N.J.: Ablex Publishing.

Bromsen, Archie. 1935. "The Public School's Contribution to the Maladaptation of the Italian Boy." Appendix E in *Greenwich Village 1920–1930*, by Caroline F. Ware. Boston: Houghton Mifflin Co.

Cohen, David K. 1970. "Immigrants and the Schools." *Review of Educational Research* 40(1/2):13–27.

The Documentation Section of the Council of Europe, ed. 1981. *The Education of Migrant Workers' Children*. Amsterdam: Swets & Zeitlinger.

Eldering, Lotty, and Jo Kloprogge. 1989. *Different Cultures, Same School: Ethnic Minority Children in Europe*. Berwyn, Pa.: Swets North America.

First, Joan M., and John W. Carrera. 1988. *New Voices: Immigrant Students in U.S. Public Schools.* Research and Policy Report. National Coalition of Advocates for Students, Boston, Massachusetts.

Fordham, Signithia. 1988. "Racelessness as a Factor in Black Students' School Success: Pragmatic Strategy or Pyrrhic Victory?" *Harvard Educational Review* 58(1):54–84.

Fourth Seminar on Adaptation and Integration of Permanent Immigrants. 1979. *International Migration* 17(1/2) [available as ERIC document ED 257 890].

Ghuman, Paul A.S. 1980. "Bhattra Sikhs in Cardiff: Family and Kinship Organization." *New Community* 8(2):308–16.

Gibson, Margaret A. 1976. "Ethnicity and Schooling: A Caribbean Case Study." Ph.D. diss. University of Pittsburgh.

———. 1982. "Reputation and Respectability: How Competing Cultural Systems Affect Students' Performance in School." *Anthropology and Education Quarterly* 13(1):3–27.

———. 1987a. "Playing by the Rules." In *Education and Cultural Process*, ed. George D. Spindler, pp. 274–81. Prospect Heights, Ill.: Waveland Press.

———. 1987b. "The School Performance of Immigrant Minorities: A Comparative View." *Anthropology and Education Quarterly* 18(4):262–75.

———. 1988. *Accommodation without Assimilation: Sikh Immigrants in an American High School.* Ithaca, N.Y.: Cornell University Press.

———. 1989. "School Persistence versus Dropping Out: A Comparative Perspective." In *What Do Anthropologists Have to Say about Dropouts?*, ed. Henry T. Trueba, George and Louise Spindler, pp. 126–34. New York: Falmer Press.

Husen, Torsten, and Susan Opper. 1983. *Multicultural and Multilingual Education in Immigrant Countries.* New York: Pergamon Press.

Inner London Education Authority. 1987. "Ethnic Background and Examination Results: 1985 and 1986." Report P-7078, prepared by ILEA Research and Statistics, 1 July. London.

Jordan, Cathie, Roland G. Tharp, and Lynn Vogt. 1986. "Differing Domains: Is Truly Bicultural Education Possible?" Working paper, Kamehameha Center for Development of Early Education, Honolulu.

Kagan, Spencer. 1986. "Cooperative Learning and Sociocultural Factors in Schooling." In *Beyond Language: Social and Cultural Factors in Schooling Language Minority Students*, pp. 231–85. Sacramento, Calif.: State Department of Education, Bilingual Education Office.

Malhotra, M.K. 1985. "Research Report: The Educational Problems of Foreign Children of Different Nationalities in West Germany." *Ethnic and Racial Studies* 8(2):291–99.

Moore, Michael. 1987. "Pride and Prejudice." *San Francisco Examiner*, 15 Nov., Image section, pp. 14–34.

Olsen, Laurie. 1988. *Crossing the Schoolhouse Border: Immigrant Students and the California Public Schools*. A California Tomorrow Research Report. San Francisco, California.

————. 1989. *Bridges: Promising Programs for the Education of Immigrant Children*. A publication of the California Tomorrow Immigrant Students Project. San Francisco, California.

Rothermund, Dietmar, and John Simon, eds. 1986. *Education and the Integration of Ethnic Minorities*. New York: St. Martin's Press.

Schermerhorn, R.A. 1970. *Comparative Ethnic Relations*. New York: Random House.

Smith-Hefner, Nancy J. 1990. "Language and Identity in the Education of Boston-Area Khmer." *Anthropology and Education Quarterly* 21(3):250–68.

Suarez-Orozco, Marcelo M. 1989. "Psychosocial Aspects of Achievement Motivation among Recent Hispanic Immigrants." In *What Do Anthropologists Have to Say about Dropouts?*, ed. Henry T. Trueba, George and Louise Spindler, pp. 99–116. New York: Falmer Press.

————, ed. 1991. *Anthropology and Education Quarterly* 22(2). Theme issue, "Migration, Minority Status and Education: European Dilemmas and Responses in the 1990s." In press.

Sung, Betty Lee. [1979]. "Transplanted Chinese Children." Report to the Administration for Children, Youth and Family, Department of Health, Education and Welfare, Washington, D.C.

Swann Committee Report. 1985. *Education for All. Report of the Committee of Inquiry into the Education of Children from Ethnic Minority Groups*. Cmnd. 9453. London: Her Majesty's Stationery Office.

Tosi, Arturo. 1984. *Immigration and Bilingual Education: A Case Study of Movement of Population, Language Change and Education within the EEC*. New York: Pergamon Press.

Trueba, H.T., L. Jacobs, and E. Kirton. 1990. *Cultural Conflict and Adaptation: The Case of Hmong Children in American Society*. New York: Falmer Press.

United States Bureau of the Census. 1983. *1980 Census of Population*. Vol. 1: *Characteristics of the Population*, chap. C: General Social and Economic Characteristics, pt. 1: United States Summary, PC-80-1-C1 (tables 123, 160, 166). Washington, D.C.

Wagley, Charles, and Marvin Harris. 1958. *Minorities in the New World*. New York: Columbia University Press.

Walker, Wendy D. 1989. "The Challenges of the Hmong Culture: A Study of Teacher, Counselor and Administrator Training in a Time of Changing Demographics." Ed.D. diss. Harvard University.

Ware, Caroline F. 1935. *Greenwich Village 1920–1930: A Comment on American Civilization in the Post-War Years*. Boston: Houghton Mifflin Co.

Wong, Eugene F. 1985. "Asian American Middleman Minority Theory: The Framework of an American Myth." *Journal of Ethnic Studies* 13(1):51–88.

Wright, Paul, and Robert W. Gardner. 1983. "Ethnicity, Birthplace, and Achievement: The Changing Hawaii Mosaic." Paper 82, East-West Population Institute. Honolulu, Hawaii.

Supplementary Readings

John U. Ogbu
University of California, Berkeley

Minorities are usually found in what are called "plural societies," i.e., societies with two or more populations within their respective political boundaries. A population within such a society or nation is a minority group not because it is numerically smaller, but because it occupies a subordinate power position vis-à-vis another population within the same political boundary. The subordinate power position has important implications both for the way the minority group is treated in various domains of life, including education, and for the way the minority-group members perceive and respond to events in those domains. However, the way members of a given minority group perceive and respond to schooling depends not only on how they are treated by the dominant group, it also depends on the terms of the initial incorporation of the minorities into the society, such as whether the minorities joined the society more or less as "voluntary" immigrants or whether they were "involuntarily" incorporated through slavery, conquest or colonization. It is, therefore, important that those who study the education of minority children, make policy affecting minority education, or teach minority children in school should have an understanding of the nature of the society in which the minorities are being educated and the status of the minority group in question. It is for these reasons that the following supplementary readings are divided into two parts. Part One consists of readings on the nature of plural societies and types of minority groups. The readings in Part Two are about the school experiences of minority groups in selected countries.

Part One:
Plural Societies and Minority Status

Banton, M. 1983. *Racial and Ethnic Competition*. London: Cambridge
University Press.

This book analyzes racial and ethnic relations through the use of
the principal theme of competition, both cross-culturally and
historically. Banton makes use of a rational choice theory of behavior,
combining elements of economics with sociological interpretations. His
theoretical position is that group competition reinforces social
boundaries marked by physical differences, whereas individual
competition eliminates these social boundaries.

Benedict, B. 1970. "Pluralism and Stratification." In *Essays in
Comparative Social Stratification*, ed. L. Plotnicov and A.
Tuden, pp. 29–81. Pittsburgh: University of Pittsburgh Press.

Benedict argues for the use of the concept of social pluralism
over cultural pluralism. He stresses the importance of studying social
structure and institutions in analyzing plural societies rather than only
analyzing cultural differences among the groups of these societies. The
relationship among the structural categories of the society must be
examined in order to analyze a society's system of social stratification.

Berreman, G.D. 1979. *Caste and Other Inequalities: Essays on
Inequality*. Delhi: The Folklore Institute.

A collection of essays by Berreman focusing on social inequality
and social justice in India, and cross-culturally. The contents include a
comparison of caste in India and the United States, empirical and
theoretical essays on various institutionalized systems of inequality—
rural, urban, large-scale and small-scale—and social organization in
India.

Bhachu, P. 1985. *Twice Migrants: East African Sikh Settlers in Britain*.
London: Tavistock Publications.

This book examines the marriage patterns of Sikhs in Britain,
based on a community with a history of migration from India to Africa,

then to Britain beginning in the mid-1960s. It analyzes the adaptation of the Sikhs, a strongly traditional group, to life in urban Britain.

Castile, G.P., and G. Kushner, eds. 1981. *Persistent Peoples: Cultural Enclaves in Perspective*. Tucson: University of Arizona Press.

A collection of articles that focuses on the phenomenon of ethnic enclavement. The analysis draws on numerous ethnic groups worldwide. These groups demonstrate a continuity of common identity in resistance to absorption by a dominant surrounding culture. Issues addressed include plural interrelationships, opposition, ritual, and applied and adaptive perspectives.

Crowley, D.J. 1957. "Pluralism and Differential Acculturation in Trinidad." *American Anthropologist* 59:817–24.

Crowley examines the differential acculturation of the numerous racial and cultural groups comprising Trinidadian society. He argues that these groups, hierarchically arranged within the Trinidadian social structure, are not functionally exclusive. Thus, members of each group have knowledge of or participate in other groups' cultures. Crowley terms this process "plural acculturation," which Trinidadians experience without loss of their original racial or national identity.

Daedalus. 1981. "American Indians, Blacks, Chicanos and Puerto Ricans." Special Issue, Spring 110(2).

This special issue of *Daedalus* examines the problems these four groups face in American society. The issue celebrates diversity, and it deplores poverty and injustice. Ethnic or racial identity, exploitation, economic inequality, language and culture, class, race and social change are topics included in this issue.

Despres, L.A. 1967. *Cultural Pluralism and National Politics in British Guiana*. Chicago: McNally.

An anthropological study through which cultural pluralism is examined during the colonial rule of Guiana. Despres focuses on the process of decolonization, the problems faced by a plural society emerging as a new, united nation, and the subsequent integration of Guyanese society. Three levels of integration are distinguished for analysis: integration of colonial society, integration of the major ethnic components, and integration of local ethnic communities.

De Vos, G.A. 1980. "Ethnic Adaptation and Minority Status." *Journal of Cross-Cultural Psychology* 11(1):101–24.

De Vos provides an analysis of how social degradation among individuals retaining their ethnic identity is related to family cohesion and peer-group interaction. Both of these are dependent on past cultural traditions. Drawing on examples from Japanese research, De Vos argues that educational studies must include psychocultural determinants which are related to social or ethnic identity and the awareness of a disparaged minority status.

De Vos, G.A., and L. Romanucci-Ross, eds. 1982. *Ethnic Identity: Cultural Continuities and Change.* Chicago: University of Chicago Press.

A collection of essays that emphasize psychocultural forms of analysis. The essays take into account the experiential and subjective forces that underlie ethnic identity and serve to maintain ethnic identity in pluralistic societies. The essays include an analysis of social disequilibrium and change in societies that have unassimilated minorities.

Dinnerstein, L., and F.C. Jaher, eds. 1970. *The Aliens: A History of Ethnic Minorities in America.* New York: Appleton-Century-Crofts.

A historical survey of the history of ethnic groups in the United States. Issues covered include: the treatment of Indians during the colonial era; black workers' experiences; the lives of German and Chinese immigrants during the period of the new republic; problems of ethnic groups involved in the industrial transformation; and, finally, an examination of ethnic minority groups in contemporary America.

Fisher, R. 1977. *Contact and Conflict: Indian-European Relations in British Columbia, 1774–1890.* Vancouver: University of British Columbia Press.

Fisher examines the mutually beneficial relations between Indians and European fur traders in British Columbia from 1774 to 1890. This is followed by an analysis of the relations between Indians and European settlers, who displaced European fur traders in British Columbia and disturbed the culture of the Indians.

Furnivall, J.S. 1944. *Netherlands India: A Study of Plural Economy.* Cambridge, England: The University Press.

A historical study of the economic and social development of Netherlands India, with emphasis on its character as a plural society. The time frame ranges from a brief history prior to the 1600s to the 1930s.

Furnivall, J.S. 1956. *Colonial Policy and Practice: A Comparative Study of Burma and Netherlands India.* New York: University Press.

Furnivall wrote the book after being asked by the Government of Burma in 1942 to present his views on reconstruction in Burma. He was to examine practices of colonial rule in Netherlands India, suggesting those which might subsequently be applied to Burma. Furnivall provides a general survey of colonial policy and practice in both Burma and Netherlands India, and contrasts British colonial policy with Dutch colonial policy.

Gordon, M.M. 1961. "Assimilation in America: Theory and Reality." *Daedulus,* Spring, 90(2):263–85.

In this article, Gordon describes and makes distinctions among three theories of assimilation: Anglo-conformity, the melting pot and cultural pluralism. He attempts to clarify the nature of the historical process of assimilation and theories of immigrant adjustment in the United States. Additionally, he examines the then-contemporary U.S. structure of society in relation to ethnic groups, followed by an analysis of the American assimilation or integration goals during the early 1960s. He posits the need for "structural pluralism."

Kuper, L. 1970. "Stratification in Plural Societies: Focus on White Settler Societies in Africa." In *Essays in Comparative Social*

Stratification, ed. L. Plotnicov and A. Tuden, pp. 77–93. Pittsburgh: University of Pittsburgh Press.

Kuper argues that plural sections of society (ethnic or racial) are not the same as stratified sections. He points out that there are class differences among members of the different races. Systems of social stratification of southern and central African societies are such that ethnic groups as well as classes are given unequal worth.

Kurokawa, M., ed. 1970. *Minority Responses: Comparative Views of Reactions to Subordination*. New York: Random House.

The selections in this book were collected for use as supplementary reading for courses in racial and ethnic relations. The articles focus on the responses of minority members to their treatment by the dominant group. The articles also address the relationship between cultural background and how power and privilege is distributed. Other areas covered are assimilation, accommodation, submission, contention and revitalization.

Lawrence, D. 1974. *Black Migrants: White Natives: A Study of Race Relations in Nottingham*. London: Cambridge University Press.

Lawrence discredits the accepted view that Nottingham city's race relations are harmonious. He formulates an analysis of sociological aspects of race relations and relates the implications of this analysis for policy formation.

Lijphart, A., ed. 1981. *Conflict and Coexistence in Belgium: The Dynamics of a Culturally Divided Society*. Berkeley: Institute of International Studies, University of California, Berkeley.

This book was developed from a 1980 conference held at U.C. Berkeley which addressed the theme: "Belgium: The Bicultural State and Society." The essays in the book deal with Belgian history, society, government and literature, with special reference to the ethnic tensions between the Flemish majority and the French-speaking minority of Belgium.

Novak, M. 1973. *The Rise of the Unmeltable Ethnics*. New York: Macmillan.

An analysis of ethnic group assimilation in U.S. society. Novak discounts the theory that all individuals must assimilate into one "superculture." Rather, he looks at the realities of subcultures in the United States that refuse to assimilate.

Omi, M., and H. Winnant. 1986. *Racial Formation in the United States: From 1960 to the 1980s.* London: Routledge and Kegan Paul.

This book presents an analysis of the principle of race in the political movements in the United States during the last decades. Omi and Winnant criticize current paradigms of ethnicity, class and nation used to understand social action. Instead, they emphasize race as a key "organizing principle" of social action.

Rex, J. 1959. "The Plural Society in Sociological Theory." *British Journal of Sociology* 10:114–24.

Rex examines the sociological study of plural societies, using theories of J.S. Furnivall, B. Malinowski, and G. Myrdal for his theoretical framework. He attempts to test and refine the concept of plural societies and argues for the use of this model for non-colonial societies.

Rubin, V., ed. 1960. "Social and Cultural Pluralism in the Caribbean." *The Annals of the New York Academy of Sciences* 83(5):761–916. Special Issue.

This issue, focusing on social and cultural pluralism in the Caribbean, includes the following topics: the range and variation in Caribbean societies; "metropolitan" influences in the Netherlands Antilles, the French Antilles and the West Indies; social stratification; politics; urbanization; communication; peasants and plantations; and cultural assimilation. Specific areas investigated are Haiti, Trinidad, Jamaica, and British Guiana.

Smith, M.G. 1969. "Some Developments in the Analytical Frameworks of Pluralism." In *Pluralism in Africa*, ed. L. Kuper and M.G. Smith. Berkeley: University of California Press.

A review of critiques of J.S. Furnivall's concept of pluralism, as well as a commentary on various analytic formulations of pluralism.

Smith presents a general theoretical framework to analyze pluralism which addresses the relationship among three levels of pluralism: structural, social and cultural..

Spicer, E.H., and R.H. Thompson. 1972. *Plural Society in the Southwest*. Albuquerque: University of New Mexico Press.

Ethnic diversity is explored in seven states in Mexico and six in the United States in this book. Four aspects of this diversity are focused on: the Indian presence, Hispano-Anglo contact, the impact of immigration, and cultural variation.

Titley, E.B. 1986. *A Narrow Vision: Duncan Campbell Scott and the Administration of Indian Affairs in Canada*. Vancouver: University of British Columbia Press.

Titley provides an analysis of the development of Indian policy in Canada during the late nineteenth and early twentieth centuries (1899–1932). He focuses on Duncan Campbell Scott's career in government as Deputy Superintendent General of Indian Affairs, whose view was that the Indians of Canada should be absorbed into the Canadian body politic. An evaluation of Indian health, education and welfare during this time period is also included.

Van Amersfoot, H. 1982. *Immigration and the Formation of Minority Groups: The Dutch Experience, 1945–1975*. London: Cambridge University Press.

An analysis of the social position of the main groups of immigrants in the Netherlands since World War II. Van Amersfoot examines the conditions under which immigration leads to the formation of minority groups. He develops a theory of race relations with respect to minority problems, assimilation of immigrants and social stratification. Four immigrant populations are investigated: returning "Indo-Dutch" Eurasians, the Moluccans, the Surinamese and labor migrants from the Mediterranean area.

Part Two:
Minority Education in Plural Societies

General

Appleton, N. 1983. *Cultural Pluralism in Education: Theoretical Foundations.* New York: Longmans.

The focus of this book is on theories of pluralism in education and their link with the effects of social and cultural biases in U.S. schools. Also addressed is how education can prepare students to function successfully in a culturally diverse society. The book includes teacher resources.

California State Department of Education. 1986. *Beyond Language: Social and Cultural Factors in Schooling Language Minority Students.* Los Angeles: Evaluation, Dissemination and Assessment Center, California State University, Los Angeles.

The work analyzes the relationship between cultural and social factors which affect minority students, beyond problems associated with language difference. Underachievement of minority students is addressed in terms of the broader social and educational contexts. Suggestions for the improvement of educational programs are offered.

Corner, T., ed. 1984. *Education in Multicultural Societies.* New York: St. Martin's Press.

A comparative approach to understanding how multicultural educational systems can work with different cultural groups, rather than trying to integrate or assimilate them into the majority group. Corner provides examples from both developed and developing countries.

Jacob, E., and C. Jordan, eds. 1987. "Explaining the School Performance of Minority Students." *Anthropology and Education Quarterly* 18(4):259–392. Theme Issue.

This issue is a collection of articles that focuses on two major frameworks for understanding school performance among minority students. Case studies, which illustrate each approach, report on comparative analyses of immigrant minority students' school performance, school failure and success among native Hawaiian and Navajo school children, achievement motivation in the context of a psychosocial model among Hispanic-American students, and educational change through educational research.

OECD. 1983. *The Education of Minority Groups: An Enquiry into Problems and Practices of Fifteen Countries.* Paris: Centre for Educational Research and Innovation, OECD.

A collection of essays which were part of the documentation of a program of inquiry carried out by the Centre for Educational Research and Innovation for the member countries of the Organization for Economic Co-operation and Development. The essays define the policies and processes which designate certain groups as being in need of special attention, and through which differential treatment is legitimated, organized and financed.

Ogbu, J.U. 1978. *Minority Education and Caste: The American System in Cross-Cultural Perspective.* New York: Academic Press.

In this book, Ogbu discredits theories that explain ethnic minority students' school performance based solely on three factors: home environment, school environment and heredity. Ogbu argues that these students' performance is directly related to expected adult postschool roles typically found among the ethnic groups. This study investigates the education of ethnic minority students in six societies: India, Israel, Japan, Britain, New Zealand and the United States.

Rothermund, D., and J. Simon, eds. 1986. *Education and the Integration of Ethnic Minorities.* New York: St. Martin's Press.

The essays in this book are the papers delivered at a workshop held in 1984 in Germany entitled: Education and the Integration of Ethnic Minorities. Issues addressed include language and the problem of the medium of instruction; the influence of the social and political context of educational systems on ethnic minority students' education; and discrimination, racism and inequality in education. The following geographical areas are covered: Germany, Japan, Malaysia, Indonesia, Israel, Nigeria, India, Sri Lanka and the United States.

Vernon, P.E. 1982. *Abilities and Achievements of Orientals in North America.* New York: Academic Press.

This book explores the achievements of Asian immigrants in education and vocation, specifically the achievements of Chinese and Japanese immigrants. Vernon reviews the literature regarding the abilities, achievements and personality characteristics of Asian immigrants and their descendants. He then relates this literature to the immigrants' cultural backgrounds and the history of their experience as immigrants in North America, using a psychological theoretical framework.

Australia

Bullivant, B.M. 1987. *The Ethnic Encounters in the Secondary School: Ethnocultural Reproduction and Resistance: Theory and Case Studies.* London: Falmer Press.

This book presents a theoretical model of cultural reproduction which combines socioeconomic status and ethnic perspectives in a theory of ethnocultural hegemony. Bullivant produces a theory of "social closure": i.e., prejudice, discrimination and sexism as being aimed at reducing ethnic groups' competitiveness in society.

Britain

Swann Committee Report. 1985. *Education for All.* Report of the Committee of Inquiry into The Education of Pupils of Ethnic Minority Groups. Cmnd. 9453. London: Her Majesty's Stationery Office.

The report focuses on problems of ethnic minority children in schools, particularly their underachievement. Ethnic communities focused on are the Asian and West Indian communities, including an interim report published June 17, 1981 regarding West Indian children in schools. Major areas of concern include language education and the role of the school regarding religion. The report reviews policies and practices in the field of multicultural education.

Taylor, M., and S. Hegarty. 1985. *The Best of Both Worlds . . .? A Review of Research into the Education of Pupils of South Asian Origin.* Windson: NFER-Nelson.

This study addresses South Asian students' education in British schools. The students' families are from India, Pakistan and Bangladesh. The authors review research already conducted on the school performance of South Asian students living within two cultural systems in Britain. Students' performance is differentiated among the three Asian groups. The previous assumption that linguistic proficiency was the source of minority students' educational problems is discounted.

Canada

Barman, J., Y. Herbert, and K. McCaskill, eds. 1986. *Indian Education in Canada, Volume 1: The Legacy.* Vancouver: University of British Columbia Press.

This first volume of two analyzes the education of Indian children by whites since the arrival of the first Europeans in Canada four centuries ago. Essays focus on tensions created by Europeans attempting to "civilize" the Indians through education, the activities of missionaries, and the regaining of control over education by the Indian community during the twentieth century.

———. 1987. *Indian Education in Canada, Vol. 2: The Challenge.* Vancouver: University of British Columbia Press.

This second volume is concerned with the changes in the education of Indian children since 1972. Issues addressed include the role played by elders in passing on traditions to the next generation and the consequences for local communities of their acquisition and control over the schooling of their children.

Kahn, L. (forthcoming). *Schooling, Jobs and Cultural Identity.* New York: Garland Publishing, Inc.

Kahn examines the impact of self-initiated social change upon the schooling of Quebecois of Canada over a twenty year period. She uses and builds upon John Ogbu's cultural adaptation model: minority school performance as both a socioeconomic and cultural response to the structure of power relations in society. She questions the role and limitations of the state in reversing social inequality through legislative reforms and changes in the educational system.

Solomon, R.P. 1991. *The Creation of Separatism: Black Culture and Struggle in a Canadian High School.* Albany: State University of New York Press.

Solomon focuses on race in educational subcultures by examining a black, working-class male subculture in a white Canadian middle class high school structure. He depicts how black immigrant students use their primary and secondary cultural differences to build an oppositional social identity. Finally, he looks at the interaction between school structures and multiple student cultures.

Ireland

O'Connell, J. 1988. *Education and Partition: A Case Study of Ethnic and Religious Minorities in Twentieth Century Ireland.* Ann Arbor: University Microfilms International.

An analysis of the role and status of four minority groups in Ireland: Protestant and Jewish minorities in Eire, and the Travelling People and Catholics in the North of Ireland. O'Connell uses John Ogbu's cross-cultural framework of the status mobility system and educability. He considers possible ways of closing the gap between school performance and job opportunities for minority groups.

Israel

Lewis, A. 1979. *Power, Poverty and Education: An Ethnography of Schooling in an Israeli Town.* Ramat Gan, Israel: Turtledove Publications Company.

Lewis examines school children in an Israeli elementary school and the problems a nation with an egalitarian ideology faces when an ethnic community remains in a low status position within their society.

He analyzes the education of children in the context of the status of the people of the community in the national, social, political and economic structure. Also under investigation is the educational process at the elementary school and the relationship between the school and the community.

Japan

Rohlen, T. 1983. "Educational Policies and Prospects." In *Koreans in Japan*, ed. C. Lee and G.A. De Vos, pp. 182–222. Berkeley: University of California Press.

This chapter analyzes the issue of ethnicity versus assimilation for Korean students in the Japanese educational system. Topics addressed include: whether the Koreans in Japan would ever return to Korea; if Japan could become pluralistic enough to accept a Korean minority as different but equal; the contradictions in Japanese government policies; and how social forces in Japanese society may influence the outcome of educational policy.

Shimahara, N. 1971. *Burakumin: A Japanese Minority and Education.* The Hague: Martinus Nijhoff.

This work examines educational problems faced by the Burakumin minority group in Japan and the responses of two schools to these problems. A historical survey of Burakumin culture is provided, as well as an examination of the community, organizations, struggles for emancipation, the nature of prejudice and discrimination, and the interaction between Burakumin and non-Burakumin people. Integral to this study is the understanding of education within the context of the culture of Burakumin and Japanese society—how education and culture relate to each other.

———. 1979. *Adaptation and Education in Japan.* New York: Praeger.

An anthropological and sociological interpretation of Japanese education and society. Adaptation and the nature of Japanese group orientation are the frames within which education in Japan is analyzed. Shimahara looks at the interaction between cultural orientations and structural conditions, or institutions, which are constantly undergoing change. He rejects the notion that education can be understood in isolation from its social context. Also examined is the stress the Japanese place on college entrance examinations, regarding them as a rite of passage into future college and employment opportunities.

United States

Carter, T.P., and R.D. Segura. 1979. *Mexican Americans in School: A Decade of Change*. New York: College Entrance Examination Board.

Carter and Segura focus on the failure of American schools to educate Mexican American students in the Southwest. Included is an assessment of educational theory and practice. Issues addressed are low academic achievement of Mexican American students; high rates of attrition; lack of skill necessary for social and economic advancement; and retention of traditional cultural forms and the Spanish language. The analysis examines the Mexican ethnic group, the school and the society.

Fordham, S. 1988. "Racelessness as a Factor in Black Students' School Success: Pragmatic Strategy or Pyrrhic Victory?" *Harvard Educational Review* 58(1):54–84.

This article examines the conflict faced by high-achieving black American students who are tied to both their identification with their indigenous black fictive-kinship system and the individualistic, competitive and impersonal system of the U.S. educational system. Fordham argues that students experiencing this conflict develop a strategy of appearing raceless in their efforts to "make it." Additionally, she argues that the organizational structure of the American educational system encourages and rewards racelessness in students.

Gibson, M.A. 1988. *Accommodation Without Assimilation: Sikh Immigrants in an American High School*. Ithaca: Cornell University Press.

Based on a two-year study of Punjabi Sikhs in a California public high school, this book offers insights into the processes that promote and impede success in school for immigrant youths. It also treats the school performance of the majority group. Issues addressed by Gibson include minority-majority relations, the processes of Americanization and assimilation, mediocrity in American high school education, parental involvement in schooling, and the educational and economic achievement patterns of Asian Americans and other immigrant groups. An important theme of this work is immigrants' use of a strategy of "accommodation and acculturation without assimilation."

Guthrie, G.P. 1985. *A School Divided: An Ethnography of Bilingual Education in a Chinese Community*. Hillsdale, N.J.: Lawrence Erlbaum Associates.

In this book, Guthrie moves beyond evaluating the academic performance of immigrant students by additionally examining how bilingual education programs are initiated, planned and implemented. The theme of "transitional versus maintenance education" is addressed. Guthrie examines the history of bilingual education in the United States; the attitudes and perceptions of teachers regarding language in relation to recently immigrated children in a Chinese community in the United States; and the perceptions and attitudes of Chinese immigrant parents and students toward bilingual education and learning English.

Harvard Educational Review. 1988. Special Issue, 58(1).

This special issue addresses questions regarding education in the United States. Issues covered are Native American schooling from 1880 to 1900; sexuality, schooling and adolescent females; and black students' strategy of appearing raceless in order to succeed in school.

Hsia, J. 1988. *Asian Americans in Higher Education and at Work*. Hillsdale, N.J.: Lawrence Erlbaum Associates.

This book considers the special problems faced by the growing numbers of Asian Americans within, and applying to, institutions of higher education. Asians are often considered to be overrepresented in many of these institutions. Hsia looks at the conflict faced by educational institutions between equality of educational opportunity and proportional representation of all ethnic or racial groups. Additionally, he addresses the different abilities and needs of the various Asian ethnic groups, and those between immigrants and native-born or long-term residents.

Ogbu, J.U. 1974. *The Next Generation: An Ethnography of Education in an Urban Neighborhood.* New York: Academic Press.

Based on anthropological research in the multiethnic neighborhood of Burgherside in Stockton, California, Ogbu focuses on the question of why many ethnic minority children do so poorly in school while others succeed. The neighborhood is composed of blacks, Mexican Americans and Asian Americans, many of whom are immigrants. Ogbu focuses on problems faced by subordinate minorities (as opposed to immigrant minorities), i.e., blacks and Mexican Americans. He argues that school failure among subordinate minorities is closely tied to lack of equal school and economic opportunities with the dominant group of whites.

Ogbu, J.U., and M.E. Matute-Bianchi. 1986. "Understanding Sociocultural Factors: Knowledge, Identity, and School Adjustment." In *Beyond Language: Social and Cultural Factors in Schooling Language Minority Students*, pp. 73–142. Sacramento, Calif.: California State Department of Education, Office of Bilingual Education.

The focus of this chapter is on why some language minorities experience persistent disproportionate school failure. The authors assess socio-cultural factors which influence minority students' school performance: group attitudes toward education, self-identity, historical experiences, cultural values, job ceiling, etc.

Suarez-Orozco, M.M. 1989. *Central American Refugees and U.S. High Schools: A Psychosocial Study of Motivation and Achievement.* Stanford, Calif.: Stanford University Press.

Suarez-Orozco examines the success of Central American immigrant children in the U.S. educational system. Issues addressed are problems students encounter in schools, how their prior experiences affect their school performance, how they adapt to change, and why their success rate is greater than that of other ethnic groups in the United States.

Szasz, M. 1974. *Education and the American Indian: The Road to Self-Determination, 1929–1973*. Albuquerque: University of New Mexico Press.

This work is an examination of the history of the failure of federal Indian education from 1928 to 1973. The book concentrates on education directed by the Indian Bureau, and, later, on schools controlled by the Indians themselves. Excluded are Indian children in eastern states and those in major urban areas.

INDEX